# Auto Repair for Dummies

## Deanna Sclar

Technical Advisors

**Don Donesley**
**Julia Hamm,** second revised edition

**Second Revised Edition**

Ten Speed Press
*Berkeley, California*

*The instructions in this book are based on generally workable principles,
but may not be applicable to your particular automobile or particular
repair problem. In using this book, you should, at all times, use extreme
care and adhere to all instructions in it and your owner's manual.*

Ten Speed Press
P.O. Box 7123
Berkeley, California 94707

Book Design by A Good Thing, Inc.

Quote on page iii is reprinted with permission of William Morrow & Company, from *Zen and the Art of Motorcycle Maintenance*, copyright
©1974 by Robert M. Pirsig.

Title by permission of Philip R. Martin, author of *Auto Mechanics for the
Complete Dummy*, ©1974

**Library of Congress Cataloging in Publication Data**

Sclar, Deanna.
    Auto  repair for dummies.

    Bibliography: p.
    Includes index.
    1.  Automobiles—Maintenance and repair—Amateurs' manuals.
I. Title.
TL152.S42    1989         629.28'722         89-4483
ISBN 0-89815-341-7

Printed in the United States of America

   2  3  4  5  –  93  92  91  90

Each machine has its own, unique personality which probably could be defined as the intuitive sum total of everything you know and feel about it. This personality constantly changes, usually for the worse, but sometimes surprisingly for the better.... The new ones start out as good-looking strangers and, depending on how they are treated, degenerate rapidly into bad-acting grouches or even cripples, or else turn into healthy, good natured, long-lasting friends.

Robert M. Pirsig
*Zen and the Art of Motorcycle
Maintenance*

# What's So Special About

**It Is *Not* Written for Confirmed "Do-It-Yourselfers"…**

It *is* for You if

- ☐ You have never held a wrench;
- ☐ You are positive that, in your case, manual labor can lead only to disaster;
- ☐ You haven't the vaguest idea of how a car works;
- ☐ You cannot identify anything you see under the hood of your car;
- ☐ You have failed shop or arts and crafts;
- ☐ You believe that if you do something wrong, your car can blow up.

**To Enjoy This Book It Would Help If:**

- ☐ You do not believe that working on your car can possibly be *fun* but are willing to give it a try for any reason whatsoever;
- ☐ You are sincerely tired of being ripped off because of your own ignorance.

**Why Should That Be Enjoyable?**

Because you will be more delighted than anyone else to find:

- ☐ Cars run on principles that are as easy to understand as common sense;
- ☐ Most of the devices on your car will not hurt you unless you really go out of your way to hurt yourself;
- ☐ Not only can you get a fair deal, but you can save a tremendous amount of money, extend the life of your car, save on fuel, do your bit for the environment, and have a hell of a good time working on your car!
- ☐ The fun comes because it's so easy and you expected to hate it or be bored or befuddled.

**Here's How *Auto Repair for Dummies* Accomplishes These Miracles**

- ☐ By starting from scratch (it even shows you what a screwdriver looks like);
- ☐ By providing step-by-step illustrated instructions for even the simplest task;
- ☐ By telling you exactly what you'll need and how to know if you've been given the wrong thing;
- ☐ By covering each system thoroughly in simple terms *before* you get to work on it. It's easier to work on something that you understand.

**There Are Fringe Benefits Too!**

- ☐ Your car will run better and live longer;
- ☐ Mechanics will respect you;
- ☐ You'll have more money to spend on other things;
- ☐ You will no longer be a dummy.

**It Tells You the Truth About**

- ☐ What makes your car go (and how and why as well);
- ☐ The easy work involved in keeping your car well tuned and running right, and how to tell what's wrong if trouble strikes;
- ☐ A program of "preventive medicine" to avoid trouble, that takes about an hour or two a month;
- ☐ Whether or not you can handle a problem yourself, and how to get it fixed at a fair price;
- ☐ How to buy a used or a new car.

**These Features Will Make Life Even Easier:**

- ☐ A Practical Glossary of Automotive Terms that are in boldface throughout the book so you can refresh your memory if you've forgotten what some terms mean;
- ☐ A detailed Index where you can look up a part, or a problem, or a symptom, or a specific job and find the page you need;
- ☐ A Maintenance Record so that you can keep track of what you've done and when you did it;
- ☐ A Specifications Record, where you can keep all the information you need to buy the right parts for your car;
- ☐ A Tool Checklist so that you can tell what you need, what you already have, and what you'd like for Christmas;
- ☐ More than 300 illustrations that show you how things look, where they are, and what to do with them;
- ☐ A checklist that tells you if a used car is worth buying and if your car is worth keeping.

**This Revised Edition Also Tells You:**

- ☐ How to keep your car clean, young, and healthy looking, and how to repair the dents, dings, and other hard knocks that life has inflicted on its body;
- ☐ A whole bunch of stuff about diesel engines, turbocharging, fuel injection, electronic ignitions, and other innovations that may come into your life, like it or not;
- ☐ How to travel happily by car and by trailer, and what to do if you meet with The Unexpected.

**You Have to Supply a Few Things Too!**

- ☐ You have to buy the book;
- ☐ You have to take the time to read it through, just once;
- ☐ You have to try to do one small, easy job yourself (and you can pick the job).

**And That's What's So Special About This Book!**

It is probably the only auto repair manual designed for people who think they *can't* do it themselves, feel they wouldn't like it anyway, but are willing to give it a try. How do I know it will work for these reluctant readers? Because it is written by a genuine, certified, ex-dummy who has found that despite total ignorance and a complete lack of manual dexterity, working on a car is enjoyable, rewarding, and easy. And, believe me, if I can do it, so can you!

DEANNA SCLAR

# Acknowledgments

Terry Miller of the Automotive Parts and Accessories Association (APAA), Tim Sullivan, Rick Johnson, and Jack Trotter—the "godfathers" of the original edition. Your good advice, bright ideas, valuable leads, and unhesitating friendship meant a lot to me. I hope the good Karma flows back your way!

Don Donesley, my first automotive guru, whose classes and advice made this book possible. Thanks for introducing me to three of the finest things in life: cars, beer, and the Mojave Desert!

Julia Hamm, automotive specialist and good friend, who brought the experience and insight of more than twenty years as a mechanic and instructor to the second revised edition. Thanks for being there when I needed you!

Tim Tierney and Bob McMinn, of the Automotive Parts and Accessories Association (APAA), who offered valuable suggestions for the revised editions. Thanks for the time and trouble!

The members of the APAA, who have provided over 250 illustrations. Thanks for keeping costs down!

Rosemarie Kitchin, Bob Rodriguez, Tom Houston, Anton Veseley, and A. B. Schuman, who provided leads and illustrations for the first revised edition. You are the kind of friendly, helpful people who make working in the automotive field a pleasure indeed!

The old Thursday Evening Auto Class at University High School, a truly communal group who shared ideas, tools, and elbow grease; served as guinea pigs for one another; changed master cylinders by flashlight; and got it all together over beer and pizza afterward. Wherever you all are now, pals, thanks for being your beautiful selves!

John Cutsinger, who provided the kind of backup that every writer needs to free her so she can write. Thanks for the hot meals, the errands run, the unfailing good humor, and the sympathy that only another car-freak can offer.

And, finally, thanks to *Tweety Bird*, faithful Mustang, who survived all the experiments and mistakes and grew up to be a fine car and a worthy steed, and to *Honeybun*, my dream car come true.

# Contents

# Preface to the Second Revised Edition

The automotive field has seen many changes since *Auto Repair for Dummies* was first published in 1976. As inflation increased, the price of automobiles soared and so did the cost of fuel. For that matter, since then the price of everything has gone up: tools, parts, labor—even the beer you may drink after the job is done. As a result, many people who never before dreamed of getting their hands greasy now think seriously about doing the basic maintenance on their cars themselves.

Money hasn't been the only motivation: many of us have become terribly concerned about the environment, particularly the air pollution that threatens to reach toxic proportions. Although the EPA has established new standards that have brought about major changes in automotive technology and design, when it became obvious that there was a direct relationship between how efficiently our cars ran and the extent to which they fouled the air, we found that owning a fuel-efficient car simply wasn't enough: if the car wasn't properly tuned and lubricated, its fuel efficiency dropped drastically. So, for many of us, maintaining and tuning our cars has become a personal contribution toward protecting our environment.

Other dramatic changes in consciousness have made it vitally important for an increasing number of people to work on their cars themselves: growing consumer awareness has changed our attitude toward saving money from "penny-pinching" to "affirmative action," and many of us no longer are willing to waste precious time and money by laying the responsibility for the care of our possessions on someone else. Women everywhere now feel powerful enough to take on tasks that had previously been exclusively relegated to males, and learning to maintain and repair a big "power object" like a car has given us confidence we've never felt before.

As all of these factors have contributed to the continuing success of *Auto Repair for Dummies*, it's been necessary for me to keep my readers up to date on changes as they occur. In 1983 I wrote a revised edition, nearly double the size of the first, which provided information on new developments and systems as well as five additional chapters of material readers had requested. Since then, advances in electronic technology have radically altered nearly every automotive system, and although the new cars generally function more efficiently and require less maintenance than older models, in many cases it's difficult and dangerous to work on them yourself. Because of this, many people have clung to their older cars (as I have), but new-car owners urgently need to know what work they can do on their high-voltage cars without damaging delicate systems—or themselves. To keep up with all of this, I've appeared on more than 400 radio and television shows as a car-care expert and consumer spokesperson; written articles for several national magazines, including regular features in *Boys' Life* and *Family Circle*; taught adult education car-care classes; produced this second revised edition; and created a home video called *Auto Repair for Dummies: The Maintenance Tape,* to serve as a companion piece to the book.

On a personal level, I've also restored two cars, a truck, and a house; changed my marital status, my hometown, and my philosophy on life; written two more books; watched my kids grow into young adults; and then sailed halfway around the world, crewing on yachts, when I knew they could make it on their own. Through all of this, I've found that I still ask myself certain questions before undertaking *any* job, and I'd like to pass them on to you:

— Do I really want to do this? Will it be fun—or horrendous? (I never do anything that doesn't *feel* good anymore, unless it's absolutely necessary.)

— Do I know how to do it? If not, where do I go to learn?

— Does it require such expensive tools that it would cost less to have someone do it for me than to buy them? Can I borrow the tools I'll need?

— If I goof, can something be seriously damaged? Can I?

— How long will it take and what is my time worth? How much money will I save by doing it myself?

— Will I violate any warranties by doing it myself?

Surprisingly, almost every job listed in this book will pass these tests. If you find one that doesn't, don't hesitate to turn it over to a mechanic—*after* you've read enough to know that the job is definitely necessary, what it entails, whether the work has been done properly, and how to get satisfaction if it wasn't.

One more thing: before you start *any* job, read "How to Disassemble Anything (and Get It Back Together Again)" on page 213. It works not only for cars but for any gadget or appliance—even toys and furniture with instructions translated loosely from Japanese. (Come to think of it, they produce so many popular cars in Japan, it's probably time someone translated this book *into* Japanese!)

And now, welcome to the second revised edition of *Auto Repair for Dummies,* which should continue to be useful until the last automotive system has been replaced by a little black box. Until then, may you and your car have a long and happy life together!

DEANNA SCLAR
SANTA BARBARA, CALIFORNIA

# How I Became Intimately Involved with My Automobile, and Why You'll Want to Do It, Too

For many of us, getting a driver's license is an event that runs second only to getting a diploma or a marriage license. We study, practice, and take the test in a state of high anticipation, marred only by the fear of failing and being "grounded" forever.

Most of us succeed in passing and hop happily into our cars, headed for the freedom of the open road. Unfortunately, most of us don't know the first thing about the machine we've been licensed to drive—and this can turn a ticket to freedom into a ticket to trouble.

I'm not necessarily talking about physical danger. Our state motor vehicles bureaus have made fairly sure that we know how to drive defensively and can handle a car under poor driving conditions. What I am referring to is the kind of trouble that comes from being dependent upon other people for the care and repair of our automobiles.

If you are like most people who don't know anything about cars, you probably tend to drive around until something goes wrong, and then incur the expense of replacing worn and burnt-out parts—or the entire engine, for that matter—when low-cost, regular maintenance could have kept your wheels turning for a long time.

Even if your mechanics are honest, they are not going to notify you, as your dentist does, when it's time for a checkup. And charitable souls that they may be, they are not going to put their time and labor into your car without charging you for them. Since they have had to order, stock, and lay out cash for parts and supplies, they are going to want to make a profit on these too. Many of us have found that it simply isn't worth the extra money to get other people to do the things we can do for ourselves. And some of us are getting tired of having other people assume, just because we are teen-agers or women, that we aren't capable of handling repairs ourselves.

As a woman who has just gotten involved with her car, I'm here to tell you that we don't have to stand for this kind of thing! Getting involved with your car is easy and enjoyable and can save you a heck of a lot of money.

Whether you are trying to cut expenses, are tired of being patronized, or have just fallen in love with your first car, this book will tell you how your car works, what it needs in the way of tender loving care, and how to keep from getting ripped off if you have to entrust repairs to someone else. By handling the simple maintenance and tune-ups yourself, by being able to diagnose trouble and perform the less complex repairs yourself, you will earn the respect of your family, your mechanic, and your car—and, most of all, you'll feel pretty good about it! I know, because I've been there....

Before I moved to California I was an ordinary urban cliff-dweller. Oh, I had a nodding acquaintance with cars; ours was locked up in a garage, to be summoned forth by Herb, who was my husband at the time, for excursions to "the country." But aside from these occasions, I tended to think of transportation in terms of subways, buses, and taxis.

All the maintenance on our automobile was done by the garage that housed it. Every few months the garageman would comment, "Seems a little rough, could use a tune-up," and Herb would agree and give him the go-ahead. My sole contribution to our automotive life was choosing the color whenever we bought a new car (the only reason I had that much responsibility was that Herb is color blind), and since we rarely managed to put more than a few thousand miles on our car each year, these occasions were few and far between.

I had gotten a driver's license a few years back so I could go to the supermarket during our summers in the country or drive down to the lake for a swim, but driving in the city seemed to be a cross between foolishness and suicide, and I rarely, if ever, did it.

How did such a scared rabbit get to be an "authority" on automotive repairs, and where did she get the nerve to write about it? Funny you should ask. . . .

When we moved to California, I must confess, my enthusiasm for a life in the sun was considerably dampened by the knowledge that this would also include a life on the freeway. For the first few months Herb dutifully packed me into the family car and drove me to work, a distance of around 20 miles. Then he would turn around and drive home again. Each evening he would pick me up at work and take me home. Now, Herb is a very nice guy. And the drive took him through some very pretty scenery. But he had a business of his own to deal with, and the extra 80 miles and hour and a half a day did nothing to improve his temperament. And I was beginning to feel my oats. It began with a solo marketing excursion, and then that marvelous feeling of freedom that comes with sliding behind the wheel began to take hold, and before I knew it, I was looking for a car of my own.

Since the family budget had been considerably strained by the move West, the best I could do was a six-year-old Mustang with more than 70,000 miles on it. A friend of mine, who had grown up in Los Angeles—and was therefore a qualified expert on cars—checked the car out and pronounced it drivable. He said it might need "a little work." We took it to a reliable mechanic, who checked it over, tuned it up, and told me that it was a "classic." "They don't make them that way anymore," he explained. "Any time you want to get rid of it, just let me know. I can always use another car."

Thus reassured, I drove the car to the motor vehicle bureau for registration. I parked the car, turned off the ignition, locked it, and found that, sitting there in the middle of the parking lot, the car was singing! A bit puzzled, I rechecked the ignition and the radio, but everything was truly shut off. And still the car sang. By the time I returned, all was quiet. But that night, when I took the family out to dinner, old Tweety Bird began to sing again. Several weeks of filling and refilling the radiator, changing the coolant, putting gunk in the radiator to block any leaks, and so on managed to reduce the singing somewhat. But when I found out, $40 later, that all she needed was a new $2 radiator cap, I was made abruptly aware of two things:

First, Tweety was mine, and my responsibility. If she didn't work, I wasn't going to be able to either. And second, it was going to be impossible to enter this symbiotic relationship properly if I didn't know anything about her, because the garage bills were going to send both of us down the drain. The idea of putting myself into a piece of machinery and driving it at least 80 miles a day, at high speeds (this was pre-energy crisis), without the faintest idea of how it worked or what to do if it fell apart on the freeway, had become unthinkable.

So, after conning a friend of mine who happened to have two sets of car tools into taking an auto shop class with me at a local adult education center, I entered into what will probably turn out to be the closest relationship anyone has ever had with an inanimate object.

Of course the term "inanimate" is not really accurate. When you realize that a car exhibits most of the symptoms of life—it is self-propelled, reacts to outside stimuli, consumes fuel and discharges wastes, and even manages to sing a little tune now and then—it is really hard not to respond to it as though it were another living thing. (How far you go along with this idea is your own business. It is not a prerequisite for getting into auto repair, but it helps.)

The first thing I discovered was that cars are pretty simple things to deal with. Instead of a bewildering array of weird metal objects and miles of hoses, which threatened to blow up if I turned a screw in the wrong direction, I soon found that a car is just a series of simple Rube Goldberg mechanisms linked together. Since each repair, problem, or tune-up involves only a few, isolated gadgets, Tweety soon stopped being a mystery and began to be fun to hang around with.

Before long, just knowing what made the car go was not satisfying enough. After hanging around the auto shop watching other amateurs work on their cars, I began to itch to get into my own. The first steps were a bit awkward; I kept expecting the darn thing to blow up or break down if I made a mistake. Then I made the same discovery I'd made about my first child—the best way to handle a car (or a baby) is to take a firm grip on things and do the job without mincing around. Both the car and the baby seem to equate a little rough handling with assurance on your part. The results make for more security all around. From there, it was only a short step to forgetting about simply being able to communicate knowledgeably with a mechanic: I wanted to be the mechanic *myself* whenever possible.

One other note for my fellow females. No matter how liberated you've become, or how committed you still are to life as a "pussycat," you cannot fail to enjoy the heady pleasure that comes with being able to stride up to a garage mechanic and tell him you've recently rebuilt your carburetor! We'll get into all the money that moves like rebuilding your carburetor will save you, but just between us, knowing as much—or more—about cars than do the men you live with, or meet, is much richer stuff!

When I began to frequent auto-parts places, to get the things I needed for my work on Tweety, they used to go into the back and call out the other guys to see "the lady mechanic." Now we all stand around, peering under the hood, exchanging ideas, and I am "one of the boys." It beats getting whistled at, and it sure beats getting ripped off! To cap my pleasure, Herb, who had never gotten involved with auto repairs, respectfully requested that I teach him how to tune his car. Oh, bliss!

As a matter of fact, I've met a great many men who are intelligent, well educated, and know a great deal about law, business, literature, medicine, and other nonautomotive subjects but know absolutely nothing about cars. For some reason, most of them are ashamed of their ignorance and live as "closet dummies" who nod and smile wisely at the incomprehensible mutterings of their mechanics and shell out money for repairs neither fully understood nor always needed. For nonmechanical males this book can be "instant macho." You can finally learn what you need to know without having to admit you didn't, and you'll probably find that you enjoy being "one of the boys" as much as I do.

To my amazement, not only did learning about the inner secrets of my car turn out to be fascinating, but working on it myself soon became a great deal of fun. There is something about doing physical work and seeing the tangible results as soon as you drive away that is very, very rewarding. Another rewarding thing is seeing the difference between what it would have cost to have the work done professionally and the little bit of expense involved in buying the stuff yourself and doing your own maintenance and repairs.

In exchange for a total of 2 to 5 hours of your time, you can save as much as $200 in a single day by doing the basic maintenance on your car yourself. Not only will you save money, but you'll have the pleasure of knowing that the work has been done—and done correctly—because you'll have done it yourself!

This holds true whether you own an older car with a distributor that needs its points replaced and its carburetor adjusted regularly or a more recent model with fuel injection and an electronic ignition system that should be serviced professionally. Why? Because even the newest, most "maintenance-free" cars still need their filters, oil, coolant, spark plugs, hoses, belts, windshield wipers, and other parts and fluids replaced. If you do it yourself, for less money, you'll find that you'll do it more often and save additional money by preventing the extra wear and tear that negligence can cause.

Since you'll be working for love rather than money, you'll not only save on labor but on parts as well. Not only do mechanics have to charge more than the basic retail price for parts to cover the costs of purchasing and stocking them, but many auto-parts stores run special sales of basic maintenance items like spark plugs, oil, and various filters. If you keep an eye out for such sales and stock up on parts for later use, you can save time as well as money because you won't have to head for the store when the urge to work on the car hits you—you'll have everything right on hand. However, when looking for bargains, beware of one thing: be sure the products you buy have been made by well-known manufacturers. In recent years, there's been a rash of "counterfeit" car parts: shoddy merchandise packaged to look like high-quality, well-established brands. So read the label carefully before you buy.

How much you actually save will vary with the situation, but here's one example: Years ago I succumbed to laziness and allowed a local service station to change my **oil** and **coolant** for me. When the bill came to more than $50, I could only feel that I richly deserved it. When you consider that, at that time, I could have bought the coolant on sale for less than $4 and flushed and filled the engine by merely turning the knob of a $3 attachment and connecting a garden hose, *and* that the oil could have cost less than $7 and changing it only involved removing the plug, allowing the **crankcase** to drain, replacing the plug, and pouring in the oil, you can see that I paid a great deal for the convenience of having someone else do it.

I'm not saying I was charged unfairly for the work I had done—the prices seemed quite standard for my neighborhood—but the mechanics did neglect to change the **oil filter**, so I had to wait until I needed another oil change to do it. Since the filter was pretty old, that next oil change came up long before it would have if I'd done the job properly myself. Besides, I probably spent as much time and trouble getting to and from the service station as it would have taken me to do the job at home!

Today, having those jobs done for me would probably cost even more; and as the cost of labor continues to rise, such services will become even more costly in the future. On the other hand, it's interesting to note that the cost of the basic *supplies* involved has remained remarkably stable. If you compare the cost of a quart of automotive oil to the cost of a quart of milk over the past five years, you'll find that the former costs little more than it did before while the latter has risen dramatically. And the same goes for coolant and many filters. On labor-intensive jobs, the difference between doing it yourself and having it done for you is even more dramatic: spark plugs may cost little more than they used to, but a major **tune-up** can run into hundreds of dollars even though the cost of the parts required is negligible.

If you are still with me and are now eager to get started (or at least are willing to read on while reserving judgment), then let me tell you a bit about what this book will cover and what it will not.

First, we'll talk about tools. Although you may not have a friend with a spare set, tools needn't be a major investment. You can borrow some of the more specialized ones, and there is really no need to go for the finest unless you are planning to start a business. There are, however, some tools that everyone should own, and we'll get into these in terms of what, to buy, how to judge quality, and what they are for.

After a brief discussion of the basic principles and parts that make your car go—just so you'll know what you are dealing with—we'll get down to basics. We'll talk about each of the major systems in turn: the **electrical system**, the **fuel system**, the **cooling system, brakes, steering** and **suspension, lubrication**, and **transmission**. We'll discuss each system in everyday terms, with no jargon and no unnecessary technical details but with lots of simple illustrations. And we'll go into the tune-up and maintenance of each system with detailed instructions that leave nothing (I promise!) to the imagination.

There will be simple drawings that show *how* something works, with no attempt to show what it actually looks like, just the clearest possible picture of *what is actually going on*—and photographs that show *where* to find the part in your car and *what it really looks like*. I've tried to make the illustrations easier to follow than those instructions that tell you how to put together the toy you bought your kid for Christmas.

There will be chapters on how to lubricate your car and change your oil and oil filter, how to inspect your brakes (although we won't get into many brake repairs here; it can be dangerous if you should goof), how to eliminate future trouble by looking at your spark plugs and **tires**, how to tune your **ignition** and **carburetor**, how to buy tires and how to change a flat, how to flush out your **radiator** and change your coolant, and how to diagnose transmission trouble. Other chapters of the book will provide information on buying and maintaining diesel engines, how to save fuel and cut down on air pollution, how to keep your car clean and rust-free, easy ways to remove small dents and touch up paint, and a host of other useful items.

There will be pre-trip safety instructions that should keep the "bugs" out of the car, even if they get into your picnic lunch; how to rent or buy a trailer and drive it safely; tips on what to pack and what to do if, despite your tender loving care, your car drops dead on the freeway or you find yourself involved in an accident.

If it is safe, and fun, to do the work yourself, I'll tell you how to do it. If it is just too hairy to deal with yourself, I'll tell you how to find and communicate with a good mechanic, how to do enough trouble shooting to have a good idea of what's wrong and what work is needed, how to make sure you get what you pay for, and what to do if you get ripped off anyway.

If all else fails and another car seems to be the only solution, I'll show you how to evaluate and get the best deal on new and used cars.

I've provided a Glossary, and throughout the book the terms that appear in it are printed in bold type, in case you forget what a **differential** is and don't want to search for the chapter that introduced you to it. There's a large Index, where you can look for a part, a system, or a problem when you return to this book for instructions. You will also find a Tool Checklist, a Maintenance Record to remind you to get busy if you've let things go too long, and a handy Specifications Record so you'll have the numbers of the parts you'll need when you go to the auto supply store.

I suggest you read the book right through the first time. After that initial excursion, just tuck the book into your trunk compartment, or under the front seat, so you can have it handy when it's time to tune up or make an adjustment or figure out what has gone wrong. I'd suggest you do your preliminary reading within walking distance of your car (you might want to curl up on the front seat) so you can open the hood and see for yourself that it's all in there just as I said. Then try an ignition tune-up for starters and, thus reassured, get into the rest of the stuff. I hope you'll find it as exhilarating as I did, and I know your car will love you for it!

# The Way to
# Your Car's Heart Is
# Through Your Toolbox

Standard Screwdrivers
Rosco Tools Inc.

Standard Screws
Jack Herlihy

Whether you are trying to cook up a decent meal, paint a picture, run an office, or work on your car, you are only going to be as good as your tools will allow you to be. Just as you can't slice things super thin with a bent, rusty, dull knife—and you can't type a professional-looking letter on a broken-down typewriter—so it is impossible to do any kind of job on your engine if you lack the means to loosen or remove parts, clean or gap them, reinstall them, adjust them, and test the results.

Now, before you run off to return this book because you aren't prepared to spend a lot of money on tools that will probably never get used again after you've ruined your engine or cut off your thumb, let me tell you that all you really need are a few basic implements and that they are not very expensive (we'll deal with the engine and your thumb later). In fact, you probably already own most of them. Prices vary widely, but if you do your shopping in a major auto-parts chain store and stick to well-known brands, you will get good value at a fair price. Be sure to watch the paper for sales; most chains have them regularly, and you can save a lot of money. Also, if you buy each kind of tool in sets of different sizes, rather than buying at random, you will save there too. Look for high-grade steel, with no rough edges. Pick out friendly-looking salespeople and ask them what kind they buy. Most of them are auto enthusiasts who will be delighted that you are planning to do your own work (and be a future customer), and they will be glad to point out the best buys.

**Screwdrivers**

First of all, you are going to need a couple of screwdrivers, so get out the toolbox and see what you already have in stock.

There are two basic types of screwdrivers, and you will need a few of each type (not just for your car but for almost anything that has to be done around the house). The most common ones are called *standard screwdrivers* (or slot screwdrivers), and the others are called *Phillips screwdrivers*. They have different heads made to fit Phillips screws. You cannot use a standard screwdriver on a Phillips screw, or vice versa. Since your car is fitted with both types of screws, in a variety of sizes, it is necessary to have several of both kinds. Using a screwdriver of the wrong type or size will result in damage to the screw, the screwdriver, or yourself. Always use a screwdriver with a tip that is the same width as the head of the screw you are working on. The shafts will vary in length too, and this is useful, because a longer shaft will provide greater leverage for hard-to-remove screws, while a shorter shaft will get into tight places more easily. You can get all the screwdrivers you need for a couple of dollars. Look for sales of plastic-handled screwdrivers, in sets of varying sizes.

By the way, if you find yourself confronted with a screw that is difficult to start unscrewing, try giving it a slight twist in the *opposite* direction (clockwise), as though you were trying to tighten it. Then loosen it (counterclockwise). If this doesn't work, rap the screw on the head with a hammer, which should loosen it a bit. This works for bolts too. If strong-arm tactics aren't getting you anywhere, you can try squirting the troublemaker with a can of penetrating oil.

Keep your temper with difficult screws; otherwise you'll risk stripping the threads and turn a fairly simple job of replacing what you've loosened into a hair puller.

Phillips Screwdrivers
Rosco Tools Inc.

Phillips Screws
Jack Herlihy

## Screwholders

Screwholders are perfectly marvelous for hanging on to screws that have to fit into tiny places. Instead of hanging on to the screw with the fingers of one hand while you wield the screwdriver with the other, you simply fit the screw into the screwholder and use the screwholder instead of a screwdriver. Some screwholders have a magnet to hold the screw; others have a little gizmo that grabs the screw when you twist the screwholder. Both are lovely.

Screwholder
Pendleton Tool Industries, a subsidiary of
Ingersoll-Rand Company

000-011

Open-End Wrench
Husky Hand Tools

Box-End Wrench
Husky Hand Tools

**Wrenches** These are probably the most basic tools for auto repair. You will need a couple of different kinds, in different sizes. Most wrenches are available in both standard measurements and in metric measurements, and you must know which system of measurement your engine is based on. Originally, most foreign cars were based on the metric system, while domestic engines used standard fractions of an inch. Then, in the mid-seventies, American car makers began to switch to metric parts. Today most cars are built entirely on the metric system. Therefore, check your owner's manual or with your dealer to see if your car requires metric or standard tools before you buy anything.

There are several basic types of wrenches, some for very specialized purposes, but the following are the kinds you will need for most jobs. Again, look for sets made by well-known toolmakers and try to buy them on sale.

Combination Wrenches
Pendleton Tool Industries, a subsidiary of
Ingersoll-Rand Company

**Combination Wrenches** There are *open-end wrenches* and *box-end wrenches,* but the very best kind to get are *combination wrenches,* with an open end and a closed end on each wrench. These wrenches come in sets of several sizes, and each wrench is made to fit a nut of a specific size, whichever end you use.

Some combination wrenches are sort of S-shaped. These are good for hard-to-reach spots and are called *offset wrenches*. You might want to add a couple to your tool kit. The most useful offset wrench is the *distributor wrench*. You use it to adjust your **timing**. Be sure to get one to fit the **distributor hold-down clamp** on your car. If you're not sure what a distributor hold-down clamp is or where to find it, see the Glossary or Chapter 5.

**Offset Wrenches**

Ignition Wrenches

Offset Distributor Wrench
K-D Manufacturing Co.

Ignition wrenches are simply sets of combination wrenches in very small sizes for ignition work. You can get a set for a couple of dollars.

**Ignition Wrenches**

Some of the screws or fastenings in your car may have oddly shaped holes in the center of the heads. These require special wrenches, which are L-shaped rods that fit into the holes. If the center hole is hexagonal, you will need an Allen wrench (sometimes called a "hex" wrench). You can buy a set of assorted sizes for under $5.

**Allen Wrenches**

"Hex" wrench

Allen or "Hex" Wrench

**How to Use a Wrench**

To use the open end of a wrench most effectively, place it around the nut you want to remove and move the wrench to the right so that the screw moves in a counterclockwise direction to loosen the nut. If the nut sticks, try a squirt of penetrating oil or give it a bang on the head with a hammer. Place your free hand over the wrench and the nut to give yourself some control and to stop the wrench from flying off the nut. When you move the wrench as far as it will go, the nut will have been loosened 15 degrees. (That's why the slot is at an angle.) By simply turning the wrench over so that the other surface of the same end is around the nut you can move the nut another 15 degrees without having to place the wrench at a different angle.

How to Hold a Wrench
Pendleton Tool Industries, a subsidiary of
Ingersoll-Rand Company

Always use the proper-size wrench. If you use one that is too big, it will slip and round off the edges of the nut. This will make the nut harder to tighten later on. It will also round off the inside edges of the wrench, with the same results.

A good set of **socket wrenches** will really make the difference between enjoying your work or killing yourself over it. These come in sets for around $20, less if you catch a sale. Your set of socket wrenches should contain the following basic items:

1　A variety of ¼-inch or ⅜-inch drive heads or *sockets*. The ½-, ⁹/₁₆-, and ¾-inch sockets are the ones you'll use the most, unless you need a metric set. The word "drive" refers to the size of the square hole in each socket where it attaches to the **ratchet handle**. It is easy to remember that the smaller the drive, the smaller the job you use it for. Quarter-inch drive is for tiny areas, ⅜-inch is standard; other drives up to 2 inches are for really big jobs. You won't need these. You can use adapters to convert sockets of one drive to fit handles of another drive.

2　A **spark plug socket**. This is the large socket with a soft lining to hold the spark plug securely without damaging its soft jacket when you are removing and inserting it, or when you drop it on the floor by mistake.

3　At least one **ratchet handle**, to which you can fit any of the sockets. Most sets have one handle with at least one adapter. You might want to add additional adapters to extend the handle to different sizes and to adapt it to different drives. A *flex-head* handle or adapter is also very useful. It enables you to hold the ratchet handle at any angle when working in tight places—and engines are full of tight places!

The way to tell a good socket-wrench set is to look at the number of teeth in the ratchet handle. Most have 20 to 30 teeth. The really good ones have up to 60 teeth. The more teeth the handle has, the better it will fit into tight places. This is because you have to move the handle only a few degrees to turn the nut as much as a cheaper handle would in many degrees. In other words, a ratchet handle with 24 teeth must be moved 15 degrees to reach its limit. A handle with 60 teeth has to be moved only 6 degrees to turn a nut as far.

**Socket Wrenches**

Socket Wrench Set
Oxwall Tool Company

Spark Plug Socket
Oxwall Tool Company

| | | | | |
|---|---|---|---|---|
| **A** | –Adapter | **K** | –Regular 6-point socket |
| **B, C, E** | –Extension bars | **L** | –Regular 12-point socket |
| **D** | –Sliding T handle | **M** | –Hollow screw socket bit |
| **F** | –Deep 6-point socket | **N** | –Universal 12-point socket |
| **G** | –Deep 12-point socket | **O** | –Flex handle |
| **H** | –Spark plug socket | **P** | –Flex head ratchet |
| **I** | –Speeder handle | **Q** | –Reversible ratchet |
| **J** | –Ratchet adapter | **R** | –Universal joint |

Ratchet Handles, Extenders, and Adapters
Hand Tools Institute, New York

### Torque Wrenches

A **torque wrench** is designed to tighten a nut, bolt, or screw to an exact degree. This is extremely handy because until one becomes familiar with a job, there is always the danger of undertightening or overtightening things. If you are replacing a spark plug and you do not tighten it enough, it will work loose and fail to deliver a spark. If you overtighten it you can strip the threads or crack the plug. Similarly, parts that have **gaskets** can leak if the bolts that hold them are not tightened enough. But if you overtighten the same bolts, the gasket will be crushed and it will leak anyway. Most really good torque wrenches are expensive, but you will find that a cheaper one is good enough to serve your purposes. If you'd rather not spend the money until you are sure you are really going to like working on your car, it might be a good idea to borrow one, just to get the feel of how tight a nut, bolt, etc., should be. Or you can just forget the whole thing. I've never used a torque wrench; my set of socket wrenches has accomplished everything quite well, but I might just have been lucky. I'll probably borrow a torque wrench soon, and if I really like it, maybe I'll invest in one someday. Anyway, if you are planning to buy one, keep these things in mind:

1 Get a wrench with a slim profile, because torque wrenches are bulky anyway and will often not fit in tight places.

2 Get the kind that has an audible click when you reach the proper degree of tightness. The dial kind sometimes cannot be seen if you are working in a dark place or "by feel" in a remote corner of your engine. There is a torque wrench with a dial that lights up when you have tightened the bolt to the proper degree, but these are expensive. A click should do—if you don't sing while you work.

3 Torque wrenches should be gripped well down the shaft (not up close to the dial) and should be operated smoothly.

4 It is best to tighten a series of bolts out of sequence, to distribute the pressure evenly, instead of in strict clockwise or counterclockwise order.

5 When tightening a series of bolts, tighten them all just until they are snug. Then go back and tighten them all a bit more. Then go back and tighten them all the way to the torque specifications. This will ensure that the entire part you are tightening is under even pressure. It will prevent leaky gaskets and increase the life of the bolt and the part. This is good advice (so is 4) to follow when using any kind of wrench to tighten anything.

(*left*) Dial Torque Wrench (*right*) Deflecting Beam Torque Wrench
Pendleton Tool Industries, a subsidiary of Ingersoll-Rand Company

Carpenter's Hammer
Channellock, Inc.

You may associate these with carpentry, but they are useful in automotive work as well. A *carpenter's hammer (or claw hammer)* is not really designed for auto repair.

**Hammers**

**Ball-peen Hammer**
Channellock, Inc.

You should have a *ball-peen* hammer. If all you have is a carpenter's hammer and you don't want to buy another one, you can probably make do with it. Just be sure that the hammer you use does not have a loose head. If the shaft is not securely sunk into the head, it can fly off and damage your car, yourself, or an innocent bystander. Claw hammers can also be dangerous because a hard, solid impact can cause the claws to break off, with dismal results.

**Needle-nosed Pliers**
Rosco Tools Inc.

**Pliers**   Rummage through the family toolbox for these. Almost everyone has *needle-nosed* and *slip-joint* pliers, and these will be useful. If you are prepared to buy pliers, however, the very best kind to get are *combination slip-joint pliers*. These general-purpose tools can be adjusted to several widths by a sliding pin. They also usually have a wire-cutting slot built into them as well. If you are the only person on your block who doesn't possess these, by all means rush out and buy them before dark. Again, they needn't be expensive. Just be sure they work easily, are made of forged hardened steel, and seem to be well finished.

**Combination Slip-Joint Pliers**
Channellock, Inc.

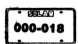

A few notes on the use of pliers. If you are working on electrical wiring and want to be sure you won't get shocked, slip a length of rubber hose over each handle, leaving the hose in one piece. This will not only insulate the pliers; it will allow them to spring open quickly. Never use combination pliers on nuts and bolts—they will round off the corners and make them harder to replace. Besides, that's what you have all your lovely wrenches for.

**Tool Kits**

If, as you read this chapter, you are made painfully aware that you are going to have to go out and buy practically everything, you might want to look into pre-packaged tool kits. Nearly every major supplier carries a tool kit with everything you need already in it, and if you are totally tool-poor, one of these may prove to be the best buy. Be sure you are getting good quality, however. It's better to have a couple of tools that work well than a large assortment of junk. And while we're on the subject, empty toolboxes are inexpensive and worth buying. They keep tools clean and in good shape and, most important, all in one place. Look for one that will fit easily into the trunk of your car. Although your tools will be useful around the house, it's very nice to have them handy if you get stuck away from home.

Cars with electronic ignitions don't need tune-ups, and they require special, expensive tools for adjustments. If you have one, forget about buying the feeler gauges, timing lights, and tach/dwell meters described below. You can consult your owner's manual to see if yours is simple enough to adjust yourself, and what tools you'd need, but chances are you will be happy to have a professional maintain the system for you.

**Gauges**

The next two items are specialized tools that are used for "gapping" spark plugs, points, and valves. They are very inexpensive—some stores give them away as

Wire Feeler Gauges
K-D Manufacturing Co.

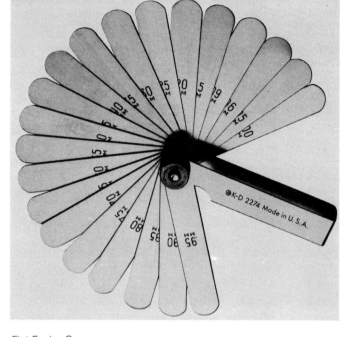

Flat Feeler Gauge
K-D Manufacturing Co.

Taper Feeler
Gauge
Snap-on Tools
Corporation

premiums. I will usually discuss specialized tools in the chapters that call for them, but I wanted to mention them now so you can pick them up while you're at an auto supply store buying other stuff.

**Wire and Taper Feeler Gauges**

Wire and taper **feeler gauges** are used for gapping spark plugs. "Gapping" simply means sliding the proper-sized wire or taper gauge between the spark plug electrodes to be sure the surfaces are the proper distance apart. This ensures that the spark can jump across the gap with the proper intensity.

**Flat Feeler Gauges**

Flat **feeler gauges** are used for adjusting valves and ignition contact points, relatively simple jobs that are impossible to do properly without a feeler gauge. Look for them as part of a set of tools—or as freebies in auto-parts stores—before you buy them.

Compression Gauges
DIXCO
Karcheck Products

**Compression Gauges**

**Compression gauges** are used to check the pressure that builds up in each cylinder as your engine runs. They also reveal damage to piston rings and valves. If your car is new, this is probably not going to be a problem for some time, but if it is older, or second-hand, this easy-to-use gauge is a good investment. It will help you spot trouble and save you money. The screw-in kind is easiest to use, but these usually cost a bit more.

**Work Lights**

Whether you plan to work on your car in your home garage, in your driveway, at the curb near your house, or in a local auto shop, you will find that the lighting will be inadequate once you get under the hood—or under the car if you are that adventurous. A **work light** will provide all the illumination you need, with the capability of shining the maximum amount of light right on the work area and not in your eyes. If you will not be working near an electrical outlet, you might need an extension cord, but these, and the work light, are not expensive items at all. Be sure your light has a protective cage around at least half of the bulb and that the cord is long enough and properly

Work Light
Guaranteed Parts Company

insulated. Look for the Underwriter's tag to be sure you are getting quality. Recently, a work light was re-called from the market because right under the bulb, there was a flexible handle with an open socket under that. You could plug additional accessories into this socket, but the convenience was considerably lessened because if you had nothing plugged into the socket, you ran the risk of "plugging yourself in" by gripping the work light on the socket area.

Most work-light cages have a hook at the top so that the light can be hung inside the hood of your car or on a nearby part. Just be certain you are not hooking the light to anything that carries electricity itself.

Get a good work light, with at least a 25-foot cord. Lights with shorter cords are cheaper, but if you need to buy a proper extension cord, it may cost you more in the long run.

You will find that a work light is useful for a variety of home repairs and for outside work at night, but if you are going to be working far from an outlet, there is also a work light that gets its power from your car's battery. I've also seen portable battery-powered fluo-rescent lanterns that are useful for night work and for camping.

**Scissor Jack**

**Tripod Jack**

**Hydraulic Jack**

Three Types of Jacks

**Jacks**  Most new cars come with a **jack** to be used when changing tires. If you have a secondhand car, or if your jack has been lying around neglected, you may need to buy one. There are several types of jacks available; just be sure the jack you buy is suited to your car's bumper design. Check your jack periodi-cally and lubricate it. Never use a jack without the base plate, and never jack your car up unless the wheels are properly blocked. We'll get into this in de-tail in Chapter 9.

One last word: Be sure your jack is in your trunk at all times. It is very depressing to know how to change a flat only to find that your jack is in your garage and your car is on the road.

Jack Stands
Foxcraft/Philmont, a Division of Gulf & Western Mfg. Co.

## Jack Stands

**Jack stands** are quite inexpensive and very important if you are going to work under your car. Get two of them and look for instructions in Chapter 9 before you use them.

## Timing Lights

A **timing light** is a specialized piece of equipment that is used to check ignition **timing**. You can find out what timing is and how a timing light is used by checking the Glossary, and full details are given in Chapter 5. It is standard equipment at every garage, and if you don't want to undertake the expense right away, borrow one from someone else in your neighborhood who works on his or her car. If you live in an isolated spot, or in an old folks' home, you might drive down to your local garage—after you've done your tune-up—and ask them to check your timing. They will promptly haul out their timing light, shine it at your engine, and give you an answer. The only trouble with this is, if your timing is off, they will not understand why they can't fix it for you. And if you tell them you are going to fix it yourself, you'd better plan to go to another garage for a timing check when you're through. Then, when you've exhausted all the garages in the neighborhood, you'll have to go out and buy a timing light anyway.

Timing Light
DIXCO

Tach-Dwell Meter
DIXCO

Generally, the more you pay for a timing light, the brighter it will be. Neon lights are the cheapest, but because they operate off the spark plug circuit and use minimal voltage, they may not produce enough light to see clearly, unless you work in almost total darkness. Xenon lights cost more, but provide more light. I'd suggest you buy a cheap light, try it out, and return it and buy the next more expensive one until you get what you need.

Be sure that the cord is long enough and that the clamps are properly insulated so that you can grab them easily without getting shocked. The light should go on and off with a "strobe" effect when the clamps are properly affixed. When you shine the light at the timing marks on the moving **crankshaft pulley** of your engine, this strobe effect will make the marks appear to stand still, so you can see if you have tuned your car properly. We'll go into the proper way to use this gadget, and what "timing" really means, in Chapter 5.

**Tach/Dwell Meters**

Although you can buy a gadget that is simply a **dwell meter**, try to find one called a *dwell/tachometer* or *tach/dwell meter*. This simply means that the gadget not only has a dwell meter for measuring your point gap but that it has a **tachometer** built in as well. The tachometer will measure the revolutions per minute (rpm) of your engine, and it is extremely valuable for adjusting your carburetor so that your car will idle properly. Look for a tach/dwell meter that has both high and low ranges on the tachometer—it will give you a more precise reading. Although you can get along without one, a tach/dwell meter (we'll just call it a "dwell meter" for short for the rest of the book) will provide a fast way to know whether you have set your **dwell** and idle properly. If you don't know what "dwell" and "idle" mean, relax. Basically they just mean that your car is running at a pace that ensures maximum mileage per gallon with optimum performance and minimum wear and tear. All shall be revealed to you in time; just have patience, fear not, and buy a dwell meter if you have the funds. If you don't, try to borrow a friend's until you are sure you are going to be working on your car regularly. I use the one at my auto shop class, but I am planning to ask Santa Claus for one this year, and if he fails me, I'll buy myself one for my birthday. If funds, friends, and Santa all fail you, don't let the lack of a dwell meter keep you from tuning your car, however. The chapter on ignition tune-ups will tell you how to do the job with feeler gauges. A dwell meter would simply be more accurate and would help in adjusting your carburetor, but it can wait.

**Fire Extinguishers**

A **fire extinguisher** is not really a tool, but it is a *must* for your car. Get the 2¾-pound dry chemical type. Engine fires do not necessarily mean that the car is ruined—if you can put them out quickly. Sometimes gasoline can leak out of your carburetor and be ignited by a stray spark from your spark plugs or from a cigarette butt thrown from a car window. The resulting fire looks awful, but it is really burning on the outside of your engine. If you put it out quickly, you may have little or no damage. Cigarette butts can also land on your back seat, and fires can be caused by ruptured **fuel lines**, flooded carburetors, and faulty wiring as well, so an inexpensive fire extinguisher may not only save you money; it may also save your life. If the flames are anywhere near the **fuel tank**, however, forget the heroics; just run for it and throw yourself to the ground if you think it might explode. Because your fuel tank is located right under your trunk compartment, keep your extinguisher under the front seat of your car, in a suitable bracket. Otherwise, it can roll under the pedals in normal stopping.

**Funnels**

Funnels are used for filling your radiator, adding oil, and adding **transmission fluid** to your car. Steal a large one from the kitchen, or buy one at an auto supply or hardware store. Either metal or plastic is fine.

**Other Things You'll Want to Carry in Your Car**

You probably have most of this stuff already, but here's a chance to check:

**Rags**

Rags should be clean and lint-free. Get rid of gasoline-soaked rags—they're highly combustible. Never keep them in closed places, but you know that already, right? Don't use an oily rag on anything that isn't oily already. Because your car contains a variety of substances that must be kept away from other substances (engine oil, transmission fluid, and grease eat rubber hoses, for instance), it is best to throw out—or wash—dirty rags, and go for a clean one each time you start a job. Keep a clean rag in your glove compartment; you'll need it (if for nothing else) to defog your windshield.

**Spare Parts**

When you replace your spark plugs and your **points**, save the old ones if they are not too worn. Carry them in your trunk compartment toolbox for a quick replacement if something goes wrong with those in your engine. The same goes for old, not-too-cruddy **air filters, fuel filters, rotors, fan belts**, and other minor gizmos. A couple of extra nuts, bolts, and screws will also help, in case you lose those you have or strip them accidentally. And hang on to extra pieces of hose, wire, etc., for makeshift repairs.

**Spare Tires**

Just a reminder to check your spare tire often. It is humiliating to go through the work of changing a tire only to find that your spare is flat, too. If your spare is worn beyond belief, most garages will sell you a not-too-hideous patched tire at a low price.

**Lug Wrenches**

A **lug wrench** is sometimes provided, along with the jack, on new cars. It is used to remove the wheel or lug nuts when you change your tires. But if you are going out to buy a lug wrench, get the *cross-shaft* kind. It will provide you with more leverage.

(*left*) Single-Shaft Lug Wrench (*right*) Cross-Shaft Lug Wrench
Alexandra Soto

**Jumper Cables**

One of the most common malfunctions of a car is the loss of power to start it, either from an old or faulty battery or because you've left the headlights on by mistake. Once in this situation, you can either wait for the AAA or a nearby garage to come and bail you out, or you can stop a passing car, whip out your **jumper cables**, attach them in seconds, and "jump a start" from the Good Samaritan's car to your own. Most people are willing to lend their cars to this sort of operation, because they lose nothing but a few minutes of their time. Full instructions for the proper way to "jump a start" can be found in Chapter 15.

You can buy a set of jumper cables for much less than you'd have to pay a garage if mechanics had to come to start your car. Good cables cost more because they have more strands of better-conducting wire which let more "juice" flow between the cars, with less loss of voltage. Sometimes the success or failure of an attempt to jump a start depends on the quality of the jumper cables and their grips. If you get a cheap set, there is an easy way to make them work better. Go under the plastic sheath that covers the place where the cables meet the grips and squeeze the connection tight with a pair of pliers. This will improve the connection, and the cheap set of cables will work beautifully—at least for the first few times.

Jumper Cables
Guaranteed Parts Company

**Snow and Ice Equipment**

If you live in an area that is cold in winter, try to carry a bag of *sand,* or *tire chains,* in case you find yourself dealing with icy conditions. A small shovel might be useful for digging out, and a scraper will help to clear your windshield if you've been parked in the snow and it has iced over.

**Flares and Flashlights**

A flashlight is always a good addition to your glove compartment. It will help your kids to locate dropped toys on the floor of the car, enable you to see under the hood if your car breaks down, and serve as an emergency light for oncoming traffic if you have to stop on the highway for repairs. You can use flares, but they can be dangerous, and many states have rules regarding their use on the highways. A flashlight with a red blinker is safer, more versatile, and just as good. Of course you will be sure to put in fresh batteries now and then, or carry a couple of extras.

**First-Aid Kit**   It is a good idea for both workshop and car to keep on hand a couple of Band-Aids, something soothing for burns, and a good antiseptic.

**Hand Cleaner**   Most of these hand cleaners are basically grease solvents. They range from heavy-duty stuff that removes the skin along with the grease; through nice, soothing, good-smelling creams that leave you feeling reborn; to pre-cleaners that you put on your hands *before* you start working, in order to be sure that the grease will slide off easily afterward. Some of these cleaners can also be rubbed into work clothes to remove grease and oil stains before you launder them.

**Gloves**   Keep a pair in the car for emergencies. Thin, tough, and comfortable surgical gloves are available at any pharmacy. They cost little and will keep the grease out from under your fingernails. One problem, however, is that gasoline or solvent will melt them. If you prefer, industrial rubber gloves, available at a swimming-pool supply store, are not affected by gasoline, solvent, or battery acid.

**Spare Tools**   If you can't carry your toolbox all the time, try to leave a couple of screwdrivers, some standard-size combination wrenches, and a can of penetrating oil in your trunk compartment. Remember, it is not necessary to buy everything at once in order to get started on your car; use the beg, borrow, and steal-from-the-family-toolbox method if you must. The important thing is to get to work!

**Hat**   To keep the dust and grease out of your hair, and to prevent long hair from being caught in moving parts, use a hat you can afford to get dirty. Painters' hats are available cheaply at hardware and paint stores.

Here is a handy checklist to help you keep track of what you have, what you need, and what you think you can do without. You can tear it out and take it to the store if you like.

## Tool Checklist
(Starred tools are optional, but definitely worth buying!)

| Tool | Have | Don't Have | Need Sizes: |
|---|---|---|---|
| Standard Screwdrivers | | | |
| Phillips Screwdrivers | | | |
| *Screwholder | | | |
| Combination Wrenches | | | |
| Ignition Wrenches | | | |
| *Distributor Wrench | | | |
| Socket Wrench Set | | | |
| *Flex-head Extension | | | |
| *Extra Handles & Adapters | | | |
| *Torque Wrench | | | |
| Ball-peen Hammer | | | |
| Needle-nosed Pliers | | | |
| Combination Slip-joint Pliers | | | |
| Wire and Taper Feeler Gauges | | | |
| Flat Feeler Gauge | | | |
| *Compression Gauge | | | |
| *Work Light | | | |
| Jack | | | |
| *Jack Stands | | | |
| *Timing Light | | | |
| *Dwell Meter/Tachometer | | | |
| *Fire Extinguisher | | | |
| Funnel | | | |
| Rags | | | |
| *Spare Parts | | | |
| Spare Tire | | | |
| Lug Wrench | | | |
| *Jumper Cables | | | |
| Flashlight | | | |
| First-Aid Kit | | | |
| Hand Cleaner | | | |
| Gloves | | | |
| Hat | | | |

SCLAR
000-029

# What Makes It Go?
# The Inner Secrets
# of Your Car Revealed

Anthropologists tell us that one of the major events that marked the transition of early man from "wise monkey" to a more civilized critter was the ability to get something else to do his work for him. Along with such major technological breakthroughs as the club and spear, the control of fire, and the invention of the loincloth was the eventual use of round logs, later called "wheels," to move things and people. Carts of various types, with wheels that allowed them to move easily, were pushed or pulled by men and animals for centuries. Eventually, some early science-fiction freak decided to invent a machine that could move itself, and the first engine appeared.

Today, most of us possess vehicles that can move themselves. True, we still have to tell our cars when to go and when to stop, and we have to steer them in the proper direction and keep them in good running order, but basically a car is simply a set of wheels and an engine to turn them.

The **internal combustion engine**, which forms the "heart" of your car, is a lightweight, fairly efficient, and relatively uncomplicated piece of machinery. It works on a mixture of gasoline and air to produce enough power to turn a shaft that turns the wheels. The basic gizmos on your car are simply the things that bring the fuel and air together in the proper quantities, ignite them, and channel the resulting power to the wheels. All the rest of the stuff is there to make this happen with ease and efficiency, to provide you with some control over what's going on, and to give you a place to sit and store your groceries. Power attachments provide comfort, at the price of additional cost and potential repairs. You pay your money and you take your choice.

O.K. Let's get down to specifics. First, let's take a look at your engine and the way it works.

Now remember, every car manufacturer has made sure to do something a little bit differently from the competition so that he can get patents and say that his cars are the best. Therefore, if any part of your car is not exactly where it is in the pictures in this book, don't panic. Just look for something that looks like it, in the same general area. Believe me, it will be in there someplace or your car would not go.

Your **owner's manual** should have a diagram that was probably gibberish to you until you bought this book. Now you can return to it and locate the parts of your car, if you can't find them on the car itself. If you are still up the wall, or if you didn't get an owner's manual, ask a friend who has the same make car, or ask your friendly garage mechanic, to point out these "missing" parts. I'm willing to bet, however, that if you read this chapter carefully, with an eye on your engine, you will be able to locate almost all the parts yourself.

By the way, if you don't have an owner's manual, ask your local distributor or car dealer to get one for you, or to tell you where you can get one. There are also **service manuals** available for every car, and it is a good idea to get one of these too. Again, ask the local distributor or dealer of your make car, or write to the company that made your car, with the words "Service Manuals" written on the envelope. The manufacturer will be very happy to sell you one. On the last pages of most owner's manuals there is information about obtaining service manuals. If all else fails, try your local public library for a commercially published service manual which deals with your particular car's year, make, and model. At first look, these seem very complicated; the schematic drawings are especially scary. But if you get to the point where you want to rebuild your carburetor, these drawings will show you where every little screw and washer fits, so you won't end up with a couple of "extra" parts at the end of the job. There's no need to rush out and get a service manual immediately, however. Most of the things we're going to cover right now can be learned without one.

And now back to our story...

First, I am going to run through the five basic systems very quickly, to give you a general idea of what goes on and how the parts and systems connect. Then we'll take it again, chapter by chapter and piece by piece, in greater detail. When we're done, you'll know about as much as I do concerning what makes your car go. Don't worry about what model you own; every car with an internal combustion engine works on the same principles in the same way.

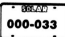

**The Electrical System**

Although we tend to think of cars as being basically powered by gasoline, there are many parts of the car that function on electricity. These include the radio, headlights, clock, etc. Of course, you could get along without these devices if you had to, but did you know that it takes electricity to get your car to *start*? This is accomplished by an **ignition system**, which works in conjunction with your car's electrical system. It provides the power that allows your starter to make your engine turn over. And once your engine turns over, it can begin to run on gasoline, just as you expected it to. Here's how it works:

All the electrical current for your car is supplied by the **battery**, which is constantly being recharged with electricity by the **generator** or the **alternator**. Unless your car is quite old, it probably has an alternator, which generates alternating current (AC) and then converts it to direct current (DC) so that it can run the various devices on the car. Older cars have generators, which generate DC directly. If you aren't sure which one you have, alternators are short, round, and silver-colored; generators are cylindrical, long, and black.

Once your car has started running, the ignition system continues to provide electric current to the spark plugs so that they can provide the spark that causes

Alternator

Ignition switch

Battery

The Charging System
Automotive Information Council (AIC)

Alternator
Delco-Remy Division, General Motors Corp.

the fuel to burn. To do this, the current passes from the alternator (or generator) to the **coil**, where it is amplified. From the coil, it goes to the **distributor**, which directs the current to the proper **spark plug** at the proper time. This is a bit more complicated than it seems, and so I have devoted the next chapter to explaining the ignition system in detail. But now, back to

Generator
Delco-Remy Division, General Motors Corp.

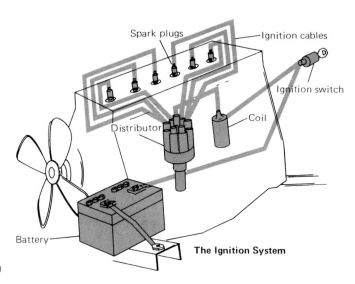

The Ignition System
Automotive Information Council (AIC)

what happens when you start your car. (Although fuel-injected cars don't have carburetors, most everything else is similar. See pages 134–138 for details.)

1 When you turn the key in your car's **ignition switch** to "Start," you close a circuit that allows the current to pass from your battery to your **starter**, via the **starter solenoid switch**.

2 Your starter makes your engine **turn over** (that's the growling sound you hear before the engine

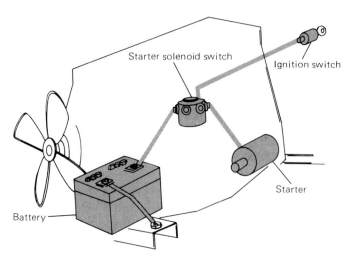

The Starting System
Automotive Information Council (AIC)

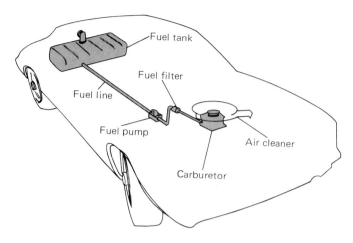

**The Fuel System**

The Fuel System
Automotive Information Council (AIC)

starts running smoothly). Once the engine is running, the following things happen:

3 Fuel (gasoline) flows from the **fuel tank** at the rear of the car, through the **fuel lines**, to the **fuel pump**, under the hood.

4 The fuel pump pumps the gasoline through a **fuel filter** into your **carburetor**.

5 The carburetor mixes each pound of fuel with 15 pounds of air to form a vaporized mixture, like a mist. Since fuel is much heavier than air, this mixture works out to something like one part of fuel to 9,000 parts of air, by volume. In other words, your car engine really runs on air, with a little fuel to help it!

6 This **fuel/air mixture** passes into the **cylinders** in your engine. Cylinders are hollow pipes with one open end and one closed end.

7 Inside each cylinder is a **piston**. These pistons fit the insides of the cylinders very closely and move up and down.

8 The piston moves *up,* trapping the fuel/air mixture in the upper part of the cylinder and *compressing* it, or squeezing it, into a very small space.

9 A spark from your **spark plug** *ignites* the fuel/air mixture, causing an explosion.

10 The explosion forces the piston back *down* again, with more *power* than it went up with.

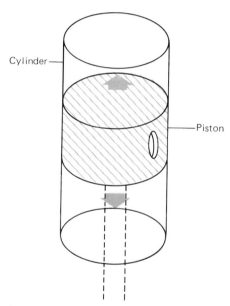

Cylinder and Piston
Alexandra Soto

**The Drive Train**

11 Attached to the bottom of the piston is a **connecting rod**, which, in turn, is attached to a **crankshaft**, which leads, eventually, to the rear wheels of your car.

12 As the piston and the connecting rod go up and down, they cause the crankshaft to turn, in pretty much the same way as when your knee goes up and down while your foot goes round and round with the pedals of your bicycle.

13 At the other end of the crankshaft is a box of gears called the **transmission**. If your car has a conventional engine, the transmission is under the front seat. If it has a **transverse engine**, the transmission is on the side of the engine, which is mounted between the drive wheels. On cars with front-wheel drive, you will find both the engine and the transmission under the hood. On rear-engine cars, they are both under the rear deck-lid.

14 If your car has a **manual** (or standard) **transmission**, you will also find your **clutch** located between the crankshaft and the transmission. The clutch tells the transmission when to connect or disconnect the engine from the rest of the drive train. In a car with an **automatic transmission**, this is done automatically.

15 When you shift into "Drive," or "First," depending on whether you have an automatic or a standard transmission, a set of gears causes the rest of the crankshaft (which is called the **driveshaft** after it leaves the transmission) to turn at a particular speed.

16 The driveshaft runs to the rear wheels of conventional rear-wheel-driven cars and ends in another set of gears called the **differential**. The differential turns the power of the engine and the transmission 90 degrees into the axles that connect the drive wheels of your car. Cars with front-wheel drive or with rear engines do not require driveshafts because the power source is located right between the wheels that are going to drive the car. On these cars the transmission and the differential are combined into a single unit called the **transaxle**, which connects directly to provide power to the drive wheels.

(*top*) Compression Stroke (*bottom*) Power Stroke
Echlin Manufacturing Company

When you ride a bicycle, your knees move up and down to turn the pedals 'round and 'round—just as the pistons and connecting rods move up and down to turn the crankshaft in circles.
Jack Herlihy

The Drive Train
Automotive Information Council (AIC)

Cutaway View of Car with Front-Wheel Drive
Ford Motor Company

The Exhaust System
Automotive Information Council (AIC)

The Cooling System
Automotive Information Council (AIC)

17 Since, on most cars, the axle is set at right angles to the driveshaft, you can see that the differential is really changing the direction of the power, so your drive wheels can turn.

18 Your drive wheels turn and push your car forward (or backward) and off you go.

Still with me? If you are confused, go back through the preceding text slowly, looking again at the accompanying illustrations, or try to explain it all to someone else. You'll be surprised at how much you know, once you're confronted by someone who knows less.

Now, let's fill in some necessary details.

**The Exhaust System**    The **exhaust gases** from the burnt fuel/air mixture that was ignited in the cylinders pass through **exhaust pipes** to the **tail pipe** at the rear of the car. On the way, antismog pollution-control devices remove some of the harmful substances. A **muffler** controls the noise of the escaping gases, which contain carbon monoxide, which is poisonous.

**The Cooling System**    Since the temperature at which the combustion of the fuel and air takes place is around 4,500 degrees Fahrenheit, the temperature must be quickly lowered below the boiling point of fluid or your engine would break down rapidly. To do this, water and coolant circulate from your **radiator** through pipes called **water jackets** in your engine to keep your engine cool. A **water pump** keeps the water circulating, and a **fan** helps to get the cooling process started.

**Oil** circulates through your engine to keep its moving parts (pistons, connecting rods, crankshaft, etc.) lubricated to move freely and to reduce the friction that causes your engine to heat up. An **oil pump** keeps the oil circulating, and an **oil filter** keeps it clean.

And, while we're at it we might as well go into what makes your car *stop*....

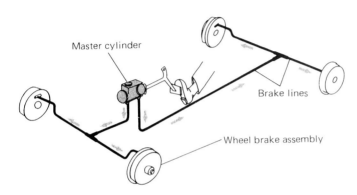

Master cylinder

Brake lines

Wheel brake assembly

1  To stop your car, you step on the **brake pedal**.
2  The brake pedal pushes against another piston in a cylinder located under the hood of your car. This is called the **master cylinder**, and it is filled with a liquid called **brake fluid**.
3  When the piston in the master cylinder is pushed by your brake pedal, it forces the brake fluid out of the master cylinder into tubes called **brake lines**, which run to each wheel of your car.

## The Lubrication System

The Engine

Oil pan

Oil filter

Oil pump

The Lubrication System
Automotive Information Council (AIC)

The Braking System
Automotive Information Council (AIC)

## The Brake System

Backing plate

Drum

Wheel cylinder   Retracting springs

Brake shoes

Drum Brake
Automotive Information Council (AIC)

4 Each wheel has a round, hollow, metal **brake drum** with another, smaller, **wheel cylinder** inside it.

5 The brake fluid goes into the brake cylinders and pushes against little **pistons** located at each end of each wheel cylinder.

6 These little pistons push against the **brake shoes**, which are curved, movable plates with friction-rough surfaces.

7 The brake shoes push against the inside walls of the brake drum, and the resulting **friction** stops your wheels from turning.

8 When you take your foot *off* the brake pedal, the whole thing is reversed. Springs pull the brake shoes back; the pistons push back into the cylinders, squeezing the brake fluid back up the brake lines to the master cylinder. Now your wheels can turn freely again.

That's all there is to it! Of course, if you have **disc brakes** on your car, there is a slight difference, which we will get into in the chapter on brakes, but essentially, the same principles apply.

Now, let's go into each of the foregoing systems in more detail. As you learn how each part works, in view of what it does for your car, you'll get a better idea of how to keep it working well and what to do if it breaks down. By looking at your car as a series of simple systems, each with a specific job to do, you will soon cease to see it as a dismaying collection of gears, hoses, and gizmos and be able to deal with it easily and effectively.

# The Electrical System:
# Your Car's
# "Spark of Life"

The **electrical system** provides your car with that vital spark that makes it start and keeps it running. Here are some of the services it performs:

1 It provides the initial power to get your engine started, through the **starting system**.
2 It fires the **spark plugs** so that they can cause the fuel and air to "combust" and drive your engine, through the **ignition system**.
3 It generates electrical power for the various systems in your car which depend on electric current, through the **charging system**.
4 It stores excess current for future needs, in the **battery**.
5 It runs a mixed bag of electrical gadgets like your car's horn, headlights, and so on, through various **circuits**.

Ignition System

Horn Circuit

Charging System

Starting System

Lighting Circuit

The Electrical System
Delco-Remy Division, General Motors Corp.

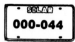
SOLAR
000-044

In order to deal with the electrical system in simple terms, let's break it down into its basic functional systems and deal with each in turn.

This is the portion of the electrical system which gets your car started. When you turn your key in the **ignition switch** to "Start," it closes a circuit that lets electrical current flow from your car's **battery** to its **starter**. On the way, the current passes through a little device called the **starter solenoid**, which becomes important only if it malfunctions. Basically, all the solenoid does is pass the current along; you don't adjust or replace it unless it breaks down. So don't bother with it now; just know where it is and what it's called so you can impress your garage mechanic if it dies.

After I took my first class on the electrical system, I went out one morning and found that my car wouldn't start. I remembered that my instructor had said that if you hear a clicking noise (that's your solenoid) but your engine won't start running, it is probably simply a loose wire somewhere between the ignition switch and the starter. So I opened the hood (it was only the second time I'd gotten that far) and peeked in. Sure enough, there was a cluster of wires on the **firewall** in front of my steering wheel. (The firewall is the divider between the interior of your car and the under-the-hood area. It runs from the windshield down.) I could see where the wires ran to the battery, along the frame of the car, but after that I got lost. I ended up calling the AAA. When they arrived, I proudly informed them that I knew what was wrong. "It's just a loose wire between my battery and my starter," I announced. "Then why didn't you fix it yourself?" the mechanic asked. "Because I don't know which gadget is the starter!" He was nice enough to keep from laughing, and I felt better when it did turn out to be a loose wire on the starter. The mechanic also pointed out the starter and showed me where the wires ran that connected to it.

Anyway, why don't you stop here for a moment and try to trace the wiring from that cluster of wires on the firewall which lead from your ignition switch to

Voltage Regulator
ACCEL, Division of Echlin Manufacturing Co.

Under-the-Hood View of the Starting System
Richard Freshman

the battery, and from the battery to your starter solenoid and starter. Then you can be a hero if your car clicks but won't start running some morning. If you hit a couple of other things along the way (like a square box called a **voltage regulator**), just ignore them. Like the solenoid, you don't have to fuss with them unless they fail, and if they fail they have to be replaced. Actually, there are several things to look for if your car won't start, and they are all covered in Chapter 15. (By the time you get there, this will seem like kid stuff!)

**How to Open the Hood of Your Car**

It occurs to me that there may be some of you who aren't sure how to get under the hood of your car. Here's how:

1 Try to remember where the thing is that the service station attendant grabs when he opens the hood to check your oil and water. Does he ask you to pull a lever inside the car? Or does he go to the front grill?

2 Look around, and through, the grill to find a handle, lever, arm, or button, or feel under the grill and behind the bumper for a handle or lever. Then, pull, press, push front to back and side to

side on the thing you find. The hood should open a little, but it may be stopped by a safety catch that prevents it from coming open, and obscuring your vision, while you are driving.

3  Raise the hood with one hand, and feel along the underside for a metal lever which, when pressed one way or the other, releases the catch. Then raise the hood the rest of the way.

4  If it stays up, fine. If not, look for a safety rod attached to the underside of the hood. This should come down and fit into a slot. Other rods lift up from the frame and fit into a slot under the hood.

5  The easiest thing to do is to forget steps 1–4 and ask the person in the service station to show you how to open the hood, the next time you go in for gas.

Now, let's take a look at each part of the **starting system** (sometimes called the *cranking circuit*) and see what it does:

The **battery** is the box that sits under the hood. It is filled with acid and distilled water, and it has a set of plates inside it. Most batteries are sealed, but if yours isn't, you can remove the caps that cover the holes on the top and check to see whether the liquid covers the tops of the plates in each compartment. If it doesn't, add distilled water. There are also two large metal terminals attached to the top or sides of the box. One is a **positive terminal**; the other is a **negative terminal**. You can tell which is which because the positive terminal is usually larger and may have a + or the word "Positive" on or near it.

**The Battery**

Most cars are *negative ground,* which means that the wire from the positive terminal leads to the starter, ignition, etc. The wire from the negative terminal is attached to the frame of the car to **ground** it. Some foreign cars are *positive ground* (or positive *earth,* as they call it in England), and this simply means that the reverse is true.

The battery stores electric current and passes it along to the parts of your car that need electric current to

1 Container
2 Cover
3 Positive plates
4 Negative plates
5 Separators
6 Cell
7 Cell connectors
8 Terminal post
9 Vent caps

**Anatomy of a Battery**
Automotive Parts & Accessories Association (APAA)

function. We'll get into the right way to keep it functioning properly in the next chapter. Right now, let's continue to explore the starting system.

**The Starter**   After the battery sends the current to the starter solenoid (which we've dealt with above), the current goes to the **starter**. If you've located the starter, perhaps you'd like to know what's inside it. Basically, it is a motor that makes your engine **turn over**. It has a shaft attached to a gear called a **starter drive**, which sits near a gear, called a *ring gear,* on the end of your **crankshaft flywheel**. When you turn your key in the ignition switch to "Start," the starter drive slides down the shaft and engages the ring gear. The motor starts the starter drive spinning, and it in turn starts the ring gear spinning. This makes the crankshaft turn, and your engine starts running because the turning crankshaft makes the **pistons** go up and down.

**Starter with Starter Solenoid**
Delco-Remy Division, General Motors Corp.

Anatomy of a Starter
Jack Herlihy

As your key returns to a vertical position, the starter drive and the ring gear disengage and your engine continues running on the fuel and air that are now being pumped into its **cylinders**. If you keep the key in the "Start" position after the engine starts running, the starter drive and the ring gear will continue to try to spin while they are still meshed together. The result is a horrible sound like metal grinding against metal—and that's exactly what's happening. If it happens too often, you will strip the teeth off the starter drive (or the ring gear) and have to get a new one. So be sure to let go of the ignition key as soon as your engine catches. When you release the key, it will automatically return to the "On" position and stay there until you shut the engine off.

O.K. Now your engine has started and is running at a nice steady rumble. This is because, as soon as the pistons in your cylinders started to go up and down, your car began to run on its usual diet of fuel and air.

**The Charging System**

000-049

And as your ignition switch went from "Start" to "On," the electric current stopped flowing from the battery to the starter but continued to flow through the **charging system**, as you will see.

### The Alternator (or Generator)

The running engine drives a belt that enables your **alternator** to produce electric current for the rest of the trip. As we've discussed earlier, the basic difference between an alternator and a generator is that alternators appear on newer cars and produce alternating current (AC), which is then converted to the direct current needed to drive various gadgets. Generators are usually found on cars built before 1964. They simply generate direct current (DC) and pass it on. To keep things simple, let's just call the gadget an alternator, because no matter which you have on your car, it will do the same thing in the long run. There are pictures of an alternator and a generator in Chapter 3, and since you won't have to take the thing apart, or adjust it, it really doesn't matter what we call it—as long as you know which one you have, where it is, and what it does. Try to find yours now.

Under-the-Hood View of Alternator
Richard Freshman

The first thing your alternator does is replace the electricity that was taken from the battery when you started the car. Then, every time your battery sends out some of its "juice," the alternator replaces it. When the alternator is generating electric current, we say that it is charging. Although most cars just have dashboard "idiot lights" that go on if the alternator isn't charging, some cars have gauges with a "D" at one end and a "C" at the other that show whether the battery is charging or discharging.

It is also the alternator that supplies your electrical system with current to run the car radio, headlights, etc., but let's go on to the ignition system.

### The Ignition System

Since a basic tune-up involves inspecting, cleaning, replacing (if necessary), and adjusting the various gadgets that make up your ignition system, this chapter will help you to get to know what you'll be working on in the next chapter, which is about tuning your car.

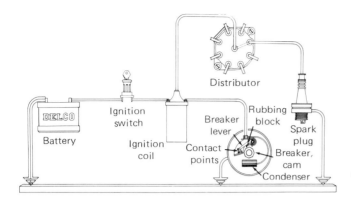

The Ignition System
Delco-Remy Division, General Motors Corp.

Meanwhile, back at the engine, the battery is busy sending the current it got from the alternator to the **coil**. Most coils are metal cylinders with three wires coming out of the top. One of the smaller wires goes to the battery via the ignition switch. The other small wire goes to the **points** and the **condenser**, which are inside the **distributor**. (Hang on, we'll clear all of this up in a minute!) There is also a big wire, which also goes to the distributor, entering through a hole in the center of the **distributor cap**. This sends current to the **spark plugs**.

**The Coil**

Anatomy of a Coil
Delco-Remy Division, General Motors Corp.

Under-the-Hood View of the Ignition System
Richard Freshman

000-051

Traditional Ignition System
Guaranteed Parts Company

The major job of the coil is to take a relatively small amount of electrical *voltage* from the battery and convert it into a big jolt of voltage and send it to the spark plugs via that large rubber-covered wire that comes out of the center of the top of the coil, travels a few inches, and enters the center of the distributor cap. In order to understand how it does this, we have to know a bit about the distributor. You will get to know your distributor quite well, because that is where a good part of your tune-up work takes place.

**The Distributor**

Your **distributor** is on either the side or the top of your engine, or up near the firewall. The coil is usually right near it. Since both are pretty distinctive-looking, they should not be hard to spot. Each of the wires that come out of the top of the distributor cap and give it its quaint, octopuslike appearance goes to a spark plug. (Except for the one that goes into the center of the cap from the coil, remember?) If you have a 4-cylinder engine, your engine will have four spark plugs and your distributor will have four wires leading from the cap to the spark plugs, plus the one to the coil. If you have an 8-cylinder engine, you will have eight wires going to the spark plugs, and your distributor cap will look like an authentic octopus. Have you found all of this on your car?

Anatomy of a Distributor
ACCEL, Division of Echlin Manufacturing Co.

Now let's take a look inside the distributor. Most distributor caps are held in place by clips or screws on either side. Clips can be removed easily with the point of a screwdriver. If you want to take yours off right away, you will find instructions for removing the cap in Chapter 5. If you're not ready for this, you can probably get all you need to know from the illustrations in this chapter. If, when you look inside your distributor cap, you do not find the parts in our diagrams, you probably have an electronic ignition system (if your car is a 1973 model or a more recent one, you probably do) and can consider yourself pretty lucky. The proud owners of cars with an **electronic ignition system** do not have to deal with traditional points, condensers, or their replacement or adjustment. All you have to do is change your spark plugs now and then and check for a defective distributor cap or rotor, if necessary. There are many types of electronic ignition systems, compared to conventional ignitions, so if you want to adjust yours it will be necessary for you to consult your owner's manual or service manual for specific instructions. Since adjustments usually require expensive tools and specialized expertise, I'd strongly advise you to rely on a good mechanic for service.

Electronic Ignition System
Zenith Ignition

Rotors
Delco-Remy Division, General Motors Corp.

000-053

**The Rotor**

Defective points

Broken strands

Loose or dirty connections

Defective condenser

Broken strands

**Typical Distributor Defects**

A Close-up of the Major Parts Inside the Distributor
DIXCO

In the traditional ignition system, inside the distributor cap, sitting on top of the **distributor shaft** is a piece of plastic called a **rotor**. This is designed to lift off and go back on in one position only (which means you have one less difficult decision to make). The tip of the rotor is made of metal, and it conducts the current that comes in from the coil through the center of the distributor cap to each of the wires that lead to the spark plugs. The way it does this is by turning with the distributor shaft. As the rotor turns, it points to each of the terminals at the base of the wires. When it is pointing at the terminal of the wire leading to your #1 spark plug, it will direct the current to that spark plug at precisely the time when the fuel/air mixture is in #1 cylinder, waiting to be exploded.

Attached to the **breaker plate** on the floor of the distributor you can see the **points** and the **condenser**. If you are looking at your own distributor, lift the rotor off to see them easily.

**The Points**

gap

Points
Automotive Parts & Accessories Association (APAA)

The **points** (short for "breaker points") are two pieces of metal joined at one end so that they can touch and then draw apart. The space where they almost meet when they are open is called a **gap**. One point is stationary, and one can move. The way they do this is simple. If you look at that same distributor shaft that the rotor was sitting on, you will see, down at the base, a roundish wheel with bumps on it. The wheel is a **cam** wheel. The bumps, one for each spark plug, are **cam lobes**. The cam wheel is attached to the base of the shaft and moves with it. As it turns, each cam lobe comes against the movable point and pushes the points *open*. When the wheel turns past the cam lobe, the points are *closed* again by a spring. Each time the points open, electric current passes to the rotor, which directs it to a spark plug wire. This causes the spark plug to "fire," producing a spark that will ignite the fuel/air mixture in its cylinder. A 4-cylinder car will have four cam lobes on this wheel, one for each cylinder. A 6-cylinder model will have six lobes, and so on.

Points close

Points open, plugs fire

Normal Point Gap
DIXCO

The gap between the points must be set at a precise width in order to ensure that each spark plug "fires" at just the right time and intensity. If the gap is too wide, the spark plugs will fire before the piston has reached the top of its path. This can cause **pre-ignition** and engine damage. If the gap is too narrow, the spark plug will fire after the piston has compressed the fuel/air mixture and has started back down. The loss of compression will result in poor combustion, loss of power, greater fuel consumption and more pollution. If the points cannot close enough to allow the current to pass properly, your car will stop completely. If they cannot get far enough apart to break the circuit, the current will arc across continuously and the points will burn out quickly. This whole problem is referred to as having your points out of adjustment, which leads to poor ignition and faulty **timing**. That's why, when you tune up your car, one of the first things you do is check with a **feeler gauge** to see whether your points are correctly "gapped." Of course, if your points are badly worn or corroded, you replace them and carefully gap the new points you've installed.

**4-Cylinder Engine**  **6-Cylinder Engine**

**8-Cylinder Engine**

Cam Wheels for 4-, 6-, and 8-Cylinder Cars
Alexandra Soto

The small metal cylinder near the points on the floor of the distributor is called a **condenser**. The purpose of the condenser is to prevent the electricity from arcing across the gap when the points are open, since this would cause the points to burn. Just how it does this is not really important for our purposes, but if you can't stand not knowing, wait until you really understand how cars work and then get a more comprehensive book that will give you all the technical details.

Anyway, since condensers don't break down (they either work or they don't), just replace yours whenever you change your points and rotor (they all come together in a tune-up kit), and make sure that it is tightly in place and connected properly. Otherwise, ignore it. Just remember that one of those two little wires from the coil connects to the condenser to help it do its mysterious job, and the other little wire runs to the battery to bring in the voltage that makes the whole thing worthwhile.

Each one of the cylinders in your car has a **spark plug** that conducts the spark that will fire the fuel/air mixture in the cylinder to provide the power that will

**The Condenser**

Condenser
Automotive Parts & Accessories Association (APAA)

**Spark Plugs**

000-055

Spark comes from distributor

Spark fires fuel/air mixture in cylinder

Spark Plug
ACCEL, Division of Echlin Manufacturing Co.

turn the wheels. If your car is properly tuned, that spark will arrive at the precise moment when the fuel/air mixture is fully compressed by the piston, and the result will be that the fuel and air will burn as intensely and completely as possible. To achieve this, the spark plug has to deliver as strong a spark as possible. The strength of the spark is determined by the distance (or **gap**) between the **electrodes** at the tip of the plug. In the next chapter, you will learn how to gap your plugs properly. Right now, look at the illustration to see what a spark plug looks like. The side of the plug in the picture has been cut away to show you the metal shaft that runs from the top of the plug to the bottom. Since the wire from the distributor leads to the top of the plug, and since the bottom of the plug (where the hooklike electrode is) emerges into the cylinder, you can see how the electric current reaches the fuel/air mixture.

### Another Way of Looking at the Electrical System

Is your head spinning? Don't worry, try looking at it this way: all that the electrical system does (all that matters for our purposes) is generate, store, and regulate the flow of electricity needed to start the car, fire the fuel/air mixture that drives the engine, and run the other electrical devices in the car. If you look at each part in terms of its position in this chain, the confusion will clear up. Let's trace the voltage once again:

**Battery:** *Stores* electricity to crank the motor and fire the spark plugs. Starts the starter.

**Starter:** Has a small motor that *starts* the crankshaft turning so the pistons can go up and down, the spark plugs can fire, and the engine can start running.

**Alternator:** *Generates* alternating current, *converts* it to direct current, and sends it to the battery. The equivalent on most older cars is called a *generator*. It serves the same function.

**Coil:** Takes a small amount of voltage from the alternator and multiplies it into a higher voltage that fires the spark plugs.

**Distributor:** Gets the voltage from the coil and *distributes* it to each spark plug in turn. Contains the points, rotor, and condenser.

**Points:** *Trigger* the flow of electricity so that it arrives at the spark plugs at the right point in time and at the right intensity.

**Rotor:** *Rotates* toward each spark plug terminal so that each plug fires in the correct order.

**Condenser:** An electrical *"sponge"* that keeps the points from burning up.

**Spark Plugs:** *Deliver* the spark to the fuel/air mixture in the cylinders at the point of greatest compression. The spark makes the mixture explode. The resulting power drives the engine and thus the car.

Try to look at the preceding in terms of the relationship between each part. You might trace the wires that carry the current from each part of your car to the next.

If you think you have it all digested, let's take a look at the rest of the electrical system, especially the gadgets that may someday need your attention.

As I've mentioned on several occasions, the alternator also supplies the electrical current for the car radio, head and taillights, etc., via electrical wiring under the dashboard. Most of this wiring is hard to reach, and since it doesn't go out of whack very often, we won't get into wiring problems here. But you should know about the fuse box that is usually located under or near the dashboard. Your owner's manual can help you find it, or you can crawl under the dashboard and trace the wires from your radio until you reach the fuse box.

(*top*) A Good Fuse (*middle*) A Burnt-out Fuse (*bottom*) Fuse Box Located Under Dashboard
Bussman Manufacturing Division, McGraw-Edison Company

**The Fuse Box**

A fuse box is easy to recognize and replacing burnt-out fuses is a fairly simple matter. If your radio, clock, map light, or other electrical dashboard appliances stop, the chances are that a fuse has blown. It is much cheaper to change a fuse (even if you chicken out and have the garage mechanic do it) than to pay for a new clock or for repairs that you don't need. So take a few minutes to find your fuse box. They're usually under the dashboard or in the engine compartment. Look for a fuse that's black inside or no longer has its filaments intact. Unless you have a blade-type fuse, with prongs, take a bobby pin, bend it, and use it to pull the bad fuse out. Now press a new fuse into place. When you've replaced all the burnt-out fuses, try your radio or clock again. If it still doesn't work, then worry about having it repaired or replaced.

**Directional Signal Flasher Lights**

Here's something interesting. Did you know that the directional signal flashers on your dashboard have been designed to provide clues to malfunctions elsewhere on your car? If one of your directional flashers should stop flashing, or should stop making that ticking noise when it flashes, this does not mean that the light is out of order. It means that your car manufacturer has cleverly utilized these lights to tell you that a light on the outside of your car is not working.

Using the left-turn signal flasher as an example, if you find that the left flasher on your dashboard simply stays on, without blinking or without making a noise, get out of the car and check to see if your left directional signal lights are on in the front and the rear of your car. If only one is out, simply replace the bulb. Once the bulb has been replaced, your dashboard flasher should work normally again.

If there is no light on your dashboard when you move your directional signal lever, then the bulb in your dashboard flasher is out.

If your left *rear* directional signal light goes on but does not blink, and your left *front* directional signal light does not go on at all, but both your *right* directional signal lights are working perfectly, then your left front directional signal bulb is bad. Once it is fixed, the left *rear* light will start to blink again.

If *all* your directional signal lights go on but they don't blink, then your flasher unit is bad. This unit usually plugs directly into the fuse box, so look for trouble there first.

Once you replace the bulb or fuse that is defective, the dashboard flashers will go back to normal. Isn't that lovely? Be sure to replace burnt-out bulbs at once.

They cost practically nothing. Most service stations will replace them for the cost of the bulb, which is usually less than a dollar. Headlights are more expensive because they have to be replaced as a unit (see below).

It doesn't hurt to wash the outside of your headlights and tailights occasionally; they will provide better visibility at night. If you still have trouble seeing at night (and you've been getting enough Vitamin A), check to be sure your headlight beams are shining straight ahead and not shining walleyed at the side of the road or in the eyes of other drivers. Check your headlights on both high and low beams. If one of your headlights won't work on low but does work on high, you will have to replace the bulb. Ask for a **sealed beam unit**. If it won't work on either high or low, you probably have a bad connection in the wiring.

Here's how to replace a sealed beam unit:

Before you can remove the bulb, you have to be careful to turn the correct screws to loosen the plate that holds the unit in place. (I'm going to refer to the sealed beam unit as the headlight bulb from now on.) There are six screws on the plate; three of them loosen the plate, and the other three adjust the angle of the bulb. If you turn the wrong screws, your headlights will go out of focus. Also, when you put in a new bulb, you have to put it back into its locking slots with the unit number at the *top*.

If you manage to goof up your adjusting screws, or if you find that your car is walleyed, or if you just aren't sure whether or not your headlights are properly adjusted, most service stations that do motor vehicle bureau inspections have the equipment to adjust your lights. Be sure to get a certificate saying that the lights have been adjusted and meet the proper standards. This certificate is usually part of the price. A cheap way to check it out is to look for a Highway Patrol station near your house. They usually have the facilities to check them for you. Or they can tell you where their current highway checkpoints are. Of course if they find that your headlights aren't in focus (or find anything wrong with your car's emissions, etc.), you will have to get the trouble fixed within two weeks or

**Headlights**

Headlight Removed to Show Adjustment Screws
Richard Freshman

Headlight Installation Screws
Richard Freshman

face a fine. If you can fix it yourself, go back to the checkpoint for an O.K.; otherwise you will have to pay some service station that does motor vehicle bureau inspections for a certificate, whether they do the work or not.

**Windshield Wipers**  Windshield wipers generally run in conjunction with the electrical system, too. The main things to check here are the blades (which can easily be replaced; most simply slide in and out, with maybe a button or a clip to hold them in place) and the fluid level in your windshield washer reservoir. More about this in the under-the-hood check section in Chapter 5.

**Other Gadgets**  If you have trouble with your car's radio, defroster, heater, air conditioner, and so on, get professional help. Later on, if you have turned into a confirmed do-it-yourselfer, there are books that deal with these.

Have you got it all now? Then you are ready to stop living vicariously and get down to the nitty-gritty (which can always be removed with cleaning solvent).

# How to Tune Your Ignition System and Do a Monthly Under-the-Hood Checkup

There are several good reasons for tuning your car yourself. First, as we mentioned in Chapter 1, it's much cheaper, and since a well-tuned car will last longer, you can tune it more often and save yourself even more. Second, a well-tuned car is a gas saver. Not only does this mean less money spent for fuel, it also means less air pollution from unburnt fuel and exhaust fumes. Third, today most cars on the road have **electronic ignition** and **fuel injection systems** which need no servicing until something goes wrong, and this turns tune-up time into a breeze. And finally, if you tune your car yourself, you'll know it's been done properly.

It's hard to write a book like this without being called on the carpet for knocking professional mechanics. I've tried very hard not to do this because most of them don't deserve it. However, although most of them know their business, they are human. At today's labor prices every minute counts; if a tune-up is unexpectedly difficult and time-consuming, it can cost both the mechanic and the customer considerable money. So if the car happens to have one spark plug that's impossible to reach without disconnecting or moving the air conditioner or hoisting the engine right out of the car—and if the car seems to be running well with that one teensy-weensy spark plug left unchanged—then you just might find that you have a freshly tuned car with all brand-new spark plugs *except* for one funky old one that's been in there since the car left the factory. I know this because it happened to me! One spark plug that is old and fouled can ruin your car's performance and increase its fuel consumption. It's like a piano that's been tuned, with one sour note left in it.

By checking them yourself, you can judge whether your spark plugs only need to be cleaned and gapped or whether you should replace them. And if you have an old-style distributor that needs to be serviced on a regular basis, you can do it yourself for a fraction of what it would cost to have it done for you. Don't worry, most of the parts involved are very easy to replace.

Of course, if you've bought this book, you've probably already decided that you want to tune your car yourself, so let's get started.

**Tune-up** intervals vary from car to car. Most older cars should be tuned every 10,000 to 12,000 miles or every year, whichever comes first. Newer cars with electronic ignition and fuel injection systems can be tuned as seldom as every 25,000 miles or two years. See your owner's manual for recommended intervals, but be aware that even if it says the car does not require any tune-ups at all, it's in your best interests to check the car periodically to be sure it's working at peak performance. If you do a lot of stop-and-go driving or pull heavy loads (like a camper or a boat), you may need to tune the car more often.

**How Often Should You Tune Your Car?**

There are only a couple of parts that you will need for your basic tune-up, but in order to buy them properly, you should know something about car **specifications**.

**Buying Parts for Your Car**

1 Your owner's manual should give you specifications for everything you'll need for a basic tune-up.

2 If you don't have an owner's manual, or if yours lacks the necessary data, you can go to the auto supply store and use a general "tune-up specification guide." These are either in pamphlet form or printed on large sheets that are displayed near the parts section of the store. If you can't find a "spec sheet" at the store, ask a salesperson to show one to you. *Don't* ask what part you should buy, as you have a very good chance of getting the wrong one. First look up the specifications yourself; then ask for the part by number.

**Where to Locate the Specifications for Parts for Your Car**

Here is the proper way to read one of these specification sheets in order to obtain the proper parts for your car:

**How to Read a Spec Sheet**

1 Know the following things about your car:

a The *manufacturer's name* (General Motors, Ford, etc.).

b The *make* of the car (Pontiac, Mercury, etc.).

c The *model* of the car (Catalina, Monterey, etc.).

d The *year* the car was built (1968, 1988).

| 1967 Make and Model | Dist. Rotation | Dwell | Contact Gap | Spark Plug Gap | Firing Order | Ign. Timing B.T.C. @RPM |
|---|---|---|---|---|---|---|
| **CHRYSLER (Neg. Grd.) (INCLUDES IMPERIAL)** | | | | | | |
| 383 Cu. In. V8 Eng. (2 bbl.) | CC | 30 | .016 | .035 | 3A | 12°@550 |
| •383 Cu. In. V8 Eng. (2 bbl.) | CC | 30 | .016 | .035 | 3A | 5°@600[52] |
| 383 Cu. In. V8 Eng. (4 bbl.) | CC | 30 | .016 | .035 | 3A | 12°@500 |
| •383 Cu. In. V8 Eng. (4 bbl.) | CC | 30 | .016 | .035 | 3A | 5°@500[52] |
| 440 Cu. In. V8 Eng. | CC | 30 | .016 | .035 | 3A | 12°@650 |
| •440 Cu. In. V8 Eng. | CC | 30 | .016 | .035 | 3A | 5°@650[52] |
| **DODGE (Neg. Grd.) (INCLUDES CHARGER, CORONET, DART)** | | | | | | |
| 170 Cu. In. 6 Cyl. Eng. | C | 42 | .020 | .035 | 5 | 5°@550 |
| •170 Cu. In. 6 Cyl. Eng. | C | 42 | .020 | .035 | 5 | 5°ATDC@650 |
| 225 Cu. In. 6 Cyl. Eng. | C | 42 | .020 | .035 | 5 | 5°@550 |
| •225 Cu. In. 6 Cyl. Eng. | C | 42 | .020 | .035 | 5 | TDC@650 |
| 273 Cu. In. V8 Eng. (2 bbl.) | C | 30 | .016 | .035 | 3A | 5°@500[56] |
| •273 Cu. In. V8 Eng. (2 bbl.) | C | 30 | .016 | .035 | 3A | 5°ATDC@650 |
| **LINCOLN (Neg. Grd.)** | | | | | | |
| 462 Cu. In. V8 Eng. | CC | 30 | .017 | .034 | 8C | 10°@475 |
| •462 Cu. In. V8 Eng. | CC | 30 | .017 | .034 | 8C | 10°@500 |
| **FORD (Neg. Grd.) (INCLUDES BRONCO, FAIRLANE, FALCON, MUSTANG, THUNDERBIRD)** | | | | | | |
| 170 Cu. In. 6 Cyl. Eng. | C | 40 | .025 | .035 | 5 | 6°@550[6] |
| •170 Cu. In. 6 Cyl. Eng. | C | 40 | .025 | .035 | 5 | 5°@550 |
| 200 Cu. In. 6 Cyl. Eng. | C | 40 | .025 | .035 | 5 | 6°@525[56] |
| •200 Cu. In. 6 Cyl. Eng. | C | 40 | .025 | .035 | 5 | 4°@500[52] |
| 240 Cu. In. 6 Cyl. Eng. | C | 40 | .025 | .035 | 5 | 6°@550[6] |
| •240 Cu. In. 6 Cyl. Eng. | C | 40 | .025 | .035 | 5 | 5°@550 |
| 289 Cu. In. V8 Eng. (2 bbl.) | CC | 29 | .017 | .035 | 8C | 6°@475 |
| •289 Cu. In. V8 Eng. (2 bbl.) | CC | 29 | .017 | .035 | 8C | TDC@550 |
| 289 Cu. In. V8 Eng. (4 bbl.) | CC | 29 | .017 | .035 | 8C | 6°@525 |
| •289 Cu. In. V8 Eng. (4 bbl.) | CC | 29 | .017 | .035 | 8C | TDC@550 |
| **OLDSMOBILE (Neg. Grd.) (INCLUDES F85, TORONADO)** | | | | | | |
| 250 Cu. In. 6 Cyl. Eng. | C | 32 | .019 | .035 | 5 | 4°@500 |
| •250 Cu. In. 6 Cyl. Eng. | C | 32 | .019 | .035 | 5 | 4°@500 |
| 330 Cu. In. V8 Eng. | CC | 30 | .016 | .030 | 3A | 8°@850 |
| •330 Cu. In. V8 Eng. | CC | 30 | .016 | .030 | 3A | 7°@850 |

e The *number of* **cylinders** in the car (4, 6, V-8, etc.).

f Whether the car has **automatic** or **manual (standard) transmission**.

g The engine **displacement**—how much room there is in each cylinder when the piston is at its lowest point. A 300-cu.-in. 6-cylinder engine has a displacement of 50 cu. in. in each cylinder. The bigger the cylinder, the more fuel and air it will hold.

h The kind of **carburetor** it has. This is generally referred to by the number of **barrels**, or chambers for mixing fuel and air (2 bbl., 4 bbl., etc.). This is where the terms "single-barrel carburetor," "**dual carbs**," and so on, come from.

i Does the car have *air conditioning*? It is necessary to take this into account when buying certain parts but not usually spark plugs or distributor tune-up kits.

j  The **horsepower** rating of the car. This is not essential, but it's nice to know.

All this information should be in your owner's manual, and most of it is also printed on metal tags or patches located inside your hood. These can be found in front of the radiator, inside the fenders, on the inside of the hood, anywhere the auto manufacturer thought you'd find them. I know of one car that has its patch inside the lid of the glove compartment. Look around, you'll find it. These ID tags also give a lot of other information about where the car was made, what kind of paint it has, and so on, but you needn't worry about these. I have included a Specifications Record sheet at the end of this book to provide a place to keep all this information handy. It also has room for you to list the numbers and specifications of the things you should be replacing at regular intervals. Once this sheet contains the necessary data for each of your cars, you will be able to take it to the auto parts store with you and keep it handy when you are working on your car. If you don't want to take the book along, and you have reservations about tearing out pages, you might want to have it photocopied before you fill it out, so you will have copies for future cars. There is also a Maintenance Record sheet to help you to keep track of what you've checked and what you've changed during your tune-ups and monthly checks. While you're at it, make copies of this one, too, so you'll have one for each car and each new year.

2  Look up your car, by make and model, under the proper year on the specifications record. For Tweety, I look under 1967, then under Ford, then under Mustang, then under "200 cu. in. 6 Cyl. Eng. (1 bbl.)"—which means she has an engine displacement of 200 cu. in., a 6-cylinder engine, and a single-barrel carburetor.

3  Take along a pencil and your Specifications Record from the end of this book and mark down the information in the columns under the following headings:

a  **Dwell**. (The number refers to the place on the **dwell meter** that the needle should point to if your points are correctly gapped. It is given in degrees.)

b **Contact gap** (the proper **gap** for your **points**).

c **Spark plug gap** (exactly that).

d **Firing order** (to help you locate your #1 plug, which you will need to know in order to check your **timing**).

e **Ignition timing**. The number given in degrees refers to the proper **timing mark** on your **crankshaft pulley** (I'll help you find it), and the number after "@" indicates at how many **rpm** to check your timing on your dwell meter/tachometer. (Don't get excited; it's not as complicated as it sounds.)

f Now, jot down the proper parts number given for spark plugs and for the distributor **tune-up kit** for your car.

4 Buy them. Most professional mechanics get a discount at auto parts stores. You might try to see if you can get one by telling them that you are going to install them yourself. It can't hurt to try. If not, you are still ahead of the game, especially if you shop at one of the discount auto shops—Sears, Pep Boys, Montgomery Ward, etc. You can use either the house brand or a very well known brand like Champion or AC. Avoid little-known brands; they may not be made to the proper tolerances, and, with automotive parts, a fraction of an inch makes the difference between moving and standing still.

**What You Will Need to Tune Up Your Car**

1 A new set of spark plugs. Buy one for each cylinder in your engine. Never change just a few plugs; it's all or nothing for even engine performance. If you are feeling especially wealthy, buy an extra plug in case you get home and find that one of them is defective, or in case you accidentally ruin one by dropping and cracking it, or by cross-threading it when you install it. If you don't use it, keep it in your trunk compartment tool kit for emergencies. Spark plugs don't get stale.

2 A tune-up kit. This will contain a new **rotor, condenser**, set of points, little capsule of **cam** lubricant, and any other things that the manufacturer thought you might like to have. Pick your kit out by part

number; then read the package carefully to make sure it says that it is for *your* make, model, year, and engine. This kind of double checking always pays off. If you don't see your car listed on the package, ask the salesman to clear up the situation.

3  Your tools. **Screwdrivers, screwholder, wrenches, feeler gauges**, a work light (or a flashlight, at least), a **socket wrench** and a **ratchet handle** with a **spark plug socket**. If possible, a **dwell meter** and a **timing light** (in case you can't get these, however, I'll show you how to set your dwell and timing without them).

4  An old blanket, mattress pad, or a shiny new vinyl car protector to place over the fender where you'll be working, so you won't scratch it. The vinyl car protectors often come with handy pockets to keep tools and little parts in while you are working. You can make one yourself by pinning up the bottom edge of your folded blanket or pad—or you can forget about it completely if you don't mind rummaging in your tool kit a lot. Just don't place tools, screws, and little parts where they can fall into the engine. It can be difficult and time-consuming to get them out of the unreachable places they invariably head for once they are in a state of free fall. *Never* attempt to drive your car with something lost in the works. Even the smallest screw can find its way into something that will react violently to the intruder, ruining itself, and you, if you are on the freeway when it happens. Just hunt around patiently until you find whatever it is you've dropped. If you are lucky, it will drop through onto the ground, so check there first and rock your car a little, by leaning on the fender, to encourage the missing item to drop down.

While we're on the subject, check under the car *before* you start working. That way you will know that any bolts, screws, or unidentifiable objects that are there after you are done have *not* come from your car. Not knowing can be disquieting, to say the least.

5  Work clothes that you won't mind getting irrevocably stained with grease, oil, and other stuff.

6  Hand cleaner.

**Safety Rules**  Before we go any further, I'd like to give you a few safety rules for working on your car:

1 Tie back long hair. If it accidentally gets into a moving fan or belt you can literally be scalped.

2 Never work on your car unless the **parking brake** is on, the car is in either "Park" or "Neutral"; and the engine is shut off. If you have to run the engine to adjust something, turn it on and off yourself to avoid the risk that a friendly helper may misunderstand and turn the engine on while your hands are in the way.

3 Never jack a car up unless the wheels are properly blocked. I'll go into this when we talk about changing tires. You won't need the jack for your tune-up.

4 Use insulated tools for electrical work.

5 Before using a wrench or ratchet on a part that is "stuck," be sure that, if it suddenly comes loose, your hand won't hit anything. To avoid this, *pull* on wrenches whenever possible, rather than *push* them.

6 Be sure the parts of the engine you are working on are nice and cold, so you won't get burned. If you are doing a job that calls for a warm engine, be very careful.

7 Don't smoke when you are working on your car— for obvious reasons!

So much for the scary stuff. It's all a matter of common sense, really. And remember, it is almost impossible to make a car "blow up" unless you drop a match into the gas tank. If you do something incorrectly, the worst thing that will probably happen is that the car won't start until you get it right. The first time I tuned my car I was sure that if I made the smallest mistake the car would explode when I started it. This seems to be a common delusion. It just isn't so. All you'll get is silence (which can be just as disconcerting, but not lethal, after all). And now, to work.

**Changing Your Spark Plugs**  Before you can change your spark plugs, you have to find them. Look for a set of thick wires (or thin cables) that enter your engine block in neat rows—

on both sides if you have a V-6 or V-8 engine, and on only the driver's side if you have a straight 4- or 6-cylinder engine (these are also called **in-line engines**). Since these spark-plug cables run from the **distributor** to the spark plugs, you can also trace a cable from your distributor to find your plugs for sure.

In all U.S.–made straight 4- and 6-cylinder cars, the cylinder nearest the radiator (nearest the front of the car) is #1. Then they run in sequence toward the **firewall**—#2, #3, #4, and so on. Some foreign-built cars have this reversed, with #1 at the rear, near the firewall. If you have a foreign car and no owner's manual, ask your local dealer where your #1 cylinder is. Your #1 plug is the spark plug in your #1 cylinder.

**Cylinder Sequence**

V-8 engines are not as easy. Most Ford V-8s have the #1 cylinder in the front on the passenger side of the car. Then, #2, #3, and #4 follow it toward the rear firewall. Number 5 is up front on the driver's side, with #6, #7, and #8 in sequence going toward the rear. On most other V-type engines, the #1 cylinder is up front on the driver's side, with #3, #5, and #7 proceeding rearward. Then, #2 is up front on the passenger side, with #4, #6, and #8 following. This goes for V-6s as well as V-8s: the three odd-numbered plugs are on one side and the three even-numbered plugs are on the other side, with the lowest-numbered plugs usually up near the radiator. Page 70 shows some examples of the **cylinder sequence** in U.S. engines.

Now, do not confuse cylinder sequence with **firing order**. Although your engine may have its cylinders in simple numerical sequence, if the cylinders were fired in that order the engine would rock violently as first the cylinders on one side (or toward the front) fired in rapid succession, and then the other cylinders did likewise. To avoid this, the firing order is carefully arranged to distribute the shock of **combustion** evenly throughout the engine. The cylinders fire in very swift

**Firing Order**

000-069

**Straight 6-Cylinder Engine**

Cylinder sequence

1-5-3-6-2-4

Firing order

**Straight 4-Cylinder Engine**

1-3-4-2

**Typical V-6 Engine**

1-6-5-4-3-2

**Ford V-8 Engine**

1-5-4-2-6-3-7-8

Cylinder Sequence and Firing Order of Popular Engines
DIXCO

sequence, and the result is a fairly stable engine. A typical firing order for a Ford V-8 engine (with cylinders #1 to #4 on one side and cylinders #5 to #8 on the other) would be #1, #5, #4, #2, #6, #3, #7, #8. The firing order has been printed inside each of the engines illustrated above. Trace the path of combustion back and forth throughout each of these engines so you can see how the shock of combustion is distributed to avoid rocking the engine. Remember, the whole thing happens very rapidly.

If you've digested all this, let's get back to work:

In order to keep the proper **firing order,** each spark-plug cable must go from the proper terminal on your **distributor cap** to the proper spark plug, so before you remove anything, you should label each cable with its proper number in the **cylinder sequence.**

1  To label your cables, place a piece of masking tape or a clothespin on the spark-plug cable near the **boot** that covers the tip of each plug. Put the proper cylinder number on each one. If you also label the boot where each cable enters the distributor cap terminal, you will never be unsure about hooking things up properly. Of course, if you make it a habit to remove the cable from only one plug at a time, and to put it back before you remove another, you won't ever get into trouble—unless another cable comes off accidentally.

2  Gently grasp the #1 spark-plug cable by the boot, where it connects to the spark plug. Never yank on the cable itself (you can damage the wiring); just grasp the boot and twist it and pull it straight out so you can pull it off the plug. The shiny thing sticking out of the engine **cylinder block** is the *terminal* of the #1 spark plug.

3  Take a nice soft rag or a small paint brush, and clean around the area where the spark plug enters the block. Or you can blow the dirt away with a soda straw. This will keep loose junk from falling down the hole into the cylinder when the plug is removed.

4  Find your **spark plug socket** (the big one with the rubber lining) and shove it down over the spark

1-8-4-3-6-5--7-2

**Many Other V-8 Engines**

plug. Exert some pressure to be sure it's all the way down. Like everything else in auto repair, don't be afraid to use some strength. Just do it in an even, controlled manner. If you bang or jerk things, you can damage them, but you will never get anywhere if you tippy-toe around.

5 Pick up your **ratchet handle** and stick the square end into the square hole in the spark-plug socket. If you can work more comfortably by adding a couple of extensions between the handle and the socket, so that you can move the handle freely from side to side without hitting anything, go ahead. You add them in the same way you added the socket to the handle.

The little knob on the back of the ratchet handle is used to make the ratchet turn the socket either clockwise or counterclockwise. You want to loosen the spark plug, so you want the handle to turn counterclockwise. You can tell which way the handle will turn the plug by listening to the clicks that the handle makes when you move it in one direction. If it clicks when you move it to the right, it will turn the socket counterclockwise when you move it, silently, to the left. If the clicks are audible on the leftward swing, it will move the socket clockwise on the rightward swing. Every screw, nut, bolt, etc., that you encounter should loosen counterclockwise and tighten clockwise. If your ratchet is clicking in the wrong direction, just move that little knob and it will reverse direction.

Now, you may have some difficulty in loosening the spark plugs for the first time. This is because the mechanic who installed it may have used a "gorilla," which tightens things much tighter than you can. To get the proper leverage, place your free hand over the head of the wrench, grasping the head firmly, and pull the handle as hard as you can, hitting it gently with the palm of your hand to get it going. If you can't budge it, don't feel like a weakling. I thought it was because I was female, at first; but the biggest man in my class had problems starting my plugs. We recently had a discussion about it, and the general opinion was that strength depended less on the size or sex of the person and more on the way in which an indi-

How to Use a Socket Wrench
Richard Freshman

vidual had been taught to focus his or her strength in the hands or the tool with which one was working. I now approach hard-to-move objects with a wrench and the conviction that I can move it by pouring all my strength down my arms into my hands. You know, it works! Also, the longer the tool, the more leverage it will give you.

You'll feel better to know that after you've installed your new plugs by hand, it will be a lot easier to get them loose the next time. Also, grease, **sludge**, or

WHAT YOUR OLD SPARK PLUGS TELL YOU
ABOUT YOUR CAR

| CONDITION | | CLUES | PROBABLE CAUSES |
|---|---|---|---|
| Normal plugs | | Brown or grayish-tan deposit on side electrode. | Everything's fine. Just clean and regap the plug. |
| Carbon-fouled plugs | | Black, dry, fluffy soot on insulator tip and electrodes. | Overly rich fuel/air mixture; malfunctioning choke; dirty air filter; or just too much driving at low speeds, or standing and idling for a long time. Switch to "hotter" plugs. |
| Oil-fouled plugs | | Wet, black, oily deposits on insulator tip and electrodes. | Oil may be leaking into cylinders past worn pistons or poorly adjusted or worn valves. Clean and regap these, or replace them, but find out where the leak is coming from. |
| Lead-fouled plugs | | Red, white, brown, or yellow deposits called scavenger deposits. | Highly leaded gas or other additives in gas or oil. Disregard, unless extensive. Clean and regap plugs. |
| | | Shiny yellow glaze. | Same as above, but you'll have to throw these away. |
| Burnt plugs | | Blisters on insulator tip, melted electrodes, burnt stuff. | Engine overheating; gap too wide, wrong or loose plugs; overly lean fuel/air mixture; incorrect timing. Replace plugs. |
| Worn plugs | | Severely eroded or worn electrodes. | Plugs have been in there too long. Replace them. |

000-072

other junk may have caused the plugs to stick in place, especially if it's been a long time between tunings. So persevere. I've never met a plug that didn't give up and come out, eventually.

6 Got it loose? Good! After you get the plug started, you can disconnect the ratchet handle, leaving the socket on the plug, and turn it the last few bits yourself so you'll know when it is free. Now take it out and remove the spark plug from the socket.

Take a look at your plug. The deposits you find on it will provide valuable "clues" to what your engine is doing. Here are a few clues to help you "read" your plugs and learn about your engine's past (and predict its future, in some cases):

1 Look at the end of your plug which was inside the cylinder. This is called the firing end. The hook at the top is the *side* **electrode**. The bump right under its tip is called the *center* **electrode**. The spark from the distributor comes up the center of the plug and jumps the **gap** between these two **electrodes**. And the gap has to be a particular distance across.

2 Take your *wire* or *taper* **feeler gauge** and locate the proper wire (if your spark-plug gap specifications said .035, look for this number near one of the wires on the gauge). Now, slip the gauge wire between the two electrodes on your old plug. It probably has a lot of room to wiggle around in. This may be because your old plug has worn down its center electrode, causing a gap that is too large. If the gauge goes in and out with a lot of room on either side, the gap is too large. If the gauge will not fit between the center and side electrodes, the gap is too small. This means that the spark plug is not burning the **fuel/air mixture** efficiently.

3 Now, look at the little center electrode bump again. It is nice and cylindrical, like the center electrodes on your new spark plugs? Or is it worn round, or worn down on one side? Chances are it's pretty worn. That's because it's old. Now that you are doing your tune-ups yourself, you'll probably check your plugs more often and replace them before they get too worn to operate efficiently. When the

**Reading Your Spark Plugs**

Anatomy of a Spark Plug
ACCEL, Division of Echlin Manufacturing Co.

center electrode wears down, the gap becomes too large.

If you should find that your plugs seem to indicate that there is something wrong with the way your engine is running, ask a professional mechanic for an opinion. If it seems to be a serious problem, requiring extensive or expensive work, get a second opinion at another station without telling that you went to the first station. This is a good policy to follow whenever major garage work is indicated. We tend to get a second opinion whenever a doctor tells us we need major surgery; why not give your car the same thorough attention? Sometimes a problem can be cured by going to a "hotter" or "cooler" burning plug. These can be identified by the plug number. The higher the number, the hotter the plug. Never go more than one step hotter or cooler at a time.

If you find that a few of your old plugs were not too worn, and in fairly good shape, clean them and regap them and keep in your trunk compartment tool kit for emergencies. When tuning your car, either replace all the plugs or clean them all and use them all. Don't mix plugs in varying states of wear. Your engine will not operate efficiently. And please don't use a *flat* feeler gauge to gap old plugs.

**Right**

**Wrong**

Why You Can't Use a Flat Feeler Gauge on Old Spark Plugs
DIXCO

**Gapping Your Spark Plugs**

1 Now, locate a place where you can keep the used plugs in cylinder order and put the #1 plug there. An egg carton works well.

2 Get out a shiny new spark plug and take a look at it. It should be clean and new-looking, with the tip of the side electrode centered over the center electrode. There should be no cracks or bubbles in the porcelain insulator, and the threads should be unbroken.

3 Take your feeler gauge, select the proper wire, and run it between the electrodes. If it doesn't go through, find the part of the feeler gauge that is used for bending electrodes, hook it under the side electrode, and tug very gently. Now run the gauge through the gap again.

4 Did it go through this time? Did it go in too easily, without touching the electrodes? Then you've got

How to Gap a Plug with a Wire Gauge
Rogers and Greenberg

the gap too wide. Press the side electrode against a clean, marproof surface, *very gently*, until it is *slightly* bent down toward the center electrode. Now try the gauge again. Does it go through fairly easily, just catching the electrodes as it passes? Fine! (If the gap is now too small again, don't feel bad. Everyone I know goes through the "too large–too small–too large" bit a couple of times for each plug, especially the perfectionists.) The wire should just "hang" in the gap but go through with a little guidance.

Now you are ready to reinsert the plug in the engine.

**How to Replace a Spark Plug**

1 Clean the hole in the cylinder block with a clean cloth. Wipe *away* from the hole; don't shove any dirt into it.

2 Slip the spark-plug socket over the new plug, pressing the plug, terminal end first, into the socket as far as it will go, leaving the threads and electrodes exposed.

3 Place the plug in the socket back in the entrance of the hole and gently turn it clockwise, by hand, as far as it will go comfortably. This is called *seating the plug*. You have to do it by hand, or you run the risk of starting the plug crookedly and cross-threading it. Cross-threaded plugs are useless, unless you know someone who has a gadget that can rethread them.

4 Attach your ratchet handle to the socket (be sure that the knob is adjusted to make it turn the socket clockwise) and tighten the plug. Don't overtighten (you can crack the plug); just get it in nice and tight with no wiggle. It should stick a little when you try to loosen it, but you should be able to loosen it again without killing yourself. Tighten and loosen it once or twice to get the proper "feel" of the thing.

If you have a **torque wrench**, look in the manual for the proper setting and use it, once you have seated the plug by hand. Then try to loosen the plug by hand. This will give you the proper "feel" for how tight it should be. Most do-it-yourselfers tend to do plugs without torque wrenches because they are difficult to work with in the small space between the block and the other parts of the car.

5 Slip the cable **boot** over the exposed terminal of the new plug and press it firmly into place.

Well, you've just cleaned, gapped, and installed your first spark plug. Don't you feel terrific? Now you only have 3, or 5, or 7 more to do, depending on your engine. (It's at times like these that owners of 4-cylinder cars have the edge on those who drive those big, expensive 8-cylinder monsters.)

6 Taking each plug in order, and working only on *one plug at a time,* gap and replace each plug. Most of them should be easy to reach. If you find that one or more plugs are blocked by an air conditioner, a power-steering device, or some other part, try using various ratchet handle extensions to get around the problem. There are *universal* extensions that allow the ratchet handle to be held at odd angles; *T-bar* handles for better leverage; and *offset* handles for hard-to-reach places. (See the tool chapter for examples of these.) Almost every car has at least one plug that is a miserable thing to reach. If you have one, save it for last. Then you can work on it with the satisfaction of knowing that, when you get the darn thing finished, you will have finished the job. I bet that when you get it out you will find that it has never been replaced during all those professional tune-ups you've paid for. And you've paid even more because that one funky plug can cut your gas mileage (and add to air pollution). Your car will be really glad to get rid of it.

If you absolutely cannot reach the offending plug, you can always drive to your service station and humbly ask them to change just that one plug. They won't like it, but it *is* a last resort. If you get to that point, you'll probably be glad to pay to have it done. But do try very hard, first. If you can't get to the plug in the ordinary way, go under, over, around, or through gaps in the thing that's blocking it. Or get someone to help you move what's in the way (but be sure that you can get it back in place correctly). Use your imagination; it's the only hard part of the job. And you won't have to do it again for a long time. Of course, if you are lucky enough to own a car without air conditioning, power steering, power brakes, etc., chances are that all your plugs will be easy to get at. Think it over next time you are tempted to buy a car with all the "extras." Those "extras" tend to block the things you want to work on, and they often go wrong themselves. Some, like air conditioning if you live in a hot climate, are worth it. Others, like power brakes on a small car, are not.

Done? Great! Go and start your car to prove to yourself that everything still works. Then wash your hands with hand cleaner. You want to be nice and fresh for your distributor. If you have had a hard time with a hard-to-reach plug, you can put off the distributor part until tomorrow, but you should be able to do both, in a couple of hours, without getting fed up.

Most cars built after 1975 have **electronic ignition systems** which require no regular servicing. All testing and servicing of these systems should be left to trained professionals because the systems are easily damaged if hooked up improperly and they employ high voltage that can also damage *you*. If your car has such a system, or no distributor at all (yes, there are such miracles these days), you can bypass this section and go on to the Under-the-Hood Check on page 99. But don't forget to change your spark plugs and check to be sure your cables and connections haven't become

**Servicing Your Distributor**

Anatomy of a Distributor
DIXCO

Removing a Distributor Cap with Screw Clamps
Delco-Remy Division, General Motors Corp.

Removing a Distributor Cap with Clips
Delco-Remy Division, General Motors Corp.

corroded or detached. If you aren't sure whether or
not your car has one of the older distributors which
must be manually serviced, note that these have one
thin wire on the side, while the electronic ones have
two wires, or more. If you're still confused, check your
owner's manual or call the service department at a
dealership that represents your car's manufacturer.

For those of you whose distributors do need servicing,
the **tune-up kit** you'll buy for this purpose contains
everything you'll need to do the job except for such
tools as a screwdriver, a screwholder (optional, but
nice), and a timing light and dwell meter, which you
can borrow if you don't want to buy them.

**Removing Your Distributor Cap**

Let's begin:

1 Find your **distributor**. If you are still not sure about
it, go back and reread the description of the distributor—where it is, what it does, and what it
contains—in the previous chapter. I'll wait....

2 Using a long-handled screwdriver, remove the **distributor cap**. Most caps are held in place by either
clips or screws. Illustrations on this page and on
page 77 show how to remove both types of caps.
Which kind does your car have?

3 Now that your distributor cap is free, remove it
without removing any of the wires that are attached
to the top of the cap. Place it to one side and take a
look inside your distributor. Does the stuff in there
look like the stuff in your kit? Look at the structure
of the **rotor** and the **points**. They should be similar,
although some parts may be made of plastic instead
of metal. If they look different, you've got the
wrong kit. Go back to the auto-parts store and start
over (Do Not Pass Go, etc.).

Various Types of Rotors
Delco-Remy Division, General Motors Corp.

**Removing Your Rotor**

Sitting on top of everything in the distributor is the
**rotor**. Rotors vary in size from small plastic gizmos
that simply lift off the **distributor shaft**, to big round
plastic plates that have two screws to remove. The illustration to the left shows different kinds of rotors.

1 Before you remove your rotor, move it on its shaft.
Does it move easily? If not, you really need this
tune-up badly!

2 Now remove the rotor from the shaft. The illustrations on this page will show you how to remove big and small rotors.

3 Take a close look at it. You can see the metal contacts that conduct current to the spark plug terminals. Are they corroded? Broken? Cracked? Then you really needed a new one! You'll put a new one in anyway, because you've paid for it and it will last longer than the one that's in there now. But don't put it in yet; you have other things to do. Just be sure to see how the old one fits onto the shaft so you can put the new one in properly, later on. All rotors will go on one way only. They either have a square-pin-in-square-hole/round-pin-in-round-hole arrangement, or they are notched or shaped so that they fit on the shaft in one direction only. Still, it is a good habit to take a long look at anything you are removing, because later on you will tend to forget how it went, and sometimes you have to make a choice. Don't be afraid to draw pictures if you aren't sure you'll remember how something fitted together.

Removing a Small Rotor
Delco-Remy Division, General Motors Corp.

Centrifugal Advance
Guaranteed Parts Co.

Removing a Big Rotor
Delco-Remy Division, General Motors Corp.

This type of rotor is released by removing the screws.

Under the rotor are the points and condenser. Under the rotor on some General Motors cars, you will find something called the **centrifugal advance**. Its function is rather complicated, and it has nothing to do with our minor tune-up and hardly ever breaks. Just leave it where it is and forget it.

**Static Shield**  On some cars, you will find a **static shield**, which you will have to remove before you can change your

Static Shield
Guaranteed Parts Co.

points and condenser. The figure shows what this shield looks like. Its purpose is to prevent radio interference. Sometimes the working of the electrical system in your car will produce strange noises on the car radio. This gizmo prevents that. It isn't hard to remove, but when you are finished working on your distributor, be careful to put the shield back the way it was. If you cannot get it back properly, your car will run perfectly without it, so just put the pieces in a paper bag and drive to your friendly service station. They'll put it back for you (although you may have to take a little kidding).

**How to Remove and Replace Your Condenser**

1 You will notice that there are two little wires, one leading to the **points**, and one to the **condenser**, that join together—usually with some sort of little screw and washer arrangement. Take a good look at how these wires fit together in the gadget that holds them (it is called the **primary terminal**). The main purpose of the primary terminal is to keep the clips at the ends of the wires (or *leads*, as they are sometimes called) from touching the floor of the distributor, which is called the **breaker plate**. If they touch this, they will short out and the car will not start. Look again. Are the little clips at the ends of the wires touching each other? Or are they separated with something? Does the screw that holds them in

place touch them? Or is there something in between? If you don't think you can remember how they go, draw a picture of them. The figures on this page show how to disconnect several types of primary terminal arrangements.

2 Now disconnect the leads. Put the screws, or other parts that came off, down on a clean area, so you'll know where they are in case you need them later.

3 The **condenser** is that little cylinder in there. Push it through the ring that holds it, and put it down near the screws. Some condensers are attached to the clips that hold them, and you will have to remove them clip and all. Wipe around the breaker plate where the condenser was resting with a clean, lint-free rag. The figures on this page show a few of the most common set-ups.

4 Now take the new condenser and slide it in where the old one was. If there is a new clip in the tune-up kit but you were able to slide your old condenser out without removing the old clip, forget the new clip as long as the old one seems to be in good condition and does not wiggle around. Congratulations, you've just replaced your condenser.

Disconnecting the Lead Wires from the Primary Terminal of Various Popular Distributors
Delco-Remy Division, General Motors Corp.

(*above*) On some types of distributors, the leads must be loosened from the primary terminal as shown. Leads should be removed from the terminal after noting their relative positions.

(*below right*) On other types of distributors, the nut on the primary terminal must be loosened to release the contact spring and lead wires. Here again the lead arrangement must be noted. (*below left*) Still another type of distributor has its leads attached as shown. These must be removed by loosening the nut at the primary terminal.

(*below*) Here is another arrangement of the primary terminal. To release the contact point spring and leads, a special tool must be used to remove the primary terminal nut.

### How to Remove Old Points

How to Remove the Condenser from Various Popular Distributors
Delco-Remy Division, General Motors Corp.

This type of condenser has one screw to remove and two locating bumps to help you position the new one correctly.

1 Take a look at the **points** in the tune-up kit. They may look a bit different from the ones in the illustration, but they work the same way. Some points are made in a single unit; others consist of two halves that fit together. Some Chrysler products have dual sets of points, but these are no more difficult to install or change. Some foreign cars have little springs that come out separately from the points. If you have points like these, be sure to hold your free hand over the distributor when you loosen the points or it will spring out and get lost. Some points have two screws that fit into slots in the points—these can be loosened, and the points will slide out. Others have a screw to hold the points down and another screw to adjust them. Which kind do you have?

2 Take your screwdriver and open the points up so you can see between them. Are the contacts rough where they meet? This is usually the result of normal wear and tear, and if they are badly burnt or pitted, they should be replaced. If the points are relatively new, excessive wear can be a sign that something is improperly adjusted or malfunction-

Other types of condensers have a locating hole in the mounting bracket.

Some types of condensers are connected to the primary terminal by a copper strap that must be released before the condenser can be removed.

Why You Can't Get an Accurate Gap Reading
on Old Points
Delco-Remy Division, General Motors Corp.

How to Remove Points
Delco-Remy Division, General Motors Corp.

Remove the screw(s) that hold the points in
place. If you have slotted points, simply
*loosen* the screw and slide the points out.

ing. Excessively worn points or burned points usually result from either poor adjustment when they
were installed (this means that they were incorrectly
gapped) or a bad condenser, or the accidental intro-
duction of oil or cam lubricant between the point
contacts. Because used points are impossible to read
accurately with a feeler gauge, you will not be able
to tell if this was a case of poor adjustment. But if
your old points looked badly burned or worn, be
sure to check your new points after about 1,000
miles of driving, and if these look bad too, ask your
garage mechanic for an opinion.

3 Remove the old points by removing the screw or
screws that held them in place. This is a good time
to use your screwholder. Because it will hold on to
the screw until you release it, it cuts down on the
chances of dropping the screw into the works, and
makes it easier to operate in the relatively tight dis-

tributor area because you don't have to cram your fingers in to hold on to the screw. Some screw holders work on magnetic principles; others have a twist handle that grabs the screw. The magnetic ones are super for retrieving metal screws, nuts, and washers that you've dropped into relatively inaccessible places; the other kind may hang on to the screw more securely. Take your pick!

4 Put your old points aside. With the clean rag that you used to clean around under the condenser, wipe the rest of the floor of your distributor (the breaker plate).

**How to Lubricate Your Distributor**

1 Here is something that seems inconsequential but is really very important. In your tune-up kit there should be a little capsule of cam lubricant. If there isn't any, you can buy a tube of it very cheaply. Take a *little bit* of cam lubricant on your index finger and wipe it around the sides of the cam wheel. Use it very sparingly. You don't want lumps, just a nice greasy finish on the cam wheel *only*. If you don't lubricate this wheel, your points could burn out very quickly. If you use too much, the

Applying Lubricant to the Cam Wheel
Delco-Remy Division, General Motors Corp.

The cam wheel should have a light coating of cam lubricant applied to its surface prior to point installation. The amount of grease applied should be kept to a minimum to prevent the grease from being thrown off at high speeds and/or at high temperatures.

Lubricating the Distributor Shaft
Delco-Remy Division, General Motors Corp.

Place a few drops of light engine oil on the wick in the shaft under the rotor, if a wick is present. Do not over oil!

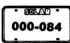
000-084

stuff will fly around inside the distributor when the wheel spins, and foul things up or cause your points to burn. Since your points open and close at around 12,000 times a minute when you drive a V-8 engine at 60 mph, you can see why the lubricant is necessary and why it might tend to fly around if you've been too generous. You want just enough to make your cam wheel lobes slide easily past the points.

2 Look at the top of the distributor shaft, where the rotor was sitting. If there's a wick inside it, place a few drops of light engine oil on the wick in the shaft. If you don't have the proper kind of oil, forget it this time and pick up some in time for the next tune-up.

Installing New Points
Delco-Remy Division, General Motors Corp.

Some points have a knob that fits into a locating hole on the floor of the distributor.

**How to Install New Points**

1 Now pick up the new points. Gently rub the two contact tips together. They usually come from the factory with some kind of coating on them, and this coating can keep the spark from going across the gap. Gently rubbing them together will remove this coating. Don't use cloth, paper, or a file to remove this coating—the lint or tiny filings will foul the points. A little rub is all you need.

2 Install the new points where the old ones were. Sometimes it is easier to connect the lead wires that come from the points and the condenser before you replace the points in the distributor. In any case, just be sure that the clips on both wires *touch each other* but *do not touch any other metal*. They are designed to go back to back so they will fit snugly into the clip on the primary terminal. Check back on page 81 to see the different types of clips and the way to assemble yours. If you don't see it and you've neglected to make a drawing of the way yours were, use your imagination. If you get it wrong, your car won't start until you get it right. Nothing else will happen, so don't worry. Just fit the wire clips together and put them in the clip so that they are not touching anything metal (this includes the side of the clip, if it's made of metal, and the distributor base). As I said before, this can be done either before or after you've got the points in place, whichever is easier.

3 If you haven't already done so, install the new

Other points fit over a locating post on the floor of the distributor.

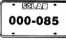

points. Don't tighten down the screws that hold them in place until you have adjusted the gap.

**How to Gap Your Points**

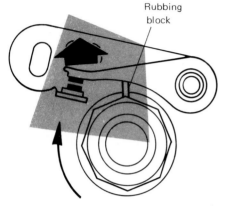

Rubbing block

How the Rubbing Block Causes the Points to Open
Delco-Remy Division, General Motors Corp.

The rubbing block is pushed upward by the highest point on the cam lobe, which causes the points to open to their widest gap.

How to Bring Points to Their Widest Gap
Delco-Remy Division, General Motors Corp.

Crank the engine with the starting motor until the point rubbing block is on the peak of the cam lobe. This is the position of maximum point gap.

Now it's time to adjust your point gap (or gap your points).

1 Look at your specifications for the proper gap. Then take your flat feeler gauge and select the correct blade. Before you can adjust the point gap, the little **rubbing block** that protrudes from the side of the points nearest the cam wheel must rest on the highest point of one of the cam lobes. This forces the points open to their widest gap—and that is the gap that you are going to adjust.

2 If the rubbing block is not resting on the point of the cam lobe, bump your starter with the ignition key until the cam wheel turns to the correct position. If you can't seem to do this, run a chalk mark down the side of the distributor and on to the base, or whatever it is sitting on. This will help you later to get it back the way it was. Then turn to page 97 of this chapter where we deal with adjusting the timing, and see how to locate the **distributor hold-down clamp**. Loosen it and turn the distributor until the rubbing block is resting on the point of the cam lobe and the points are wide open.

3 Slide the blade of the feeler gauge between the points. Is the gap too small to let the blade in? If you left it like that, your car would be hard—or impossible—to start and your points would get burnt and pitted. Is the gap so wide that the gauge doesn't touch both surfaces as it goes in and out? This would result in a weak spark and poor engine performance at high speeds. So, if your gap is either too wide or too small, it needs adjusting.

4 There are three basic kinds of point-adjusting set-ups. Let's see which one your car has. Some cars have an *adjusting screw* (in addition to the screw or screws that hold the points in place). Other cars have an *adjusting slot*. Still others have a little *window* in the distributor cap which allows you to adjust the points without removing the distributor cap.

*If you have an adjusting screw:*

a Loosen the screw or screws that hold the points in place.

b Turn the off-center adjusting screw.

c Place the feeler gauge between the point contacts (these should still be at their widest gap; if they aren't, turn the distributor shaft until they are).

d Turn the adjusting screw until the gauge can slip in and out between the contacts, just touching them as it slides. There should be a minuscule grab as it goes through, but it should go through easily. If you aren't sure, try the next thicker and thinner gauges. Neither should work properly.

e When you've got the gap just right, tighten up the screws that hold your points in place (*not* the adjusting screw) and recheck with gauge.

f If you have moved the distributor, put it back where it was, with the chalk marks lined up.

*If you have an adjusting slot:*

a Loosen the locking screw or screws that hold the points in place.

b Making sure that the points are at their widest gap (if they aren't, move the distributor shaft until they are), insert the tip of your screwdriver into the adjusting slot and, by moving it one way or the other, open the gap so that the correct feeler gauge blade can slip in.

c Insert the correct feeler gauge blade and, using your screwdriver in the adjusting slot, adjust the contacts to allow the feeler gauge to slide in and out properly. It should just touch both contacts as it moves, but it should move easily, with just a little bit of grab as it goes by.

d Tighten screws that hold points in place and recheck with gauge. If you have moved the distributor, put it back the way it was, with the chalk marks lined up.

*If you have an external adjustment window:*

a Reassemble your distributor and put the distributor cap back on. (You'll find instructions for do-

**Adjusting Screw-Type Points**
Delco-Remy Division, General Motors Corp.

Insert a *flat* feeler gauge between points and turn adjusting screw until points grasp gauge firmly but not so tightly as to obstruct its movement. (Do *not* use wire gauge shown in illustration.)

**Adjusting Slot-Type Points**
Delco-Remy Division, General Motors Corp.

Insert tip of screwdriver into adjusting slot and twist until points grab feeler gauge firmly but not enough to impede its movement. (Use *flat* gauge rather than wire gauge shown in illustration.)

ing this on the next page or so.) Your points will probably *not* need adjusting—they come preset from the factory—but if you do need to adjust them, then follow the rest of these instructions. You will know if they need adjusting if your car won't start and if you've hooked the wires from the points and the condenser together so that they don't touch any other metal but each other.

b (Only if your points need adjusting) If the car won't start, use a wrench as in c below to turn the adjusting nut. If turning it one way won't get the car started, try turning it the other way. Start your car and leave the engine running with the emergency brake on and the car in either "Park" or "Neutral" gear.

c Use the little "hex" wrench in the tune-up kit, or your own, to turn the adjustment nut behind the sliding window in the distributor cap. Turn the nut clockwise until the engine starts to "miss." Then turn the screw *half a turn* counterclockwise, remove the wrench, and close the window.

Adjusting Points with an External Adjustment Window
DIXCO

Insert "hex" wrench into adjustment nut. With engine idling, turn nut clockwise until engine "misses," then half a turn counterclockwise.

How to Replace a Defective Distributor Cap
Delco-Remy Division, General Motors Corp.

To replace a defective cap, place old and new caps side by side in same relative position, noting locating lugs or slots. Remove one lead at a time from the old cap, placing it in the same relative tower on the new cap. Lead must first be pushed to bottom of tower and then the rubber boot replaced securely.

### How to Reassemble
### Your Distributor
**Replacing the Rotor**

Some distributor caps have either a locating lug that fits into a slot in the cap spring hanger, or a groove or slot in the cap which fits over a boss on the distributor housing.

After replacing the cap, with the locators in place, fasten it to the housing by either (a) pressing on the center of the cap spring, forcing the spring over the mounting lugs on the cap, or (b) by pressing down on the screw and turning it until the clamp is under slot on the bottom of the housing.

How to Replace Your Distributor Cap
Delco-Remy Division, General Motors Corp.

000-090

1 You've got your points adjusted, the condenser in place, and the little lead wires screwed into the clip, right? Now install the rotor from the tune-up kit, making sure that you put it back the way it was. (Of course if you have one of those **static shields**, you want to put that back before the rotor.) All rotors will fit properly one way only.

2 Turn your rotor to see if it settles back in place easily. Can you turn it in more than one direction? If you can, you don't have it back in place properly.

3 Pick up the distributor cap (don't let any wires come off) and take a look inside it. Wipe the inside clean with a lint-free rag. Are there any cracks in the cap when you hold it up and shine a light through it? If there are, you can buy another cap very cheaply. (The wires snap in and out of the cap, and as long as you hold the two caps in the same direction and pull the wires off the old cap and insert them in the new cap *one at a time* in the *correct order*, you should have no trouble.)

4 Look at the inside of the cap where the wires enter it. Push gently on each wire where it enters its "tower," and make sure it is in tightly. Are the insides of the towers clean? Each little metal thing you see inside the cap is an electrode that transfers the electricity to the rotor, so you don't want them to be too fouled to conduct the electricity. If they look dirty, scrape them with a small screwdriver to remove the carbon. If they are very dirty, or burnt, you may need to replace your wires. At this point, you are probably better off having someone do this for you. Later, when you are more confident, you can do these things yourself and wonder why I suggested you have someone else do the job. But I don't want to hit you with too many things at once.

If you are satisfied that all is well, replace your distributor cap, making sure it is on securely and will not budge when you wiggle it. Be sure you've got all the clamps or screws back in place. Now start your engine to see if you've got everything right. If your car won't start (this is not unusual), go back and recheck the following:

a Is your car still in "Park" or "Neutral"? It won't start in any other gear.

b Is your distributor cap on correctly? If it is, take it off.

c Are the lead wires from the condenser and the points correctly replaced and tightened down? If they are touching anything metal but each other, the spark is grounding out instead of passing through the points while they are closed.

d Are your points properly gapped? Check them with the feeler gauge. Sometimes they move back together when you tighten them down after adjusting them. Run a bit of very clean, lint-free cloth between them—maybe something got in there and is preventing the spark from going across. Do they close completely? They must open and close to work.

e Did you accidentally disconnect any other wires while you were working?

One of these questions will solve your problem.

Now, put your distributor cap back again and start the engine. It should start this time. Don't panic if you have trouble—everyone does the first time. But you ran the car after you changed the spark plugs, so if there is a problem it has to be in the distributor, right?

If you still can't get started, remove the new condenser and put the old one back in. Maybe the new one is defective. This could also be true of the points or rotor. I'm pretty sure you are not *going to resort to this strategy* without being able to start your car, but if you do, and nothing is still happening, the worst that can happen is that your friendly garage mechanic will come and get you out of the hole. So how bad can it be?

Anyway, for the nine-hundred-ninety-nine out of a thousand of us who have managed to start our cars, now it is time to check the **dwell**, if you are lucky enough to have a **dwell meter**. The difference between the cost of doing this tune-up yourself and having it done for you is probably what a dwell meter and maybe even a **timing light** would cost, so why not get them?

## Checking Your Distributor with a Dwell Meter

Points close — Points open, plugs fire

**Normal Gap, Normal Dwell**

Small dwell

**Wide Gap, Insufficient Dwell**

Large dwell

**Small Gap, Excessive Dwell**

"Cam angle" or "dwell" is the time the points are closed, measured in degrees of cam rotation. Point gap, therefore, has a definite bearing on the cam angle. Both cam angle and point gap should be checked when new points are installed.

What "Cam Angle" or "Dwell" Means
DIXCO

A **dwell meter** is a handy gadget for determining whether or not your points were properly gapped—a wise double-check, even for a professional—and whether your distributor is operating properly. It checks the distance that your distributor shaft rotates when your points are closed—which is the same as saying that it measures how long the points stay closed (or "dwell together"). This distance is called the *cam angle* and, like all angles, it is given in degrees.

1 Here's how to hook up two of the most popular types of dwell meter:

*The kind with two clips:*

a With the engine shut off, hook the RED clip to the clamp that holds the little wire on the side of the **coil** that leads to the distributor.

b Hook the BLACK clip to "**ground**." "Ground" can be anything that is made of metal, through which electricity can pass back to the battery. In this case, it can be any part of the metal frame of the car, but the best ground is an unpainted pipe or bolt bolted directly to the engine (but not too near the carburetor, please!).

*The kind with three clips:*

a Connect the RED clip to the positive terminal of the battery.

b Connect the BLACK clip to the negative terminal of the battery.

Black — Engine ground

Red

Ignition switch

Distributor — Coil — Battery

How to Hook Up a Dwell Meter with Two Clips
DIXCO

**CONNECTIONS:**

How to Hook Up a Dwell Meter with Three
Clips
Actron Manufacturing Co.

c Connect the GREEN clip to the clamp that holds
the little wire on the side of the coil which leads
to the distributor.

If you have a Ford, see the figure to the right.

2 If your dwell meter has one, turn the *calibrated* knob
to set it.

3 Turn the proper knob to the number of cylinders
that your car has.

4 Start the engine and let it idle, with the emergency
brake on, in "Park" or "Neutral" gear.

5 Look at the dwell meter, on the line that has the
same number of cylinders as your car. Is the needle
pointing to the correct figure listed under "Dwell"
on your Specifications Record sheet? It can
be + or − 2 degrees (if your spec sheet shows a
dwell of 38 degrees, the dwell is fine if it is
anywhere between 36 and 40 degrees). If it is further off than that, you will have to readjust your
points.

6 a If you have a distributor with an external *adjusting window*, let the engine idle and keep the dwell

Using a Ford Adapter Clip
Actron Manufacturing Co.

Late model Ford cars have an insulated
slip-on terminal on the wire lead from the
distributor to the ignition coil. Lift this
terminal and slide the Ford adapter clip in
place as shown, then push the terminal
down. Attach the GREEN clip to the adapter
clip as shown.
Do Not Allow the Ford Adapter Clip or the
Green Clip to Touch Any Other Metallic Part
of the Coil Case or the Engine.

meter in place. Then open the little window in the side of the distributor cap (it slides up) and turn the adjustment screw with the hex wrench until the needle on the dwell meter points to the correct number.

b If you have the kind of points that adjust with an *adjusting screw or slot,* you will have to shut off the engine, open the distributor cap again, and readjust your points to the correct gap with your feeler gauge. When you are sure you've got it right, put everything back and check the dwell again. Sorry, but that's life.... If the dwell is too low, the gap is too large, and *vice versa.*

Everything on target? Then it is time to check your **timing**. Did you get a timing light? I hope so. I've heard of a variety of ways to check your timing without one, but none of them has proved very accurate, and many turned out to be impossible. So, beg or borrow one if you can't buy one, or, as a last resort, ask your garage to check your timing.

7 If you have a *tach/dwell* meter (a dwell meter with a **tachometer** built in), then turn the knob to set it to the tachometer readings. Some tach/dwell meters have both Hi and Lo readings; if yours does, choose either line for right now. Start your engine and let the car idle. After it warms up a bit, check the tachometer to see at how many rpm the car is idling. Try to keep the tach/dwell hooked up while you check your timing, but if it is too difficult to clip both the tach/dwell and the timing light to the battery terminals, disconnect the tach/dwell and keep it handy.

### How to Check Your Timing with a Timing Light

1 Read the instructions that came with the light. This is a good idea with any piece of new equipment. Then, hook up your **timing light** as they suggest. Most lights have three clips on them. Cheap neon timing lights have a clip and a plug that fits a wall outlet. These lights are generally too dim to read by in anything but total darkness, so try to avoid this kind when you go out to borrow or buy one. If you have no instructions, the ones in this book will work for most timing lights with three clips.

How to Hook Up a Timing Light
DIXCO

2  Be sure your engine is shut off.

3  Clamp the big RED clip to the **positive terminal** of your car battery.

4  The big BLACK clip goes on the **negative terminal** of the battery. Make sure the battery terminals are clean enough to allow current to pass through them. If they look *very* funky, scrape the clip around on them a little, or wash off the junk with a clean rag dipped in water and baking soda. Don't get the stuff from the terminal on your hands—it has acid in it. But if you do get it on your hands, just wash them off with water; it won't burn holes in you right away.

5  The third clip, with the thickest insulation, attaches to your #1 spark plug. Way back on page 70 there is an illustration that will tell you where the #1 plug is on your car—in case you've forgotten. You can either place the clip by removing the **boot** from the plug; putting the clip on the terminal end of the plug, where it is sticking out of the engine; and replacing the boot so that it fits snugly and allows the current to pass through from the cable to the plug. Or you can use a small metal spring or clip that will fit over the end of the plug, leaving a gap between the boot and the plug on which to clip the third clip from the timing light.

To distributor

Spring connector

Using a Spring Connector
DIXCO

If your #1 spark plug is hard to get at, you can attach the third clip to the distributor terminal tower where the cable from the #1 plug enters the distributor cap. Just trace the cable from the plug to the distributor, remove the boot from the distributor cap terminal, add a metal extension (usually supplied with the light), replace the boot, and clamp the clip to the extension.

6  Keeping your engine shut off, try to pull up on your fan belt with one hand to tighten it, and turn the fan with the other hand in order to rotate the wheel that has the fan belt hooked around it (the lower wheel). This wheel probably has your **timing marks** on it. It is called the **crankshaft pulley** (or the harmonic balance wheel). On some cars, the timing marks are located elsewhere, so if you cannot find yours on the crankshaft pulley, consult your owner's manual for their location, or call your dealer. If you cannot move the fan by hand,

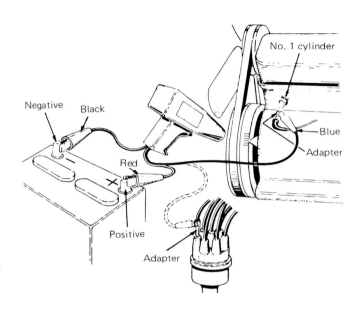

How to Attach the Third Clip to the #1 Spark Plug or the #1 Distributor Terminal
Actron Manufacturing Co.

Timing Marks on the Crankshaft Pulley of a Car
DIXCO

remove the big wire from the center of your distributor cap and lay it on something metal to ground it. Then turn the key in the ignition to "bump" the starter without starting the engine. This will turn the pulley, and as it turns, a set of lines should come into view. These are your timing marks. A pointer attached to the engine block usually points to these marks. To set your timing, you will have to get the pointer to point to the correct timing mark while the engine is running.

7 Look at your spec sheet to see what your timing degree should be. It will say something like "10°@ 550," which means that you want to line the pointer up with the 10° timing mark when the engine is idling at 550 rpm. It may say something about "BTDC" or "ATDC." This simply means that your timing marks will have a line labeled "0," with marks above and below it, and these will be the marks that come before and after the "0," which is "top dead center" (**TDC**). Depending on the direction that the wheel rotates, the lines that come into view before the "0" (or TDC mark) are "before top dead center" (BTDC), and the ones that appear after TDC are "after top dead center" (ATDC). In case you are curious, "top dead center" is the point at which the piston has reached its

highest point in the cylinder and compression is greatest. (How's that for cocktail party chatter?)

8 Have you found your timing marks? Do you know which mark you want to set your timing at? Then use a piece of chalk to make that mark stand out. You can also chalk the tip of the pointer to make it more visible.

9 Attached to the side of your distributor is a round gizmo called a **vacuum advance**. Disconnect the little rubber hose that comes from it, and put a piece of tape on the end of the hose—or stick a screw in it—to seal it off.

10 Start your engine, making sure that your emergency brake is on and that you are in "Park" or "Neutral," and let the car warm up.

11 If your dwell meter/tachometer is still hooked up, look at the rpm line to see if the car is idling at the proper speed. If it isn't, you will have to adjust your **idle**. You will find instructions for doing this in Chapter 7. It is a simple matter of turning one screw, so don't be dismayed. And just think, if your idle is off, you have been wasting fuel and your car hasn't been running properly.

12 Is your car idling properly now? Fine! Now aim the timing light at the timing marks and press the button on the light. The fact that the light is hooked to your #1-cylinder spark plug means that current will pass through the light every time your #1 plug "fires." This makes the light go on and off with a strobe effect. The timing marks should appear to be standing still, although the crankshaft pulley is actually turning rapidly. Is the pointer pointing to the correct mark? If it isn't, you must adjust your timing.

Timing Mark Locations on Various Popular Cars
DIXCO

Plug end of vacuum line

The Vacuum Advance Shown Disconnected
Actron Manufacturing Co.

1 On the base of your distributor shaft, below the distributor, is a nut called the **distributor hold-down clamp**. Use a combination wrench to loosen this nut so the distributor can turn a bit on the shaft when you grasp the vacuum advance and move it back and forth. If you have trouble reaching the hold-down clamp, use your *distributor wrench*.

**How to Adjust Your Timing**

### How to Adjust Your Timing
Delco-Remy Division, General Motors Corp.

To change the timing, the clamp holding the
distributor to the engine block must first be
slightly loosened. The entire distributor is
then turned in the direction of rotation of the
rotor to retard the timing. To advance the
timing, turn the distributor in the direction
opposite the rotating rotor. Tighten the
hold-down clamp securely after adjustment is
completed.

Offset Distributor Wrench
K-D Manufacturing Co.

2 Move the distributor *a little bit* on the shaft, then
shine your timing light at the timing marks again. Is
the pointer nearer the right mark? Is it farther
away? Then you have moved the distributor in the
wrong direction. Go back and move it the other way.

3 Now go back and check again with the timing light.
Continue doing this until the pointer is pointing to

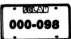

the correct timing mark. If your idle speed changes, adjust your idle to specifications and recheck your timing. Then tighten the distributor hold-down clamp again, making sure you don't move the distributor when you do it. Check again with the light. Are the timing marks dead on? Good! (You can be off a little bit without causing trouble, but be as accurate as you can without driving yourself crazy.) You now have your car timed perfectly, and this will lead to much better engine performance and fuel consumption. And cut down on air pollution.

4 Shut off your engine, and disconnect the timing light and the tach/dwell meter. Be sure to remove the metal extension if you've used one on your #1 plug, and put the boot back on the plug.

Well, you've changed your spark plugs, serviced your distributor, and checked your dwell, idle, and timing. You have just completed a basic tune-up! If you've had a little trouble, would it have been worth big bucks to avoid it? (As I write this book, the cost of tune-ups seems to be going up daily.) And you *know* that all the work has been done, and done properly. If you are still game, there are a couple of other things that you can do to be sure your engine is operating at peak efficiency. If you are pooped, you can check them tomorrow, or next weekend, without ruining anything. Then, make it a habit to set aside an hour or two on a specific day each month for your under-the-hood check.

We all know people who are chronic "tire kickers." These are the people who habitually walk around their car, kicking the tires to make sure they aren't flat, before they get in and drive off. These are the same people who habitually open and close all the cabinet doors in the kitchen and turn the gas jets to make sure they are completely off, every time they go past the stove. We tend to laugh at them, and yet they are probably rarely caught with flat tires, open cabinets, or leaking gas. We can learn a little from these people and make a habit of checking the little things under the hood of our cars—maybe not *every* time we go

**Under-the-Hood Check**

anywhere, but definitely once a month and before starting out on long trips. I've provided a Maintenance Record sheet at the back of this book to help you keep track of what you've checked and what you've replaced.

What should you check now? Well, you are probably already doing a lot of these things. Here they are:

**Radiator Check**

1 Open the cap on your radiator and check to see if the water in it is running low. You should be able to see the water a couple of inches below the cap. If the level is low, add water or coolant. Tap water is fine. You should always do this when the engine is cold, to avoid the possibility of being burned. If you ever have to remove a radiator cap from a car that has been running, be sure to see page 160 for instructions.

If your car has a coolant recovery reservoir (a plastic bottle connected to the radiator that holds an extra supply of liquid), there is no need to open the radiator cap. Just check to see if the liquid reaches the level indicated on the bottle and remove the bottle cap to check the quality of the liquid inside. You'll find more about these handy gadgets, some of which you can install yourself, on page 178.

If the liquid looks pink, green, or yellow that's the coolant, or antifreeze. If the water looks rusty or has things floating around in it, you should flush your radiator and add new coolant. Instructions for when and how to do this start on page 175.

2 While you are messing around with your radiator, feel the big hoses that go into the top and come out of the bottom of the radiator. If they are leaking, cracked, bulgy, or squishy, they should be replaced. Easy instructions begin on page 171.

**Fan Belt Check**

Take a look at the belt that goes around the fan and the alternator (or generator) on your car. Is it cracked or frayed inside or outside? If it is, it should be replaced. Is the inside of the belt glazed and shiny? This means it should be replaced, too. Does the belt "give" more than half an inch when you press on it midway

How to Replace Your Fan Belt
The Gates Rubber Company

1. Loosen the alternator (or generator) by loosening the pivot bolt.

2. Loosen the adjustment bolt.

3. Move the alternator toward the block by grasping the belt and pulling sharply upward. If the belt is broken or missing, use a hammer handle to move the alternator.

4. Remove the old belt by slipping it off the alternator pulleys and working it up and over the fan blades.
   NOTE: On some cars the fan is too close to the radiator to slip it into the crankshaft and alternator pulley grooves.
5. With a new belt, reverse the process. Work the new belt down and over the fan blades and slip it into the crankshaft and pulley grooves.

6. Pull the alternator by hand until the belt is snug. Then use a hammer handle to apply leverage until there is about ¼ to ½ inch of "play" on the belt. Use that hammer handle carefully to avoid applying pressure to parts of the engine or alternator which could be damaged. Tighten the adjustment bolt.

7. Run the engine for about 15 minutes at varying speeds, and check the belt again for the proper amount of tension. After about 100 miles of driving, check the belt again. New belts will stretch. If it has more than ¼ to ½ inch of play, readjust the tension.

Two Types of Battery Covers

between the alternator and the fan? You might be able to adjust it if the belt is otherwise in good condition. If not, replace it.

Here's how to tighten your **fan belt:**

1 Loosen the nuts and bolts that secure the alternator bracket.

2 Pull the alternator back, away from the fan end of the belt, so that the belt is drawn tighter. Then tighten the nuts and bolts. Check again after about 100 miles of driving to see if it has loosened again.

If you want to do it yourself, go to the auto-parts store with the year, make, and model of your car. Buy the fan belt you need. Then follow the instructions in the "How to Replace Your Fan Belt" illustration.

Keep the old belt in the trunk of your car for emergencies. If replacing it yourself does not seem worth the effort, you can have the fan belt adjusted or replaced at almost any service station.

1 Open those little caps, or remove the bars, on the top of your battery. Look inside. If you can see the tops of the plates inside the battery, add distilled water, or water with a low mineral content. (If you have a sealed battery, you will not be able to do this.)

*Caution:* Never open a battery with a lighted cigarette in your mouth. For that matter, don't smoke when working around your car. Batteries are filled with acid, which generates hydrogen gas, so you want to be careful when working around them.

2 The cruddy deposits that form in lovely colors on the top of your terminals are made by this acid. Brush it off with a wire *battery brush,* or remove it with some baking soda and water. Try to avoid getting the powdery stuff on your hands or clothes, but if you do, just wash it off with water *right away* and neither you nor your clothes will be damaged. If you coat the terminals with grease or petroleum jelly, you can help to prevent these deposits from forming.

**Battery Check**

Battery Brush
K-D Manufacturing Co.

Frayed or
Broken Cables

Overfilling

Water

Corrosion

Dirt

Loose
Hold–Down

Cracked
Case

Low
Electrolyte

Cell
Connector
Corrosion

Cracked
Cell Cover

Check Your Battery for These Problems
Automotive Parts & Accessories Association (APAA)
Battery Tester
K-D Manufacturing Co.

3 Check to see that the wires leading to the terminals are not frayed. If they are, they should be replaced, or the battery may short circuit. A battery that is kept clean and filled with water should last a long time. By the way, if those caps or bars look beyond help, you can buy replacements cheaply at the auto supply store.

4 Check the rest of these trouble areas shown in the illustration.

5 If your battery has been acting up lately—if you are having trouble starting your car or your lights dim out—or if the battery is very old, buy a battery tester and check to see if the acid level is high enough. These testers cost only a few dollars, and you simply draw some of the battery fluid (**electrolyte**) into the tester and look at the floating balls inside it. A scale on the tester will tell you the condition of the battery fluid. If you get a very low reading, you can get the fluid changed at a service station. But if they tell you that the condition of the plates inside the battery is also deteriorating, you are probably going to have to buy a new one. Don't put an expensive battery with a 5-year guarantee on a car you hope to get rid of in a year or two.

**Hose Check** Walk around the hood area, squeezing every hose you encounter. If you meet any that are leaking, bulgy, soft and squishy, or hard and brittle, turn to Chapter 8 for instructions on how to replace them. Replacing a hose is an easy job. It pays to replace hoses *before* they break; any saving of time or effort is not worth the aggravation of having your trip come to an abrupt stop on the freeway because of a broken hose. Most emergency trucks do not carry spare hoses (they'd have to carry too many different kinds, and they don't have the time to change them on the road), and you may end up paying an expensive tow charge for a couple of dollars' worth of hose that could have been replaced ahead of time in about 10 minutes.

**Oil Check** Sticking out of the side of the engine block is a little **dipstick** with a ring on the end of it. That's the one the gas station attendant is always showing you and

Where to Find the Oil Dipstick on Many
Popular Cars
Richard Freshman

saying, "Looks like it needs oil. Shall I add some?"
Now, look at it yourself. First, be sure that your engine is cold or has been shut off for a few minutes.
Then, pull the little stick out and wipe it off on a
clean rag. Now shove the stick back in again. If it gets
stuck on the way in, turn it around. The pipe it fits
into is curved, and the metal stick will bend naturally
in the direction of the curve if you put it back the way
it came out. Now pull it out again and look at the tip
of the stick. You will see a film of oil. Does the oil film
reach only to where it says "add oil" on the dipstick?

Or does it reach to where it says "full"? Is the film of
oil on the dipstick very black and gooky? Stick the tip
of your finger in it. Does it leave your fingertip dirty
when you wipe it off? Then you should probably have
your oil changed. Chapter 12 will tell you how to
change your oil yourself. It's easy and will save you a
lot of money.

Let's say that your oil looks clean enough but that it
only reaches to the "add oil" level on the dipstick. You

An Oil Dipstick
Richard Freshman

can get some oil next time you fill up at the gas station, or you can buy a can at the auto supply store and add it yourself. Chapter 12 will help you to determine the proper weight oil for your car, and provides instructions for locating the place to add it.

**Automatic Transmission Fluid Check**

Where to Find the Transmission Dipstick on Many Popular Cars
Richard Freshman

Look for another dipstick handle toward the rear of the engine. This one is sticking out of your **transmission**, where the end of the crankshaft meets the gears and turns miraculously into a driveshaft, remember? Let your engine run with the car in "Neutral" or "Park." When it's warm, leave the engine running and pull out the dipstick. Wipe it with a clean, lint-free rag. Reinsert it and pull it out again. If the stick shows that you need more **transmission fluid**, use a funnel to pour just enough fluid down the dipstick tube to reach the "Full" line on the stick. Do not overfill!

There are two major types of transmission fluid, Type F and Dexron II. Each is made for a specific type of automatic transmission. Since there are so many different kinds of transmissions in use these days on the various models put out by each car maker, you must check with your owner's manual or car dealer to find out which type of fluid your car requires.

Of course, if you have a car with a manual (standard) transmission, disregard all of this. The level in **manual transmissions** must be checked with the car on a hoist, to enable the mechanic to easily reach a plug in the bottom of the transmission. It's best not to monkey around with this yourself. But the next time your car is in for repairs, or for lubrication, have them check the level for you.

If the transmission fluid on the dipstick looks or smells burnt or has particles in it, have the fluid drained and changed by a mechanic. It should be pinkish and almost clear.

Incidentally, if your car has been hesitating when you change gears, the first thing to check is the transmission fluid level before you let anyone start talking about "bands." If you are burning white smoke from under your car, you probably need transmission fluid badly, although it can also be a bad **vacuum modulator**. If the smoking has been going on for a long time, you may need a new transmission!

On the driver's side of your car, usually up near the firewall, is a little box or bottle with pipes, or a pipe, coming from it. This is your **master cylinder**. It holds the **brake fluid** that gets pushed down the lines to each wheel of your car when you step on the brake pedal. If there is insufficient brake fluid, your car won't stop properly. So, let's check to be sure that there's enough brake fluid in your master cylinder. You can find instructions on how to open your master cylinder and how to buy the proper brake fluid in Chapter 10. Most master cylinders have two chambers as a safety feature. This way, if one well of brake fluid goes dry—owing to a leak in the brake lines, or something like that—then the other chamber still has enough fluid in it to stop the car. Is the brake fluid up to within ½ inch or so of the cap? Then you are O.K. If it isn't, get some brake fluid and add it. Be careful not to get brake fluid on anything painted. It eats paint. If there are spills, wipe them up and get rid of the rag. Be sure not to get grease or oil into your brake fluid (you can cause this by wiping your master cylinder with a greasy or oily rag), because either will ruin your hydraulic brake system. One more thing: Don't open a can of brake fluid and leave it standing around. If the air gets to it for as little as 15 minutes, the fluid is ruined. (Air oxidization lowers its boiling point.) So keep it tightly closed until you are ready to use it, and if you have some left over, throw the stuff away.

**Brake Fluid Inspection**

A Transmission Dipstick
Richard Freshman

Where to Find the Master Cylinder on Many Popular Cars
Richard Freshman

**Power-Steering Fluid Check**

Locate the **power-steering pump** in your car. Your owner's manual should tell you where it is. Unscrew the cap and check to see that the fluid is up to the fill mark on the dipstick, or near the top of the bottle. If it isn't, check your owner's manual to see what kind of fluid it requires.

NOTE: If any of the water, oil, transmission, brake, or power-steering fluid levels are very low and it has been only a short time since that particular fluid was added to your car, it might be a wise idea to find out why you are losing fluid. Your garage attendant has a special device to locate leaks in your cooling system. It is a replacement radiator cap that has a short hose attachment that leads to a meter and a hand pump. If you ask him to pressure-test your radiator, he will put the cap on your radiator and use the pump to pump air into your cooling system. This increases the pressure in the cooling system to where it generally is when your engine has been running. (The meter tells him when the proper pressure is reached.) If you have a leak in your cooling system, the pressure will make the water squirt out of wherever the leak is.

Similar devices will give you the answers to other fluid-loss problems. It is usually simply a leaky hose, or a gasket that has come loose. Sometimes a loss of

Where to Find the Power Steering Pump on Many Popular Cars
Richard Freshman

transmission fluid, or radiator water, can be cured with a single dose of the proper **sealer**. It is wise to get professional advice about leaks, but be sure that they cover the simple, inexpensive answers (like changing a hose or adding sealer) before you let them sell you expensive parts (like water pumps) or major overhauls.

**Windshield Washer Fluid Check**

Under your hood there is a plastic bottle or bag that connects to the washers on your windshield wipers. Is it full of liquid? If not, you can fill it with any one of a variety of windshield washer solutions. Some are concentrated, and are mixed with water before adding, or you can use a home window cleaner. Don't use detergent, however. It can leave a residue that can plug up your lines, and it isn't easy to drive with suds all over your windshield!

If you live in an area that gets cold in the winter, you can buy a premixed washer solution that contains antifreeze. This comes in quart and gallon sizes and will keep your windshield clean while it prevents the liquid from freezing up in cold weather.

If your wipers have been making a mess of your windshield, buy new blades for them. These are generally inexpensive, and usually just slide or snap into place. Consult your owner's manual, if you can't figure it out by looking—or ask the person in the auto parts store to tell you how the blades are inserted.

**Wiring Check**

Feel the wires that you encounter under the hood. If they feel hard and inflexible, if there are bright metal wires showing through the insulation, or if the wires look corroded or very messy where they attach to various devices, they may need to be changed before they short out. Have a garage do the rewiring until you really get to be an expert.

**Tire Pressure Check**

And lastly, for those tire kickers among us, buy an accurate tire gauge (they aren't expensive) and check the pressure in each of your tires. Chapter 11 has full instructions on how to perform this easy task. Tires that are low wear down faster and make your car harder to steer. Tires that have too much pressure may blow out or steer erratically. So try to keep them within the manufacturer's specified range.

You're through for the day! You know that your car is in tune and that it has had everything it needs in terms of fuel, oil, water, and other exotic beverages. And you did it all yourself! Doesn't it feel good? There is nothing like working on your own car for instant rewards. Get in and drive it around. It feels smoother, right? The pickup is better. The car is happier, and you can hear the engine purring. Your car knows that *you* did it, and it has drawn you closer. Silly romanticizing? Well, either I have an extremely affectionate car or a wild imagination.

For more tangible evidence, I offer this: When I was married, I showed my husband (who used to run at the sight of anything mechanical) how to do everything in this chapter. After just changing his spark plugs and servicing his distributor, his mileage increased from 10 miles per gallon to 17.5 miles per gallon. He was so impressed that the next weekend he changed his radiator hoses and did his under-the-hood inspection (which involved fixing a windshield washer pump that had gotten stuck), and now he is a confirmed do-it-yourselfer. This was a relief to me, because I had visions of taking care of *two* cars, and that is *one* car too many for a "working girl"—unless she is a garage mechanic!

Now that you are hooked, let's get on to the Fuel System so that you can see what *really* makes that engine run and can learn to tune your carburetor.

# The Fuel System:
# The Heart and
# Lungs of Your Car

Let's go back to our earlier discussion of how an **internal combustion engine** works. We zipped through it rather quickly, way back in Chapter 3, but now you are sufficiently sophisticated about cars to bear a couple of additional technical details. It is always easier to work on a machine that you understand, and if you are going to get involved with your **fuel system**, you should be able to relate to it in terms of what it does to make your engine operate efficiently.

Basically, the fuel system stores the fuel for the car; passes it along to the **carburetor**, which mixes it with air; and sends it on its way to the engine. Probably the most coherent way to get this stuff across to you is to take each step in the process separately, discuss its form and function, and let the total picture emerge from the relationship of its parts. With characteristic perversity, let's begin at the rear of the car and work our way forward...

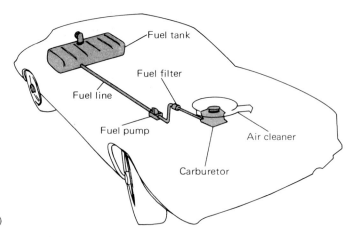

The Fuel System
Automotive Information Council (AIC)

### The Fuel Tank

The **fuel tank** is a metal container located under the trunk compartment of most cars, although others have some fairly interesting other locations for it. Your owner's manual will tell you where yours is located, but since fuel tanks very rarely go wrong, you probably won't have to deal with it personally.

Inside the fuel tank is a little float that bobs up and down on the surface of the fuel. It sends messages to the fuel gauge on your dashboard so you can tell when it is necessary to buy more gasoline.

Since the rest of the space in the fuel tank, above the fuel level, is filled with air—and since air contains quite a bit of water vapor—on cool mornings the water in the air tends to condense on the sides of the fuel tank, and elsewhere. This water vapor can rust the insides of your fuel tank, it can mix with the fuel, and it can act in a variety of pesky ways to keep your car from operating efficiently. Of course, if you keep your fuel tank well filled, there will be less room for air and therefore less water vapor hanging around. This is an excellent reason for *not* driving around until your fuel gauge reads "Empty."

Another reason for making those extra trips to the gas station is that the rust that is formed by the water vapor in the air tends to sink to the bottom of the fuel tank. These sediments can do no harm as long as they are happily sloshing about in the bottom of the tank. But if you let the fuel level in the tank get too low, the fuel that gets fed to your engine could be like the last bit of coffee in the bottom of the pot—full of sediment that tends to stick in the throat. Some tanks have filters to prevent this, but they can get choked up if you consistently drive on an empty tank.

**Why You Should Keep Your Fuel Tank Full**

It might make those refueling trips more fun—and cheaper too—to turn them into another do-it-yourself adventure. Since the energy crisis, some gas stations have offered their customers the option of operating the pumps themselves and buying the gasoline at a lower price. This kind of consumer self-sufficiency has a lovely "rightness" about it. Everybody wins. The station attendants can devote their time to more financially-rewarding projects, and the customer gets a lower price.

Here's how to pump your own gas:

1 Look at the price window on the pump. If there is a price registered there, have the attendant clear the machine so that the price window reads "$0.00."

2 Move the little handle on the pump to the "ON" position.

3 Remove the cap from your fuel tank.

4 Take the pump nozzle off the pump and place it into the fuel tank opening.

**How to "Fill 'Er Up" Yourself**

5  There is a trigger on the pump nozzle. When you press it, gasoline flows out of the hose and into your fuel tank. There is usually a little latch near the trigger which will keep the trigger open so that you don't have to stand there holding it. Don't worry about overflows; these pumps automatically stop pumping gasoline when your tank is almost full.

6  When the gasoline stops flowing (you'll know because those numbers in the window of the pump will stop moving), remove the pump nozzle from your fuel tank. If you want to bring the price up to an even figure, you can add a small additional amount of gasoline by pressing the trigger on the pump nozzle and watching the figures on the pump. I don't do this, because I don't want to overfill my tank—if the gasoline is right up to the top of the tank, it might leak out. Another reason for not "topping off" your tank is that if you fill up when the car is cold and then park in the sun, the gas will expand and run out through an overflow outlet, causing waste, pollution, and a fire hazard.

7  Return the pump nozzle to the pump. Find the attendant who will then write the bill for the amount shown on the pump. *Don't* clear the pump, or you will find yourself unable to prove how much gasoline you've taken, and that could lead to a very unhappy station-attendant/customer relationship!

While you are standing around waiting for the fuel tank to fill up, you can divert yourself in a variety of ways. You can get a couple of those treated towels and some water and wash your windshield. Or you could whip out your tire gauge and check your tires and maybe add some air. Most pump areas have water faucets, towels, and air hoses near them. Or you can kibitz with the attendant about cars and what you've been doing to yours. Most attendants are totally enchanted with customers, especially female customers, who do their own work. I haven't encountered any attendant whose first reaction was that I was going to deprive the station of its income. Most of them are delighted to have found a fellow car freak. Once you've made friends, they won't react too badly if you have to drop in occasionally to get a little help.

O.K., now your fuel tank is nice and full. What happens next?

The **fuel pump** under the hood of your car pumps the gasoline through the **fuel lines**, which run under your car from the fuel tank to the **carburetor**.

We aren't going to get into the inner secrets of the fuel pump, here. If your fuel pump goes wrong, I'd let a professional take care of it, for now. *But,* before you let anyone talk you into buying a new one, be sure the trouble really does reside in the fuel pump. Remember, any problem that seems to be the result of a faulty fuel supply could be caused by a variety of other things. There could be a block in the fuel lines, your fuel filter could be stuffed up, or the problem could be in your carburetor.

An easy way to see if fuel is getting pumped to the carburetor is simply to locate the hose that carries the fuel from the fuel pump to the carburetor, unhook it at the carburetor end, and stick the end of the hose in a clean can. Then have someone crank the car while you see if fuel comes out of the hose. Be careful not to spill the gasoline—it can cause a fire. If fuel comes out of the hose, your fuel pump is doing its job and the trouble is farther up the line, in the carburetor, the fuel filter, etc. Be sure to shut the engine off before the fuel overflows the can.

If your fuel pump does need replacing, a rebuilt one is often as good as a new one, and a lot less expensive. So ask your garage to locate a rebuilt fuel pump for your car. Some manufacturers supply rebuild kits and you can take your pump apart with a screwdriver and rebuild it for a few dollars, if you are ambitious.

Between the fuel pump and the carburetor is a little metal cylinder called a **fuel filter**. It does exactly that. As the fuel passes along the hose, it goes through this thing, and a small screen inside it traps the dirt and rust that might have got into your fuel (especially if you've been riding around most of the time on a near-empty tank). Some cars have additional fuel filters between the fuel tank and the fuel pump. Change fuel filters every tune-up or according to the manufacturer's maintenance schedule.

## The Fuel Pump

The Fuel Pump at Home
Richard Freshman

## The Fuel Filter

**The Carburetor**  The **carburetor** is probably the most easily located part under the hood of your car. It usually sits under a large, round, pot-shaped thing that dominates the view under your hood. This is called an **air cleaner**, and it is usually removed by unscrewing the wing nut situated in the center of the lid, opening any clips, and lifting off the air cleaner. Some cars, especially foreign cars and sports cars, have more than one carburetor. Fuel-injected and diesel cars have none, but do have air cleaners.

The main job of the carburetor is to mix the proper proportions of air and fuel together and pass them along in the proper quantity to the engine. Along the way the carburetor performs a couple of other functions, and we'll get into these as we go along.

You may remember that the proper proportion of air to fuel is *one* part of fuel to 15 parts of air, by *weight*. Since air is considerably lighter than gasoline, if we were to view this in terms of the amount of space taken up by these parts, it would come out to one part of fuel to 9,000 parts of air, by *volume*. That's enough air to fill a room 10 feet square for every gallon of gasoline we burn!

10 Feet
10 Feet
10 Feet

1 Gallon

(*above*) For Every Gallon of Fuel, Your Car Consumes Enough Air to Fill a Room 10 Feet Square!
Alexandra Soto

(*right*) The Carburetor and the Air Cleaner
Guaranteed Parts Company

Air filter

PCV air filter

Idle stop solenoid

Gaskets

Idle mixture screws

PCV valve

Luckily, the car does not have to store air; it simply draws in astonishing quantities of it through the **air cleaner**. The air passes through an **air filter** located inside the air cleaner and then goes down the throat, or barrel, of the carburetor.

Since dirt and dust particles are extracted from the air by the air filter, you will want to change it at least once a year, as well. We'll get into how you tell if the air filter needs replacement, and how to do it, in Chapter 7.

The air travels down the **carburetor barrel**, and on its way, it passes a small pipe that leads to a fuel reservoir called a **float bowl**, which holds a small supply of gasoline.

**The Float Bowl**

This small chamber on the carburetor is located next to the carburetor barrel. It contains a small amount of raw fuel to ensure a readily available fuel supply when you start or accelerate the car. This is more efficient than having to pump each new portion of gasoline all the way from the fuel tank at the rear of the car. The amount of fuel that stays in the float bowl is controlled by a little float (surprise!) that bobs up and down on the surface of the fuel in the chamber. The float bowl is kept filled by a hose that leads to it from the fuel pump.

Fuel inlet

Internal vent

Needle and seat assembly

Float

The Float Bowl
Echlin Manufacturing Company

000-117

If your car has too little fuel in its float bowl, it is going to hesitate or stall when you want that extra surge of power or when you try to start it in the morning. The float in the float bowl is adjustable, but adjusting it involves taking apart at least a portion of the carburetor. This isn't too hard, but putting the thing back together again can get hairy; so again, if you think your carburetor needs overhauling, let a professional do it. Of course, there are overhaul kits with instructions available, and if you are determined to do the job yourself, look for a good auto repair course and do it under the instructor's supervision.

**The Fuel/Air Mixture**

As the air passes the small opening at the end of the little pipe that leads to the float bowl, it picks up fuel, and the result is a mist, or a vaporized **fuel/air mixture**. The air and the fuel travel in this form to the cylinders, where combustion is going to occur.

How does the vaporizing process take place? The principle is the same as the one that operates "flit guns." If you look closely at one of these insecticide sprayers you will see that when you push the plunger, you are sending a jet of air past an opening in the top of the chamber where the liquid is stored. The air rushing past the opening creates a vacuum that draws the liquid out of the storage chamber and mixes it with the air. The carburetor works the same way.

**The Venturi**

Because the faster the air moves, the more liquid it will pick up, the carburetor has been very cleverly designed so that air will pick up speed as it passes through the barrel. Inside the barrel is a chamber called a **venturi**. This gets narrower as it nears the opening that leads to the float bowl. When the air gets to this narrow part of the venturi, it picks up speed, creating a vacuum just at the point where the opening occurs. This draws the fuel out of the float bowl and mixes it with the air. The resulting fuel/air vapor is carried to the cylinder.

In case you are wondering why all this is necessary, you must remember that liquid gasoline will not explode. Oh, it will burn all right, if you drop a match into it, but it will not explode. And it is the pressure caused by the rapid expansion of exploding gases that drives the engine. The only way to get gasoline to explode is to mix it with air. Gasoline/air vapor is explosive; plain old gasoline isn't. This, incidentally, is why so many accidents occur with near-empty gasoline cans. We tend to think that if a can of gasoline is almost empty, it is harmless. This is just when it is at its most dangerous! The "empty" can still contains a tiny bit of gasoline, and remember, we need only one part of gasoline to 9,000 parts of air to get a combustible mixture! So, if there is a lot of gasoline sloshing around in the can, there might be *too much* gasoline to explode. But if all there is is a bit of gasoline vapor, or fumes, it can mix with the air in the "empty" can, and any kind of spark can set off a really big explosion. Gasoline/air vapor is more explosive than TNT! Now you can see why we are not encouraged to store gasoline around the house or in the trunk of the car. If you have an old gasoline can around, throw it out! Fill it with water before you dispose of it so it doesn't do any damage to any innocent bystanders it may encounter. Some people keep gasoline to clean parts with. This is dangerous. Mechanic's Solvent, available at gas stations or auto supply stores, works better, and it has been treated with a flame retardant to keep it from burning too freely.

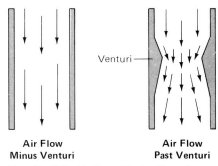

**Air Flow Minus Venturi**  **Air Flow Past Venturi**

Venturi

How Air Picks Up Speed in the Venturi
Echlin Manufacturing Company

**Single-, Double-, and Four-Barrel Carburetors**

To increase the amount of fuel/air mixture that is passed along to the engine, auto manufacturers have developed carburetors with more than one barrel. A double-barrel carburetor has two venturis, and a four-barrel carburetor has four venturis. These are generally found on large engines, like V-8s, where more fuel and air is needed fast to supply all those cylinders with stuff to feed on. In a four-barrel carburetor, two of the four barrels are reserved for extra power at high speeds or stress, and you can see why V-8 engines consume more fuel than most four- or six-cylinder engines do. Of course they put out more power, too. And if you like to drive a big, impressive car around—or if you want to drive up hills at high speeds—that's the kind of engine you need. Just don't confuse *power* with *efficiency*. A smaller engine will do just as good a job, if it is not hauling a lot of extra junk around.

You may ask, If that is all the carburetor does, what are all those other gizmos attached to it? Good question. Let's take them in order.

**The Choke**    At the top of the carburetor, looking up at you after you've removed the air cleaner, is the **choke**. This consists of a little **butterfly valve** that can open and close, and a means of adjusting it.

When your car is cold, the butterfly valve will stay closed. This way, when you go out to start your car in the morning, the choke will help you get the car started and warmed up faster. Here's how it does this:

1 When you start your car and the engine is cold, the gasoline condenses on the cold metal parts. As much as ⅓ of it can settle out in this way, leaving only ⅔ of the fuel/air mixture on its way to the engine. This is not enough for proper combustion, and your car won't start properly. The mixture must be enriched.

2 The choke limits the air supply by closing the butterfly valve at the top of the carburetor barrel(s) so there is a greater vacuum created in the venturi.

(*below right*) When You Look Down the Carburetor Barrel, You Can See the Choke Butterfly.
Richard Freshman

(*below left*) The Choke Butterfly Can Restrict the Amount of Air Entering the Venturi.
Echlin Manufacturing Company

Choke butterfly

Float

Venturi

Throttle

Butterfly

Fuel inlet

This causes more fuel to come out of the pipe that comes from the float bowl. This larger quantity of fuel mixes with the restricted amount of air, forming a richer mixture. Now, even though some of the fuel condenses on the walls of the pipes leading to the engine, there is still enough left for proper combustion.

3 When the engine warms up, the butterfly valve opens, letting more air into the barrel(s), and the fuel/air mixture returns to normal.

Remember, the choke limits the supply of air entering the venturi. It does not prevent all the air from coming in. The resulting fuel/air mixture is richer than the stuff you usually drive on, but it returns to normal when the car warms up enough to stop the fuel from condensing. Simple, isn't it?

Cars used to have manual chokes, which you controlled by a knob on the dashboard. Today, most cars have an **automatic choke** that works by means of a spring that coils and uncoils in response to the amount of heat present. It is this spring that eventually causes the butterfly valve to open and close.

If you have an automatic choke (see illustrations on pages 150–151 in Chapter 7), chances are it is controlled by a thermostat located on the outside of the carburetor, either at the top of the barrel near the butterfly valve, or near the carburetor at the end of a long rod. The first type looks like a little round cap, and there are little arrows on it that say "Lean" and

**Automatic Chokes**

The Choke Thermostat Causes the Butterfly to Open and Close.
Guaranteed Parts Company

"Rich." By turning this knob, you can adjust the proportion of air that is allowed into the carburetor barrel past the butterfly. The second type uses a rod attached to the thermostat to make the butterfly open and close. In the next chapter, we'll get into how, and when, to adjust your automatic choke.

**How to Tell If Your Choke Is Working**

If you want to see whether or not your choke is working (and, if you have trouble getting started in the morning, it may not be working properly), take the air cleaner off some morning before you start your car. Does the butterfly valve seem to be closed? If it isn't, step on the gas pedal a couple of times before you start the car and it should close. Now, run the car for a few minutes. (You can run your car with the air cleaner off, but never drive around like that. The amount of dirt that gets into your engine will determine the life of your car. This dirt creates the kind of

Accelerator Pump System
Echlin Manufacturing Company

wear that causes engines to break down.) By the time the car is warmed up, the butterfly should open so that you can see down the barrel of the carburetor. If you are driving a car with a manual choke, see if the butterfly valve opens and closes when you push the knob on the dashboard in and out, but don't let anyone accelerate the car while you are looking down the carburetor. It could backfire.

If the butterfly valve refuses to open or to close, it may simply be stuck because of poor lubrication or dirt. Try wiggling it with your finger. If that doesn't work, squirt a little carburetor cleaner or automatic choke cleaner on the moving parts. Then wipe them dry and put a drop of oil on them. If this doesn't work, the next chapter will tell you how to adjust your choke properly.

**The Accelerator Pump**

Have you ever stopped to wonder just what makes your car speed up when you step on the gas pedal? It's really a very simple device, so unsophisticated that you'd think the inventor would have been embarrassed to suggest such a "mickey mouse" gadget.

When you step on the gas pedal to accelerate, there is a rod that connects the pedal to a little lever located on the outside of the carburetor. This little lever pushes on a little piston inside the carburetor which squirts a little extra fuel into the venturi. That extra fuel creates a richer fuel/air mixture, which explodes with a bigger bang in your cylinders, and your car gets that extra push we call "acceleration."

If you have the air cleaner off your carburetor, look for the little lever on the side. (Not the big one, that's the throttle; and we'll get to that in just a minute.) If you push that little lever in, even if the engine is not running, you will see a little squirt of fuel inside the barrel of your carburetor. So, if your car has been hesitating when you step on the gas, it may be that your **accelerator pump** is not working properly. If no gasoline squirts into the carburetor when you push the lever, or if the lever won't move when you try to push it, then that's where the trouble is.

If your **accelerator pump** is not working properly, your carburetor will probably have to be rebuilt (which means taking it apart, cleaning it, and replacing various parts) or replaced. Again, if you need a new carburetor, you may be just as well off with a cheaper, rebuilt one. Ask the person who is going to do the work to try to get one for you.

**The Throttle**

And now for the bigger lever on the outside of your carburetor. This is the *throttle arm*. It too is attached to your gas pedal. It controls the **throttle**, a butterfly device, very much like the choke butterfly but located at the *bottom* of the carburetor barrel, where it joins the **intake manifold**. The intake manifold is a pipe that branches into as many smaller pipes as you have cylinders. It carries the fuel/air mixture to each cylinder.

Fuel inlet

Arm

Filter

The throttle controls the amount of fuel and air that comes into the carburetor. The more air, the higher the vacuum developed in the venturi. The greater the vacuum, the more fuel is drawn out of the float bowl and mixed with the air. The richer the fuel/air mixture, the faster the car will go. At high speeds, the throttle is wide open to allow a lot of air to come into the carburetor. At low speeds, the throttle closes, so less air can get in. If you get someone to sit at the wheel of your car, with the emergency brake on and the car in "Park" or "Neutral," and have them step on the gas pedal while you look at your carburetor, you will see that every time your friend revs up the engine, the throttle arm moves. Now, with no one stepping on the gas, and the car just idling by itself, press the throttle arm with your finger. The car will rev up just as though you were stepping on the gas pedal. What a very simple device! And yet it controls that most important flow of fuel and air which determines how effectively your car performs!

There are a couple of other gizmos on your carburetor that make your car run smoothly. I'll show you in the next chapter how to adjust them, but I thought I'd introduce you to them here:

(*top*) The Accelerator Pump Arm Is Located on the Outside of the Carburetor.
Richard Freshman

(*bottom*) The Throttle Arm Is Also Located on the Outside of the Carburetor.
Richard Freshman

The **idle speed screw** is a little screw located at the bottom of your carburetor, on the outside, but right near the throttle. It keeps the throttle from closing completely when your foot is off the gas pedal and the car is idling. (Idling is what the car is doing when it just sits there humming to itself without moving. Cars **idle** while they wait for stoplights to turn green.) It is important that you locate this screw on your carburetor, because it is easy to adjust and will do wonders for your engine performance and fuel consumption if it is set properly after you've tuned your ignition system. The next chapter is going to tell you how to do this, so get out your owner's manual and hope that it tells you where the idle speed screw is. If not, look at your carburetor and try to identify it. It is near the throttle on the outside of the carburetor. If you turn it clockwise, with a screwdriver, your car will idle faster; counterclockwise, and it will idle more slowly. Do not get it confused with the **idle mixture screw**, however (see page 126).

**The Idle Speed Screw**

Idle mixture screws

Idle speed screw

Some of the newer cars do not have only an idle speed screw and an idle mixture screw; they have an **idle stop solenoid** as well. This is really easy to spot. You can see one in the figure on page 148. Cars with engines with controlled exhaust emissions tend to idle at faster speeds. Often, if such an engine is shut off abruptly, the engine simply cannot stop fast enough and it keeps going, or dieseling. The idle stop solenoid prevents the car from continuing to idle after it has been shut off.

If you think you have an idle stop solenoid on your car, look for a little can-shaped device attached to the carburetor near the throttle. When it is time to tune your carburetor, read the instructions in the next chapter about adjusting the idle stop solenoid.

Some cars do *not* have an idle speed screw. They have an **idle air bleed screw** instead. The theory behind this one is that when the throttle is closed during idling, there should still be some air coming through

**The Idle Stop Solenoid**

Idle mixture screws

Idle speed screw

Idle Speed and Idle Mixture Screws on Two Popular Carburetors
Actron Manufacturing Company

**The Idle Air Bleed Screw**

to prevent the formation of carbon and gum deposits that tend to collect around the throttle area. The idle air bleed screw, or *idle air adjusting screw,* as it is sometimes called, simply determines how much extra air is allowed to come in when the throttle is closed. By turning this screw clockwise, you can decrease the amount of air that gets in and slow down your idle. By turning it counterclockwise, you get more air and more idle speed. Wait for the next chapter before fiddling with it. Air bleed screws are usually found on Lincolns, Caddies, and other big cars.

**The Idle Mixture Screw**

(We're almost through with the carburetor gadgets now; don't lose heart!)

The **idle mixture screw** looks like the idle speed screw, but it controls the *proportion* of air and fuel that get to your engine while your car is idling. By turning this screw, you can determine how rich the fuel/air mixture will be. If you adjust it properly, you can get maximum engine performance and still save fuel.

Carburetors with more than one barrel can have more than one idle mixture screw. The screw (or screws) can be found in a variety of locations, depending on your car. It can be identified by the fact that if you turn it counterclockwise, the end of the screw will come out of the carburetor. However, because of state and federal smog standards most car manufacturers place limiter caps on the idle mixture screws or hide them behind metal plugs to prevent owners from adjusting them. Even if your car lacks these antitampering devices, it would be wise to leave adjustments to a mechanic.

I realize that all of this has been a bit complicated. Before we continue to follow that fuel/air mixture into the engine, it might be wise to check yourself to be sure that you have it all straight. Try to see if you can find the following parts on your carburetor, and then tell yourself what each one does. If you have problems, reread the chapter until you get it straight. It may seem like gibberish at first, but I promise you that it will all fall into place! My instructor used to make us promise not to think about what he'd told us until the next class. He'd say, "Forget everything I've said. It will just confuse you if you think about it. When you start to actually work on the car, it will become clear." And you know, it did!

O.K., find these:

Automatic Choke
Butterfly Valve
Float Bowl (just the outside will do)
Accelerator Pump Arm
Throttle Arm
Idle Speed Screw, or, if you don't have one:
Idle Air Bleed Screw
Idle Mixture Screw (see page 126)
Idle Stop Solenoid (you may not have one)

Do you know what these mean?

Venturi
Single-, Double-, Four-Barrel Carburetor
Throttle
Fuel/air Mixture (and what causes the fuel to vaporize)

You do? Then you are ready to get into your engine!

**The Engine Block—Where the Action Is**

If you take a look at what we've covered in the past few chapters, you will see that you now know about the source, and control, of the three things you must have to drive an **internal combustion engine**. These three things are *air, fuel,* and *fire.* (Of course we're not dealing with actual fire here, but rather with a spark that ignites the air and fuel. One should really say "air, fuel, and *ignition,*" but "air, fuel, and fire" has a more poetic ring to it—and it's easier to remember.)

Well, if you've got the air and fuel coming together, in the form of a vapor, and you've got the spark plugs and the distributor timed to provide that all-important ignition spark; then all you need is a spot for that passionate meeting to take place. That rendezvous occurs in the cylinders of your engine, and it is truly a triumph of timing (as all successful rendezvous must be!).

This is what happens:

**The Intake Manifold** The fuel/air mixture travels past the throttle at the bottom of the carburetor to the **intake manifold**. (We've already described this cluster of iron pipes, remember?) There are actually *two* sets of manifold pipes. The other set is the **exhaust manifold**, which carries the carbon-monoxide and other vapor wastes away from the engine for disposal. The intake manifold pipes are generally found near the top of the engine, between the carburetor and the engine block. The exhaust manifold is either lower down on the same side of the engine, or on the other side of the cylinder heads.

Inside the engine there are a variety of fascinating objects. At the top are the **cylinder heads**, which contain the mechanisms that allow the valves to open and close to let the fuel/air mixture into the cylinders and allow the burnt gases to leave. You open the cylinder heads to adjust your **valves**.

Below the cylinder heads is the **engine block** itself. This contains the **cylinders**, which in turn contain the **pistons**.

At the bottom of the engine is the **crankcase**, which houses the **crankshaft** and the **oil pan**. Water circu-

The Fuel/Air Mixture Travels from the Carburetor, Through the Intake Manifold, to the Combustion Chamber, Where Ignition Takes Place.
Echlin Manufacturing Company

Cylinder head

Engine block

Crankcase

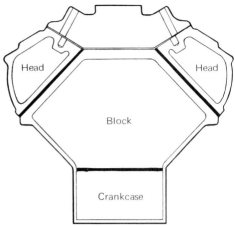

Head

Head

Block

Crankcase

Cylinder Head, Engine Block,
Crankcase—The Main Parts of the Internal
Combustion Engine
Automotive Marketing Division, Dana Corp.

lates throughout the engine to keep it cool, and oil circulates, as well, to keep the parts moving freely.

Let's look inside one of the cylinders and see what goes on in there.

**The Cylinders**

A **cylinder** is an empty iron pipe. A **spark plug** is inserted in the pipe, with its **electrodes** available for action. Inside the pipe there is a metal **piston**, which fits snugly against the walls of the cylinder, so nothing can get past it. There are **piston rings** on the outside of the piston that ensure that it fits snugly. Those "ring jobs" that people have to pay for involve taking the engine apart to replace the rings on the pistons. This is a time- and labor-consuming job, so it usually costs a good deal of money. If your car needs one you generally have to "bite the bullet" and pay. But sometimes people pay for these jobs when they don't really need them. Or people need ring jobs when simple maintenance could have prevented the trouble. If you know how your engine works, you are in a better position either to prevent the trouble or to determine if such costly work is really necessary. And that is what this book is all about.

The piston rides up and down, inside the cylinder, on a **connecting rod** that attaches to the **crankshaft**. (You remember that from Chapter 3, right? If you don't, take another look at that chapter; it will make this a lot easier to grasp.)

There are two other openings in the cylinder besides the ones for the spark plug and the piston. These are for the **intake valve** and the **exhaust valve**.

**The Four-Stroke Power Cycle**

Inside the cylinder, the piston (as we've said) goes up and down. Each movement it makes—either up or down—is called a **stroke**. It takes four strokes—down, up, down, and up—to complete the cycle that creates the power to drive the engine.

Spark plug

Intake valve

Piston

Intake stroke

**Intake Stroke**

1  When the piston moves *down*, it creates a vacuum in the top portion of the cylinder (where the piston was at the end of its last upstroke). Air cannot get in from the bottom of the cylinder, because the rings on the piston have sealed it off.

2  The **intake valve**, conveniently located at the entrance of the **intake manifold** pipe to the cylinder, opens up and lets the fuel/air mixture into the cylinder. It rushes in to fill the vacuum left by the piston.

**The Compression Stroke**

1  The piston moves back *up*, compressing the fuel/air mixture into a tiny space between the top of the piston and the top of the cylinder. This space is called the **combustion chamber**. It also happens to be where the spark-plug electrode end enters the cylinder. The fuel/air mixture is compressed into about 1/10 the space it occupied before the piston moved up, and this 10:1 **compression ratio** increases the pressure in the combustion chamber to about 200 psi (pounds per square inch). Normal air pressure is 15 psi. The reason this is necessary is that compression will make the explosion much more intense than it would have been if the fuel/air mixture had been allowed to spread out. So, when the compressed mixture is ignited, the pressure will increase another *four times*, creating a heck of a lot of power when it explodes!

2  At this point, the intake valve has closed, so the compressed mixture can't get out. Both the intake and exhaust valves have seals to ensure that nothing can get past them when they are closed.

Compression stroke

1 The spark plug produces a spark across the gap between its electrodes, which ignites the compressed fuel/air mixture.

2 The burning fuel/air mixture explodes, creating intense pressure that forces the piston *down* again. The power that pushed the piston down is transmitted, via the **connecting rod**, to the **crankshaft**. It then travels, via the **drive train**, through the **clutch**, the **transmission**, the **driveshaft**, to the **differential**, and so on to the wheels. (Aren't you glad you reread Chapter 3?)

**The Power Stroke**

Power stroke

1 The piston moves *up* again, pushing the burned gases up with it.

2 The **exhaust valve** opens and lets the burned gases out into the **exhaust manifold**.

3 From there, they travel through the exhaust system (which, on newer cars, includes antipollution devices), through the **muffler** and out the **tail pipe** into the air.

**The Exhaust Stroke**

Exhaust valve

Exhaust stroke

The Four-Stroke Power Cycle
Echlin Manufacturing Company

Now you can see why your ignition tune-up is so important. If it is done properly, it will ensure that a full measure of electricity is transferred from the battery, amplified by the coil, and directed by the distributor to the proper spark plug at the proper time. If the spark was insufficient, or if it arrived before, or after, the fuel/air mixture was at full compression by the piston, the result would be less power and poorly burned fuel. Consequently, your car would produce more air pollution and use more gasoline—a dangerous, and costly, price to pay for laziness or ignorance.

## Stratified Charge Engines

In their efforts to design and build cars with a greater degree of fuel efficiency, car makers have had to deal with a frustrating paradox: it takes a *lean* fuel/air mixture (one that has relatively little fuel in proportion to air) to cut down on the hydrocarbons and carbon monoxide which pollute the air, and to provide maximum fuel economy; but it takes a *rich* mixture to cut down on nitrogen oxides, which also pollute the air, and to attain greater power. How to get the benefits of both, while avoiding the pitfalls? The answer came in the form of the **stratified charge engine**, which can be found in several relatively new cars.

Stratified charge engines are basically the same as conventional internal combustion engines, with one major difference: they provide both a lean mixture of fuel and air *and* a rich mixture to the cylinders, and keep them separated until the vital moment when combustion takes place. Then the spark plug fires the rich mixture, which in turn ignites the leaner mixture. Since the fuel/air ratio for a conventional engine is around 15:1, and a stratified charge engine can use a mixture as lean as 30:1 (some have even worked successfully with mixtures of 200:1!), you can see why these new engines have stacked up such sensational ratings for fuel efficiency and clean emissions.

The basic design of a stratified charge engine varies with the manufacturer. One of the most outstanding was pioneered by Honda in their CVCC. They used a **pre-chamber** (short for pre-combustion chamber) to keep the rich mixture from mixing with the lean one.

**Four-Stroke Power Cycle for a Stratified Charge Engine**

Here's how it works:

1 The cylinder head has a little chamber, called a pre-chamber, which has its own little intake valve. The spark plug is also located in this chamber.

**Intake Stroke**

2 On the intake stroke, the little valve opens and allows a very rich mixture of fuel and air to enter the pre-chamber.

On the same stroke, the regular intake valve opens up and brings a very lean mixture of fuel and air into the cylinder itself.

**Compression Stroke**

3 The compression stroke compresses the lean mixture at the top of the cylinder in the combustion chamber, and brings the two mixtures into contact with one another.

**The intake stroke**

**Compression stroke**

A lean mixture (1) is drawn through the main intake valve (2) into the main combustion chamber (3). At the same time, a rich mixture (4) is drawn through the auxiliary intake valve (5) into the pre-chamber (6).

**Exhaust Stroke**

**Ignition Stroke**

| KEY | |
|---|---|
| ▨ | **LEAN MIXTURE** |
| ▨ | **MODERATE MIXTURE** |
| ▨ | **RICH MIXTURE** |
| ▨ | **FLAME AREA** |
| ▨ | **HOT GASES** |

Four-Stroke Power Cycle of Stratified Charge Engine
American Honda Motor Co., Inc.

**Ignition Stroke**  4 During the ignition stroke, the spark plug fires the rich mixture in the pre-chamber. It burns fiercely and ignites the leaner mixture in the combustion chamber. This forces the piston down and provides the power that moves the car. Because the lean mixture burns more slowly, the fuel is burned more thoroughly, and this is why stratified charge engines get better mileage and put out cleaner exhaust fumes.

**Exhaust Stroke**  5 On the exhaust stroke, the exhaust valve opens and sends the burned gases on their way out of the car, via the exhaust system.

Other stratified engines use a depression in the piston's surface to provide space for the rich mixture to be ignited, instead of a pre-chamber. This *open chamber* design has performed efficiently in a variety of other cars. If you are thinking of buying a new car, you might want to check out whether the models you like have fuel-efficient engines such as these. However, there are other cars that utilize fuel injection systems which are quite efficient too. Let's talk about these and other "cars without carburetors":

**Cars without Carburetors**  If your car does not have a carburetor, it has a gasoline or **diesel engine** with a **fuel injection system**. (Unless, of course, it's run by steam or electricity!) Because diesels have become much more popular in recent years, I've devoted an entire chapter to understanding, buying, and maintaining diesel cars (see Chapter 14, "Diesels for Dummies," for more illustrations of fuel injection system components). At present, most fuel injection systems are still too difficult to repair yourself, but if you know a bit about how they work, you will be able to communicate with a mechanic more knowledgeably and this should save you time and money. *Caution:* Never attempt to test a fuel injector yourself. It operates under such pressure that it can squirt fuel *right through your finger!*

1 Electronic control unit
2 Injection valve
3 Air-flow sensor
4 Temperature sensor
5 Thermo-time switch
6 Start valve
7 Electric fuel pump
8 Fuel filter
9 Fuel-pressure regulator
10 Auxiliary-air device
11 Throttle valve switch
12 Relay set

Atmospheric pressure ($p_0$)

Pressure in
intake manifold ($p_1$)

Fuel

Coolant

L-Jetronic fuel injection system
Robert Bosch Sales Corporation, Inc.

000-135

**Fuel Injection Systems**

In a gasoline engine, fuel injection eliminates the need for a carburetor by bringing the fuel and air together right in the **intake manifold,** just outside the combustion chambers of the engine. A constant supply of air is drawn through the **air cleaner** and past a **throttle** into the intake manifold. Here, tubes of equal length deliver an equal amount of air to each cylinder. This air is mixed with varying amounts of fuel from **fuel injector valves** located close to the combustion chambers. Some systems work mechanically using a meter and a pump to regulate the action of the valves. In other systems the valves respond to commands from an **electronic sensing device** which receives data on intake manifold pressure, intake air temperature, the position of the throttle, and the temperature and speed of the engine. The longer a valve is open, the more fuel it delivers to the combustion chamber. The richer the resulting fuel/air mixture, the more power it delivers.

One exciting way that fuel injection systems are being perfected is the tendency to replace moving parts with stationary ones, and "solid" parts with intangible substances. By reducing the number of mechanical parts car makers hope to reduce production costs and create devices that are less subject to breakdown due to physical stress. Here's an example: The Robert Bosch Company developed an air-flow-controlled (AFC) fuel injection system called L-Jetronics. At first, this system used an air flap which responded to the air moving through the throttle by wiping a contact across a resistor which sent the signals to a computer. By monitoring the volume of air, the computer could then regulate the amount of fuel to be injected into the cylinders. Then someone thought, "Why bother with an air flap that takes two- or three-tenths of a second to respond to a change in air flow?" Systems using platinum wires and sonic waves swiftly followed, and then completely computerized systems.

Now, I am all in favor of simplification, ever since my mother taught me to always buy the washing machine with the fewest gadgets on the principle that the fewer parts involved, the fewer things there are that can break down. But I keep having this fantasy that if they continue to replace mechanical car parts with miniaturized and computerized equipment, eventually we may lift the hood of the car and find nothing but a little black box! At that point, when things go wrong, we'll probably have to seek the services of ¿ wizard, rather than a mechanic! Still, I like the pro⌐pect of using less metal, plastic and rubber, because it will place less of a strain on our dwindling supply of raw materials, the amount of energy consumed by production as well as driving, and the number of disposal facilities required to trash all the worn and broken stuff we'd have to throw away.

**Throttle body fuel injection** is another type of carburetor-less system which mixes the fuel and air together right in the throttle of the car instead of using individual injectors to pump the fuel into each cylinder. These systems are less complicated than individual fuel injection systems and are generally cheaper. Some of these systems use **solenoids** to spray the fuel into the airstream in the throttle through a fuel injector nozzle. Here's how it works:

**Throttle Body Fuel Injection**

1 An electrical fuel pump pumps gasoline to a fuel pressure regulator located in the engine compartment.

2 The pressure regulator adjusts the force of the fuel until it is at the right pressure to operate a spring in the regulator. When the spring opens up, the fuel is at just the right pressure to be injected into the airstream. All the excess fuel is sent back to the fuel tank.

3 A computer tells the solenoids when and for how long to open the valves in the fuel injector nozzles, which spray the fuel into the air as it passes through the throttle on its way to the engine.

Chrysler has designed a system which uses a little bar with holes in it to spray the fuel into the airstream as it travels down the throttle. This system uses an interrupted light beam to measure the amount of fuel traveling through the system.

**Turbochargers and Superchargers**

Both **turbocharging** and **supercharging** are used to increase the power of the engine, with turbocharging doing the job more efficiently in terms of fuel economy. Since it is especially effective on diesel-powered cars, I've placed most of the information on turbochargers in the diesel chapter with the information on superchargers immediately after it.

Although they are more expensive to service than carburetors, in recent years fuel injection systems with computerized electronic sensing devices have shown sufficient sensitivity, accuracy, and dependability to repay their cost with better performance, greater fuel economy, cleaner exhaust emissions (some of the newest models are reported to be 95 to 100 percent clean-burning!), and more controllable power. Innovations in design are constantly producing cheaper and more durable systems. Today, just about every new car is fuel-injected.

If you are driving an older car, the chances are that it still has a carburetor. You will be happy to know that the carburetors on most cars work on the same principles. They may look a bit different, vary in size and the number of barrels, but they all do the same job and are adjusted in the same manner. So, unless your car has a diesel engine or a fuel injection system, just remove your air cleaner (or air cleaners), take a look at what you've got, and try to relate the information in this chapter to the carburetor(s) on your car. If you really have a rough time finding the adjustment devices on your carburetor, either ask a mechanic to point them out to you or get a service manual for your car (you can probably borrow one at the local public library or buy one at an auto parts store). The service manual will have a picture of your carburetor, with all the parts labeled. It might be wise to make a photocopy of the page and keep it in this book, for future reference. Some owner's manuals have this information, so check yours before you buy elsewhere.

In the next chapter, we'll discuss the proper way to keep your fuel system in tune. By adjusting the carburetor, you will enable your car to use a minimum amount of gasoline to produce the maximum amount of power. And the best thing about carburetor tune-ups is that they can cost *nothing*—if you do them yourself.

# How to Keep Your Fuel System in Tune

If your car has a carburetor, it requires periodic tune-ups to keep it operating at peak efficiency. If it is fuel-injected, skip the sections on the following pages that involve adjusting the carburetor and simply have it checked periodically to be sure it's performing well. Regardless of what kind of fuel system your car has, it will probably still require the other basic maintenance mentioned in this chapter. Maintenance doesn't usually involve hard, or messy, work, and if you've already acquired the tools to tune your ignition system, you probably possess all the tools you need to complete this job, as well. All the work is under-the-hood stuff, so you won't need to jack up your car and you probably won't have to indulge in any acrobatics to reach the scene of the action.

Filters on all cars should be replaced on a regular basis according to your owner's manual or the intervals suggested in this book, but if your car isn't starting right up in the morning, idling without conking out at stoplights, or producing readings within the acceptable range on your tach/dwell meter or on the electronic analyzer at your service station, it probably needs the work outlined in this chapter. Since there's little or no expense involved, it's worth giving it a try before you head for a mechanic and major repair bills.

### How to Replace Your Air Filter

If you unscrew the wing nut on the lid of your **air cleaner** and undo any other devices that hold it down, you will find an **air filter** inside. Although most cars come with doughnut-shaped, pleated-paper filters that can be replaced for a few dollars, a few older models have permanent air filters, which should be cleaned according to instructions in your **owner's manual**.

To see whether your air filter needs replacement, just lift it out (it isn't fastened down) and hold it up to the light. Can you see the light streaming through it? If not, try dropping it *lightly*, bottom side down, on the ground. This should jar some dirt loose. Don't blow through it—you can foul it up that way. If it is still too dirty to see through after you've dropped it a few times, you need a new one.

It's a good idea to change these filters at least every year or every 20,000 miles, whichever comes first—unless yours gets very dirty before then. If you do most of your driving in a dusty or sandy area, you may need to replace your air filter every 5,000 miles, or less.

To replace your air filter, just go to your local auto supply store, tell them the make, model, and year of your car, buy a new one, take the old one out, and drop the new one in. Look for well-known, quality-brand filters; you can often get them quite cheaply at a discount store. Unknown brands sell for very little, but they are not always of good quality, and if your air filter lets a lot of junk get into your carburetor, you may find that a cheap filter is very costly in the long run. Be sure the filter you get matches your old filter in size and shape. That way you'll be sure you've been sold the proper filter for your car.

The Air Filter is Inside the Air Cleaner.
Richard Freshman

Take the rest of the air cleaner off your car—it will just lift off. Underneath is your carburetor, and inserted into the little hose or pipe that comes out of the carburetor and leads to the fuel pump—usually just an inch or two away from the carburetor—there often is a little metal or plastic cylinder called the **fuel filter**. On most cars, the fuel filter is held in place by metal clamps on either side of it, either in the fuel line or in the carburetor inlet fitting. These are called *in-line* filters. Some cars have the fuel filter inside the carburetor or the fuel pump, but it is no more difficult to get at these. They are called *integral* filters. If you haven't already found yours, find it. It is important to get in the habit of changing your fuel filter every time you tune your car, especially if you tend to ride around with an almost-empty fuel tank.

To replace your fuel filter, buy a new one at the auto supply store (on the basis of your car's make, model, and year—plus type of carburetor, in some cases).

## How to Replace Your Fuel Filter

Filter

An In-Line Fuel Filter Near the Carburetor
Richard Freshman

**In-line Filter**      **Integral Filter**

Replacing In-Line and Integral Fuel Filters
R&S Auto, Division of Roth-Schlenger

Again, go for well-known brands at discount prices. Buy new gear-type clamps, too, if yours look old, rusty, brittle, or are the wire-ring type illustrated on page 172. The filter and the new clamps should cost only a few dollars.

Back home, simply unfasten the clamps that hold the filter in place, slip the filter out, slip the new one in (there's usually an arrow on it to show you which way it goes, or look at the way the old one is pointing before you remove it), and replace the clamps. If you get the clamps on nice and tight (without cutting or shutting off circulation in the hose), there will be no leaks and no trouble.

## How to Tune Your Carburetor

There are several things you can do to keep your carburetor in tune. You can adjust the **idle speed screw** to keep the car idling at the proper number of revolutions per minute (rpm); readjust the **automatic choke** if your car is not starting properly in the morning; adjust the **idle stop solenoid** to prevent dieseling when you shut the engine off; check and clean your **PCV valve** or, if necessary, replace it; and determine if more radical surgery is in order. I'll show you how to do all these things in the following pages.

Carburetor barrel
(Venturi)

Choke butterfly

Fuel filter

Accelerator pump arm

Idle bleed screw

Float bowl

Throttle arm and
accelerator pump arm
linkage

Typical Carburetor
Echlin Manufacturing Co.

**An Exploded Drawing from a Carburetor Kit**

Ref.
No.    Nomenclature

1      Clamp screw
2      Thermostatic cover clamp
3      Thermostatic spring cover
4      Thermostatic cover gasket
5      Choke baffle plate
6      Retainer clip
7      Washer
8      Fast idle link
9      Pin spring
10     Choke housing screw and washer
11     Choke housing assembly
12     Choke housing assembly
13     Air horn screw and washer
14     Air horn
15     Air horn gasket
16     Screw and lockwasher
17     Choke seal retainer
18     Choke rod seal washer
19     Choke rod seal
20     Float pin retainer
21     Float assembly
22     Float pin
23     Needle and seat assembly
24     Needle seat gasket
25     Pump discharge nozzle screw
26     Pump discharge nozzle screw gasket
27     Nozzle and venturi assembly
28     Venturi assembly gasket
29     Pump discharge ball
30     Main metering jet
31     Pin spring
32     Pump rod
33     Pump cover screw and washer
34     Pump cover assembly
35     Pump diaphragm return spring
36     Pump diaphragm assembly
37     Pump inlet ball retainer
38     Retainer gasket
39     Pump inlet ball
40     Economizer screw and washer
41     Economizer valve cover
42     Economizer valve cover gasket
43     Economizer valve assembly
44     Economizer valve gasket
45     Idle mixture screw
46     Idle mixture screw spring
47     Main body
48     Pump cavity filler
49     Pump diaphragm return spring
50     Elastomer inlet check valve
       (When used, replaces parts 37–39)
51     Idle limiter cap (Beginning 1968)*

*Do not remove unless new cap is
available.

Late design
replaces 20

Late design
replaces 36

Late design
replaces 36

Accelerator pump design
beginning late 1964

000-143

If your carburetor doesn't respond to any of these, and is still carrying on by causing your car to stall, accelerate improperly, burn enormous quantities of gasoline, etc., *and* if the inside of your carburetor looks foul and gunky, you might want to have it rebuilt. This can be accomplished by using an inexpensive kit, but it's a difficult job and I'd suggest that you either have a mechanic do it or—if you have a very simple carburetor and a lust for adventure—ask a friend who's already rebuilt one to help you. The basic problem is not one of *skill,* or of mechanical genius, but simply that the darn things have so many nuts, screws, washers, and gizmos that it can be very difficult to remember where everything goes when it's time to reassemble. The kits come with "exploded" drawings, but these can be confusing unless you've had some experience. If you have no mechanically inclined friends, you might want to find yourself an auto repair course at a local school and try the job under the supervision of an instructor. Right now, let's get back to the easy jobs!

### How to Check Your PCV Valve

When your car is running, a certain amount of fuel and exhaust fumes find their way past the piston rings and into the crankcase. Originally, these fumes were simply dispelled into the air through a tube, because if they were left to accumulate, they would foul the oil in the crankcase. In the early sixties a new method, called *Positive Crankcase Ventilation* (PCV), was put into general use. This was much more efficient because, instead of allowing these fumes to pollute the air, it rerouted them back to the carburetor so that they could be reburned in the cylinders along with the rest of the fuel/air mixture. This was much more desirable. It increased fuel economy, since the engine could now run on the fuel in the exhaust fumes as well as on the regular fuel/air mixture.

Not every car has a **PCV valve,** but most do. If your car has one, every time you do a tune-up, check the PCV valve to be sure it hasn't become clogged with sludge from the contaminants in the exhaust fumes. If it ceases to function, the fuel/air mixture that has been

PCV Valve
Automotive Marketing Division, Dana Corp.

adjusted to take these fumes into consideration will go out of balance and your car will not operate as efficiently. Most car manufacturers suggest that PCV valves be cleaned or replaced after about 12,000 miles of driving. Here's how to check your PCV valve:

1 Look for the hose that leads from the bottom area of the carburetor to the top of the **valve cover** or to the **oil filler hole**. (If your car has *both,* you want the one that does *not* lead to the oil filler hole.) Some PCV valves screw into the base of the carburetor; some push into a rubber grommet in the cylinder head valve cover, at the end of the hose that leads from there to the carburetor; and still others screw or push into the oil filler cap or tube. If you can't find yours, consult your **owner's manual** or dealer.

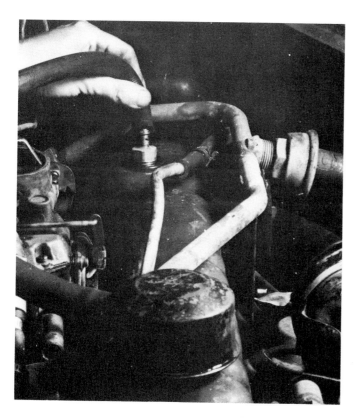

A PCV Valve Located on the Cylinder Head with the Hose That Leads to It Removed
Richard Freshman

One Way to Check Your PCV Valve
R&S Auto, Division of Roth-Schlenger

2 With the engine idling, pinch the hose hard to shut off any air that may be going through it. Don't puncture the hose, however. If the PCV valve is operating, the idle speed should drop perceptibly. You'll be able to *hear* the change. If your car has been idling roughly, you might want to check the PCV valve before you make other adjustments.

3 You can also check your PCV valve by removing it from the valve cover, with the hose still attached, and placing your finger over the open end of it. If it is working well, you will feel a strong suction.

4 Another way to check your PCV valve is to remove the oil filler cap from the valve cover and place a stiff piece of paper over the opening. The paper should be sucked against the hole within seconds if your PCV valve is working properly.

5 If your PCV valve is not working and you have the kind that comes apart, you can clean it yourself. Just take it apart and immerse it in carburetor cleaner or PCV solvent, if you can get some cheaply. Lacquer thinner and fuel oil can also do the job. There should be no gummy deposits or discolorations on a clean valve. If your PCV valve must be replaced, buy a new one.

6 While you have the valve off, check the hose by removing it and blowing through it. If the hose is dry, brittle, soft and spongy, or full of sludge or hard deposits, replace it. When everything is shipshape once more, reassemble hose and valve and replace them.

**How to Check Your Accelerator Pump**

Check to see that, when someone steps on the gas pedal (with the emergency brake on and the car in "Neutral" or "Park"), the **accelerator pump** arm moves freely. If it catches, bend it a little to clear the obstruction. Some accelerator pumps have more than one hole where the arm hooks up, to allow you to adjust it. Adjusting for a shorter stroke will give you a leaner mixture of fuel and air; a longer stroke will give you a richer one. If your accelerator pump arm is moving when the gas pedal is stepped on, and if you are still having "getaway" problems, try adjusting the arm for a longer stroke. Did you look into your carburetor barrel to see if fuel is squirting in when the accelerator pump arm moves? We talked about this in the previous chapter.

1 You've already located your **idle speed screw** after reading the last chapter, right? Now, get out your tach/dwell meter (a plain tachometer will do as well, but a dwell meter without a tachometer is useless here) and hook it up according to the instructions that came with it. (If you have no instructions, refer back to Chapter 5.)

2 With the emergency brake on, and the car in "Neutral" or "Park," start your motor and let it run until the engine is hot and the choke butterfly is fully open.

3 When the engine is hot enough, turn the knob on the meter to "tach" and look on the rpm line of the tach/dwell meter to see at how many rpm your car is idling. Check this against your spec sheet or owner's manual to determine at how many rpm it should be idling.

4 If your car is not idling at the proper number of rpm, check your owner's manual to see whether idle speed should be adjusted with the air cleaner off or on the carburetor. Most cars are adjusted with the air cleaner off. If there is a hose that goes from the carburetor to the air cleaner, plug the hose after you take the air cleaner off.

5 With a screwdriver, turn the idle speed screw until the tach/dwell needle rests on the proper number of rpm. Turning the screw *inward* (clockwise) will *increase* idle speed; turning it *outward* (counterclockwise) will *decrease* it. And that is all there is to it.

**How to Adjust Your Idle Speed Screw**

Typical idle speed adjustment screws

Typical Idle Speed Adjustment Screws
Karcheck Products, Otsego, Michigan

**How to Adjust Your Idle Air Bleed Screw**

If you have an **idle air bleed screw** instead of an idle speed screw, just do exactly the same thing to adjust it. However, in this case, turning the screw *clockwise* will *decrease* idle speed, and turning it *counterclockwise* will *increase* idle speed. Otherwise, they are just the same in terms of adjustment.

**How to Adjust Your Idle Stop Solenoid**

If you have an **idle stop solenoid**, you will probably find a tag somewhere under the hood of your car that will give you special instructions on how to adjust it. If you can't find yours, and your owner's manual either is not helpful or is too difficult to follow, and you have hooked up your dwell/tach and found that your car is *not* idling at the proper speed, then do the following:

1 Adjust the nut on the end of the solenoid until your car is idling at the proper number of rpm (at least 700 rpm is usual).
2 Disconnect the little wire that runs from the end of the solenoid to whatever it leads to. Your idle speed will drop.
3 Then adjust your **idle speed screw**, following the instructions above.

Your manual will usually indicate that this last adjustment is at a lower number of rpm. This is called *shutdown idle speed,* and it is the reduced speed that allows your engine to stop running when you shut off the ignition.

Idle stop solenoid

An Idle Stop Solenoid Is Sometimes Located on the Outside of the Carburetor
Guaranteed Parts Company

**How to Adjust the Idle Mixture Screw(s)**

If you feel that your fuel/air mixture needs to be adjusted because your car is not idling smoothly now that you've corrected its idle speed, the **idle mixture screw** (or screws) on your car can do just that. *But,* because of federal and state smog standards, since 1981 these screws have been covered by metal plugs, or by plastic limiter caps which either do not allow you to adjust the screws or limit adjustments to around a quarter of a turn. This was done to keep you from adjusting for a too-rich mixture that would result in an increase in the exhaust emissions that pollute the air. On Tweety-Bird I adjusted to make the mixture as "lean" as possible, to see how far I could cut down on fuel without affecting the smoothness of the idle. If your car has limiter caps, leave them alone. The idle mixture screws were preset at the factory and are probably set properly. If you're having problems that nothing else seems to cure, have a mechanic take a look at it.

If your car has a single-barrel carburetor with no cap on the idle mixture screw, use your owner's manual or service manual to locate the screw. With the car at idle speed, turn the screw inward until the engine starts to falter. Then turn it back the other way, about half a turn. If the engine is idling roughly, continue to turn the screw outward until the engine smooths out. If you turn the screw too far outward, the too-rich fuel/air mixture will cause the engine to run roughly again. If you're using a tach/dwell meter, you'll know the engine is properly set when it returns to the highest idle speed after its initial drop when you turned the screw inward. Two- and four-barrel carburetors have more than one screw. Do them one at a time.

NOTE: Some cars are adjusted according to special instructions provided on a tag or decal under the hood. You can find these tags almost anywhere, usually on the cylinder head cover or on the air cleaner lid or up front on the frame. If you have one, follow the instructions on the tag instead of those given above.

Typical idle mixture adjustment screws

Typical idle mixture adjustment screws

Typical Idle Mixture Adjustment Screws
Karcheck Products, Otsego, Michigan

## How to Adjust Your Automatic Choke

Many cars have a **thermostatic spring choke.** Some are riveted in place and can only be overhauled by a mechanic, but if you have an older car and have trouble starting in the morning, you may be able to adjust yours.

1 Check the specifications for your automatic choke, and see if it is properly set (if the proper notch on the carburetor housing is opposite the indicator on the plastic cap). If it isn't, then you will have to adjust the thermostatic spring choke to the proper setting. If it *is* properly set and you are still having trouble getting the car started in the morning, first wait until the car is very cold (like the next morn-

Baffle plate    Choke housing

Choke valve

Vacuum port

Choke piston

Thermostatic spring

Vacuum passage

Thermostatic Spring Choke
Echlin Manufacturing Company

The Three Screws to Loosen When Adjusting
a Thermostatic Spring Choke
Richard Freshman

ing), step on the gas pedal, and check to see if the **butterfly valve** is closed before you start the car. If it *isn't* closed, then it may need adjusting or cleaning, in case it is simply stuck. The butterfly valve should open again after the car has been running for a few minutes and is sufficiently warmed up. If the butterfly valve is not closed and the car won't start properly, you can try adjusting the thermostatic spring choke to a richer setting.

2  First loosen the three screws that keep the plastic cap in place.

3  Next, turn the cap until the notch lines up with the proper mark on the carburetor housing. You will notice that on the back of the cap, there are the words "Lean" and "Rich" with arrows to indicate direction. Your specifications may read "one notch Lean," in which case you would turn the cap until the indicator lined up with the first mark on the "Lean" side of the carburetor housing. If your car was already set at the specified mark, just turn the cap one notch to the richer side and see how that works the next morning. If it is still not starting properly, try one notch richer. Never adjust more than one notch at a time. These chokes are generally set on the lean side, so they often run better cold when set a notch richer. Don't forget to tighten down the three screws when you are finished.

If your automatic choke is the **thermostatic coil** type, it will have a rod leading from the top of the carbure-

Choke valve

Vacuum
diaphragm unit

Diaphragm

Engine
manifold
vacuum

Rod to
thermostatic
coil

Thermostatic
coil

Thermostatic Coil Choke
Echlin Manufacturing Company

tor near the choke butterfly to a small box mounted not far away, usually on top of the exhaust manifold. Unless it's been tinkered with since the car came from the factory, an automatic choke of this type stays set properly until it breaks down. It is quite cheap to replace, and if you think your choke is not working properly—either because the butterfly won't close when the car is cold or won't open when it warms up, or because you can't get the car started properly in the morning—get a new one, for a couple of dollars. You can install it yourself if you want to.

There are other types of automatic chokes, but these should be adjusted by a professional. If you have one of these and your choke does not seem to be working properly, ask your garage mechanic to have a look at it. Be sure that all the above-mentioned gizmos are checked before you let them talk you into a new carburetor or any other major expense. If you are told that your carburetor needs replacement, get another opinion (without telling the second garage that you've been to the first one). You can probably get a **rebuilt** carburetor for your car at a much lower price than a new one would cost. Ask whoever is going to do the work to find a rebuilt one, if possible—they usually work just as well, and should be guaranteed for thirty days—or call the auto wreckers to locate a rebuilt carburetor and either bring it with you or install it yourself.

**Installing a New or Rebuilt Carburetor**

You can probably install another carburetor yourself, with the help of a knowledgeable friend or an auto shop instructor. It's easier than overhauling one!

1 Go down to the local auto parts store or auto wrecker. Ask them for a rebuilt carburetor for your car. Give them the make, model, year, how many cylinders the car has, how big the engine is, etc. If your carburetor still has a metal tag on it, bring the tag along; that will tell them what they need to know. Check out a couple of places by telephone, using the Yellow Pages. Prices can differ drastically from one place to another. Ask for a mechanic's discount, since you are going to do the job yourself. (Who knows, you might get it!) Or ask if they will accept your old carburetor in exchange for a discount.

2 When you get the carburetor, there will be a **gasket** with it. The gasket goes between the carburetor and the thing it sits on. Compare the new gasket with the one under your carburetor. They have to be the same; if not, you have bought the wrong carburetor. Now, before you go any further, skip ahead to Chapter 10 for instructions on How to Disassemble Anything (and Get It Back Together Again).

3 Remove the throttle arm and choke linkages (the things that attach the moving parts of your old carburetor to the other parts of your car), and all the pipes, hoses, and other things that connect your old carburetor to your car. (Leave the other ends attached to the car so you can hook them to your new carburetor.) Be sure to remember, or draw, the way they were attached.

4 Remove the carburetor nuts that fasten the base of your old carburetor to the top of your engine, and lift the old carburetor out of your car. If fuel spills out, wipe it up—and for heaven's sake! *don't smoke* while you do this job! There will be fuel in the float bowl of the old carburetor and in other parts of it, so handle it carefully and dispose of the old fuel before setting the old carburetor aside. Don't throw the old carburetor out—you may be able to sell it to a place that can rebuild it and sell it again.

5 Clean the gasket surfaces where the old gasket was. If the old gasket is stuck to the car, clean it off and be sure to keep the pieces of the old gas-

ket from falling down the manifold. Maybe stuff a clean, lint-free rag into the top of the hole while you are getting the junk off—just don't forget to remove it before you put the new gasket on!

6 Be sure the new gasket goes on the way the old one was. If you are afraid you'll forget, draw a picture before you take the old one off.

7 Never use anything to cement the new gasket in place. Just place it where it belongs. The weight of the carburetor will hold it in place.

8 Place the new carburetor on the gasket and replace the carburetor hold-down nuts. Don't get these, or any other bolts, too tight; you don't want to break them, or crush the gasket. Have an experienced friend check it over when you are through—or ask your auto mechanic to check it for you. It is impossible to *tell* someone how tight or loose to make a bolt—you have to *feel* it for yourself. And only experience can bring that sense of tightening something properly.

9 Assemble the linkages, pipes, hoses, etc., in the reverse order in which you took them off. If you still think you won't remember, write little numbers next to each thing you disconnect as you disconnect it. Again, remember to have someone with experience check your work when you are through, before you head for the freeway.

10 The idle mixture and the idle speed adjustments are preset.

**Float Level Adjustments**

As we mentioned previously, if the float in your **float bowl** is set improperly, you may find that your car will hesitate or stall when it is accelerated, or it may be hard to start. Since the float level is pre-set, it will only be incorrect if someone has worked on it since the carburetor was installed. If you suspect that this is your problem, then have a professional overhaul your carburetor and reset the float level to the manufacturer's specifications. If he finds that the float level was correct, then chances are that the tiny passages in the carburetor have become plugged with dirt. An overhaul (dismantling and cleaning of the carburetor) will correct this. As I've said before, don't try this yourself unless you have at your elbow someone who has done it before.

**What to Do When All Else Fails** If you've made all the adjustments in this chapter and your car is still not idling properly; is not starting up in the morning without a hassle; or is hesitating or stalling at corners or when it is accelerated sharply, then you are going to need extra help. *But,* you don't want to seek help like a lamb being led to the slaughter. If you want to drive into the service station like someone who knows the score and is prepared to judge intelligently whether or not the proposed remedies are necessary or not, here's what you should do:

1  Take the car to your friendly garage mechanic and ask him (or her) to use an **oscilloscope** to test your ignition system, in case that is the culprit.

2  Then ask them to use their *exhaust gas analyzer* to test your exhaust to see if your car is running on a fuel/air mixture that is too lean or too rich. The easy way to spot this for yourself is to run your finger around the end of the inside of your tail pipe (when the car is cold, please) to see if there is a black, *sooty* deposit there. If there is, your fuel/air mixture is too rich. If there is a black, *greasy*, or *shiny* deposit, you are burning oil. A car that is running "too lean" runs poorly only when it is cold. A choke adjustment should help. In either case, you will need a professional for the necessary carburetor adjustments if the adjustments you've made to the idle mixture screw and the choke haven't helped.

After the garage has isolated the problem, remember to get a second opinion if the remedy seems costly or overly drastic. Also, remember to request a *rebuilt* carburetor, if you need a replacement.

You have just finished the most difficult jobs in this book! If you've gotten this far, what is to come should be a breeze. The next chapters will deal with the rest of the systems at work in your car. None of them are so complex, and none of them need the kind of adjustments that your ignition and fuel systems did. So, if you've just finished your tune-up work, relax and enjoy yourself—you're practically a professional! And if you've "chickened out" so far, there are still a lot of things you can do to save money and keep your car running well.

# The Cooling System:
# How to Keep
# Your Car from
# Getting Heartburn

The Cooling System
Automotive Information Council (AIC)

With all that "air, fuel, and fire" stuff going on in its engine, your car needs something to help it keep a cool (cylinder) head! Since water is cheap, plentiful, and readily available, car manufacturers have found it to be the simplest answer to the problem. (Except for a few who found that air was even cheaper and more abundant. They designed the air-cooled engine. If you have a pre-1975 Volkswagen, you won't find a drop of water in it.)

Of course, nothing is as simple as it seems, and so the car manufacturers have added a couple of gimmicks to keep the water from boiling too easily. These include a **water pump** to keep the water moving; a **fan** and a **radiator** to cool it off; a **pressure cap** to retard boiling; a **thermostat** to help you warm the car up fast on chilly mornings; and **antifreeze/coolant** to raise the boiling point of the water, keep it from freezing in the winter, and keep it from rusting your engine. Put them all together, and you have the **cooling system** in your car. This system is highly efficient. It requires almost no work to keep it operating—only a watchful eye for leaks, and an occasional check or change of coolant, should do it.

Let's take a look at the way the system works; then we'll discuss the things that you can do to help your car keep its cool. If your car has been overheating lately, it may *not* be the fault of the cooling system, and we'll get into the other possibilities as well.

Water Circulates Between the Radiator and the Engine via the Radiator Hoses.
Jack Herlihy

### The Radiator

When the fuel and air mixture is ignited in the cylinders, temperatures can reach *thousands* of degrees Fahrenheit! It takes only *half* that heat to melt iron, and your 500-pound engine would be a useless lump of metal in about 20 minutes if you couldn't keep things cool. Naturally, the water that circulates around the cylinders in the engine block gets very hot, and so it is continually circulated back to the **radiator**, where it cools off before heading back to the scene of the action.

The radiator is designed to cool the water quickly by passing it over a larger cooling surface. The water enters the radiator through a *radiator hose* that is usually connected to the top of the radiator. As the water descends, it runs through channels in the radiator which are cooled by air rushing in through *cooling fins* between the channels. When the water has cooled, it leaves the radiator through another hose that is generally found at the bottom of the radiator.

It is easy to see how air rushing through the radiator can cool things off when we are driving merrily down the freeway—but what happens when the car is standing still or crawling its way through heavy traffic? To keep a fresh supply of air moving through the radiator fins, there is a **fan** located behind the radiator. It is positioned so it can draw air through the radiator.

Originally, a fan belt drove the fan as long as the engine was running. Now, fan clutches on many cars automatically limit the fan's movement at speeds over 25 mph. Since the air rushing past them allows these fans to simply "coast" at high speeds, the engine doesn't have to work as hard or burn as much fuel to supply the power they would normally consume. Most cars with transverse engines have electric fans, some of which continue to run for a short while after the engine is shut off.

The fan belt is also connected to the **water pump**. This pump draws the water from the radiator through the *bottom* radiator hose and sends it to the engine, where it circulates through **water jackets** located around the cylinder combustion chambers and other hot spots.

### The Fan

The Fan Draws Air Through the Radiator to Cool the Water Even When the Car Isn't Moving.
Jack Herlihy

### The Water Pump

Water pump

(*left*) The Water Pump Forces the Water from the Radiator Through the Water Jackets in the Engine.
Jack Herlihy

Water pump

**Antifreeze/Coolant**  To keep the water in the cooling system from boiling or freezing, the water is mixed with **antifreeze/coolant**. This contains a chemical called "ethylene glycol," which can keep water from freezing at temperatures far below the 32 degrees Fahrenheit usually required to freeze water at normal pressures and can retard boiling so that the resulting mixture of water and antifreeze/coolant will not boil and turn to steam until it reaches a much higher temperature than the 212 degrees F. normally required.

Most antifreeze/coolant (after this, let's just call it "coolant," for short) contains about 95 percent ethylene glycol, plus rust, corrosion, and foaming inhibitors. This means that coolant does more than just keep the water in the system in a liquid state. It helps to prevent the formation of rust on the metal surfaces of the engine and the radiator, lubricates the water pump, and keeps the liquid from foaming as it circulates through the system. Since the early 1960s, car

Antifreeze (Coolant) Raises the Boiling Point and Lowers the Freezing Point of the Water in Your Cooling System.

manufacturers have designed the cooling systems of most cars for a 50–50 mixture of ethylene glycol and water—and that is generally considered the proper proportion of coolant and water for the cooling system of your car.

If your car's cooling system is operating properly, you should not have to keep adding water to it. The more water you have to add, the more you dilute the coolant in your system. Since the generally recommended proportion of coolant and water is 50–50 (although you can use a higher proportion of coolant if you need it), sooner or later you are going to tip that balance in favor of water if you keep adding it without adding coolant. Even if your car is not losing water, you should flush the system and replace the coolant at least once a year. We'll get into how to do this as soon as we finish with the technical stuff.

**Anti-freeze/Coolant**

To further retard the boiling point of the liquid in the cooling system, the entire system is placed under pressure. This pressure generally runs between 7 and 16 pounds per square inch (psi). As the pressure goes up, the boiling point rises as well. This combination of pressure + coolant results in the ability of the liquid in your cooling system to resist boiling at temperatures that can rise as high as 250° F., or more, in some new cars.

The illustration on the opposite page gives you an idea of the ways in which coolant and pressure affect the boiling and freezing points of the water in the system.

To keep the lid on the pressure in the system, and to provide a place to conveniently add water and coolant, each car radiator has a removable **radiator pressure cap** on its **radiator fill hole**. These are relatively inexpensive, but if you have a cap that is not working properly, or if you have the wrong type of cap, you will be amazed at the amount of trouble it can cause. A modern cooling system that has been designed to operate normally at temperatures over 212 degrees F., and that is filled with water and in perfect condition, will continually boil over if the radiator cap is no good.

## The Radiator Pressure Cap

Pressure

**Sealing Position**

**Pressure Released**

Overflow
tube

Filler neck
radiator

Pressure released

**Pressure Escaping**

How a Safety Pressure Cap Works
Stant Manufacturing Company, Inc.

If the gasket (rubber ring) inside the cap is not work-ing, the pressure in the system will escape, allowing the water to boil at a lower temperature. As the water boils, it will escape through the overflow pipe in the form of steam. The car will overheat, and the result-ing inconvenience and possible danger to your engine—and yourself—are just not worth the risk.

Most cars come equipped with a simple radiator pres-sure cap that resembles the lid of a jar. You just screw the cap on and off the **radiator fill hole**. If you have this kind of cap on your radiator, *get rid of it,* whether or not you are losing water!

What you want is a **safety radiator pressure cap** be-cause it will help to keep you from getting burned if it becomes necessary to remove the cap before the car is cool.

Most safety caps have a little lever on them. Whenever you want to remove the cap, you lift the lever *first.* This allows the pressure to escape (it sounds like the "poof" you hear when you open a fresh can of coffee) *before* you unscrew the cap.

Since the stuff in the radiator has been restrained from boiling by the pressure in the system, if you just whip off the radiator cap the pressure in the system will go down suddenly and the liquid in the system will boil instantly. The result can be a terribly hot spray of liquid and/or steam which can scald you badly. So, whether or not you already have a safety cap on your radiator, it is important that you know how to remove the cap safely.

**How to Remove a Radiator Cap
and Add Water or Coolant to
Your Radiator**

1 First of all, *never* remove the cap from a radiator when the engine is hot. If your car overheats on the freeway, get to the side of the road and shut off the engine. Then just sit there for 15 or 20 minutes un-til things cool down. You can lift the hood to help the heat escape, but leave the radiator cap alone. Since it is automotive suicide to add cold water to a hot engine (see No. 6 below), there is no need to get the cap off until the engine cools down. Keep your cool until your car regains its own!

2  For nonemergencies, just do what the garage attendants routinely do when they check the liquid level in your radiator. First, lift the lever on the safety cap, to allow the pressure to escape. Then turn the cap counterclockwise to remove it. It's a good idea to place a cloth over the cap after you've raised the lever, to keep the cap from burning your hand if it is hot.

3  If you don't have a safety cap, place a cloth over the cap and turn it counterclockwise to its first stop. This will allow the pressure to escape. If you see liquid, or a great deal of steam, escaping, retighten the cap and wait for things to cool down. If not, continue to turn the cap counterclockwise to remove it.

4  When you remove the cap, *tilt* it as you remove it, so that the opening is away from you (and anyone else around). In this way, if there is still enough heat and pressure to spray hot stuff around, it will land on the engine, or inside the hood, where it can do no harm. Be particularly sure to do this if you haven't bought a safety cap.

5  Of course, if the car is completely cold, there is no risk at all, so try to do routine peeking into your radiator in the morning, before you warm up the car. If you get in the habit of checking the liquid level in your radiator every week, you won't have to bother the gas station attendants with it, and they will be free to devote themselves to cleaning your car windows instead.

6  *Never* add cold water to a hot engine! Adding cold water to an engine that is hot can crack the engine block, since the hot metal contracts sharply when the cold water hits it. If you must add water to an engine that is still *warm*, always do it with the engine running. This allows the cold water to join the stream of hot water that is circulating through the system, rather than falling all at once into the system when the engine is started again.

7  If you keep the radiator filled to within a couple of inches below the cap—or to the fill line if you have one—there will never be any need to have the gas station add water to your warm engine. Plain old tap water will do—you can use the garden hose if

How to Remove a Radiator Cap Safely
Richard Freshman

you like, but try to maintain a good coolant level, too. If you are unsure about what the liquid level should be, just be sure that it covers the radiator tubes that are visible when you look down the hole. If you overfill, the extra liquid will get hot, expand, and flow out of the **overflow pipe**, coolant and all.

8 When you are finished, replace the cap by screwing it on, clockwise, and then push the lever down again.

Radiator safety caps cost very little. Almost every gas station stocks them, but they are cheaper in auto supply stores. Check your manual for the amount of pressure in your system and look for the proper number of psi on the new cap.

These safety caps are well worth the money. I know of one person (myself) whose mysterious car problems were eliminated by a new safety cap (see Chapter 1 for *that* adventure!). In my case, I got off with only about $40 in unnecessary repairs, but I recently met someone who had been through $200 worth of new water pumps, radiator rebuilding, and assorted other unnecessary heartaches and expense before he discovered that all he needed was a new radiator cap.

You know, that really sums up the major difference between doing the work yourself and taking it to a professional. If you don't know exactly what is causing your trouble, there are usually several possibilities to consider. Professional mechanics may go for the most potentially lucrative solution first. If that doesn't do it, they try the next thing, and continue to try things until they hit the right one. This method can cost you a bundle.

On the other hand, when *you* are the one who is doing the diagnosing, you tend to try the cheaper solutions first. So, if your car has been overheating consistently, you would first replace the radiator cap, pressure-test the system, check the coolant level and the thermostat, *before* you go for a new pump. If the pump wasn't leaking, you'd check the radiator thoroughly too. And, if it finally came down to changing the pump, you would try to find a rebuilt one and you might consider installing it yourself (this is not usually difficult). The money you would save would be well worth the effort of doing it yourself.

Piston

Spring

Upper
gasket

Lower
gasket

Copper
cup

Pellet

Anatomy of a Thermostat
Fulton Sylphon Division, Robertshaw Controls Co.

The last link in the cooling system does *not* help to keep the car cool. In fact, it helps it to warm up on cold mornings so your engine can operate efficiently.

The **thermostat** is usually located where the upper radiator hose meets the top of the engine. On a few foreign cars it is found where the bottom hose joins the engine. Your owner's manual should tell you where yours is.

Here's how the thermostat helps your car to heat up:

1  In the morning, when you start the car, the engine turns the fan, which is attached by a fan belt to the water pump.
2  The pump draws water and coolant from the radiator, through the bottom hose, into the engine.
3  The liquid leaves the cold engine via the upper radiator hose, on its way to the radiator, as usual. But on the way it passes through the thermostat.

**The Thermostat**

Thermostat

The Thermostat Keeps the Hot Water from Leaving the Engine Until the Car Warms Up.
Jack Herlihy

000-163

**Thermostat Valve Closed
(Engine Cold)**

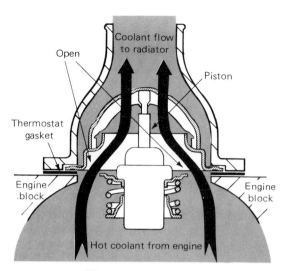

**Thermostat Valve Open
(Engine Hot)**

How a Thermostat Works
Standard-Thomson

4 The thermostat is just a small metal part that is sensitive to heat. When it feels hot liquid, it allows it to pass through. But when it feels that the liquid is cold, it shuts and does not allow the liquid to circulate through the radiator.

5 As a result, the liquid stays in the engine, where it gets hot as the engine warms up, and in turn, the increasing heat of the liquid helps the engine to warm up more quickly. As a result, the car runs efficiently and burns less fuel.

6 When the engine has reached the proper temperature, and the liquid reaches anywhere from 180 to 205 degrees, the thermostat begins to open and allows the liquid to circulate to the radiator and cool off.

This supply of hot liquid is also used by your car's heater when you want to heat the interior of your car. Blowers force the air that is heated by exposure to the hot liquid in the heater through vents to the passenger compartment.

And that is all you need to know about the cooling system in your car! Oh, some cars have more complicated systems, or variations on the theme. (For instance, Jaguars and VW Rabbits have two fans that are run by electric thermostats that are not connected to the water pump at all. These go on independently and draw air in to cool the engine when necessary.) But in general, if you understand the way the basic cooling system works, you should have little trouble handling the one in your car. Most cooling systems need little maintenance, and if things break down, you generally have to replace them completely or get professional help.

There are, however, a couple of things that you can do to be sure that your car's cooling system is operating efficiently. You should make it a habit to check it out fairly often—once a month for a new car, every week for an older model, right away if the car has been overheating or losing liquid regularly.

1 *Check your radiator cap.* If you don't have a safety cap, or if you haven't replaced yours in two years, buy one, whether your car is working well or not. Give the salesperson the make, model, and year of your car, but check the pressure limits on the cap against your manual to see that it is the proper cap for the amount of pressure in your car's system.

2 *Look under your car* in the morning to see if there is any liquid on the ground under it. If there is, stick your finger in it and smell it. If it's oil, see the chapter on lubrication (oil is black and greasy). If it's transmission fluid, see your mechanic (transmission fluid is pinkish and greasy). If it's coolant, then look around the parts of the car that are over the puddle and feel around for wetness.

3 *Check all the hoses* under the hood of your car whether or not you have been having trouble. If you find a hose that is:

a soft and squishy

b bulgy

c hard or brittle

d cracked or leaking

e marked with a whitish deposit where stuff has leaked and dried

you should replace it immediately. If, however, you find a hose that has collapsed when the engine is cold and that springs back when you remove the radiator

**How to Check for Leaks**

| | | | | | | | |
|---|---|---|---|---|---|---|---|
| **1** | External leakage | **6** | Air suction | **11** | Heater control valve |
| **2** | Internal leakage | **7** | Clogged air passages | **12** | Hose deterioration |
| **3** | Rust deposits | **8** | Stuck thermostat | **13** | Fan belt deterioration |
| **4** | Heat cracks | **9** | Sludge formation in oil | **14** | Pressure cap leakage |
| **5** | Exhaust gas leakage | **10** | Transmission oil cooler | **15** | Leaky core plug |

Cooling System Trouble Spots—Where to
Check for Leaks
Union Carbide Corp.

pressure cap, it is the cap and not the hose that is at fault. For instant panic, there is nothing like having a hose burst while you are driving. If it's a radiator hose, the resulting shower of steam is frightening at best and dangerous at worst. If it is a vacuum hose that goes, the sudden loss of vacuum can stop your car in the midst of traffic. Watching your hoses and replacing the funky ones is the kind of preventive medicine that can save your nerves and your pocketbook in the long run. Later in this chapter, I'll show you how to replace your hoses.

4 *If you can't locate the source of the leak* and your car is losing liquid from the radiator on a regular basis, there is a more "professional" way to find the leak and to check out your radiator cap.

There is a "cooling system pressure tester" sold that consists of a gauge, a hose that leads to what looks like a radiator cap, and a little hand pump or bulb. These gadgets can cost quite a lot, so if you are tired of buying tools, just drive to your gas station and ask them if they will use theirs. They may do this for nothing, if they are nice. All it entails is replacing your radiator cap with the fitting on the pressure tester and pumping air into the cooling system with the hand pump until the dial on the gauge reaches the amount of pressure that your cooling system is supposed to operate under. (So if your car operates at 15 psi, they will pump the system until the needle on the gauge reaches the 15.) At that point, if there are any leaks in the system, the gauge needle will drop and liquid may start squirting out of the leaky places right before your eyes! Simple, isn't it...?

A cooling system pressure tester
Stant Manufacturing Company, Inc.

5 *If no leaks appear* as a result of the pressure test, have them remove the radiator cap from their pressure tester and replace it with the radiator cap from your car. The same gauge will show whether your cap can withstand the 15 psi pressure. If it can't, you've found the culprit. If you've used the tester at your gas station, it might be nice to buy the new safety radiator cap from them, as a thank you. (Never let some strange gas station attendants hook you into buying a new radiator cap unless you make them test your old one with this type of tester. It might be smart to have them test the new one as well. I've been sold faulty caps to replace faulty caps.)

Once you've found the leak, you will have to decide whether you can handle it yourself or if you must use a professional. Here are a few pointers to help you decide:

**What to Do After You've Found the Leak**

**Radiator Leaks**

1 Look around your radiator for whitish deposits or rust-colored stains. These indicate old leaks that have dried. They may not be very old; water tends to evaporate quickly on a hot radiator.

2 If the radiator is leaking badly, see a reliable radiator repair shop (doctors aren't the only specialists, you know). If you are on good terms with your local garage, they may be able to steer you to one. They just take the radiator out of your car and send it to radiator specialists, so you might as well go directly to the specialist yourself and discuss the matter in person.

3 Ask the radiator specialists what they intend to do, and if they cannot be firm about the costs involved, request a written estimate *before* they do the work. If the estimate seems very high, call another radiator shop (use the Yellow Pages), tell them what needs to be done, and ask them for an estimate. Never let anyone undertake major work on your car without a *written* estimate. Some of the trusting souls among us have found that the final costs were hundreds of dollars more than they expected, and current law in some states allows the garage to *sell your car* and keep the money if you refuse to pay their bills! The same law requires them to honor a written estimate and to lose the additional money if they do extra work and do not notify you first. If you have no written estimate, the sky's the limit! Many states are working to change these laws, but it is best to be cautious. If you have a hassle about getting a written estimate, look elsewhere.

**Leaks in the Engine-Block Core Plugs**

On the sides of the engine block you will see little circular depressions. These are called **core plugs**, or **freeze plugs**. They plug the holes where the sand was removed when they cast the engine block. If you see rusty streaks leading away from the core plugs on your engine block and you have been losing liquid lately, you may have to have the core plugs replaced. It is best to seek professional help on this one.

Sometimes a leak right under the **cylinder head** can be the result of an ill-fitting gasket, or the fact that the bolts that hold the cylinder head on the engine block are too loose or too tight. It is possible that if you try to tighten these bolts yourself you might damage the gasket, so I think that the best thing to do would be to get professional help here too. If they just have to tighten the bolts, the cost will be minimal. If the gasket needs replacing, remember that even if you can't do the job yourself, you are still ahead if you go to a professional mechanic with a good idea of what is wrong and what it will take to correct it.

**Leaks Near the Cylinder Head**

Often a **water pump** that is about to break down will send out noisy warning signals and then start to leak before it goes completely. You can check your pump by either shaking the fan when the engine is shut off to make the pump rattle, or by removing the fan belt, which drives the water pump, and running the engine to see if the noise has stopped. If it has, the water pump was the noisy culprit.

**Leaks in the Water Pump**

If the pump is leaking in the front where it rotates with the belt, it must be replaced. If the leak is around the gasket that lies between the water pump and the engine, you may be able to stop it by tightening the bolts that hold the water pump in place. If this doesn't do the job, then you probably will need a new pump.

## How to Replace a Water Pump

It's a lot easier to replace a water pump than it is to fix one. If they're available for your car, you may be able to get a rebuilt or remanufactured pump for about half the price of a new one. Be sure to ask for a 90-day written guarantee. Since you'll have to pay labor charges to have the pump installed by a mechanic, if you replace yours yourself you'll be way ahead of the deal whether you buy a rebuilt pump or a new one.

If you want to do the job yourself, be prepared to do the following:

1 Drain all the liquid out of your cooling system by opening the drain cocks in your radiator and letting

the rest of the stuff drain out when the pump is removed. (It doesn't all have to go, but most of it will.)

2  Remove the fan and the fan belts (see Chapter 5 for instructions on how to remove and replace fan belts).

3  Unscrew the bolts that hold the water pump in place. Be sure to lay everything you've removed down in the order in which you removed it, with each part in the same direction as it was on the car. This will help you to put everything back in reverse order, with no guessing about which end was up or which bolt went where.

4  Disconnect the hoses that led to and from the pump. If the **hose clamps** look funky or brittle, replace them with new ones of the gear type.

5  Remove the pump and its gasket. Scrape the spot clean, put some water-resistant sealing compound on the area, and put down the new gasket.

6  Replace the pump, the bolts, the hoses, the fan and fan belt and test-drive the car to see if there are any leaks.

If all this seems like too much of a challenge, by all means have a professional do it for you. But call around for prices on a rebuilt pump first and bring it to the mechanic. Make sure the pump comes with a gasket that matches the old one.

**A Word About Sealer**  If you find a leak in your radiator or engine block—and if the leak is just a small one (a couple of drops a day, with no need to add water more frequently than once a week)—you might want to try a **sealer** before you head for the repair shop.

Sealer is something you add to the liquid in your cooling system. It circulates around with the water and the coolant and when it finds a hole where a leak is occurring, it plugs it up.

There are several kinds of sealers, or "stop-leaks," as they are sometimes called. The trick is to choose one that will do the best job without gumming up the cooling system. Ask for advice on this at the auto supply store. It is especially important that the sealer be compatible with your coolant. The label should tell you.

Sealers are added through the radiator just as you add water and coolant. Some coolants have a sealer built in, but these are rarely strong enough to deal with established leaks. If you try a sealer and the leaks recur in a couple of days, you'd better get professional help.

On the other hand, if the leaks occur in any of the hoses, it is quite simple to replace them yourself.

If you have checked the hoses in your car and found a leak in one of them, or if they are deteriorating in any of the ways listed on page 165, it is a simple and inexpensive matter to replace them, *with two exceptions:* First, *both* ends of the hose must be accessible. Some heater hoses disappear through the firewall and under your dashboard. I'd much rather pay a mechanic than hang upside down in a cramped space until I'd located and replaced one of these. Second, and much more important: Never, *never* attempt to replace the hoses connected to your air conditioner (if you have one) or to deal with the air conditioner itself. Air conditioners and their hoses contain a special type of refrigerant, under pressure, that can literally blind you. If you have any air-conditioning problems, or if the hoses leading to and from the air conditioner do not appear to be in good shape, let a professional deal with the problem. Nothing is worth the potential danger involved.

So much for the scary stuff. Although the instructions below deal with replacing radiator hoses, they can be adapted easily to other hoses in your car:

1  If you have another way of getting to the auto supply store, remove the hose and take it with you. That way you can check the one they give you, right on the spot, to be sure it's the correct hose for your car.

While you are removing the hose, take a look at the clamps that are holding it in place. If they are cruddy and brittle, or are the wire hose clamps mentioned below, buy new gear-type clamps when you buy the hose. These are very cheap, and since wire clamps are difficult to remove and replace, why not substitute clamps that are easy to deal with?

**How to Replace a Radiator Hose (and Almost Any Other Hose, for That Matter)**

**Gear-Type Clamp**

**Wire Hose Clamp**

**Screw-Type Clamp**

Hose Clamps
Everco Industries, Inc.

A Preformed Radiator Hose
The Gates Rubber Company

a *Wire hose clamps:* I hate these. You need a special kind of tool to deal with them. It is called a "wire hose clamp pliers," and it comes with a slit inside each side of its jaws for gripping the ends of these clamps. If you are going to replace a hose that has these clamps, buy a new set of gear-type clamps and throw the old wire ones away.

b *Gear-type clamps:* These are installed with a screwdriver. Just turn the screw to loosen the clamp, slip it over the hose, slip the end of the new hose in place, and turn the screw clockwise to tighten the clamp. Easy? These are my favorites.

c *Screw-type clamps:* These are hard to loosen, so they are used on radiator hoses and the like to keep them in place. Unscrew the screw completely. When you've removed the screw, slip a screwdriver under the clamp and loosen it. When you replace the hose, throw away the clamp, unless it has been *most* cooperative, and use one of the gear-type clamps to install the new hose.

2 If you must drive the car to the auto supply store, take along the spec sheet with the make, model, and year of your car. They may also want to know the size and type of engine and whether or not your car has air conditioning—depending upon which hose you are buying. But by now you have all that information at your fingertips, right?

3 Tell them which hose you want:

a If it is a *top radiator hose,* I recommend you get one that does *not* have wire inside it. Radiator hoses have to bend to fit properly between the radiator and whatever they lead to. Some hoses are straight tubes, with wire coiled inside the rubber casing. These are called "universal" hoses; they are designed to be bent to fit many cars. Often the wire will break or work its way through the top covering of the hose and cause the hose to leak.

The kind of hose to look for is called "preformed" hose. It is made with the proper bend already in it. There is no wire inside the rubber.

Another reason why you do not want a top radiator hose with wire inside it is that it should be squeezable. This way, if you have problems with your cooling system, you can squeeze the hose to see if the system is operating under pressure. A dangerously pressurized hose which is hard to squeeze warns you not to remove the radiator cap until the car cools down and the pressure is reduced.

b If it is a *bottom radiator hose* that you need, it *must* have a wire coil inside it to help it keep its shape and withstand the vacuum caused by the water being drawn out of the radiator by the water pump. In this case, look for a hose with a wire coil insert inside it.

c If it is any other hose, either drag the salesperson outside to see which one it is, or indicate in the following terms which hose you need:

—its *name,* if you know it

—what it *connects* (e.g., the rubber hose that runs between the carburetor and the fuel pump)

—the *diameter* of the hose. Most hoses are sold by their *inside* diameter, and you may have to take one end of the hose off, measure its inside diameter, then put it back on and drive to the auto supply store. (They will also need to know *how long* a hose you need in this case.)

Don't forget to buy new clamps, if you need them. They should be large enough to fit the outside diameter of the hose.

4 If possible, check the hose against your own before you remove your own hose. If the hose does not look, feel, or seem to be the same size as your old one, take it back.

5 Now you are ready to replace the old hose. If it carries water or fuel, you will need something to catch the liquid that will run out when it's removed.

a Hoses that carry fuel will lose only the fuel in the hose. This is because when your engine isn't operating, the fuel generally remains in the gas tank. All you need is a can in which to put the first end of the hose that you remove, in order to catch whatever drains out of it.

b If you are going to change a radiator hose, espe-

A Flexible Radiator Hose with Wire Insert
The Gates Rubber Company

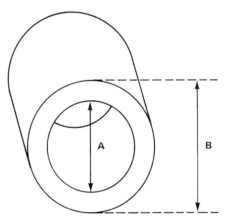

How to Measure the Inside and Outside Diameters of a Hose
Alexandra Soto

How to Install a Hose
The Gates Rubber Company

1. Wipe pipe end clean.
2. Use sealer if you want to—or try doing without it first.
3. Install clamps and tighten with screwdriver.
4. That's all there is to it!

cially the bottom one, you will need a bucket to catch all the liquid that drains out of the radiator and the hose. (If you haven't had your coolant changed for almost a year, it might be a good idea just to let the stuff drain and combine replacing the hose with flushing your cooling system and adding new coolant. Instructions follow on how to do that.)

6 Remove the clamps at either end of the hose. If liquid drains out, catch it as we've described above. If you are going to replace the clamps with new ones and the old ones are hard to remove, you can saw them off if necessary. Wipe the pipe ends clean.

7 If you are replacing a hose that normally contains liquid under pressure, some manuals advise putting a water-resistant sealer on the ends of the pipes to which the hose connects. This is to prevent leaks. Because these sealers tend to make the hoses very hard to remove when it is time to replace them again or to do minor repairs, I would suggest you try it without sealer. Then if the hose leaks, you can always go back and use the sealer as recommended. In most cases, if the hose is the proper one and the clamps are on tight enough, you should be able to get by without sealer.

8 Attach the new hose, attaching and clamping one end in place before you tackle the other end.

9 If it was a radiator hose, you will have to replace the water and coolant that drained out. If the coolant is new and the water looks free of rusty junk, just remove the radiator cap and pour the liquid back through the opening after the new hose is in place. Use a funnel if necessary.

If it was a fuel hose, dispose of the fuel that leaked out when you removed the hose. If there is a lot of it and if you managed to catch it in a clean container, you can put it back into your fuel tank.

10 Check, with the engine running (make sure that the parking brake is on and that the car is in "Neutral" or "Park"), to be sure that the clamps are nice and tight so that no air, water, fuel, or whatever was in there to begin with, leaks out. You don't want your clamps so tight that they can cut

the hose—but if you leave them too loose, the hose will either leak or come off.

It is impossible to tell someone, in a book, how tight or loose a clamp should be. Use your best judgment. If the clamp is so tight that it appears to be cutting into the hose, loosen it. If you can hear or see air or liquid escaping from the ends of the hose, the clamp should be tighter. In any case, the worst that can happen is that the hose will come off, and then you just have to put it back in place and tighten the clamp some more.

## How to Flush Your System and Change Your Coolant

There are three things that you should do to keep your cooling system in good shape: check for leaks, replace worn hoses before they split, and flush the system and change the coolant at least once a year. We've already discussed the leak situation, and you now know how to change your hoses, so let's get on to the proper way to flush your system and change the coolant in it.

This is definitely a job that you should do yourself. It is very easy, and the difference in cost is tremendous. Remember, not only will your service station expect to make a profit on the coolant (they bought it and stocked it, didn't they?) but they will charge you for labor. Even if the "labor" consists of just waiting around for the radiator to flush, they will still charge you for that time. So be smart; do it yourself.

### How to Tell If Your Coolant Needs Changing

There are two situations when you should definitely change your coolant. The first is if you haven't changed it in a year. The second is if your car has been losing water for some time and is overheating easily. The reason for this is that, after continually adding water to your cooling system, you have probably significantly lowered the level of the coolant in the system to less than half the mixture.

If neither of the above is true, you may still be in need of a change, so here are a couple of things that you can do to ascertain whether or not you should do the job:

The correct mixture of radiator coolant will help prevent costly freeze-ups and boil over.

**K-D TOOLS** / LANCASTER, PA. 17604 U.S.A.

Number of floating balls indicates degree of radiator protection.

| BALLS FLOATING | ANTIFREEZE PROTECTION TO: | BOILING POINT° PROTECTION TO: | % OF ANTIFREEZE IN SOLUTION |
|---|---|---|---|
| 1 | +20°F | +255°F | .25% |
| 2 | +5°F | +257°F | .30% |
| 3 | −10°F | +261°F | .40% |
| 4 | −25°F | +266°F | .50% |
| 5 | −40°F | +271°F | .60% |

°Using a 15 lb. pressure cap at sea level.

A Coolant-Protection Level Tester
K-D Manufacturing Co.

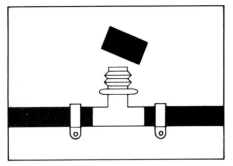

How to Use a Flush 'N Fill Kit
Union Carbide Corp.

1. Remove cap from tee. *(continued on next page)*

1 Unscrew the radiator cap and look in. Is the liquid inside clear? Or are there "things" floating around in it? Does it look rusty? Coolant can be pink in color, so don't mistake coolant for rust. Rusty water has particles floating around in it. Coolant can also be green, greenish yellow, or blue.

2 Have you been adding water every couple of days or weeks? Then your antifreeze/coolant protection level is probably low. There are little testers for sale that will tell you if you have enough coolant in your system. These are cheap and easy to use, and you might want to use one to check protection level, especially if coolant has been changed recently but you've had to add a lot of water. The instructions are on the package. They usually involve drawing a bit of liquid out of the radiator into the tester. Then little balls or a float in the tester will tell you whether you need to add coolant. While you're at it, you might check the liquid in the tester for rust.

3 If you live in a place where it gets very cold in the winter or very hot in the summer, be sure you have enough coolant in your system before extreme weather sets in. In most areas, a 50–50 solution of water and coolant is recommended for year-round use. If the weather turns *extremely* cold, you can add a higher proportion of coolant without hurting your cooling system at all. You should also be aware that, although the air conditioner in your car does a fine job of keeping the interior of the car cool, it also raises the temperature in your engine. So if you have an air conditioner, be sure to have at least a 50–50 mix during the months when you use your air conditioner most. If during your seasonal check, you find that the level of coolant is very low, it might be a good time to flush your cooling system.

**Flushing Your Cooling System Can Be as Easy as Washing the Dishes**

Your owner's manual will give you difficult instructions to follow when it comes to flushing your cooling system. Ignore them. There is a gadget on sale that costs very little and makes flushing the system and changing the coolant a breeze. It is called the "Prestone" Flush 'N Fill Kit, and it is available in auto supply stores. Instead of having to disconnect hoses, drain the radiator, haul and measure water and coolant, all you have to do, once the Flush 'N Fill tee is installed, is unscrew your radiator cap and the little cap on the tee, screw on the end of your garden hose, and let the water run right through the cooling system and out the radiator fill hole to the ground. This flushes the entire system, not just your radiator! When the water has run for several minutes and is coming out of the system as clear as it went in, you just add the proper amount of coolant through the radiator fill hole. This displaces an equal amount of water at the other end through the tee. You screw both caps back on, and you are finished! There's no mess, no measuring, no dirty hands. The whole thing takes less than 10 minutes—5 of which are engaged in watching the water run out, or in sunbathing.

There are instructions on the package, but just in case you are worried about the difficulty involved, here's all there is to it. After you locate the proper hose on your car (they tell you how to find it easily), you loosen your radiator cap and:

1 You cut the hose.
2 You insert the tee.
3 You clamp the tee in place (the clamps are the easy kind you install with a screwdriver).

That's all! *(See illustration on page 178)*

You can consult your owner's manual, the back of the coolant jug, or the charts that the coolant manufacturers supply, for the number of quarts your cooling system will hold. Then simply divide the amount by two and buy that amount of coolant. This will give you a 50–50 water/coolant mixture, which is fine for everything but extremely cold weather. If you want to beef up the level of coolant in your system at any time, with the flushing tee installed (it stays in place permanently), just open your radiator cap and the cap on the tee and add additional coolant down the fill hole. An equal amount of liquid will come out of the tee at the other end. Then just shut both caps, run the engine until the car heats up, and add more water or coolant if the level of liquid in the radiator drops.

2. Connect garden hose.

3. Remove radiator cap and insert splash tube in fill hole. Let water run through system.

**How to Install the Flush 'N Fill Kit**

4. When water runs clear, remove splash tube and hose and pour anti-freeze/coolant into radiator.

**How to Tell How Much Coolant You Need**

5. An equal volume of water will leave the system through the tee. *(continued on next page)*

**Cooling System Cleaners**

6. Replace tee cap and radiator cap.

If your car is old, or if your cooling system seems to be rusting a lot, you may want to use a cleaning chemical when you flush the system. There are several different types, but they are all easy to use. Just follow the directions on the package. They all involve adding the stuff to the system and then flushing it out again. With that flushing tee, it's no extra trouble.

**Coolant Recovery Systems**

Today, most cars come with constant recovery systems like the ones that are described on the next page. If your car lacks such a system and it overheats, you will often notice liquid pouring out from under the car—especially if you are using your air conditioner on a very hot day. This liquid is usually colored, and it sometimes has white foam on it. It is just the water/coolant mixture pouring out of the overflow pipe on your radiator.

When your car heats up, the pressure in your system rises, and if it exceeds the level of pressure that your radiator cap is built to withstand, the liquid in the sys-

How to Install a Flush 'N Fill Kit
Union Carbide Corp.

1. Cut hose.

2. Insert tee.

3. Tighten clamps.

tem will bypass the radiator cap and escape through an **overflow pipe** located near your fill hole. This pipe is there to provide a safe way for your car to "let off steam." Of course, if this kind of overflow occurs often, your car will lose enough water and coolant to substantially lower the level in the cooling system. You will have to keep adding water, and eventually, the level of coolant protection will be inadequate. To prevent this, there is an inexpensive gadget on the market that you might like to try.

A **coolant recovery system** is simply a plastic bottle with two little hoses coming out of the cap. One leads to the radiator and the other serves as an overflow pipe for the bottle. The bottle holds an extra supply of water and coolant, in case the system loses any. When your cooling system heats up and starts to overflow, instead of pouring out of the radiator overflow pipe and onto the ground, the liquid pours into the bottle. When the system cools off, the pressure drops and the liquid is drawn out of the bottle and back into the radiator. Most recovery systems are considered "sealed," since you can check to see if your coolant needs changing and can add water and coolant by opening the cap on the bottle. You can also check the level of liquid in the system by seeing if it reaches the fill level shown on the side of the bottle. If you open the radiator cap, be sure that you fill the radiator right to the top before replacing the cap. This "bleeds" the system by forcing any air that may have gotten into it into the bottle and out through the overflow pipe when the car heats up.

Coolant Recovery Kit

**How to Install a Coolant Recovery Kit**

If your car lacks a recovery system, you can buy and install one yourself. Installation is simple: you usually just attach the bracket that holds the bottle to the frame of your car under the hood, so that the bottle will sit slightly lower than the overflow pipe from your radiator. Then, one of the hoses from the bottle is usually connected to the radiator overflow pipe. You then replace your original radiator cap with the cap that comes in the kit. And that's it!

**What to Look for If Your Car Is Overheating and You Can't Find Any Leaks**

If you have not been able to locate any leaks and if your car is overheating constantly, you will have to check out a different set of alternatives:

**How to Replace Your Thermostat**

If your car has been overheating or does not warm up properly, you may need to replace your **thermostat**. You will recall that this little gizmo simply stays closed and keeps the liquid in the engine block until the car heats up. Although it is a simple device, it can malfunction. If it sticks in the *open* position the thermostat will not keep the liquid in the engine long enough, and you will have trouble getting your car warmed up. If it sticks *shut*, the liquid will not be allowed to get to the radiator, and overheating will result.

It is quite a simple matter to replace a thermostat, and since they are quite inexpensive, you might want to try this before going on to more drastic measures:

1 Locate your thermostat, if you haven't already done so. Since most of them are found where the top radiator hose joins the engine, let's deal with this type. If your thermostat is in the bottom radiator hose, the principle is the same.

2 Get a new one. Supply the usual information (make, model, etc.) to the auto supply store. You should be an old hand at this by now, and they will probably say, "Here comes the sixty-seven Mustang" (or whatever you drive) when you come in the door.

3 Unscrew the clamp that holds the end of the radiator hose where your thermostat is located.

4 Pull off the hose. Some liquid will escape, so have a bucket handy to catch it, and return it to the radiator when you have finished the job or use this golden opportunity to change it.

5 Remove the bolts that hold the thermostat housing in place, and lift out the old thermostat. There is a gasket around it. Get that off too. Scrape off the pieces of gasket that may be stuck, but be sure not to let these pieces fall into the hole.

6 Lay the new gasket in place. If it doesn't match the old one, you probably have the wrong thermostat.

7 Drop in the new thermostat. Be sure to place the spring side *down*. Then replace the bolts.

Thermostats Are Replaced Spring-Side Down. Stant Manufacturing Company, Inc.

8 Replace the hose, and screw down the clamp. Screw it down tight but not tight enough to cut the hose.

9 Replace whatever liquid ran out of the hose by pouring it out of the bucket and into the radiator fill hole (of course your bucket was clean when you put the stuff in it, right?).

## Other Things That Can Cause Your Car to Overheat

If your car continues to overheat, with the new thermostat in place, then you will have to look elsewhere for the cause.

### Timing

If you haven't tuned and timed your car recently, it may be the fault of your timing. Late timing sometimes produces an overheated engine by having the spark fire the fuel/air mixture after the piston has moved back down from the top of its stroke. This causes the spark plugs to fire too late to allow all the gases to burn properly, and more heat will burden your cooling system. Late timing alone will not cause a car to overheat by more than a few degrees, but coupled with other problems, it can bring the temperature to a critical point. The remedy is simple: just check your timing and adjust it as in Chapter 5.

### Plugged Radiator

Some radiators get so plugged up with rust, sediment, or small insects that even cleaning and flushing them does not do the trick. Since plugged passages cut down on the circulation of the liquid in the system, it cannot cool efficiently. The remedy is to have the radiator removed and steam-cleaned by a radiator specialist.

### Slipping Fan Belt

Check your fan belt to be sure that there is no more than about ½ inch of "give." If it is looser than that, it may not be driving your water pump properly, and that can impair circulation and overheat the cooling system. If your fan belt seems loose or very frayed, replace it according to the instructions in Chapter 5.

### Collapsing Bottom Radiator Hose

Occasionally, a bottom radiator hose will begin to collapse under the vacuum created by the water pump, and the impaired circulation will cause overheating. If your car starts to overheat, stop and open the hood, with the car in "Park" and the parking brake on, without shutting off the engine. Then take a look at the bottom hose (be careful not to get your hair or clothing caught in the fan or the fan belt) and see if it has collapsed. If it has replace it.

**Low Oil Level**   Check your oil dipstick if you still can't find the cause of overheating. If your car is low on oil, it will tend to overheat because the oil removes from 75 to 80 percent of the "waste heat" in your engine (besides doing its other numbers). If you are one quart low in oil and your car holds 5 quarts, there is a 20 percent reduction in the amount of heat that the oil can carry away (it cools off in the crankcase).

**What to Do If Your Car Overheats from Natural Causes**   Even the happiest, most beautifully tuned car will overheat occasionally. If you find yourself in stop-and-go traffic, on a rotten hot day, the chances are that your car's dashboard temperature indicator will rise. There are a couple of things you can do to help your car keep its cool under these circumstances:

1 At the first sign of overheating, shut off your air conditioner and open your car windows. This will decrease the load on the engine and help it to cool off.

2 If you continue to overheat, turn on the car heater and blower. This will transfer the heat from the engine to the interior of the car. (It will do wonders for your overheated engine but very little for you!)

3 If you are stopped in traffic and the temperature gauge is rising, shift into "Neutral" and rev the engine a little to make the water pump and the fan speed up and draw more liquid and air through the radiator. The increased air and liquid circulation should help to cool things off.

4 Try not to "ride your brakes." Brake drag increases the load on the engine and makes it heat up. Lag behind a bit if traffic is crawling, and then move up when the gap between you and the car in front of you gets too wide. Try to crawl along slowly, on little more than an idle, rather than moving up quickly and braking to a stop.

5 If you think your car is about to boil over, drive to the side of the road, open the hood, and sit there until things cool off. Remember, *don't open the radiator cap* under these circumstances, and if your engine has boiled over, *don't add water* until the car is quite cool again. If you must add water when the engine is still a little warm, add the water while the engine is running in neutral gear.

I ought to say a word about a condition that may occur under overheated circumstances. This is called **vapor lock**, and it can be quite disconcerting if you don't know what is happening.

**Vapor Lock**

Occasionally a car will get so hot that the gas boils in the fuel line. When it boils, it forms bubbles that keep the fuel pump from pumping the gasoline to the carburetor. This situation is easy to spot. Your car just suddenly stops going. And the condition is easy to fix once you know what has occurred.

1 If you are on the freeway, stay in your car until a member of the highway patrol comes along and helps you get to the side of the road. If you are in normal traffic and it is safe to get out and push the car to the side of the road, do it.

2 Once you are at the side of the road, lift the hood and place a wet cloth on the fuel line and the fuel pump. (You remember where to find them from Chapter 6, right?) If you have no place to wet a rag, you'll just have to sit and wait until things cool off naturally. The wet rag does it much faster.

3 Once you have cooled the line until the gasoline is no longer boiling and the bubbles have dissipated, wrap the rag around the line (some tinfoil wrapped around the line helps tremendously. If you often get vapor lock, carry some foil in the trunk of your car) to help keep the gasoline in the line from overheating again. You can also place metal clothespins along the fuel line to radiate the heat.

4 Get back on the road as though nothing had happened. This sort of thing will occur only under extreme conditions; in most cases, if you are traveling at speeds under 25 mph or idling a lot, the fan in

the car will keep the fuel cool enough to avoid vapor lock.

**If Your Car Is a Chronic Hothead**

If your car is a chronic overheater, you might want to consider replacing its radiator with one with a greater cooling capacity, or installing a separate cooling device where the trouble occurs. There are devices sold to cool transmission systems, for instance. Often, these coolers are sold as part of a trailer-towing package, because most cars were not designed to tow or carry very heavy loads for long periods of time. The resulting strain will cause them to overheat. Again, a professional you can trust is the proper one to consult if you think you may need these extras. (The last chapter of this book will show you how to choose mechanics who are honest and competent and what to do if you are dissatisfied with their service.)

Now, before we get into the mysterious secrets of the brake system, let's take a little time to go over something everybody is supposed to know (and surprisingly few of us do)—how to jack up your car without hurting it and yourself and how to change a flat tire....

# How to Jack Up
# Your Car and
# Change Your Tires

Up to now, most of the work we've discussed has been the "under-the-hood" kind of stuff that did not require you to get underneath your car. However, if you've reached this chapter you are probably ready to contemplate the nether regions of your automobile without flinching, so this seems as good a place as any to tell you how to jack up your car with relatively little effort or danger. And while we're at it, we'll get into the proper way to change a tire. Even if you are a member of the AAA, there is always a chance that you will find yourself stuck with a flat tire on a remote road with no telephone in sight. On these occasions, all traffic generally vanishes, leaving you helpless unless you know how to do the job yourself. We all have a general idea of what's involved, but there are a couple of places where the job gets sticky, and unless you are properly equipped, you can find yourself out of luck and in for a long wait for help to come along.

Jack Stands Hold Your Car Up Safely
Petersen Industries, Inc., Fredonia, W.I.

We've already discussed **jacks**, way back in Chapter 2, and, I hope, you've already checked to see that the jack that came with your car is working properly. If you feel that you need a new jack, you can buy either the tripod or the scissors type, or if you plan to get into under-the-car work, such as lubrication, you might want to invest in a 1.5-ton **hydraulic** jack, which is faster and safer than the other kinds and not terribly expensive.

You will also need a pair of **jack stands** if you plan to work under your car. With these, you can jack up the car, place it on the jack stands, and remove the jack. The stands will keep the car off the ground with less danger of slipping and will enable you to jack up more than one side of the car at a time.

Substituting boxes, or stones, or bricks, is very dangerous. They can slip out or break while you are under the car. A jack can do the same thing, so if you are going to work under your car (and you should plan to change your own oil and do your own lube jobs), be sure to buy a pair of jack stands. The money you save by getting under there yourself will easily pay for the stands in no time.

If you are going to spend a lot of time lying around under your car, you will probably want a **creeper**. That's just a board with casters under it. You can lie on it and move around easily. You can make one yourself from some plywood and a couple of old roller-skate wheels, but if you were that mechanically inclined, you probably wouldn't be reading this book. Try lying on an old bedboard or a ratty old blanket instead if you are fed up with buying things.

If you are not yet game for a lot of under-the-car work, and you just want to change your tires, change your oil, and be done with it, forget about the creeper and just be sure you have a jack and jack stands that work properly and that you know how to use them. Your owner's manual will tell you how to use the jack that came with your car, or you can take the jack to an auto supply store and ask them to show you how it works.

**What You'll Need**
**A Jack**

**Jack Stands**

**A Creeper**

A Creeper Makes Working Under Your Car More Comfortable.
Sparkomatic Corp.

**How to Jack Up Your Car**

1 Check your manual for the proper place to position the jack for your model car. Remember, there is a difference in where you place the jack stands for a one-wheel job like tire changing or brake checking, and where you place them for a two-wheel whole-end job like lubrication and repairs.

2 Never place the jack so that the weight of the car rests on something that can bend, break, or "give." If your manual is incomprehensible, or lacking in this kind of information, try to place the jack so that it will touch either the car frame or the big bar that supports the front wheel suspension. Jacks can also be placed near the rear wheel **axle**. Until you become more proficient at this, I'd stick to jacking up one wheel at a time. It may mean more work, but the practice will be good for you.

3 Place the jack under the part of the car that it should contact when raised. If you have jack stands, place them near the jack.

4 *The following is important!* Before you attempt to jack up your car, observe these safety precautions:

a *Always park the car on level ground before you jack it up.* If you get a flat tire on a hill and can't coast to the bottom without killing the tire completely, then park it close to the curb, turn the wheels toward the curb, and block the downside wheels securely to prevent the car from rolling. Even with these precautions, however, I'd be nervous.

b *Never jack up a car without blocking the wheels.* Even if the car is on level ground, use bricks, wooden wedges, or metal wheel chocks to block the wheels at the opposite end of the car from the end that is to be raised. This will keep the car from rolling after it has been jacked up. Keep the blocks in the trunk of your car so you won't have to go hunting around if you have to change a tire on the freeway. If you find yourself faced with the job of changing a tire and you have been foolish enough to disregard all these italics and have nothing with which to block the wheels, then at least park it near the curb with the wheels turned in. This may not keep you from getting hurt if the car rolls off the jack, but at least innocent motorists and pedestrians will not have to deal with a runaway driverless car!

You Can Use a Screwdriver to Pry a Hub Cap Loose.
Richard Freshman

SCLAD
000-188

c *Be sure that your car is in "Park" and that the emergency brake is on, before you jack it up.* The only time you don't want the emergency brake on is if you have to be able to rotate a *rear* wheel or remove the rear brake drums to inspect the brakes.

5 If you are going to remove a wheel to change a tire or check your brakes, remove the **hub cap** and loosen the **lug nuts** *before* you jack up the car. Once the car is jacked up, the wheel will turn freely, and it will be harder to get the hub cap off and almost impossible to start the nuts.

**How to Remove a Hub Cap**

1 Use a screwdriver or the flat end of a **lug wrench** to pry the hub cap off. Just insert the point where the edge of the cap meets the wheel and apply a little leverage. The cap should pop off. You may have to do this in a couple of places; it's like prying a nonscrew cap off a jar of jelly.

2 Lay the cap on its back so you can put the lug nuts into it to keep them from rolling away and heading for the nearest sewer.

**How to Loosen Lug Nuts**

1 These are those big nuts under the hub cap that hold the wheel in place. They are usually retightened with a power tool by most garages, and unless you've done the job yourself by hand, they are going to be pretty hard to get started. If you've taken my earlier advice and bought a cross-shaft **lug wrench**, now is the time to pat yourself on the back. Before you begin, you will have to ascertain whether the lug nuts on the wheel you are working on are right-hand threaded or left-hand threaded. This is not a "left-handed hammer joke"; the threads determine which way you have to turn the wrench. The lug nuts on the right side of a car are always right-hand threaded, but the nuts on the left side *may* be left-hand threaded. Look at the lug nuts on your car. In the center of the lugs you will either see an "R" or an "L" or no letter at all. Lugs with an "R," or with no letter, are right-threaded. Lugs with an "L" are left-threaded. You turn right-threaded nuts *counterclockwise* to loosen them. You turn left-threaded nuts *clockwise*. Frankly, the whole thing

A Hollow Pipe and a Cross-Shaft Wrench Can Loosen the Tighest Lug Nuts.
Richard Freshman

seems crazy to me, but that's how it is, friends. For the purposes of sanity, let's assume that your car has right-threaded nuts. If you have a couple of lefties, just use the wrench in the opposite direction, O.K.?

2 Find the end of the wrench that fits the lug nuts on your car and fit it onto the first nut. Always work on lug nuts in rotation. That way you won't forget to tighten any later. Apply all your weight to the bar on the *left*. This should start the nut turning *counterclockwise*, which will loosen it. If the nut has been put on with a power tool and you can't get it started, a piece of hollow pipe, fitted over that left-hand arm of the cross-shaft wrench, will magically add enough leverage to start the nut easily. After you've replaced the nut yourself, this aid will no longer be necessary. But remember, the longer the arms on your lug wrench, the more leverage it will give you.

3 Do not remove the lug nuts completely, just get them loose enough so you can remove them by hand once the car has been raised.

**Back to the Jack**  Now you can use the jack to raise the car. Apply nice even strokes, taking the jack handle from its lowest to its highest point on each stroke, to cut down on the labor involved. When the car is high enough so that the wheel is completely clear of the ground and you can easily reach and see whatever part concerns you, you can stop. Then, do the following:

1 If you have jack stands, place them under the car, near the place where the jack is touching the car. Raise the stands until they are high enough to just fit under, and lock them in place. Lower the jack until the car is resting on the jack stands. Then re-move the jack.

2 Before you begin to work, wiggle the car a little to make sure it is resting securely on the jack or the jack stands. This will also tell you if you have the wheels blocked properly. It is better if the car falls while all four wheels are in place (it will just bounce a little). If you remove a wheel and begin to work without checking to be sure you've jacked it and blocked it securely, it will do itself—and you—a lot

of damage if it falls. This is not meant to frighten you away from jacking up your car and working on—or under—it. It should simply dramatize that a few simple precautions will remove any danger.

3 Everything secure? Fine! Then you can go ahead and remove the lug nuts and put them into the hub cap.

Now that we've got the car up and the lug nuts off, here's the proper way to change a tire:

**How to Change a Tire**

1 Remove the spare from the trunk, if you haven't already done so. Actually, it is easier if you do this before you jack up the car. If you haven't checked your spare recently, keep your fingers crossed that there is enough air in it! Roll the spare to the scene of the action.

2 Grasp the flat tire with both hands and pull it toward you. It is sitting on the exposed bolts that the lug nuts screwed onto. The flat should slide along the bolts until, suddenly, it clears the end of the bolts and you find yourself supporting its full weight. Tires are heavy, and you will be quite happy to lower it to the ground (if you haven't already dropped it).

3 Roll the flat along the ground to the trunk, to get it out of the way.

4 You are now going to have to lift the spare onto the lug bolts. Since tires are heavy, you may have a little trouble lifting it into place—especially if you are not accustomed to lifting heavy things. If this is the case, a bit of ingenuity will help.

I have a friend who is a newly liberated female of small stature. Recently, when her first flat occurred while she was on the road, she found herself in the infuriating position of being unable to lift the heavy spare onto the lug bolts—while a macho truck driver, whose offers of help she had spurned, enjoyed the scene (he'd decided to hang around and watch the "little lady" change her tire). After hearing her sad tale, I suggested that she cut an old wooden crate into a ramp that could get the tire high enough to fit onto the lug bolts, and that she

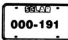

should keep the ramp in the trunk of her car for future tire changes. She did it and is now gloriously independent once more. In fact, she now gets her kicks by stopping to offer bewildered males her services when they are stopped at the side of the road with a flat tire and a lack of knowledge about how to change it! The illustration shows how to make a ramp like hers.

5 After you have the spare tire in place, replace the lug nuts and tighten them by hand. Give them each a jolt with the wrench to get them firmly into place, but wait until the car is on the ground before you really try to tighten them down.

6 Replace the jack and lift the car off the jack stands, if you've used them, and lower the car to the ground. Once the car is resting on the ground, use the lug wrench to tighten the lugs as much as you can. You don't want to twist them off the bolts or ruin the threads, but you don't want the wheel to fall off, either. Use your hollow pipe, if you are worried about tightening them sufficiently, or step on the right-hand arm of the lug wrench after the nut is tight. Remember, right-hand threaded nuts tighten in a clockwise direction, lefties go the other way.

7 Now place the **hub cap** against the wheel and whack it into place with the heel of your hand. Cushion your hand with a soft rag first so you won't hurt it.

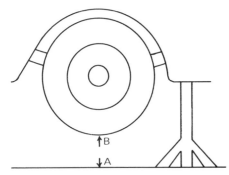

1. Measure the distance from the ground (A) to the bottom of the tire (B) while the car is jacked up.

2. Nail some boards together to form a ramp of the same height as AB above.

How to Build a Ramp
Jack Herlihy

3. Now you can roll your wheel up the ramp and just push it into place without having to lift it yourself!

Don't hit the hub cap with a wrench or a hammer—you'd dent it. Whack it a couple of times, in a couple of places, to be sure it's on evenly. Even second-hand hub caps can cost as much as $20 to $50 apiece to replace. If it is too much of a hassle, or if you don't have the time to replace the hub cap, you can take it home and install it later; it is mostly ornamental and you can drive for a while without it. But *do* replace it soon because it helps keep dust and dirt out of your brakes and bearings.

8 Put the flat into the trunk, where the spare was located, and put your tools away. Don't forget to remove the wheel blocks, and *don't forget to have that flat fixed!*

Be sure that your flat tire will be repaired properly. Instead of dismounting the tire from the wheel rim, inspecting it, fixing it, and remounting it, some service stations simply plug the flat from the outside. Several states now outlaw this procedure, known as "outside-in" repair.

If you get caught in the middle of nowhere with a flat tire and are unable to change it yourself, there is a way to get rolling again without riding on the flat. If you carry an aerosol can of *inflator/sealant,* you can simply screw the nozzle of the can onto the valve stem of the flat tire and it will fill the tire with air and some sort of goo that temporarily seals the puncture. Since there is still some question about how permanent this is and its ultimate effects on your tire, use it *only* in emergencies, get to a service station as soon as possible, and ask them to try to remove the stuff before they fix the tire.

You may not find the prospect of fixing your own flat tires especially alluring, but isn't it nice to know that if a crisis does occur and you are not near a phone or haven't got the time to wait for the AAA, you have the ability to get yourself rolling again in less than 15 minutes? To make the job easier, should an emergency arise, you might want to go out and check the lug nuts on your car now. If they are on hideously tight, loosen them with a wrench and a pipe and retighten them to a reasonable tension so you won't have to struggle at the side of the road.

# How to Be a Buddy to Your Brakes

Your car is sitting happily at the curb. It has a smug sort of look. Its ignition system is in tune, its carburetor is clean and well fed, and it hasn't overheated in a long time. You are both quite pleased with yourselves by now—and you should be. You can raise the hood with a practiced air and contemplate the gadgets in there with the eye of an old friend (well, maybe a new acquaintance). But before you relegate this book to the "guess-I'll-finish-it-later" pile and go on to learn macrame or fly-tying, we'd better talk about an aspect of auto repair and maintenance that most of us take for granted, even though it deals with practically the only system in your car that can kill you if you don't keep it in good repair. As you've already guessed—especially if you read chapter titles—I'm talking about your **brakes**.

Most cars today are equipped with a **hydraulic brake system**, which we've already discussed in Chapter 3. (If you've forgotten, you might want to go back and reread it now. I'll wait....)

Since 1968, most cars are also equipped with *dual* brake systems to ensure that, if one set of brakes fails, the other set will still be able to stop your car; and with a dashboard light to warn you if your front or rear brakes fail.

Let's go over the brake system in greater detail and talk about the differences between **disc brakes** and **drum brakes**, between *manual* and **power brakes**, and so forth, so you can be perfectly familiar with what *should* be happening when you stop your car. Then, at the end of this chapter, I'll show you how to inspect your brake system to be sure it is in good shape; how to keep it in good shape; and how to keep from being ripped off when it is time to have your brakes adjusted or **rebuilt**.

Although it is possible to do most of the work yourself—there is nothing terribly complicated about it—I don't think that you should do any major brake work without supervision. If you don't get things back properly, you'll risk losing much more than you'd gain! However, if after reading this chapter you simply can't stand the idea of having a total stranger replace your worn **brake linings**, you can always get

Disc brake
(front)

Brake line

Master cylinder

Brake warning
light switch

Power brake
(optional)

Brake pedal

Drum brake
(rear)

The Brake System
The Bendix Corp.

yourself to a good auto repair class and do the work under the watchful eye of the instructor. Auto classes generally have the hydraulic hoists, **brake drum** lathes, and other expensive equipment that you'd need to do a really good job; so even if you are sure you need no further instruction after reading my enlightened and crystal-clear prose, it would still be worth the price of enrollment to have the equipment and the instructor's expertise available.

Whether you decide to do the work yourself or not, there is still a lot of ground we can cover, and a lot of preventive checking and maintenance you can do to spot trouble before it occurs and to enable you to deal on an informed level with your auto mechanic or brake specialist.

To recap: Getting your car to stop is a relatively simple matter. The hydraulic brake system is designed to operate on a very simple principle with a minimum of parts and maintenance.

In the system shown on p. 196 there is a **power booster**, and disc brakes on the front wheels. Your system may not have power brakes or may have disc or drum brakes all around. The principle's the same in any case. Let's start at the first point of contact between you and your brakes and then work down the line to the brakes themselves.

The *brake pedal* in your car is attached to a shaft that leads to the **master cylinder**. When you step on the brake pedal, a small piston in the master cylinder forces **brake fluid** out of the master cylinder and into the **brake lines**. If your brakes are working properly, the pedal should stop a couple of inches from the floor. It should push down easily, stop firmly at its lowest point without feeling spongy, and stay put instead of sinking down slowly when you put normal pressure on it. Power brakes stop closer to the floor, with as little as one inch of clearance. We'll check yours later.

**The Brake Pedal**

Master Cylinder with Plastic Reservoir and
Power Booster
Richard Freshman

**The Master Cylinder**    Look under the hood of your car, up near the firewall on the driver's side. You should see either a metal box or a plastic bottle. Have you found it? This is your **master cylinder**. It is full of brake fluid and is connected to your brake pedal, with brake lines leading from it to the four wheels of your car. When you step on the brake pedal, fluid will go out of the master cylinder into the brake lines. When you release the pedal, the fluid will flow back into the master cylinder. Don't mess with yours now; I'll show you how to get it open later on in this chapter, when we begin to check the brake systems on your car.

**Dual Brakes**    A *dual* brake system simply means that the inside of your master cylinder is divided into *two* compartments, each filled with brake fluid. One compartment has brake lines that lead to the brakes on your front wheels; the other compartment has lines leading to your rear wheels. If you should develop a leak, or a block, in one set of lines, the fluid in that compartment will be lost or useless. But you will still have the other compartment and set of brakes with which to stop your car. It may not stop smoothly, but it will stop, and in such a case, that's all that counts! This simple modification has saved countless lives.

Metal Master Cylinder
The Bendix Corp.

If after checking your brake system you find you have a leak, or have to **bleed** your brakes, you will have to go to the auto supply store to buy some **brake fluid** in order to restore the fluid in your master cylinder to its proper level. Here are some things you should know:

1  Always use top-quality brake fluid, from a well-known manufacturer. Brake fluid for disc brakes has a higher boiling point than brake fluid designed for drum brakes and can be used on cars with any kind of brakes. However, drum brake fluid cannot be used with disc brakes.

2  If you have front disc brakes and rear drum brakes on your car, you probably have disc brake fluid in both chambers of your master cylinder.

3  *This is important!* Brake fluid becomes swiftly contaminated by exposure to air. The oxygen in the air oxidizes it and lowers its boiling point. It also has an affinity for moisture, and the water vapor in the air can combine with the brake fluid to form ice crystals that make braking difficult in cold weather. If you add water-vapor-contaminated fluid to your brake system, it can rust the system and create acids that will etch your **wheel cylinders** and master cylinder and foul your brakes, causing them to work poorly—or not at all. Therefore, if you are going to add brake fluid to your system, buy a small can, add the fluid to your master cylinder, and *throw the rest away,* or use it only in emergencies. The stuff is pretty cheap, and your car should not need more fluid after a leak has been fixed. If you keep a can with only a little fluid left in it, the air that fills up the rest of the space in the can will contaminate the fluid, no matter how quickly you've recapped it. One more thing, keep brake fluid away from painted surfaces—*it eats paint.* (If this stuff seems scary, remember that many of the same statements can be made about turpentine or nail polish remover.)

**Brake Fluid**

Dual-Chamber Master Cylinder
The Bendix Corp.

Leading away from the master cylinder, along the frame of your car to each wheel, are the **brake lines**. These are made of steel except for the portions that lie right near your front wheels and your rear **axle**. These portions of the brake line are made of rubber

**Brake Lines**

Drum

Backing plate

Wheel cylinder    Retracting springs

Brake shoes

Anatomy of a Drum Brake
Automotive Information Council (AIC)

that is flexible enough to contend with the greater amount of movement that takes place in these areas when you steer your car.

Up to now, most of the brake systems on your cars have been pretty much the same. But now we get to the major differences between the various kinds of hydraulic brake systems. Although older cars have **drum brakes** on all four wheels, today most have drum brakes on the rear wheels only and **disc brakes** on the front wheels. Still others have four-wheel disc brakes. Then there are cars with *power-assisted* drum or disc brakes. And to confuse you completely, since 1963 most brakes are *self-adjusting*, but there are still a couple of oldies with *manually adjusted* brakes around. Your owner's manual will tell you what kind(s) of brakes you have on your car, in case you don't already know, but it's more fun to see for yourself. I'll describe each type of brake in detail and then show you how to check each part of your car's brake system to see if it needs help.

**Drum Brakes**

**Wheel Cylinders**

1  In this type of brake system, the brake fluid that has been forced through the brake lines by the piston in the master cylinder goes into a **wheel cylinder** located inside the **brake drum** on the **brake backing plate**.

2  The fluid then activates the two small pistons located inside the wheel cylinder by forcing them farther apart.

1. Before Braking.

2. Fluid in the Wheel Cylinder Pushes the Piston Outward.

3. As the Brake Shoes Are Forced Against the Drum, the Car Stops.

The Brake Fluid in the Wheel Cylinder Pushes the Brake Shoes Outward, Forcing the Linings Against the Drum.
The Bendix Corp.

3 The fluid pushes against the *pistons,* forcing them to emerge from either end of the wheel cylinder and push against the **brake shoes**, which forces the **linings** against the brake drum.

4 Seals inside the wheel cylinder, called *cups,* keep the brake fluid from leaking out of the wheel cylinder.

5 *Dust boots* on each end of the wheel cylinder prevent dirt and dust from entering and fouling the cylinder.

New linings are thicker and push the pistons farther into the center of the cylinder when they return to their original position after the brake pedal is released. If there is dirt in the cylinder, the cylinder cups get jammed against it and become malformed, causing leaks. For this reason, when the brakes are relined, each cylinder should be taken apart and honed with a special tool, providing the diameter of the cylinder remains thick enough to meet specifications. If the walls become too thin, have the cylinder replaced.

(*above*) Exploded View of a Wheel Cylinder
Delco Moraine Division, General Motors Corp.

(*left*) Anatomy of a Wheel Cylinder
The Bendix Corp.

**Brake shoes** are curved pieces of metal which stop the car by pushing against the inside of the brake drum. They are attached to a set of springs that draw them back into place when you take your foot off the brake.

**Brake Shoes**

A Brake Shoe
The Bendix Corp.

Lining goes
here

If you are told by a mechanic that your brake shoes need to be replaced, remember that almost all "new" brake shoes are really **rebuilt** ones! When the mechanic replaces your old brake shoes, they are returned to a company that removes the old linings and attaches new ones.

**Brake Linings**

Either bonded or riveted to the brake shoes are curved **brake linings** of tough material which is very resistant to heat. Traditionally made of asbestos, new brake linings are now available of longer-lasting semimetallic and nonasbestos materials. When the brake shoes are forced against the insides of the brake drum, the linings create friction which causes the brake drum to stop turning. This in turn forces the wheels to stop turning, which stops the car. Brake linings should be checked for wear every 10,000 to 20,000 miles.

**Adjusting Devices**

Located at the bottom of the brake backing plate is either a *manual adjusting wheel* or a *self-adjusting device*. These are used to adjust the distance between the surface of the brake lining and the inside of the brake drum when you step on the brake pedal. As your brake linings become worn, the distance increases, and this adjustment compensates for it. If you didn't have this gadget and your linings became very worn, eventually the brake shoes would not reach the inside of the drum and your car would not stop.

Return spring

Wheel cylinder

Return spring

Adjusting
link

Actuator
return
spring

Brake
shoe

Brake
shoe

Connecting
spring

Star wheel adjuster

Self-adjusting Delco Moraine Brake: When you back up, the adjusting links and springs adjust the brakes automatically.

Adjusting Devices on Three Popular Brakes
Delco Moraine Division, General Motors Corp.

*Manually adjusted brakes* are almost never found on cars built since 1962. If your car is old and has manually adjusted brakes, they must be adjusted periodically. Only a professional mechanic should do this.

*Self-adjusting brakes* should not require any work. When you drive and stop your car in reverse, the mechanism is automatically adjusted. So if you think your brake pedal is too low, something may be wrong with the self-adjusting device, since under normal conditions we all tend to back up enough to keep our brakes in adjustment.

**Brake drums** are hollow steel cylinders located in back of each wheel. Because those same lug bolts go through them that go through the wheel, they turn when the wheel turns. If you keep your brakes in good condition and change your brake linings before they become too worn, your drums should last for the life of your car. If they become worn, they can be "reground" or "turned" to a smooth surface—unless they are worn over .060 of an inch. Then, you'll need new ones.

If you are told that your brake drums cannot be turned and must be *replaced,* ask your mechanic to let you watch while he checks them with a special instrument called a brake drum *micrometer.* The instrument will show you whether the drums are worn over the legal level.

If it looks as though you must have a new drum, ask your service station to get you a used reground one. These are much cheaper than new ones and should be just as good if they are not too worn. If your garage says they can't find any, try calling a couple of auto wreckers yourself (see the Yellow Pages) and ask for used drums for your car's make, model, and year. Be sure the drums look *exactly the same* as your old ones, and don't forget to specify drums for *front* or *rear* wheels. Have a professional mechanic install them for you, as the brake shoes must be adjusted to fit. Brake drums must be replaced with drums of the same size for even braking performance.

Manually Adjusted Brake: You turn the star wheel adjuster by hand to adjust the brakes.

Self-adjusting Bendix Brake: When you back up, the adjusting cable is automatically tightened and the brakes adjust themselves.

The Brake Drum in Place
Delco Moraine Division, General Motors Corp.

**Advantages of Drum Brakes**

The main advantage of drum brakes is that they require less hydraulic pressure to stop your car, because the brake shoes tend to screw themselves into the brake drums once they have been pushed there by the pistons in the wheel cylinders. The brake linings on the front wheel brakes have a larger surface than those on the rear wheels because the front wheels bear most of the pressure of stopping since the weight shifts from the rear to the front when you brake. However, on each set of brake linings, on any given wheel, the lining toward the rear of the car is larger and often is a different color.

**Disc Brakes**

**Disc brakes** are composed of a flat steel *disc* (surprise!) sandwiched between a pair of **calipers**. These calipers contain one or more pistons that are forced into the disc by the brake fluid in the brake lines. Between the disc and the pistons are *brake pads,* which operate in the same way as brake shoes do: they grab the disc with their rough asbestos linings and force the disc to stop turning, which in turn forces the wheel to stop turning and the car to stop moving. The effect is the same as on a bicycle when the brakes grab the wheel directly to stop it from turning.

As you can see, the **hydraulic** principle (which means liquid under pressure, in this case) is the same for drum brakes as for disc brakes. But disc brakes do have advantages. Because they operate in the open air (instead of inside brake drums) they are less prone to overheating. They are also affected less by water, because the leading edge of the brake pads scrapes the water away before it can get between the pads and the disc. When drum brakes get wet, the brake linings don't grab the brake drum satisfactorily, and often the car won't stop.

Disadvantages include the difficulty of attaching an **emergency brake** to the rear disc brakes, and the fact that disc brakes usually need to be power-assisted.

Disc — Caliper

A Typical Disc Brake
The Bendix Corp.

Many car manufacturers compromise by producing cars with disc brakes on the front wheels and drum brakes on the rear wheels. This is fine, since the front wheels do most of the job of stopping the car.

Disc brakes need very little service and require no adjusting. A set of them will usually perform better than either conventional drum brakes or power drum brakes—particularly under high-speed, wet, or over-heated conditions.

If your car is braking properly, everything is probably fine. If the disc brakes are squealing, groaning, or rattling, have a professional take a look at them.

Today, **power brakes** are found on most cars. Power brakes, or "power-assisted brakes," are simply conventional brakes that are hooked to a device called a **power booster** that uses engine vacuum to help you push the brake pedal down. They are considered most necessary on cars with disc brakes and cars that are big and heavy. I didn't realize how necessary the power brakes on our old macho-mobile were until they failed one night and we had to drive home with only the basic brake system. I had to *stand* on the brake pedal to stop the car even though we were traveling very slowly. I just can't see the logic of buying a car with a big frame that weighs so much that you need power brakes to stop it, power steering to steer it, a big engine to move it around, and a lot more fuel to keep the whole mess running. That's a big price to pay for "status," and why should obvious waste be a status symbol anyway? If you want a car with status, try a beautifully made, highly efficient, well-designed small car. They can be expensive too.

If you have power brakes on your car, and it gets really hard to push the brake pedal down, your power booster is probably the culprit and your brakes may be O.K.

Without getting too technical, here is how power brakes work: There is a power booster between the brake pedal and the master cylinder which contains a diaphragm. A metal arm runs from the brake pedal,

**Power Brakes**

The Power Booster Is Located Right Behind the Master Cylinder
*Brake and Front End* magazine

Master cylinder

Vacuum on both sides of diaphragm

Brake pedal up

☐ Vacuum
▨ Air

Diaphragm plate — Diaphragm

**Brakes Released**

Vacuum in front of diaphragm · Air to rear

Brake pedal down

Hydraulic pistons move forward

Hydraulic push rod

Diaphragm and diaphragm plate move forward

▨ Vacuum
▨ Air

How a Power Booster Works
The Bendix Corp.

**Brakes Applied**

through the diaphragm, to the piston on the master cylinder. When you step on the brake, a valve opens in a pipe connecting the booster to the engine vacuum. That vacuum sucks the diaphragm forward, which moves the arm attached to it. Since the arm is really an extension of the brake pedal, it pushes the piston in the master cylinder, which forces the brake fluid out into the brake lines. So, all that is really happening is that you are using engine vacuum to help you push on that piston instead of just doing it yourself via the brake pedal alone.

Here are a few final notes about the anatomy of brakes: Because most of the weight is in the front of the car (on front-engine cars), the front brakes bear most of the brunt of stopping the car. Consequently, the front brake shoes are usually longer and wider than the rear ones. A friend of mine had his brakes relined recently and complained that they worked miserably. We took them apart and found that the brake "specialists" had installed the larger brake shoes on the *rear* wheels and the shorter shoes on the front! Isn't that a good reason for finding an auto repair class and—under supervision—doing the job yourself?

**Parking Brakes**

A Transmission-Type Parking Brake System
The Bendix Corp.

The **parking brake**, or emergency brake, is usually attached to the rear wheels of your car. On cars with drum brakes, the parking brake is attached with cables to the rear brakes. The cables run underneath the car and can be easily adjusted by turning a screw that controls the tension on the cable. These are called *integral* parking brakes.

On some cars, other devices do the same job. Some parking brakes are linked to the transmission, and rather than activating the rear brakes, they stop the driveshaft from turning the rear wheels. With these *transmission-type* parking brakes, the band and lining are attached to a drum on the transmission. When you pull the lever, the band squeezes the lining against the drum, and the driveshaft stops turning. If you can't find a typical parking brake linkage under your car, you may have this type of brake. If it doesn't seem to be performing properly, have it checked by a professional.

You will know when your parking brake needs adjusting because it will fail to keep your car from moving when you try to drive with the brake on. Also, as the mechanism loosens up, the brake will have to be pulled up farther (if it is a hand brake), or it will end up nearer the floor (if it is a foot pedal), before you can set the brakes properly. To be set properly a good parking brake has to be moved only about one third of the total distance along its shaft to set the brake.

An Integral Parking Brake System
The Bendix Corp.

**How to Check Your Brake System**

Now that you understand how the brakes on your car work, you are in a good position to check them and be sure they are working properly. Check your brakes every 10,000 to 20,000 miles, depending on the age of your car, the history of its brakes, and how much stop-and-go driving you do. If you tend to "ride your brakes" when you drive, they are going to get that much more wear and should be checked more frequently. Riding your brake will cause your brakes to overheat more often, and you will pay the price in worn linings, worn drums, or brake shoes that have warped out of shape. Although it is always a good policy to be cautious, try to anticipate stopping situations well enough in advance to be able to slow down by releasing the pressure on your gas pedal, whenever possible, and then using your brake pedal for that final stop. If you have a **manual transmission, downshift** to take the pressure of stopping off your brakes. In situations that call for slowing down, rather than stopping, it is better to pump your brake pedal a couple of times to reduce speed than to jam on your brakes and screech to a halt. Good driving is guaranteed to make your brakes last longer than the most expensive maintenance.

Let's go back over the brake system in your car and check each part for wear and proper performance. Whenever it is safe for you to do the necessary maintenance, I'll tell you how to do it. If it is relatively complicated, I'll recommend professional help and tell you what that professional *should* be doing. Don't forget to ask to watch the mechanic test your old drums with the micrometer to be sure they're worn over the legal limit of .060 of an inch before agreeing to replace them.

Checking Drum Wear with a Micrometer
Delco Moraine Division, General Motors Corp.

**How to Check Your Brake Pedal**

1 With the car at rest, apply pressure to the brake pedal. Does it feel spongy? If it does, you probably have air in your brake lines. This is not difficult to correct; you can probably do the job yourself with the help of a friend. For instructions, see the end of this chapter under "How to Bleed Your Brakes."

2 Apply a slight amount of pressure to your brake pedal when it is once again at rest. Does it stay

where it was when you stopped depressing it? Or does it seem to sink slowly to the floor, away from your foot. If it sinks, your master cylinder may be defective and illegally unsafe.

3 Drive the car around the block, stopping every now and then, without driving the people behind you crazy. The pedal should stop more than 3 inches from the floor if you have ordinary self-adjusting brakes. If you have power brakes, the pedal should stop in an inch to an inch and a half. (Always test power brakes with the motor on.)

4 If you feel that your brakes are "low" (that the pedal goes down too far before the car stops properly), try pumping the brake a couple of times while you are driving around. Does it come up higher? If so, a brake adjustment is probably in order. After we check the brake fluid situation, if you find that you are *not* low in fluid, drive to your friendly service station and ask them to adjust your brakes. After that, the pedal should not travel as far down before your car stops.

5 While you are driving around, take time to notice how your total brake system is performing. Ask yourself these questions:

a Does the car travel too far before coming to a stop in city traffic? If it does, your brakes need adjusting or you need new linings.

b Does the car pull to one side when you brake it? You may have a leak in one of your wheel cylinders, which will cause the brakes on that wheel to "grab." Or your brake drum may be warped. We'll get to checking wheel cylinders and drums in a minute.

c Do your brakes "squeal" when you stop fairly short? This condition can impair your car's braking efficiency if that squeal means that your linings are worn down to the metal. If when you check your brake linings, you find that they are not terribly worn, just slick or glazed-looking (glazed linings reflect light like a mirror), you can roughen them up a bit with sandpaper. Just be sure that you get every last bit of sand and dust off them before you reassemble the wheel. Use nothing but sand or flint paper—carbide, emory, or aluminum oxide paper will leave a residue, and the teeniest bit of grit will cause your drums to wear out more quickly. Glazed linings are not the worst thing you can have, so if your linings seem to be wearing well and your car is braking efficiently—and if you can stand the noise—you may be better off just leaving them alone.

d Does your car bounce up and down when you stop short? Your **shock absorbers** may need to be replaced. We'll get to them in another chapter.

If any of these checks shows that you have a problem, finish this chapter and then *take care of the situation immediately.* Never put off brake work. If your brakes fail, you (and a lot of other people) may be in serious trouble. Other kinds of automotive trouble may keep your car from going—brake trouble keeps your car from stopping.... The rest, and you, may be history.

**How to Check Your Master Cylinder**

Releasing the Lid of a Metal Master Cylinder with a Screwdriver
Richard Freshman

1 Open the top of your **master cylinder**. If you have the kind with a little plastic bottle on top, just unscrew the cap. If you have a metal one, use a screwdriver to pry the retaining clamp off the top. Be sure not to let any dirt fall into the chambers when you open the lid. If your hood area is full of funky grime and dust, wipe the lid before you remove it.

2 Take a look at the lid. Attached to the inside surface is a rubber diaphragm with two rubber cups. As the brake fluid in your master cylinder recedes (when it is forced into the brake lines), the diaphragm cups are pushed down by air that comes in through vents in the lid. The rubber cups descend and touch the surface of the remaining brake fluid, to prevent evaporation and to keep the dust and dirt out. When the fluid flows back in, the rubber cups are pushed back up. If your fluid level is low, or if the rubber cups are in their descended position when you remove the lid, you will have to push them back up with your finger before you replace the lid.

3 Look inside the master cylinder. The brake fluid should be up to the fill line or within half an inch of the top of the chamber. If it isn't, you will have to buy brake fluid and add it.

A low brake-fluid level may not mean anything if it has been a long time since any fluid was added, and if your car has been braking properly. If you have reason to believe that your brake fluid level has dropped because of a leak, then check the rest of your system very carefully as we go from part to part, looking for leaks.

If you are going to buy brake fluid, reread the brake fluid section in this chapter to be sure you are buying the proper kind. Be sure that your fluid does not become contaminated by oxygen or water vapor in the air.

4 If both chambers of your master cylinder are filled with brake fluid to the proper level, close it up carefully, without letting any dirt fall into it. If dirt gets into your master cylinder, it will travel down the brake lines. If it doesn't block them, the dirt will end up in your wheel cylinders and damage your brakes.

5 Remember, brake fluid evaporates easily, so don't stand around admiring the inside of your master cylinder. Close it quickly, and be sure that the cover is securely in place. Since most master cylinders are pretty airtight, you should not lose brake fluid in any quantity unless it is leaking out somewhere else. If your fluid level was low, we'll find the cause as we continue to check the system.

6 Take a flashlight, or a work light, and look for stain marks, wetness, or gunk under the master cylinder and on the firewall near it. If your master cylinder is—or has been—leaking, there will be evidence.

7 It's a good idea to check your master cylinder every couple of months; more often if it was low in fluid when you last checked it. This should be part of your regular under-the-hood check.

You Can See the Rubber Cups Inside the Lid of This Master Cylinder.
Richard Freshman

**How to Check Your Brake Lines**

1 If the fluid level in your master cylinder remains full, chances are that there is no need to check for leaks in the **brake lines**. If, however, you find that you are losing brake fluid, or if the insides of your tires are wet and look as though something has been leaking and streaking them, it could be a

brake fluid leak in the wheel cylinders or the lines—
or a visit from a neighbor's dog!

2  The easiest way to check brake lines is to put the
car up on a hydraulic hoist, raise it over your head,
walk under it, and examine the lines as they lead
from the hood area to each wheel. There may be
leaks coming from holes in the lines—or where the
steel lines become rubber ones—or where the brake
lines connect with the wheel cylinders. Check carefully along the lines for wetness and for streaks of
dried fluid. If you see rust spots on your lines, gently sand them off and look for thin places under
them that may turn into holes before too long. Feel
the rubber parts of the brake lines for signs that the
rubber is becoming sticky, soft, spongy, or worn.
Your brake lines should last the life of your car. If
they look very bad, have a professional take a look
at them and give you an idea of whether or not
they should be replaced. If the car is fairly new and
the brake lines look very bad, I'd go back to the
dealer with the problem and ask him to replace the
lines free of charge.

3  If you do not have access to a hoist at the auto repair shop at your local school, or at a friendly garage, then you will have to jack up your car, one
end at a time, and get down there with a flashlight
or work light to look at your lines. Before you do
this, be sure to check for instructions and safety tips
in the chapter on how to jack up your car! Remember to look at the insides of your tires for drippy
clues about leaking wheel cylinders.

**Getting at Your Brakes**    The next thing to do is to check your brakes in order
to see whether they are in good condition. This is not
as scary as it sounds; in fact, it's quite a simple job—
with two qualifications. The first is that you do not
attempt to fiddle with anything unless I tell you to.
The second is that when you go about disassembling
the stuff that covers your brakes, you do so in the
proper manner. This will keep you from getting into a
situation where you cannot put the pieces back together again. It is this fear that keeps most of us from
poking around in our cars, which in turn prevents us
from discovering the cause of most trouble ourselves.

We turn to others for the diagnosis and then get angry when they come up with the wrong answers.

Once you learn to take a mechanical gadget apart properly, you will be able to put it back together again without trouble. Over the years, Don, my instructor, has given a lot of thought to this and has come up with as foolproof a set of instructions as possible. With them he has enabled hundreds of students to take apart brakes, carburetors, and other automotive gizmos, with no fatalities! I pass them along to you:

1 Before you start, get a *clean rag* and lay it down on a flat surface, near enough to reach without having to get up or walk to it. As you remove each part, you are going to lay it on this rag. Consequently, the rag should not be in an area where oil or dust or anything else will fall on it and foul the parts. If you are going to use something that blasts air for cleaning purposes, you can leave enough of the rag uncluttered to lap it over the parts resting on it while you blast.

2 Before you begin to remove each part, stop and ask yourself the following questions:

a What is this thing?

b What does it do?

c How does it do it?

d Why is it made the way it is?

e How tightly is it screwed on (or fastened down)? Most amateurs tend to put things back very tightly, in the hope that the part won't fly off. But there are things like the bolts that hold **rocker-arm cover** gaskets in place that should not be tightened too securely, because the **gasket** would be squeezed out of shape and whatever it is holding in would get out, or the bolt threads could be stripped. So try to remember how hard each thing was to remove. If you are worried about forgetting, make notes.

3 As you remove each part, lay it down on the rag *in clockwise order, with each part pointing in the direction it lay when it was in place.* This is the key to the whole thing. It will tell you when to put each thing back,

**How to Disassemble Anything (and Get It Back Together Again)**

and how it went, when it is time to reassemble things. If you are making notes about tightness, etc., just call each part by the number in which you removed it—part #1, #2, etc. If you work systematically and understand the function of each thing, you won't be left with those little "extra" nuts and bolts at the end of the job. You can even put numbers on them with masking tape if you are afraid the rag might be moved accidentally.

4   Remember, if you take something off that looks too difficult to trust your memory about, write yourself a note. It needn't be a long one, just something like: "Part #6—the hook at the end of the arm on the left hooks on to the little knob to the right of part #7." With a picture, if it will help.

5   Never, never, do a job in a hurry. Allow yourself plenty of time. If things get rough, have a soft drink or a cup of coffee. You may get a whole new perspective when you go back to work. Keep the kids and the dog away and relax. If you hit a snag, sit quietly and think about it—don't panic. If the thing fitted together before, it will fit together again.

This kind of procedure works for anything—brakes, toasters, bicycles, etc. I've never been able to follow the instructions to put my kids' toys together, but I can take a carburetor apart and get it back together again—slowly but accurately. Actually, your brakes are a good place to test this procedure on yourself. They aren't hard to disassemble, and we're not going to touch anything that will keep your car from braking properly if you goof, so get up your nerve and let's go!

**How to Check Drum Brakes**   Check one of your front brakes; the linings wear faster on the front brakes than on rear ones. If you have a front-wheel drive car, it will not conform exactly to the description below. You can still check the brakes, but you won't be able to repack the bearings.

1   Remove a *front* wheel according to the instructions in the previous chapter. Observe safety precautions with that jack!

2 Use a pair of combination slip-joint pliers to pry the grease cap off the end of the hub.

3 Look at the **cotter pin** that sticks out of the side of the *castellated nut* or nut-lock-and-nut combination. In which direction is it lying? How are its legs bent? How does it fit through the nut? How tight is it? Make a sketch, if necessary; then use a pair of needle-nosed pliers to straighten it out.

4 Pull the cotter pin out and put it on your rag (where the grease cap is already residing, right?), and be sure to lay it down in the same direction as it pointed when it was in place.

5 Slide the castellated nut or nut-lock-and-nut combination off the **spindle**. If it is greasy, wipe it off with a lint-free rag. Lay it on the rag next to the cotter pin.

Note that some cars have a nut with a cotter pin sticking through it, others have a nut-and-nut-lock combination. Which kind does your car have?

6 Grab the **brake drum** and pull it toward you. *Do not slide the drum off the spindle yet.* Now push the drum back into place. The things that are left on the spindle are the *outer wheel bearings.*

7 Carefully slide the outer **bearing**, with the washer in front of it, off the spindle. If you see little specks of silver in the grease, or the rollers are pitted or chipped, you need a new bearing. As long as you're removing your bearings, you might as well repack them, provided they're repackable. All this involves is squishing wheel bearing grease back into them. Instructions in Chapter 12 show you how to do this wonderfully sensual job.

8 If you don't want to get into packing your bearings right away, *do not* attempt to wipe any grease off the bearings, no matter how icky they look. Just put them in a little plastic bag and lay them on your rag, pointing in the right direction. The bag will keep dust from getting into them. A speck of dust can quickly wear a bearing out.

9 Look at the drum again. In the center hole you can see another set of bearings. These are your *inner wheel bearings.* If you are *not* planning to

The Things You Have to Remove to Get at Your Brakes
Delco Moraine Division, General Motors Corp.

repack them, *do not* attempt to take them out of their seat in the drum. This would break the **grease seal**, and you would have to get a new seal to replace it.

10 Carefully slide the drum off the spindle, with the inner bearings still inside it, if you aren't repacking them now. Work in a well-ventilated area and be very careful not to inhale the dust from the drum because it probably contains asbestos; if you get it in your lungs, you run the risk of asbestosis and asbestos emphysema. For safety's sake, *never* attempt to blow away the dust with compressed air. Instead, saturate the dust completely by spraying the drum with brake-parts cleaner according to the instructions on the can. Wipe the drum clean with a rag; then place the rag in a plastic bag and dispose of it immediately.

11 Take a look inside the drum. There are probably grooves on the inner walls from wear. If these grooves look unusually deep, or if there are hard spots or burned places, you should have your mechanic check the drums out with that special micrometer that we mentioned before. If the drums are not worn past legal tolerances, they can be reground (or turned) rather than replaced. There is a special machine called a "brake-drum lathe" that does this job in a relatively short time. It should not be a major job in terms of expense. You could do it yourself at a school auto shop, as most classes have the machine.

12 Now, look at the rest of your brakes, which are still attached to the **brake backing plate**.

a Your **wheel cylinder** should show no signs of leaking brake fluid.

b Your **brake linings** should be evenly worn, with no bald spots or thin places. They should be at least ¹⁄₁₆ inch thicker than any rivet. They should be firmly bonded or riveted to the brake shoes. Most brake linings will give from 10,000 to 20,000 miles of wear. Some will last even longer. If yours have been on your car for some time, they will have grooves in them and may be somewhat glazed. If your brake drums have

Drum

Backing plate

Wheel cylinder    Retracting springs

Brake shoes

Anatomy of a Drum Brake
Automotive Information Council (AIC)

been wearing evenly and your car has been braking properly, disregard the grooves and the glazing unless your linings look badly worn.

c If your linings are worn, have them replaced at once. This will involve replacing the brake shoes with "new" ones that have new linings on them.

d Do not attempt to replace shoes, linings, or wheel cylinders yourself unless you do it under the eye of an auto shop instructor. If you choose to do this, the money you save will more than pay for your tuition! The job is neither difficult nor complicated. It just needs supervision.

e To have the work done for you, find a reliable brake shop. Try the Yellow Pages, or have the mechanic at your local service station steer you to one. Call a couple of places and ask for estimates on rebuilding your brakes. Avoid the cheapest place as well as the most expensive!

f Always replace **brake shoes** in sets (four shoes for two front or rear wheels is a set) for even performance. Replacing them all at once is even better.

g Take a look at the self-adjusting devices on your brakes. Trace the cable from the anchor pin above the wheel cylinder, around the side of the backing plate, to the adjuster at the bottom of the plate. To help you, there are illustrations of the most common self-adjusters in the earlier part of this chapter. Is the cable hooked up? Does it feel tight? If your brake pedal manages to apply your brakes before it gets halfway down to the floor, the adjustment is probably just fine. If not, and if the cylinders, linings, shoes, etc., are O.K., then the adjusting devices may be out of whack. Just making a couple of forward and reverse stops should fix them. If this doesn't work, you may need an adjustment at a service station. Don't attempt to fiddle with these yourself.

When you have finished inspecting your brakes, it is time to replace everything. Here's how to do it:

**How to Reassemble Drum Brakes**

1 As you did with the drums, saturate the dirt on the brake backing plate with brake-parts cleaner; then wipe it off with a clean, *grease-free* rag and throw the rag away. Don't blow the dust around—it can contain asbestos and cause serious lung damage. If you'd rather not deal with it at all, just leave it alone.

2 Replace the wheel hub and brake drum on the spindle. If the drum isn't clean inside, you can wipe it with a lint-free rag and some alcohol, but don't use water, don't inhale the dust, and wrap the rag in a plastic bag and dispose of it immediately.

3 If you've followed the instructions in the next chapter and have repacked your wheel bearings, check those instructions again and replace the grease seal and the inner bearings.

4 Replace the outer wheel bearings and the washer. Don't let any dirt get on these! Take a look at how you've laid the bearings down on your rag, checking with the illustration on "things you have to remove to get at your brakes," to be sure you will put them back properly. Don't wipe off the grease!

5 Replace the adjusting nut by screwing it on firmly and then backing it off half a turn and retightening it "finger tight." Another way to do this is to back the adjusting nut off one full notch (60°) and, if the notch doesn't line up with the hole in the spindle, back it off just enough until it does. Then, spin the wheel by hand to be sure that it is turning freely. If it isn't, loosen the nut a bit more.

6 Insert the cotter pin into the hole in the castellated nut. It should clear the outer grooves and go all the way through.

7 Bend the legs of the cotter pin back across the surface of the nut to hold it in place.

8 Replace the grease cap.

9 Follow the instructions in the last chapter for replacing your wheel, lug nuts, and hub cap.

10 Go clean yourself up with some nice hand cleaner.

Here are a couple of "nevers" to remember when working on your brakes:

—Never step on your brake pedal when you have the drum off your brakes. You can literally blow the brakes apart! The pistons can fly out of the ends of the wheel cylinders because the brake shoes will not be stopped from moving outward by the drum.

—Never use anything but brake fluid in your brakes.

—Never get oil anywhere near your brake system. It blows up rubber and will destroy the cylinder cups and dust boots on your wheel cylinders. If it gets on your brake linings, they will not grab the brake drum.

—Never get brake fluid on a painted surface—it will destroy it.

—Never remove wheel cylinders, brake shoes, or tamper with the self-adjusting device on your brakes without supervision.

1 Follow the instructions for jacking up your car and removing a front wheel in the previous chapter.

2 Look at the disc. Do not attempt to remove it from the car. Check it for heavy rust and for uneven wear. Rust generally does no damage unless the car has been standing idle for a long time and the rust has really built up.

3 If your brakes have not been working properly—if they've been grabbing or causing the car to swerve to one side—remove the two screws from the **splash shield**.

4 Look at the brake pads inside. If the linings look very worn or unevenly worn, they will probably have to be replaced. If the linings have worn to the metal pads, the disc will probably have to be reground as well.

**How to Check Disc Brakes**

Disc linings should be checked every 10,000 miles. Relining, caliper maintenance, and disc grinding should be left to a professional unless you do the job at school. Go to a brake shop (use the Yellow Pages or ask a friendly mechanic to steer you to one) for this kind of work rather than to the corner garage. Call a couple of shops and ask for an estimate. Choose neither the cheapest nor the most expensive. And read all the "nevers" mentioned above.

**How to Reassemble Disc Brakes**

1 Screw the splash shield back on (if you've removed it).

2 Lift the wheel back onto the spindle, making sure the bolts for the lug nuts go through the holes. Finish replacing the wheel, lug nuts, and hub cap according to the instructions on tire changing.

If the first set of brakes you look at seems to be in good condition, and if your car has been braking properly, there is probably no need to check on the other three. Just remember to check a different set the next time. However, if your car has not been behaving properly, then go on checking each set until you've found the culprit. Don't be surprised to find that the brakes on your rear wheels seem a bit different. There are no wheel bearings on rear wheels, and the shoes and linings are shorter and narrower. Also, your parking brake is usually hooked up to your rear brakes if you have drum brakes on your car.

Drum brake
Bleeder nozzle

**How to Bleed Your Brakes**

For those of us with squishy-feeling brakes, an easy way to get the air out of the lines is by **bleeding** the brakes. To do the job, you will need either a *brake bleeder wrench* or a combination wrench which fits the bleeder nozzle on your car, a can of the proper brake fluid, a clean glass jar, and a friend.

1 Behind each of your brakes is a little nozzle called a *brake bleeder nozzle*. It may be easier to reach this if you jack up the car. If you are going to crawl underneath, lay an old blanket, or a thick layer of newspapers, down first to keep from getting chilly on the cold cold ground.

2 Find the ignition wrench that fits the nozzle and loosen the bleeder nozzle. Now tighten it again (not too tight).

3 If you have a small piece of flexible hose that will fit over the end of the bleeder nozzle, attach it and place the end of the hose in the jar. Then fill the jar with brake fluid to cover the end of the hose. If you haven't anything that will fit, just keep the jar near the nozzle so that any fluid that squirts out will land in the jar.

4 Have your friend pump your brake pedal a few times. If the car is jacked up, be sure that the wheels are blocked in the direction in which the

Disc brake
Bleeder nozzle

Bleeder Nozzles on Drum and Disc Brakes
Richard Freshman

Using a Bleeder Hose to Bleed Your Brakes
The Bendix Corp.

How to Bleed Your Brakes
The Bendix Corp.

car would roll, and that the car is not parked on a hill, before you let your friend get into the car with you underneath it. Leave your tires in place so the car will bounce and leave you some clearance if it should fall.

5  Have your friend say "down" when pressing the brake pedal down, and "up" when releasing it. This will sound like an exercise class, but what the heck!

6  When your friend has pumped the pedal a few times and is holding the pedal *down,* open the bleeder nozzle. Brake fluid will squirt out (duck!). If there is air in your brake lines, there will be air bubbles in the fluid. It is easiest to see these bubbles if you are using the hose-in-the-jar method, but you can also see them without it.

7  *Before* your friend releases the brake pedal, *tighten the nozzle.* If you don't do this, air will be sucked back into the brake lines when the pedal is released.

8  Tell your friend "release" and listen for "up." Then repeat the whole loosening and tightening sequence again and again until there are no more air bubbles coming out with the fluid. Do this to one brake after another until the air is out of each brake line.

9  *This is important:* After you have finished bleeding *each* brake, open your master cylinder and add some more brake fluid to the fill line. If you ne-

Bleeding a Master Cylinder
Delco Moraine Division, General Motors Corp.

If you have a bleeder nozzle, use the hose-and-jar method. Or bleed the cylinder at the brake line connections.

glect to do this before going on to the next brake, you run the risk of draining all the fluid out of the master cylinder and drawing air into the lines from the top. Now, that isn't fatal—it simply means you would have to go back and bleed your master cylinder until you had sucked the air out of that end of the system—but who needs the extra work? In case you goof and have to bleed the master cylinder, it's the same deal as bleeding your brakes (friend and all). Just bleed it at the point where the brake lines attach to the cylinder, and at the master cylinder bleeder nozzle if there is one. Meanwhile, back to the brake lines...

10 When you have finished the job, and brought the brake fluid level in the master cylinder back to full for the last time, drive the car around the block. The brake pedal should no longer feel spongy when you depress it. If it does, check the master cylinder again to be sure it's full and try bleeding the brakes one more time (this is not unusual, and it doesn't take as long as it sounds). If there is no air left in the lines and the brakes still don't feel right, you may need a new master cylinder. You should definitely consider installing it yourself—at an auto shop. All it involves is disconnecting the old one (a bolt or two and the hoses leading to the brake lines have to be released), removing it without spilling brake fluid on anything painted, installing the new one, filling it with brake fluid, and bleeding it. If it seems like too much of a hassle, then have a professional do the job. There shouldn't be much labor to pay for, and if you choose a brake shop wisely, the whole deal shouldn't cost too much. But I had Tweety's master cylinder replaced before I got smarter, and it cost me about $60. Later, I helped a friend to replace a master cylinder with a rebuilt one. The rebuilt master cylinder cost $28, instead of the $40 I'd paid for a new one, and there were no labor charges (naturally). Whatever you do, just be sure that, when the job is finished, they (or you) bleed the brakes and the master cylinder to get all the air out of the lines.

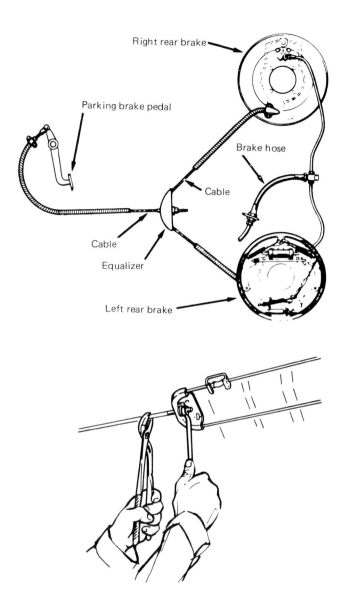

Right rear brake

Parking brake pedal

Brake hose

Cable

Cable

Equalizer

Left rear brake

Equalizer

Intermediate lever

Slot

Rear cables

Front cables

Front cable

Equalizer

Rear cables

Integral Parking Brakes and How to Adjust Them

Bendix Corp. and Delco Moraine Division, General Motors Corp.

They may look different, but they all adjust in the same way.

**How to Adjust Your Parking Brake**

Here's how to adjust your parking brake: These instructions will work only if you have **drum brakes** on your *rear* wheels. If you have a **manual transmission** you may have a transmission-type parking brake, and this should be adjusted professionally. Your service manual may tell you which kind you have, or you can crawl under the car and see for yourself. Since most of us have the traditional kind (sometimes called *integral* parking brakes), let's deal with them:

Under-the-Car Views of Two Popular Parking
Brake Adjusters
Richard Freshman

1 Jack up the car (a hoist would be lovely) and make sure it is secure. You can also slide underneath with a work light if you don't want to jack it up. Leave your parking brake off.

2 Trace the thin steel cables that run from each of your rear wheels until they meet somewhere under the back seat of the car.

3 Where they meet, there should be a device (usually a bar and a screw) that controls the tension.

4 Turn the screw (or whatever else you've got) until the cables tighten up. Then tighten the screw nuts to hold it in place. You may have to hold the cable to keep it taut.

5 Get out from under there and test-drive the car to see if the parking brake is working. It shouldn't have to be pulled or pushed to the most extreme level to make it work. As the cables loosen up again, you will have to pull the handle up higher, or push the pedal down lower, to engage the brake. You should not be able to drive with the brake on.

6 While you're at it, is the parking brake warning light on your dashboard working? If not, check or replace the bulb or fuse. If that doesn't work, get someone to check the connection between the light and the brake; there may be a short in it.

Well, that's it. If you get in the habit of checking your brakes every 10,000 miles (and more frequently as they get worn), you will be able to stop worrying that they might fail you at a crucial moment. If you are a good buddy to your brakes (and this involves driving properly as well as those periodic visits), they will prove to be your very best friends. After one of those breathtaking emergency stops on the freeway, I always say "Thanks, pals" and promise myself that I'll peek in soon to check on my brakes and lines to be sure they are in good shape.

# Wheels and Tires: How to Keep Your Car from Getting Sore Feet

Now that we've covered your brakes, let's talk about your **tires**. There is a two-way relationship between your brakes and your tires. Just as poor braking action will result in increased tire wear, if your wheels are properly balanced and aligned, and if your tires are properly inflated and in good condition, they can help to stop your car up to 25 percent faster!

There is also a strong correlation between tire inflation and tire wear. If your tires are underinflated, the outer treads will wear out faster. If they are overinflated, the center of the tread area will go. So to get more mileage from your tires, plus better braking action and a smoother and quieter ride, you ought to know a bit about buying, checking, and maintaining the tires on your car.

In this chapter, I'll tell you something about the different kinds of tires available. There are many different types, made of several different materials, and just as you wouldn't choose sneakers for a formal evening (or wear your finest shoes to the beach), you don't want to be silly about putting the most expensive, long-lasting, high-speed radials on an old car that is just going back and forth to the shopping center.

We'll go into how to check the tires on your car and how to "read your treads" for clues about how well your car is performing. If these clues show that you need to have your wheels balanced or aligned or your tires replaced, I'll provide enough information for you to be sure the work is done, done properly, and for the right price. Your treads can also tell you if you've been driving properly, and we'll go into that too.

There is practically nothing you'll have to do (in terms of physical labor) with this chapter, so just find a comfortable place to read this, relax, and enjoy it.

**Tire Construction**    Every tire has three major parts:

**The Tread**    The *tread* is the rubber part of the tire that gets most of the wear and tear. The tread patterns help the tire to grip the road (as the ad used to say) and to resist puncturing. These patterns are also excellent indica-

Anatomy of a Tire
The Goodyear Tire & Rubber Company

tors of tire wear, and we will get into reading these clues later in the chapter.

**The Bead**

The *bead* is a strip of steel wire that is wrapped around and around to help hold the tire on the rim of the wheel.

**The Casing**

It is here that the specific character of the tire is determined. The *casing* helps the tire to keep its shape when inflated, instead of blowing up like a balloon. It is basically made up of various materials, called *cords,* that are wrapped around the *bead* in different ways. The cords can be made of different materials, and it is

The Three Basic Types of Tires
The Goodyear Tire & Rubber Company

Bias-ply

Bias-belted

the type of material and the way it is wrapped that determine the kind of tire and its price. Originally, cotton was used for the cords in the casing, but this soon gave way to other materials with greater advantages. Here they are in order of durability and cost:

1 *Bias-ply tires:* Also called "diagonal" because the cords are wrapped around the bead at angles that form overlaps. They come in a variety of materials:

  a *Nylon:* Very strong and relatively low-cost. The basic disadvantage of nylon cord tires is that they tend to lump a bit when the car is not being used. Consequently, drivers experience a slightly bumpy ride for the first few minutes. After a short time, the cords smooth out and the ride is smooth for the rest of the trip. This condition is called *flat-spotting.* If you don't mind a little roughness at first, nylon cord tires are still a good buy, especially if you tend to drive locally in street traffic and don't do a great deal of long-distance, high-speed driving.

  b *Rayon:* These are also quite strong. They cost a little more than nylon but do not develop flat-spotting.

  c *Polyester:* Even stronger, with no flat spots and a smooth ride. They last longer but are more expensive. If you don't expect to get more than another 20,000 miles out of your car, or don't want to keep it for more than two more years, forget these.

2 *Bias-belted tires:* These are constructed in the same manner as bias-ply tires but feature belts of another material which wrap around the circumference of the tire to give you longer wear, to resist punctures, and to provide more directional stability. This last feature cuts down on "tire squirm," a term used by manufacturers to indicate a tendency of unbelted tires to move from side to side as they track down the road.

  a *Glass-belted tires:* Usually made of polyester, in the same manner as the bias-ply polyester tires, but have fiberglass belts for better high-speed performance.

  b *Steel-belted tires:* The same, but with steel belts for greater strength and longer wear.

3 *Radial-ply tires:* These are quite different in structure from bias-ply and bias-belted tires. They provide better handling, especially at high speeds; tend to grip the road more, especially when cornering; and can deliver twice the mileage of bias-ply and belted tires. Most of the radial-ply tires available are steel-belted, but there are glass-belted radials and others belted with synthetic materials, too.

Radial–ply

Now, before you rush out and buy a set of steel-belted radial tires, there are a couple of other things to think about. Tire wear is affected by a number of factors besides construction: the condition of the car's braking and suspension systems; inflation and alignment; driving and braking techniques; driving at high speeds, which raises tire temperatures and causes them to wear prematurely; how great a load you carry; road conditions; and climate. With all of this in mind, let's take a look at the various types of tires in terms of cost and average mileage:

*Bias-ply or diagonal tires* are the cheapest new tires you can buy. They'll average 15,000 to 25,000 miles.

*Bias-belted tires* cost about 30 percent more but they're good for roughly 25,000 to 35,000 miles.

*Belted-radial tires* can be more than twice as expensive. Wear varies from 25,000 miles and up, depending on the material the belts are made of, but top-of-the-line steel-belted radials can provide from 40,000 to as much as 60,000 miles, under average conditions.

Before making a decision, take a close look at your own situation. Are your driving habits hard on tires? If you tend to "burn rubber" when cornering, starting, and stopping, you know where that rubber will come from. Do you do most of your driving on high-speed freeways or in stop-and-go traffic? On unpaved rocky roads? Is your car exposed to long hours in the hot sun? Do you carry heavy loads? How much driving do you do?

If you only drive a couple of thousand miles a year, don't expect a pair of 40,000-mile radials to last forever. Rubber treads tend to rot eventually because of the ozone in the air, which causes cracks and hard spots in the sidewalls. The condition is called **ozone**

**checking.** For this reason, if you've used your tires for more than 40,000 miles, even if the treads are in good shape, have the tires checked to be sure they haven't become prone to blowouts and leaks from deteriorating rubber.

Above all, how long do you intend to keep your car? It's foolish to put a pair of expensive steel-belted radials on a car you intend to get rid of in 10,000 or 20,000 miles. Oh, it's possible to put well over 100,000 miles on a car—especially if you're maintaining it yourself—but if you have more than 60,000 miles on your car and you drive it pretty hard and don't intend to do a major restoration on it, I wouldn't buy a pair of 40,000-mile tires for it. Your car may surprise you and outlive its tires, but chances are it won't. I'd gamble the other way. If your car turns out to be a Motorized Methuselah, the worst that can happen is that you'll have to buy it another pair of cheapos, for those last few, sweet miles together before they all go to the "great used-car lot in the sky."

**The Secrets on Your Sidewalls, Revealed!**

Many people are willing to spend extra dollars for tires with names like "MACHO WILD-CATS" or "TOUGH GUYS" embossed in large white letters on the sidewalls, but did you know that there's a wealth of information embossed on them in quiet little black letters that can be more valuable in the long run? And it's *free*—if you know how to decode it. Even if you're not the inquisitive type, the following data will help in buying and maintaining tires:

**Tire Size Codes**

Until around 1978, tire sizes were indicated by alphanumeric codes, such as D78-14. Then, with the adoption of the metric system, the codes changed drastically. Today the new codes are much longer and provide more information. Tire dealers are required by law to have leaflets available which explain tire grades and ratings. They can also tell you which metric codes replace the old alphanumeric designations.

Here is the information provided by a common metric tire code, P205/75R-14:

P   = *Passenger* (T = *Temporary*)

205 = *Tire width,* measured across the tread, from one sidewall to the other, in millimeters (205 mm)

75   = *Tire series:* the ratio of the tire's height to its width

R   = *Tire type* (R = radial, B = bias-belted, D = diagonal or bias-ply, E = elliptic)

14   = *Diameter of the wheel,* in inches (14″)

The proper tire size for your car can be found in the **owner's manual** or on a sticker affixed to the vehicle. If neither exists, ask your dealer. Although you should never buy tires that are smaller than those specified for your car, you can buy tires a size or two larger (providing the car's wheel clearance allows it), for better handling or load-carrying ability. Ask your mechanic or a reputable tire or car dealer for advice on this one.

**Tire Quality Grade Codes**

The Uniform Tire Quality Grading System rates tires for treadwear, traction, and temperature but, because these ratings are set by the *manufacturer* and not by an objective testing service, they may not be accurate. If you want to use them to compare various brands, consult *Uniform Tire Quality Grading,* a free consumer pamphlet published by the National Highway Traffic Safety Administration, 400 7th St. S.W., Washington, DC 20590. Your dealer should have a copy on hand. Look for these grades on the sidewall or on a sticker affixed to the tread. Here's what they mean:

*Treadwear:* A comparative number grade based on carefully controlled testing conditions. In the "real world" a tire rated 200 would have twice the tread wear of one rated 100—*if* all other wear factors were equal.

*Traction:* This A, B, or C grade represents the tire's ability to stop on wet asphalt and concrete pavement under controlled conditions. The grades are based on straight ahead braking only, not on cornering or turning.

*Temperature:* A, B, or C grades that represent heat resistance and ability to dissipate it if the tire is inflated properly and not overloaded. C meets U.S. minimum standards.

**DOT Identification & Registration**

The DOT identification number on the sidewall tells where and when the tire was manufactured. For example, here's how to decode DOT WOKAABC 262:

DOT means the tire meets or exceeds U.S. Department of Transportation safety standards
WO identifies the plant where the tire was made
KA is the tire size (P194/75R14)
ABC identifies the brand or characteristics of the tire
262 says the tire was made during the 26th week of 1982

The DOT number serves as a registration number for the tire, in case of a recall. *When you buy new tires, make sure that they are properly registered.* Under federal law, the dealer is required to put the DOT number of the tire and the name and address of the dealer on a form which is then sent to the manufacturer. Although tire outlets owned by manufacturers and certain brand-name outlets must send them in, independent tire dealers can simply fill out the forms and give them to the customer to mail to the manufacturer. Unlike guarantees and warrantees, *in case of a recall you won't be eligible to receive replacements unless your tires have been properly registered and you respond to the recall within 60 days.*

**Other Sidewall Information**

Check sidewalls to see how many plies and cords the treads and sidewalls contain and whether the tire is tubeless. Look for the following safety data, too:

MAX LOAD: How much weight the tire can bear safely, usually expressed in kilograms (kg) and pounds (lbs)
MAX PRESS: How much air pressure the tire can safely hold, usually expressed in pounds per square inch (psi)

**Tips for Buying Tires**

—Never use two different-size tires, especially on the same **axle**.

—If you are replacing just one or two tires, put the new ones on the rear wheels for better traction.

—Never buy fewer than two bias-*belted* tires at a time if your others are bias-*ply*. Put the new pair in the rear.

—Never buy less than a full set of radial-ply tires. The ride is so different that these tires would throw your car out of **alignment** if you tried them in combination with traditional tires.

—Remember that new tires must be "broken in," so don't drive faster than 60 mph for the first 50 miles on a new tire or spare.

—If you buy retreads, be sure they're from a well-known, major manufacturer.

—To store tires that are not being used, keep them in the dark, away from extreme heat and electric motors that create ozone.

**Tire Rotation**

There are two points of view on tire rotation. Some say you can get up to 20 percent more wear if you rotate your tires. Others caution against rotating them because it might tend to hide the distinctive tread-wear patterns that provide clues to poor **alignment**, worn **shock absorbers**, and defective **brakes**. If your tires seem to be wearing evenly and you haven't had any of these problems, then rotate them if you like—but look at them first.

**Wheel Balancing**

**Wheel balancing** does a lot to eliminate some of the principal causes of tire wear. Since balancing is a job that should be done with the proper equipment, and since that equipment is costly and tire balancing is generally cheap, go to a professional and have them do the job for you. Just remember that there are two kinds of wheel balancing: *static* and *dynamic*.

*Static balancing* deals with the even distribution of weight around the axle. You can tell if you need to

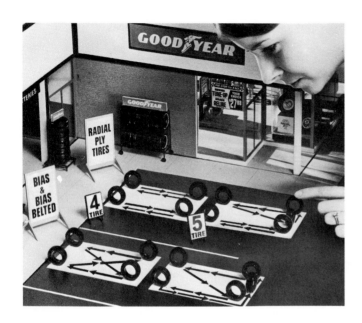

How To Rotate Your Tires
The Goodyear Tire & Rubber Company

have your wheels statically balanced if the wheel tends to rotate by itself when the car is jacked up so that the wheel no longer touches the ground. It rotates because one part of the wheel is heavier than the rest. The mechanic will find the heavy spot and apply tire weights to balance it out.

*Dynamic balancing* deals with the even distribution of weight along the spindle. Wheels that are not balanced dynamically tend to wobble and to wear more quickly. Since imbalance can only be detected when the tire is rotated and centrifugal force can act, correcting dynamic balance is a relatively complex procedure. Some service stations have computerized balancers that will not only balance the wheels but will locate the places where the weights are needed and decide how much weight to add. It should not cost more than a few dollars to have your tires balanced both statically and dynamically.

If you plan to have your wheels balanced professionally, it is a waste of time to rotate your tires yourself beforehand. The mechanics will have to remove them to balance them, so they might as well rotate them, too. If you want to make sure the garage does the job properly, the illustration above shows the proper sequence for bias and radial tires, with or without a spare tire. Note that radial tires should not be moved from one side of the car to the other, only from front to rear on the *same* side of the car.

If you own a front-wheel-drive vehicle, rotate the tires as though they were radials, *no matter what type of tires they are.*

A cheap and easy way to substantially improve your car's handling and extend the life of your tires is to be alert to signs of misalignment and have your wheels aligned immediately if the signs appear. This job is usually called **front-end alignment**, because it is the front wheels that generally get out of line. They get that way because of hard driving with dramatic getaway starts and screeching stops, hitting curbs hard when parking, accidents, heavy loads, frequent driving over unpaved roads or into potholes, and normal wear and tear as the car gets older. Occasionally the rear wheels will need realignment as well, but usually only on cars with independent rear suspension like VWs, Corvettes, etc.; or on heavy-duty equipment, cars that pull trailers or boats, or cars that have had an accident that threw the frame out of line.

I used to think that front-end alignment involved taking a car that had been bashed out of shape and literally pulling it back into line. Untrue. All they do is adjust your wheels to make sure they track in a nice straight line when you drive. To do this, they use special equipment to check six points:

1 **Caster** has to do with the position of your wheels in relation to the spindle support arm. If properly adjusted, it will make your wheels track in a straight line instead of weaving or shimmying at high speeds.

2 **Camber** is the inward or outward tilt of the top of the wheels when viewed from the front of the car—how "bow-legged or knock-kneed" they are. If they don't hang properly, your tires will wear out more quickly and your car will be harder to handle.

3 **Toe-in** involves placing your tires so that they are ever so slightly "pigeon-toed" when the car is standing still. This keeps them from being forced too far out when the car is running at high speeds. The

## Wheel Alignment

Caster

Camber

Toe-in

Moog Automotive, Inc., St. Louis, Missouri

result should be a nice straight track when the car is moving quickly.

4 **Toe-out** is the opposite of toe-in (how about that!). It affects the way your car tracks on turns. No wheels should toe out. If yours do, you're in for some very freaky steering!

5 **Turning radius** is the relation of one front wheel to the other on turns. If you turn to the right, the right front tire is going to make a smaller circle than the left front tire does. To the left, the reverse holds true. Bent steering arms can cause this kind of misalignment. If your tires are "squealing" sharply on turns, this may be your problem.

How do you know if your wheels need aligning? There are two things to check: your steering equipment and your tire wear. Do this at least once a year, more often if you have been involved in any of the situations mentioned previously.

## How to Check Your Steering

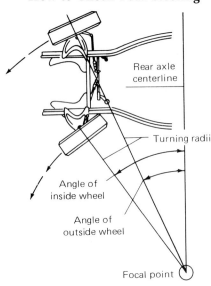

Turning Radius
Moog Automotive, Inc., St. Louis, Missouri

This is easy. Just stand outside your car, near the door on the driver's side. Stick your hand through the open window and move the steering wheel, with your eye on the left front tire. If you can move the steering wheel at all before the tire starts to move, then you need to have your steering and your alignment checked. There should be no play in the steering wheel before the signal is transmitted to the tires.

As you drive your car, be alert to signs that it is not handling as easily as before. If it seems to have a mind of its own and begins to resist you on turns (and pulling out of turns), take a good look at your tires for signs of wear caused by misalignment.

If you want to determine whether or not you should (a) buy new tires, (b) have your wheels balanced, (c) have your front end aligned, or (d) change your driving habits, you can tell a lot by simply reading your tire treads for clues. The chart on this page and the illustrations on this and the next page will show you what to look for.

1 Look at each tire. Are there nails, stones, or other debris embedded in the treads? Remove them. *But,* if you are going to remove a nail, first be sure your spare tire is inflated and in usable shape. If when you pull a nail, you hear a hissing sound, push the nail back in quickly and take the tire to be fixed. If you aren't sure if air is escaping, put some water on the hole and look for the bubbles made by escaping air. If you're still not sure whether the thing may have caused a leak, check your air pressure and

**How to Check Your Tires for Wear**

It's Time for New Tires When Tread-Wear Indicators Appear.
The Goodyear Tire & Rubber Company

## How to Read Your Treads

| Clue | Culprit | Remedy |
|---|---|---|
| Both edges worn | Underinflation | Add more air Check for leaks |
| Center treads worn | Overinflation | Let air out to manufacturers specifications |
| One-sided wear | Poor alignment | Have wheels aligned |
| Treads worn unevenly, with bald spots, cups, or scallops | Poor alignment | Have wheels aligned |
| Edges of front tires only worn | You are taking curves too fast | Slow down! |
| Saw-toothed wear pattern | Poor braking habits | Learn to pump your brakes or slow down |
| Whining, thumping and other weird noises | Poor alignment, worn tires or shocks | Have wheels aligned or buy new tires or shocks |
| Squealing on curves | Poor alignment or underinflation | Check wear on treads and act accordingly |

Severe underinflation   Overinflation        Poor alignment      Poor alignment

What the Signs of Poor Tread Wear Mean
Moog Automotive, Inc., St. Louis, Missouri

then check it again the next day to see if it is lower (I'll show you how to do this next). Tires with leaks should be patched by a professional. If the leak persists, get a new tire.

2 Look at the treads again. Most tires have **tread-wear indicators** built into them. These are bars of hard rubber that appear across treads that have been worn down to $\frac{1}{16}$ of an inch of the surface of the tire. If these indicators appear in two or three different places, less than 120 degrees apart on the circumference of the tire, the tire should be replaced. If your tires don't show these indicators and you think they are worn, place a thin ruler into the tread and measure the distance from the base of the tread to the surface. It should be more than $\frac{1}{16}$ of an inch deep.

3 If your front tires are more worn than your rear ones and show an abnormal wear pattern, you probably need to have your wheels aligned.

4 If you keep losing air in your tires, have your local service station check them for leaks. Sometimes a leak is caused by an ill-fitting rim. The garage has a machine that can fix this easily.

5 If the garage cannot find a leak and if your rims fit properly, and you are still losing air, you probably have a faulty **tire valve** that is allowing air to escape. You can buy snap-in tire valves to replace the ones on your car. Look for the number molded into the base of the tire valves on your car; then buy new ones. At least one of the four valve caps should have a notched end for removing and replacing tire valves. If you don't have one, buy one.

**How to Check Your Air Pressure**   Tires should be checked at least once a month and before every long trip to see that they are inflated properly. Underinflated tires wear out faster, create excessive heat, increase fuel consumption, and make the car harder to handle. Overinflated tires can "blow out" more easily, wear out faster, and make the car unstable and unsafe to handle. Here's how to check yours:

1 Buy an accurate *tire gauge* at a hardware or auto supply store.

2 To determine the proper air pressure for your tires, look for "MAX PRESS" on the sidewalls to see how many pounds per square inch (psi) they should contain. Some tires give you a minimum amount, as well. You can find the same data in your owner's manual or on a sticker somewhere on your car. If all else fails, ask your dealer. Some manufacturers suggest you put more air in the front tires than in the rear ones, for easier handling and better traction. Keep the tires on the same axle at equal pressure.

3 Remember that in hot weather the pressure in your tires will rise as the air in them heats up and expands. This is also true after you have heated up your tires with a lot of driving, so check tire pressure in the morning before you use the car.

4 Conversely, in cold weather the pressure will fall as the cold air contracts. If it gets very cold and it looks as though it will stay that way for some time, you might want to add a bit of air to bring the pressure back up if you get a low reading. Generally though, tires that are correctly inflated will tend to wear properly in spite of weather ups and downs. Just check them every couple of weeks to keep things under control, and try not to check them under extreme temperature conditions or after you've been driving around.

5 *To use the tire gauge:*

a Remove the little cap from the **tire valve** that sticks out of your tire near the wheel rim. There is no need to remove your hub cap to do this.

b Place the rounded end of the tire gauge against the valve so that the little pin in the gauge contacts the pin in the valve.

c Press the gauge against the valve stem. You will hear a hissing sound as the air starts to escape from the tire.

Press the round end of the gauge against the pin in the valve stem and read the numbers on the stick that emerges from the bottom of the gauge.

Use a Tire Gauge to See If Your Tires Are Properly Inflated.
Richard Freshman

d At this point, you will see a little stick emerge from the other end of the tire gauge. It will emerge partway almost as soon as the air starts to hiss, and it will stop emerging almost immediately. Without pushing the stick back in, remove the gauge from the tire valve.

e Look at the stick without touching it. There are little numbers on it, and the last number showing is the amount of air pressure in your tire. Is it the right amount? If it seems too low, press the gauge against the valve stem again. If it still doesn't move, you need more air. Do this for each tire, and don't forget the spare!

6 If your tires appear to be "low," note the amount that they are underinflated, then drive to your local gas station. At this writing, it costs nothing to use the air hose at most stations. Isn't it nice to know that some things are still free? But, since it's free, you're probably going to want to do it yourself. Here's how:

a Remove the cap from the tire valve.

b Check the air pressure in the tire with *your* gauge to see how much it's changed so you can add the same amount of air the tire lacked before you drove to the station.

c Add air in short bursts, checking each time with *your* tire gauge. The gauges on many station air hoses have been found to be inaccurate.

d If you add too much air, let some out by depressing the pin on the tire valve with the back of the air hose nozzle or with the little knob on the tire gauge.

e Check again until you've got it right. No one hits it on the head the first time.

O.K., you've kept your hands clean long enough. It's time to get back to work. All this running to professionals for wheel balancing and alignment and stuff has probably made you soft and lazy. So get prepared to do another job—not a big or difficult one—that can save you money and improve the life of your car and its fuel consumption if you do it more often and you do it yourself. What am I talking about? Those "lube and oil jobs" that service stations keep throwing at you…

# 12

# Lubrication and Suspension: How to Give Your Car a Long and Happy Life

When we think about "the good life" we tend to think in terms of freedom from pressure, discomfort, and "friction." If your car could talk (mine can only sing), it would probably agree. When you consider that the temperature in your car's combustion chambers can get as high as 4,500 degrees F., with high pressures, the shock of combustion, and many metal parts rubbing and grinding against one another, you can see that a car that is *not* adequately protected against heat and **friction** will come swiftly to an untimely death. Luckily, this kind of protection is cheap and easy to ensure. It is simply a matter of providing sufficient lubrication to keep things running smoothly and then making sure your car gets regular attention.

**A Tragic Tale**

Before we came West, my husband's car resided, as I've mentioned before, in a garage, where it was looked after by professional mechanics. Herb was always willing to agree when he was told the car needed **oil** and **lubrication**. Yet when we took the engine apart recently, we found that a lack of proper lubrication had led to trouble, for the **camshaft** had been practically worn away! When this happens, you choose between major and expensive surgery or you get rid of the car. We got rid of the car, in favor of a new, and saner, small car with lower fuel consumption and a higher potential resale value in these economy-conscious times. As we sadly watched the macho-mobile vanish into the sunset, the major question in our minds was, "How did it happen?" The answer, unfortunately, was that we had been dependent on someone else for lubrication reminders, and we had trusted someone else to do the job properly. Not only had we been paying at least twice as much as it would have cost to do the job ourselves, but we had ended up paying to replace a car that could have gone almost twice as far if it had been lubricated properly.

If this sad story inspires you to undertake your own lubrication work, then dear old m-m will not have been towed away in vain. Besides, it is just plain silly to pay someone a lot of money to do something you can do yourself in a couple of minutes. And if you can unscrew the top of a jar and use a can opener, you can change your oil without any trouble.

**The Engine**

Oil pan

Oil filter

Oil pump

The Lubrication System
Automotive Information Council (AIC)

Unless your **oil filter** and/or your **oil drain plug** is *very* hard to reach, there are good reasons why you should change your oil and oil filter yourself. It's cheaper, and believe it or not, it will save you time! Changing your oil yourself takes about 15 minutes and very little work. All you have to do is unscrew a plug and a filter, let the oil drain out, and pour some new oil in. If you have to telephone the garage to make an appointment, then drive the car in and either wait for it or find a ride home and back again to pick it up, and then wait until they've got your bill made up, it will take much, much longer. So even if you don't do another thing to your car, if you don't try changing your oil yourself, I'll confiscate your copy of this book! If you can't reach the filter or plug, or you want to chicken out of the **lube job** now and then, the good news is that most garages have low-priced oil and lube specials.

**Why You Should Change Your Oil Yourself**

To choose the proper kind of oil, you should know what the oil will be called upon to do. When your car is at rest, the oil slops around quietly in a container located at the bottom of the **crankcase**, just below your engine. This container is called the **oil pan**. When the car is operating, the oil is circulated through special channels in the engine, where it helps to cool and clean the engine and to provide a nice slippery cushion that keeps the moving engine parts from grinding one another into oblivion.

**How to Choose the Proper Kind of Oil for Your Car**

Since the oil pan is lower than the engine, and since it is located where the air that rushes past the moving car can cool it, the oil can pick up some of the heat as it travels around inside the engine and then cool off when it circulates through the oil pan. Although this is not enough to keep most engines sufficiently cool without water, it helps.

**How Oil Cools Your Engine**

Most engine oils contain some detergent, which helps to flush out the grunge and muck that accumulate inside your engine. Not only will detergent oil remove

**How Oil Cleans Your Engine**

and dissolve this old **sludge**; it helps to prevent new gobs of the stuff from forming. Believe me, you have no idea of the meaning of any of those yucky words until you've looked into the engine of a car that has not had its oil changed often enough. There are masses of black slimy stuff, hunks of undefinable vileness, and pebblelike particles clinging to everything. It is hard to see how these engines function at all. Even more depressing are the all-too-visible signs of wear on steel parts that have been eroded away by this ugly stuff. If your car hasn't had its oil changed in at least 6,000 miles, you can consider the growls coming out of its engine as cries of pain!

Brush the tears from your eyes—we're past the tragic part.

### How Oil Cuts Down on Friction and Does Other Nice Things

By far the most important thing that the oil in your engine does is form a cushion between moving parts which helps them to slide past one another easily. This cuts down **friction**, which in turn dramatically reduces the heat and wear that friction can cause. An engine that is keeping its cool, and operating with less effort, uses less fuel. So if you change your oil on a regular basis, you can cut fuel consumption and reduce air pollution. To illustrate this, let's take another look at something we discussed earlier.

If you recall, each piston is attached to a **connecting rod**, which has a hole in it for the **crankshaft** to fit through. This makes the crankshaft and the connecting rod operate together. Take a closer look at that hole in the enlarged portion of the illustration. As you can see, there is a space around the hole that is always filled with oil. When the car is running, the oil pressure forms a cushion that keeps the connecting rod (and its bearings) from ever touching the crankshaft. Instead, each moves on its cushion of oil to prevent friction and wear, which is important since the rod exerts 4000 pounds of pressure every time it moves down. This same principle is applied to other moving parts in your car.

Oil Forms a Cushion to Keep Your Crankshaft and Your Connecting Rod from Wearing Each Other Away.
Jack Herlihy

Oil also retards corrosion in your engine by enveloping the particles of water and acid which are present. These particles, plus the solid particles that it holds in suspension, are what turn oil black and thin it out. We change the oil to get rid of this stuff before it can build up to the point where the oil cannot do its job properly.

### How Often Should You Change Your Oil?

Some manufacturers suggest that oil should be changed every 7,500 miles, but they're the guys who'll get to sell you a new car if your old one wears out prematurely. To be on the safe side, I change oil every 3,000 miles or three to six months, whichever comes first. Cars that do a lot of short stop-and-start driving in city traffic never get hot enough to evaporate the water that forms in the crankcase and builds up the sludge I've so graphically dealt with above. Older cars generally carry around a collection of yuck that has accumulated over the years, and this stuff will foul up your nice clean oil fairly rapidly. Dirty oil just doesn't do the job as well as fresh oil does. The additives boil out; sulphuric acid forms in the crankcase and eats metal parts; and water collects over a period of time and forms sludge. Also, the oil holds more and more abrasive particles of metal suspended in it, and these particles wear away the parts of the engine which the oil was supposed to protect.

All oil looks pretty black within a couple of days after an oil change, so the only way to avoid running on oil that is so dirty it has become a liability is to keep a record of when it was last changed and to change it frequently—even as often as every 2,000 miles if necessary. By changing your oil frequently you can probably get *twice* the mileage out of an otherwise good engine!

### How to Tell Which Kind of Oil to Buy

Oil is rated and identified by its **viscosity**, or its ability to flow. In cold weather, oil thickens and becomes less able to flow through your engine. In hot weather it thins out, and although it flows well enough, it might become so thin that it would not prevent friction. The questions to consider when buying oil are:

1 What kind of oil have you been using?
2 What kind of oil does your owner's manual recommend?

3 Do you live where it is very cold? Hot? Is it mountainous?

4 Are there sharp changes in temperature where you live or where you are going?

5 How old is the oil in your car? How many miles have you driven it?

6 Is your car still under **warranty**?

There are two types of oil on the market, *single-viscosity* oil and *multi-viscosity* oil. (These are also called "single-weight" and "multi-weight.") Most multi-viscosity oils also have detergent added to them to help clean your engine. Most of the single-viscosity oils have detergent, too, but a few don't.

In recent years, multi-viscosity oils have come into their own, and most cars from 1968 on are designed to use them. The most common is 10W–40, which doesn't thicken when the weather is cold and won't thin out when the temperature gets hot. This oil is fine for all year round and especially good if you're driving from a warm sea-level climate to the mountains, where it is colder. The most common single-viscosity oil is 30 weight, which is generally considered to be the best-weight oil for older cars which are *not* going to face extremes of temperature. If you normally use 30 weight oil, in really hot weather you might switch to 40 weight, which is thicker. If it gets really cold, 10W (the "W" means the oil is recommended for use during the winter) will be better because it is thinner and will flow more easily after the cold thickens it. Or you can use 10W–40 all year if you want to be covered for all weather conditions.

"Aha!" you might say, "all I have to do is buy 10W–40 oil and I'm covered for everything!" Maybe, but not definitely. There are several things to consider:

1 If you have an older car that has been running on cheap 30 or 40 weight oil for most of its life, it has built up quite a bit of sludge because some of the single-weight oils don't have detergent in them. If you suddenly switch to a multi-viscosity oil, the detergent in it would free all that gook in your engine and it would start to slosh around and really foul things up. It's better to let sleeping gook lie unless

you want to invest in having your engine disassembled and cleaned. If your car is running well, don't do it. The engine would have to be taken apart and put back together again, and you might start trouble where none existed before. Just stick with the same old nondetergent stuff you've been using and forget the new-fangled stuff.

2  If your car has been logging a great many miles, and has been running on 30 or 40 weight oil, the 10W–40 stuff is not going to be consistently thick enough to lubricate the worn engine parts, which have become smaller while wearing down, leaving wider spaces between them. To keep the oil thick enough to fill these gaps, you should switch to heavier oil as your car gets older and starts to run more roughly or to burn up oil more quickly. So if you've been running on 30 weight oil, you would switch to 40 weight, at least during the summer, when oil tends to thin out. Tweety's manual called for 10W–40 oil, but I have her on straight 40 weight oil now that she has more than 80,000 miles to her credit. There is even 50 weight oil for the real oldies!

3  If you have a brand-new car, it probably has "break-in" oil in it. You must use this stuff for the first 6,000 miles; then you can switch to whatever they specify. It will probably be 10W–40, unless you live in the desert or on top of a high mountain. Then, when your car gets much older, you can switch to a heavier single-viscosity oil if you need it. Be sure to use whatever the owner's manual recommends while your warranty is in effect, or you can invalidate it.

One last note about this. No matter what you are using, if you are planning on a driving trip into the high mountains, at any time of year, use 10W–40 oil for the trip, and go back to your usual stuff when you return.

Whenever you buy oil, look for the major brands, like Pennzoil, Quaker State, Valvoline, or check *Consumer Reports*. There is a lot of reclaimed oil on the market. No matter how crazy about recycling you are, cheap reclaimed oil is junk. Stay away from it. The good stuff is often on sale in supermarkets and at auto supply stores. If you spot a sale, buy a case and stash it away.

**Synthetic Oils**

The major brands of synthetic oil are excellent investments if your car has a new or nearly new engine and doesn't leak oil. Synthetic oil can cost over five times as much as ordinary oil, but it can last 20,000 miles and requires fewer oil filter changes. Follow instructions in your owner's manual or the label on the can. The best test is how it works in your car. If your car doesn't run as well on synthetic oil, it's not the stuff for you.

**Oil Classification Codes**

A number of classification codes have been established for automotive oils for gasoline engines. You may see these codes on the oil you buy. Here's what they mean:

SA—Utility Gasoline. The lowest grade. Avoid it.

SB—Minimum Duty Gasoline. Not durable enough. Avoid it.

SC—1964 Gasoline Engine Warranty Maintenance Service. For 1964 to 1967 cars and trucks. The base minimum. Avoid it if you drive a newer car, and consider it a last resort for older cars.

SD—1968 Gasoline Engine Warranty Maintenance Service. Designed for maintenance of 1968 through 1970 models. May also be O.K. for 1971 cars.

SE—1972 Gasoline Engine Warranty Maintenance Service. For 1972 to 1979 models.

SF—1980 Gasoline Engine Warranty Maintenance Service. Until superseded by SG, this will provide maximum protection against oil oxidation, high-temperature engine deposits, rust, and corrosion. Even if your car is an older model and its owner's manual specifies an earlier-rated oil, you can use this top-rated oil with better results.

If you drive a **diesel** car, you will find the codes for diesel lubrication in Chapter 14.

There are three basic types of **additives**. The first type extends viscosity. The second loosens junk and dissolves gummy deposits. The third acts as a friction lubricant to make the oil "tougher" under high extremes of temperature and usage.

Most popular additives are basically viscosity extenders. They thicken your oil when it starts to thin out. They also keep the oil from foaming at speeds of over 100 mph. And by making the heavy-weight oil even thicker, they can also keep a very very old engine that is running poorly on 40 or 50 weight oil from clanking. Other additives have already been added to the oil you buy to help it in the following ways:

1 To pour better in cold weather.
2 To prevent corrosion of the metal parts of the engine.
3 To cut down on friction between moving parts.
4 To prevent foaming at high temperatures.
5 To clean the engine.

Remember that most oils that do not advertise the presence of additives already have most of this stuff in them. Also, no amount of additional additives will improve the performance of oil unless the oil you started with was of the best grade. So if you buy a well-known brand, you are going to get all the protection you need in these categories if your engine is in reasonably good shape. If you use high-grade oil of the proper weight and classification and change it often, you would do well to leave the rest of the additives on the store shelves. They may provide *temporary relief* if your engine is in the process of disintegrating, but they are not a *cure* for a worn-down, filthy, miserable, old engine.

If you have one of those sad, clanking workhorse engines, you must investigate the following alternatives:

1 Put the car out of its misery. You might be able to sell it to a wrecker, because junkers will sell its body parts.
2 Find out if it would respond to rebuilding. The price will depend on how many parts have to be replaced and how much work is involved. Prepare

**A Word About Additives**

SCLAD
000-249

to pay up to $2,000, or even more, for this. Is the car worth it?

3 Buy a new engine or a good **rebuilt** one, and have it installed. This is still expensive, and I'd do it only for a classic car.

4 Just keep putting in heavier and heavier oil, get used to the noise, and drive it into the ground.

**What About Oil Filters?**

Under the hood of your car, sticking out of the engine, is what looks like a tin can screwed into your engine block. This is your **oil filter**. As the oil circulates from the oil pan through your engine, it passes through this filter, which cleans it and removes some of the sludge. The oil filter should be changed every time you change your oil, especially if you are going to do it less frequently than every 3,000 miles. Oil filters sell for very little at auto supply stores; at a service station you'll pay more.

Most filters screw on and off. If your old filter hasn't been changed in a long time, you may need an oil filter wrench to unscrew it. But tighten the new one by hand to avoid crushing the seal.

Oil Filter

Oil Filter Wrench
K-D Manufacturing Co.

**How to Change Your Oil**

1 Check your owner's manual for the type of oil recommended for your car. If you have no manual, call your friendly neighborhood service station (the ones who changed it last time), and ask them what weight oil they used in your car. If you can't do that, call a local dealer who sells your kind of car and ask him. Also find out from one of these sources how many quarts of oil your car requires.

Most cars require around 5 quarts of oil.

2 Go to the auto supply store and buy your oil. Also buy an oil filter for your make and model car. An **oil drain plug** gasket is also cheap, and it is wise to buy one in case the one on your car needs replacing. If it doesn't, just save the **gasket** for later.

3 Find an old basin that is low enough to fit under
your car without having to jack the car up, and
large enough to hold all the old oil in the car (usually about 5 quarts). Line the basin with a large
plastic garbage bag, opened so it can catch the oil,
leaving the basin clean.

4 Take all this stuff, plus a funnel or an oil can
spout (if you have neither, a screwdriver or a beer-
can opener will do), to your car. You should also
have a lint-free rag and a dirty old thick rag as
well.

5 Warm up your car so that the gook will get
churned up and will flow out of the engine easily.
You *don't* want it so hot that you will burn yourself. When the car is fairly warm, shut off the
engine.

Oil Can Spout

6 Look under your car. You should be able to see
and reach a large nut located under the **oil pan** at
the bottom of the engine. This is the **oil drain
plug**. It unscrews with the aid of a combination
wrench. Feel around to see what size wrench you
will need. If the plug is too hot to touch, let the
car cool off for a while longer.

7 If you cannot reach your oil drain plug easily, you
will have to either crawl under your car to reach it
or jack up the front end. If you choose to jack up
your car, be sure to reread Chapter 9 to be sure
you do it *safely*. Use jack stands and don't jack it
up too high, or the oil may not drain out of the oil
pan completely.

8 Push the basin or container under the oil drain
plug so that it can catch the oil. It would be wise to
place all the stuff you are going to use within easy
reach, so you won't have to jump up and run
around in the middle of the job.

9 With your combination wrench, unscrew the oil
drain plug until it is *almost* ready to come out.
Then take that dirty rag in your hand and give the
plug a last quick turn by hand to release it. Pull

The Drain Plug Is Located at the Bottom of
Your Oil Pan.
Richard Freshman

An Oil Filter Is Screwed into the Side of Your Engine.
Richard Freshman

your hand away quickly so you will not get oil all over it. If the plug falls into the container, you can retrieve it later. The oil will now drain out of your engine into the container. While it is doing this, get out from under the car and take a look under the hood.

10  Remove the cap from the **oil filler hole** at the top of your engine. This large cap is easy to recognize: it lifts or screws right off, revealing a largish hole.

11  Under the hood, and sticking out of the side of your engine, is your **oil filter**. As I've mentioned before, it looks like a tin can.

On some cars, you can easily reach the oil filter by leaning under the hood. Unfortunately, other car manufacturers have placed the filter so that it must be reached from under the car. If your car is one of these, you will have to get under your car. When you really get down to it (no pun intended), jacking the car up and getting under it isn't really too horrendous. It only takes about three extra minutes of your time, and if you lie on an old blanket or mattress pad, you won't find the task more tiresome than changing a light bulb on a ceiling fixture. Not the stuff that dreams are made of, but not a nightmare either.

Unscrew the oil filter with an oil filter wrench if you can't do it by hand. Remember that, like most other things you'll find on a car, the oil filter unscrews if you twist it counterclockwise. The filter will have oil in it, so be careful not to dump it on anything when you remove it. Throw the old oil filter away, and make sure the gasket of the old filter has been completely removed from the engine.

12  While the old oil is draining out of the engine, open a new can of oil. Here's the best way to do it:

a  If you have an oil spout, just jam the end into the can. It will open the can and form a handy spout for pouring. If you have no oil spout, put the can on the ground, place one foot on the can to steady it, and jab a long screwdriver into the top of the can near the rim. That will make a hole for the oil to pour out of. (Of course, you can always use a beer can opener, but the screwdriver has more macho in automotive circles.) Don't make more than one hole; you don't want the oil to pour too fast or you'll get it all over the engine before you hit the fill hole.

13 Dip a finger in the new oil and moisten the gasket on the top of the new oil filter. Then screw the new filter into the engine where the old one was. Follow directions on the filter, or turn it gently until it "seats" and then turn it a half or three-quarter turn more. Unless the filter manufacturer specifically recommends it, never use an oil filter wrench to tighten a filter. It should fit tightly, but you don't want to damage the gasket, because it will leak.

14 Now get under the car again and wipe around the place where the oil drain plug goes. If your oil drain plug hasn't been leaking, and the old gasket looks (or feels) all right, just wipe the area and replace the plug.

If you need a new gasket, scrape the old one off the outside of the oil pan with a screwdriver or a paint-scraper and place the new one on the pan before you replace the plug.

If you don't use the new gasket and, later on, you find that your car is leaking oil from around the plug, it's not the worst thing that can happen. Just remove the plug again, catch the oil in a nice *clean* container, and pour it back into the **oil filter hole** when the new gasket is in and the plug is back in place. Most gaskets will hold through several oil changes. I've never replaced mine.

15 Here is a helpful hint that I got from Don, my advisor: Always use a *system* when you do an oil change. This means you should do each part of the job in order and not change that order from job to job. This may sound unduly restrictive to those of you who like to improvise, but if you ignore this advice, you may find you've added the new oil before replacing the plug or before changing the filter. In either case, you're going to wind up with your brand-new oil all over the ground

Pour Fresh Oil down the Oil Fill Hole at the Top of Your Cylinder Head Cover.
Richard Freshman

An Oil Dipstick
Richard Freshman

and not enough oil in the engine to drive to the store for more. Also, the *minute* you replace the oil drain plug, *always* tighten it completely and put the new oil in. That way you won't forget to put in the new oil (don't laugh; people have done that and ruined their engines in a couple of miles).

Here's how to add new oil:

16  When the oil filter is installed and the oil drain plug has been replaced, use a funnel, an oil spout, or just good aim to pour fresh oil into the oil filler hole. Stop 1 quart short of the amount your car should hold.

17  Replace the oil filler cap and run the engine for 30 to 60 seconds while you check for leaks from the oil drain plug and around the filter. The oil pressure light on your dashboard should go out in 10 or 15 seconds (or if your car has an **oil gauge**, the needle should move off "Low"). If this fails to happen, check under the car and around the engine for leaks. Running the engine circulates oil into the new oil filter, and since filters hold from a half to a full quart of oil, you want to be sure your filter is full in order to get an accurate reading on the oil dipstick.

18  Shut the engine off and wait 5 to 10 minutes for the oil to settle into the oil pan. Then remove the oil dipstick, wipe it with a clean, lint-free cloth, and shove it back in. Pull it out again and check it. Keep adding oil, a little at a time, and checking the stick until you reach the "Full" line on the dipstick.

19  Remove the basin from under the car, drive around the block a couple of times, let the oil settle down again, and recheck the dipstick and the dashboard indicator. Remember, *never* drive a car that's telling you its oil pressure is low. Since oil not only lubricates but also helps cool the engine, you can ruin your engine if you drive even a short distance with insufficient oil or with a defective oil pump.

Oh, what do you do with the plastic bag full of old oil? Remove it from the basin, tie it off, and take it down to the nearest service station that still changes oil for its customers. Since they sell their old oil to recyclers, why should they refuse to accept your donation?

Although this took 19 steps to explain, it should not take more than 15 minutes to accomplish once you've bought the necessary stuff. When you see how easy it is, you will tend to change your oil more frequently and your car will ride better, last longer, and burn less fuel. And you will feel pretty happy with yourself, too!

If you are really feeling good about the oil change and you've got the car jacked up anyway, you might want to consider doing the lube job now.

**What a "Lube Job" Involves**

Basically, a **lube job** involves applying lubricants (various kinds of **grease** and oil) to some of the moving parts under your car, and to some of the rubber parts to keep them supple. This is what you will need:

1 *A decent grease gun:* Borrow one at first; if you hate it, you won't have made a big investment. If you can't borrow one, buy a cheap one. You can always sell it to a friend who is just getting into auto maintenance and buy yourself a super one if you plan to do the job repeatedly. Most **grease guns** come with a couple of adapters to fit the grease fittings on your car, and with an extender for hard-to-reach places. If your gun doesn't have these, you can get an adapter or an extender for a couple of dollars if you need one. (You may not. Some grease guns are fitted to take grease cartridges, which save you the time and mess of loading them.)

2 *The proper kind of grease:* Consult your owner's manual, service manual, or the salesperson at the auto supply store. They have manuals that tell all.

Your **transmission fluid** and **brake fluid** are lubricants, too. See Chapter 5 about checking these, if you haven't already done so.

There are other parts of your car that need periodic lubrication. These can include **steering** parts, **trans-**

**mission** shift linkage, **clutch** linkage, **parking brake** cables, **differential,** and **driveshaft universal joint** fittings. Since some of these are hard to find, hard to reach, and most require a special kind of lubricant, and since you can get into trouble if you don't deal with them properly, I'd suggest that once or twice a year you take the car to a good dealer with service facilities and have him lubricate *everything,* including your distributor. The rest of the time, just lubricate the things I point out and you will be way ahead of the game.

O.K. Just what *are* you going to lubricate? First, the **grease fittings** under your car:

**Everything You've Always Wanted to Know About Grease Fittings (and Probably a Good Deal More...)**

Grease fittings are those places on your car that hold lubricants that protect moving parts from one another. These parts must be kept packed with grease to keep them moving freely without friction. Naturally, these are usually the parts that move the most, aside from the parts inside your engine (which are lubricated with oil).

Think about your car. Where does most of the movement take place when you drive? (Not counting the kids in the back seat, if you have any.) Well, the front wheels turn on **wheel bearings,** and they can change direction when you steer because of the **steering linkage** between the steering wheel and the front wheels.

Where Most of the Movement Takes Place When You Drive
Moog Automotive, Inc., St. Louis, Missouri

The car moves up and down on its **suspension system** and **shock absorbers**, which keep the car level although the wheels may be bobbing up and down on a rough stretch of road. All these areas can have grease fittings called **lubrication points**, and replacing, repacking, or replenishing the grease in them is called a "lube job," a "grease job," or a "chassis lube," depending on who is doing the talking. Your car should be lubricated every 3,000 miles.

**The Steering Linkage and Ball Joints**

The steering linkage and ball joints are the areas that you are going to go after with your grease gun. The steering linkage is the system that connects your steering wheel with your front wheels. When you turn your steering wheel, the steering linkage causes your front wheels to respond by moving in the proper direction. Along the steering linkage, whenever two parts meet, there is a type of **ball joint** called a **tie rod end** that is filled with grease. As the two parts of the linkage move against each other, they are cushioned by the grease in these tie rod ends. This keeps them moving freely and prevents friction that would wear them away.

The steering linkage actually connects to the wheels,

Tie rod end

Idler arm ball joint

May have ball joint

Tie rod end

Steering Linkage
Automotive Marketing Division, Dana Corp.

Zerk fitting

A Closer Look at a Tie Rod End Grease
Fitting
Moog Automotive, Inc., St. Louis, Missouri

which are held in place by a **spindle** that goes through
the wheel and is attached to upper and lower **control
arms**. (That's the same spindle as the one the brake
and bearing assembly fitted onto in Chapter 10.) The
control arms allow the wheels to turn in any direction.
To keep things moving freely, ball joints are located at
the points on the control arms where the movement
takes place. We keep the ball joints (and the tie rod
ends) filled with grease to cut down on friction. Each
ball joint and tie rod end should have a grease fitting
that allows you to lubricate it.

On some cars, all or some of these ball joints are designed for *lifetime lubrication,* which means that the
grease has been pumped in and sealed so it can't get
out. Because this kind of sealed system also prevents
dirt, air, and water from getting *in,* these lifetime lubrication systems seem to last pretty well. And you
don't have to lubricate them yourself, ever. Of course
if they break down, it is a bit more expensive to install
a whole new part, but they don't break down very often. If your owner's manual tells you that your car has

Tie Rod Ends
Moog Automotive, Inc., St. Louis, Missouri
Tie rod ends cushion the friction caused by
steering your car.

one of these, be happy, skip the rest of this portion, and go on to the **suspension system**.

For the rest of us, each ball joint has two basic parts: a rubber ball-shaped **boot** and a little metal nozzle called a **zerk fitting**. Some cars come with *plugs* on the ball joints instead of with zerk fittings. You can replace the plugs with zerk fittings by unscrewing the plugs and screwing in the fittings. The fittings then become permanent fixtures on the ball joints, and you can throw the plugs away (or save them for a rainy day).

The boot holds the grease, and the zerk fitting lets the grease into the boot and keeps it from getting out again. Most ball joints are sealed, in the sense that the only place for the grease to go in and out of the joint is through the zerk fitting. If you fill this type of joint too full, the boot will burst and have to be replaced or lubricated more frequently (as were the joints on cars before the booted ball joint was invented).

Other ball joints are designed to allow the grease to escape so that the new grease you insert pushes the old grease out the other end. Be sure to check under your car to see which type of ball joints you have. Your car dealer can also tell you if you aren't sure whether those gooey ball joints are sealed ones that have burst or the kind that are supposed to have a back door.

Another way to tell is, if only *one* of the ball joints has a mound of grease coming out of it when you put the new grease in, then it is probably a sealed joint that has burst. If they all tend to leak grease when you add more, they are probably supposed to do so. In any case, *never* add grease until the ball is tightly packed. There should be plenty of "give" when you squeeze the sides of the ball. Simply wipe the zerk fitting, fit the grease gun onto it (use an adapter if you need one), and *gently* squeeze a *little* grease into the joint.

If you squeeze too much grease in and the ball feels hard, you will have to unscrew the zerk fitting with an ignition wrench and squeeze enough grease out of the ball joint to relieve the pressure. Then you will have to screw the zerk fitting back into place. This is not a terribly pleasant thing to have to do—it is time-

Upper control arm

Lower control arm

Ball Joints Are Located on the Upper and Lower Control Arms.
Moog Automotive, Inc., St. Louis, Missouri
Each front wheel has an upper and lower ball joint, mounted on the control arms. Ball joints permit the steering and suspension movement of the wheels.

Zerk fitting

A Closer Look at the Zerk Fitting on a Ball Joint
Moog Automotive, Inc., St. Louis, Missouri

Boot

Housing socket

Rubber pressure ring

Zerk fitting

Anatomy of a Ball Joint
Moog Automotive, Inc., St. Louis, Missouri

consuming and messy—so be careful to squeeze the grease in a little at a time. I know this because I've done it, and those teeny greasy zerk fittings are hard to hang on to. But if you goof, take heart. If "Thumbs" Sclar can do it, so can you!

"Fine!" you say, "but how do I find the ball joints in the first place?" O.K., here's where to look:

1 Some of the more enlightened owner's manuals will tell you, but not many of them.

2 The service manual for your car will tell you the location and nature of each lubrication point (or grease fitting or ball joint or whatever they call them in your book).

3 Every service station has a *lubrication manual* that is published by one of the major oil companies each year. These manuals show every lube point and grease fitting for every car manufactured during the year of publication. Your service station probably has the last couple of years on hand. If you don't have a service manual for your car, ask to see the lube manual if you are having trouble locating the lube points on your car.

4 Before you go down to the service station, however, why don't you try to find them yourself by looking under the front end of your car. Trace the bar that runs from one front wheel to the other. Grease fittings are usually found at the base and top of the arms that attach your wheels to the steering linkage (these are the **steering knuckles**) and at the center of the steering linkage where the tie rods meet the center. Some cars have as many as 8 or 10 of these fittings. Others have none. Most have 4 to 6.

If you really have trouble finding yours and you are unwilling to throw yourself at the mercy of your service station for just a look at the lube manual, then give in and take the car in for a lube job someplace where they will let you hang around and ask questions. Casually ask for a look at the lube manual, or ask them to point out the lube points that they are going to work on. Say, "How many lube points does this model have?" They will usually be happy to show you and to answer your questions. People who work on cars love to talk shop (and most of them never suspect that

Some of the Places to Look for Grease Fittings on Your Car
Moog Automotive, Inc., St. Louis, Missouri

"civilians" are secretly planning to do the work themselves next time). If you get a real talkative one, you've found a gold mine, and be sure to ask about the rest of the job too.

For you lovers of recipes, let's go over the whole thing again, one step at a time:

1  Find out how many, and where, your lube points are.

2  Wipe off the first zerk fitting and try to fit your gun to it. Does it fit? If not, you may need an adapter. Can you reach it? If not, you may need an extender.

3  Load your grease gun with grease. The kind you want is called *suspension* **lube grease**.

4  Place the grease gun to the fitting and *gently* squeeze a little bit of grease into it. If the joint looks too hard and full, squeeze some out if you have the kind of fitting that has a back door. If you have a sealed joint, just add enough grease to fill it out a little. It should not be hard and full of grease. If the joint looks full before you start, don't add any grease at all; just go on to the next joint.

5  Repeat this until you have serviced all the joints.

6  If you've overfilled a sealed joint, take an ignition wrench of the proper tiny size and unscrew the zerk fitting (counterclockwise). Squeeze the excess grease out and replace the fitting.

Grease Gun with Adapter and Zerk Fitting
Richard Freshman

7 If one or more of your ball joints boots has burst, have it or them replaced *immediately*. The parts these joints protect get a lot of action, and you can be in for a very expensive job (or risk losing your ability to steer) after a very short trip on a nonfunctioning ball joint.

When you buy a new car, ask the service manager if there are any trouble spots on that model that might benefit from having a grease fitting inserted. I had several installed on my new truck, for very little money. If you have a persistent squeak you might want to check to see if having a grease fitting installed in the area will quiet things down.

Now let's talk about the rest of the suspension system.

**Lubricating the Suspension System**

The **suspension system** technically includes the steering linkage, but in my mind, it is easier to deal with these things in terms of the function they perform. Therefore, try to see the steering linkage as concerned with the *horizontal* directions in which the car can go, and the suspension system as concerned with the *vertical* movement of the car as it travels over the road. An automotive engineer might quarrel with these distinctions, but we are basically concerned with understanding how a car works and how to fix it, and for these purposes, the two systems should be viewed separately.

**What Does the Suspension System Consist Of?**

Underneath your car are the main elements of the suspension system that supports your car and keeps the passenger compartment relatively stable on bumpy roads. Many of the key parts are made of hard rubber. In the interests of preventive maintenance, get under the car and check for torn rubber fittings like ball joints and for damaged rubber bushings between tie-rod ends, idler arms, and other places where moving parts of the suspension fit together. (If you find the idea unappetizing, ask your mechanic to check these the next time you bring your car in to be serviced.)

Assuming you're adventurous enough to get a little dirty and are willing to crawl under your car, you're probably curious about how the system works, so here's a general view of the basic parts of the suspension system.

There are various types of **springs** used to absorb the bumps and keep your car level on turns. These can be **coil springs, leaf springs**, or **torsion bars**—or a combination of more than one of these. A good many U.S. cars have leaf springs at the rear wheels, and coil springs at the front wheels. Some trucks and buses have air suspension systems, but this is rarely, if ever, used for passenger cars.

**Leaf springs** are usually made up of several metal plates, piled one on top of the other. These are called *leaves*. The reason for using several relatively thin metal leaves instead of one thick metal bar is that, as a bar bends, the top of the bar has to stretch a little. If the bar bent too far, it could split from the top down. The leaf springs can bend more flexibly because each leaf bends independently and they can slide on one another instead of breaking. Each end of a set of leaf springs is attached to the *frame* at the rear of the car

**Springs**

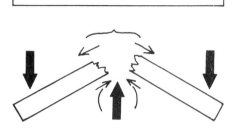

Leaf Springs Bend but Do Not Break Because They Can Slide Flexibly on One Another.
Alexandra Soto

Leaf Springs Have Rubber Bushings to Cushion Them.
Automotive Marketing Division, Dana Corp.

000-263

Dampening or steering resistance ball joint

Weight or load carrying ball joint
Note: control arm supports bottom of spring

If vehicle is equipped with torsion bars, they will usually be located as indicated

Dampening or steering resistance ball joint

Weight or load carrying ball joint
Note: control arm supports bottom of spring

Control arm bushings (upper)

Control arm bushings (lower)

**Shock Absorbers**

Front and Rear Coil Springs
Automotive Marketing Division, Dana Corp.
(*top & middle*) Front coil spring can sit on either the upper or the lower control arms. They are cushioned by the ball joints. (*bottom*) Rear coil springs have rubber bushings to cushion them.

SCLAU
000-264

with fittings that allow the springs to bend and move freely. These fittings usually have rubber **bushings** that allow the fittings to bend and twist freely and also absorb some of the vibration and prevent it from reaching the passenger compartment. These rubber bushings should be lubricated with rubber lube.

**Coil springs** look like old-fashioned bed springs. They are usually found at the front of the car, although they can be at both the front and the rear. At the front end, they help to cushion the bumps, vibrations, and steering movements. At the rear, they are suspended between control arms that have rubber bushings that should be lubricated with rubber lube.

**Torsion bars** are used mainly in Chrysler products. These are located in the front of the car, connected to the lower control arms. They twist to accommodate differences in the load that the car may be carrying, allowing the front wheels to move up and down freely.

There are other kinds of suspension systems, but the main thing to know is that most of them involve the use of rubber bushings to cushion the shock of the bumps and to allow the metal parts to move. Look near the wheels to find most of them. There are also various kinds of **stabilizers** in use. These keep the passenger part of the car from swaying and lurching on sharp curves and turns and when the wheels are traveling over uneven ground (a better solution than the legendary mountain goat that had its legs shorter on one side than the other for traveling along slopes!). Again, all you need to know is that you can lubricate the rubber parts yourself. If the suspension system gets out of whack, get a professional to diagnose and deal with the trouble.

**Shock absorbers** do most of the work of protecting the passenger compartment from bumps. These are located near each wheel. The way they cut down on vertical movement is interesting. When a car wheel hits a bump, it will tend to keep bouncing up and down long after the bump has been left behind, unless this is controlled. The bouncing effect is not only due to the fact that the wheel has an inflated rubber tire. It is also due to the fact that a coil spring that is either pulled or compressed will not just snap back into its former shape but will keep *oscillating,* or moving up and down, for some time afterward. Since the wheels are connected to the springs, they would move up and down with the springs until the motion finally died out. Shock absorbers allow the springs to compress freely and to return or rebound slowly—like the door check on a storm door that opens quickly and easily but closes slowly. For this reason, you can tell if your car needs new shock absorbers by leaning heavily on a fender or placing your weight on a bumper, and then releasing it suddenly, watching to see if the car returns slowly to its original position. (If it continues to bob up and down you need new shocks.) Another way is to stop fairly short. (If your car dips up and down a couple of times before coming to rest, you need new shocks.) Bad shock absorbers also increase tire wear, and they can cause you to lose control of the steering if you go over bumps and dips at high speeds. If any of these things seems to be happening to you, you should have your shocks replaced. Many cars now feature MacPherson strut suspension. This simplified and improved system takes up less space and is well worth having. The downside is that because MacPherson struts are surrounded by and assembled with the suspension springs, they are always under spring pressure and therefore *must* be replaced professionally. You can be taking your life in your hands if you tamper with them. Although it's not hard to replace *standard* shock absorbers, it can be a brutal job if you have to jack up your car and crawl under it. Unless you can do it under supervision on the lift at an auto class, I'd strongly recommend having a mechanic do it for you. To save money, if you see a super sale, buy the shocks yourself and just pay a mechanic to install them. The store will know what type of suspension system your car has and what kind of shocks it needs. Within limits, you do have a choice: "Heavy-duty" shocks provide a slightly harder ride; other shocks may not do as well with the entire family and two Great Danes in the car, but give a softer ride. Some shocks even provide automatic level control for vehicles that carry loads ranging from very heavy to almost weightless. Suit yourself. So much for the suspension system. Here's one more thing you can do yourself that involves lubrication:

Chrysler Products Have Torsion Bars for Load-Carrying Stability.
Moog Automotive, Inc., St. Louis, Missouri

MacPherson Strut
Monroe Auto Equipment Company

Standard Shock Absorbers
Monroe Auto Equipment Company

000-265

## How to Pack Your Wheel Bearings

This job can be done when you are checking your brakes or as part of a lube job. I prefer to do it when I'm checking my brakes because I have the wheels off and the whole thing taken apart anyway, and that's most of the work involved. First, check your owner's manual or dealer to see if your car's bearings are sealed. Front-wheel drives have sealed front bearings but some have packable rear ones. CAUTION: The bearings on four-wheel-drive vehicles are quite complicated and should be repacked professionally.

Wheel bearings come in pairs of *inner* and *outer* bearings. They allow your wheels to turn freely over thousands of miles by cushioning the contact between the wheel and the spindle it sits on with frictionless bearings and lots of nice gooey grease. This grease tends to pick up dust, dirt, and little particles of metal although the bearings are to some extent protected by the hub and the brake drum. It is important to check the bearings at least as often as you check your brakes, to be sure the grease has not become fouled with this stuff. If it has, the particles will act abrasively to wear away the very connection it is designed to protect, and the result will be a noisy, grinding ride. In extreme cases you could even lose the wheel! So be sure to check your bearings, and if they look cruddy, either repack them yourself or get a professional to do it. A good time to have your wheel bearings repacked is when they do a front-end **alignment** or a brake job, because they will have the wheels off anyway and this will eliminate paying for duplicate labor.

To check your bearings, or to repack them, here's what you do:

Wheel Bearing
Jack Herlihy

1 Turn back to Chapter 10 and, starting with "How to Disassemble Anything" on page 213, follow the instructions right through to the part about "How to Check Drum Brakes." Keep reading, even if you have disc brakes, because these instructions will show you how to get at your wheel bearings.

2 When you get to the part about sliding the outer bearings off the spindle, slide them off and take a good look at them. They are, usually, tapered *roller bearings,* not ball bearings (although I've heard that some cars have ball bearings).

3 Look in the spaces between these bearings. Do not wipe the grease off! Look at the grease. Does it have little sparkly silver slivers or particles in it? If it does, you must replace the bearings. If there are no particles in the grease, then you can start repacking your bearings with nice fresh grease (see 6 through 8 below for instructions) and then go on to the inner bearing.

4 Now, you cannot remove the inner bearing from its seat in the hub unless you have a new **grease seal** for it. So if this is just a checking expedition, leave the inner bearings alone until you're sure from the condition of the outer bearings that repacking is in order. Generally speaking, if the outer bearings look O.K., the inner ones are O.K. too. Just check each wheel, and put everything back according to the instructions for reassembling drum brakes in Chapter 10.

5 If, however, you are planning to repack your bearings, then slide the drum toward you, with the inner bearings still in place; but do not slide the drum completely off the spindle. Instead, screw the adjusting nut back in again and pull the drum or disc toward you and push it back. The adjusting nut should catch the inner bearing and its grease seal and free them from inside the hub. (If you have disc brakes, you will have to remove the **caliper** to get the disc off the spindle. If you have to get a disc caliper off to get at the inner bearings, I think you should do the job under supervision. It is not a difficult job; it's just that you might not get the calipers back on right, and that could cause your brakes to misfunction—which might be another good reason to consider an auto repair course.)

6 Take a good gob of wheel bearing grease (this is different from most chassis-lube grease), and place it in the palm of your left hand (if you're a righty). You might want to invest in a pair of cheap throw-away plastic gloves for this job, but there's something kind of nice about fresh, clean grease, and if you use gloves, you'll miss one of the more sensual aspects of getting intimately involved with your car. Hand cleaner will get the grease off easily, in any event.

How to Pack Your Bearings with Your Bare Hands
Jack Herlihy

7 Take the bearing and press it into the gob of grease with the heel of your other hand. This should force the grease into the bearing and displace the old grease out the other end. Be sure the grease is worked into every gap in the bearing. You want it nice and yucky. Now put your bearing down in a clean place, and do the inner bearing the same way.

8 Take a rag and wipe out the hole in the hub of the drum or disc where the inner bearing went. Then take another gob of grease and smooth it into the hole. Be sure the grease fills the *races* inside the hub where the bearing fits. Wipe off excess grease around the outside of the hole, or it will fly around when the car is in motion and maybe damage your brakes.

9 Insert the inner bearing into the hub, with the small end first. Take a new grease seal, and spread a film of grease around the sealing end—the flat, smooth side.

10 To fit the new grease seal into place properly, it should go in evenly, or it will bend or break and you will lose your grease. You can use a hollow pipe or a large socket from a socket wrench set that has roughly the same diameter as the seal. With the flat, smooth side of the seal toward you, place the seal in the hub opening, and use the pipe or socket to move it into the hub gently and evenly. It should end up flush with the outside of the hub or slightly inside it.

11 Now wipe the dirt off the spindle, and slide the drum or disc back on. Do it gently so you don't unseat the grease seal.

12 Now replace the outer bearing, smaller end first.

13 Then replace the rest of the stuff according to the instructions in Chapter 10, and be sure the adjusting nut is properly adjusted. If this has involved turning back and forth between chapters, please forgive me. The alternative was to say it all twice, and that would have increased the cost of this book. The effort should be worth the savings. In partial compensation here is a repeat of the diagram, anyway, to make things easier.

How to Get at Your Bearings
Delco Moraine Division, General Motors Corp.

That's all. You will be glad to hear that there are no wheel bearings to pack on your rear wheels (unless your car has front-wheel drive and the manual says the rear bearings can be repacked). There are *axle bearings*, however, but these must be replaced if they wear out; you cannot repack them. If your car is quite old and you hear a clicking or grinding noise from the vicinity of your rear wheels, you should have these bearings checked and replaced if necessary. It is easiest to hear worn axle bearings when you drive down an alley or a narrow driveway as the noise will echo loudly.

If you have found that your car needed most of the attention called for in this chapter, the chances are the other parts that are more difficult to lubricate should be attended to as well. Go to a good dealer with a service area, and ask them to lubricate your steering gear, power steering unit (if you have one), transmission shift linkage, clutch shaft, differential, distributor, and anything else that needs help. These parts don't have to be lubricated nearly as often as do bearings, but you should remember to have them professionally lubricated at least once a year (more often is better). There are instructions for checking and lubricating your differential in Chapter 13.

You will be pleased to know that this ends the dirty work that you can do on your car. If you've enjoyed tuning your car and caring for its various systems and you want to continue and do more-difficult work, by all means enroll in an auto repair course at a local school. Otherwise, do not attempt to do anything else yourself, no matter how easy it looks. I have deliberately left out those repairs that can get you into trouble if you attempt to do them without supervision. You might want to move on to a more technical repair manual just to decide whether the more difficult jobs are worth doing yourself in terms of time and trouble, but don't attempt to open your engine or to rebuild your brakes or to fiddle with your air conditioning, power accessories, etc., by yourself. Of course there are things you can do to improve the looks of your car—washing, waxing, and polishing it, cleaning and restoring the interior, and even minor bodywork. Chapters 16 and 17 will show you how.

But before you get started (or head for the showers) you may be interested in knowing how your transmission works, in case you are ever called upon to decide whether or not it should be repaired.

# Take the Drive Train: How to Understand Your Transmission System Without Losing Your Mind

The **transmission** system of your car is probably its most complex system in terms of automotive mechanics. It enables your car to move forward and backward at varying speeds, with maximum efficiency and minimum loss of power. In this sense, it is vitally connected to fuel consumption because the more power it takes to move the car, the more fuel it takes to provide that power.

Transmission systems vary from car to car. There are **manual transmissions**, for which you supply part of the power by shifting the gears and operating the clutch yourself, and there are **automatic transmissions**, which do these jobs for you.

Manual transmissions are fairly easy to explain, but I am convinced that the principles of automatic transmission were brought to Earth by some kindly extraterrestrial creature that came from a culture that operated on a very exotic system of logic. My attempts to fully penetrate the secrets of automatic transmission have been mind-boggling, and since the idea of ever fixing the thing yourself is unthinkable—except for people who have devoted their lives to it—let's be content to deal only with *what* automatic transmissions do, rather than go into detail about *how* they do it. This should give you a good idea of what should be done to keep your transmission in good condition, a good feel for diagnosing possible trouble, and at least a rudimentary knowledge of what should be done to fix your transmission if something goes wrong with it.

All cars have the capacity to move forward at varying speeds, to stop, and to move backward. Every time your car changes direction from forward to reverse, the rear wheels (or the front wheels on cars with **front-wheel drive**) have to be told which way to rotate. They must also know how fast to turn, and they must be supplied with extra power for starting, climbing hills, and pulling heavy loads.

As I've already mentioned in Chapter 3, the **drive train** on your car transmits the power from the engine to the wheels that move the car. You might want to go back to that chapter and reread the section on the drive train to get a general idea of what we're going to deal with. Start on page 38.

Still confused? O.K., let's look at it another way. Imagine that you are the captain of a ship. You have a lovely set of engines down in the engine room which are manufacturing power to move your ship. You are up on the bridge, surveying the blue ocean with your binoculars, when suddenly you see an iceberg dead ahead! You do not wish to run down to the engine room and personally reverse the propellers so that the ship will move backward. Instead, you pick up the intercom and call the engine room. You say, "This is the captain speaking. Reverse engines!" The person in the engine room hears you and does what is necessary. The ship is saved.

In a car, with a crew of one, you may be at the wheel giving orders. But you are giving them to a car that cannot hear you. How do the wheels know whether to move forward or backward? You need a piece of machinery to communicate with another machine. In this case, it is your **gearshift**. By moving the shift with your hand you can tell the transmission (the person in the engine room) what to do. Then the transmission tells the wheels via the **driveshaft**. Not only can you tell your wheels to go forward or backward, you can tell them how fast to go as well.

When you step on the **accelerator**, you are forcing the engine to produce power, but that power has to get to the wheels in the proper way for the wheels to respond most efficiently. There are ways to convey that extra power to the wheels by controlling how fast they turn in relation to the speed of the engine when you are going up a hill, pulling a heavy load, or just trying to overcome inertia and get the car started. So, your transmission has more than just forward and reverse gears; it has low and high gears too. Some transmissions have as many as five forward gears to control power and speed efficiently. The *lower* gears provide *more power* at *lower speeds*. The *higher* gears provide *less power* but allow the car to move at *higher speeds* because the wheels can turn faster in these gears at any engine speed.

Whether your car has an automatic transmission or a manual (sometimes called *standard*) transmission, you should understand how the manual transmission works. The principles involved are fairly simple, and an automatic transmission basically does the same things, but without a manual clutch and with less manual shifting.

## Manual Transmissions

A manual transmission consists of a **gearshift**, located either on the floor or on the steering column, which you operate by hand to tell your transmission what to do; a **clutch**, which you operate with your left foot to disconnect the transmission from the engine so that the gears in the transmission can change without getting tangled up with one another; and the **transmission** itself, which contains the gears and responds to messages from the gearshift and the clutch.

To get the complete picture, try to see the transmission as part of the **drive train**, which conducts the flow of power from the engine to the wheels.

In the old "toe-bone-connected-to-the-foot-bone" tradition, let's trace the flow of power down the drive train, from the engine to the drive wheels. You can follow it through, for a conventional rear-wheel-driven car, on the illustration on this page. The illustration on page 275 shows how the power flows through the drive trains of **front-wheel drive** or rear-engine cars with **transverse engines**. Notice that these do not have **driveshafts** because of their proximity to the drive wheels. Instead, the transmission and the **differential** (we'll get to that in a moment) are combined into a single unit called the **transaxle**, which powers the axle that drives the wheels. Except for this, although things may be in a slightly different order, the general setup is the same as in conventional cars.

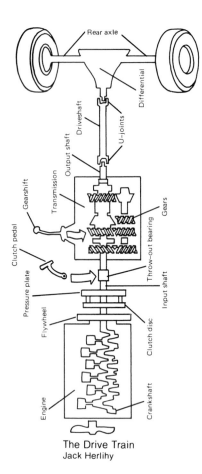

The Drive Train
Jack Herlihy

Cutaway View of Car with Front-Wheel Drive and a Transverse Engine
Chrysler Corporation

1 The running engine produces power that causes the **crankshaft** to turn at a particular rate of speed. The faster the engine runs, the more power it produces and the faster the crankshaft will turn.

2 At the end of the crankshaft is the **engine flywheel**. This is a disc-shaped plate that turns at the same rate, and in the same direction, as the crankshaft.

3 Facing the flywheel is the first part of the **clutch**. It is called a **clutch disc**, and it, too, is a disc-shaped plate. It has a tough asbestos covering. When you are *not* stepping on the *clutch pedal*, this disc is forced against the flywheel. The two plates adhere to each other, which forces them both to turn at the same speed.

4 Next to the clutch disc is the clutch **pressure plate**. This is the thing that forces the clutch disc against the flywheel or allows it to move away from the flywheel when it is time to change gears. Here's how it does that:

a When you step on the **clutch pedal** to disengage the clutch and disconnect the engine from the transmission, a clutch *release arm* forces a **throwout bearing** into the pressure plate's *release levers*. As a result, the pressure on the clutch disc is removed, and the disc can turn independently of the flywheel.

b After you have moved the gearshift to the proper gear, you release the clutch pedal. This causes springs in the pressure plate to force the disc against the flywheel again, and both the disc and the flywheel resume spinning together, at a new speed.

In this way, the clutch disc can catch up with an engine that is now turning faster—or more slowly—than before and can transmit its motion to the transmission.

5 On the clutch side of the flywheel, the drive train continues, but its name changes. It is not called the "crankshaft" anymore. It is now called the *transmission input shaft* because it carries the power, via the turning shaft, *into* the transmission. It rotates at the same speed and in the same direction as all the parts we've covered up to now.

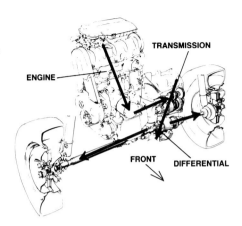

On a car with a transverse engine the power flows from the engine to the transmission and differential, which are combined into a single unit called the transaxle. From there, it flows to the drive wheels mounted at either end of the axle.
Chrysler Corporation

The Differential Makes the Axle and the Rear Wheels Move at Right Angles to the Spinning Driveshaft.
Jack Herlihy

6 Inside the transmission is a group of gears of varying sizes. These gears can move together and apart, in various combinations, to determine how fast and with how much power the wheels of the car will turn, and in which direction they will turn.

7 Another part of the **drive train** emerges from the other side of the transmission, with another new name. This time it is called the *transmission output shaft* because it is transmitting the power that the transmission is now putting out to the **driveshaft**.

8 The driveshaft of a rear-wheel-driven car with a conventional engine has a **U-joint** (short for **universal joint**) at either end to allow it to move freely without affecting the more rigid transmission shaft at one end, and to absorb the vertical movement of the rear axle and wheels at its other end. On cars with transverse engines, the U-joints can be found where each axle joins the transaxle and where each connects with the drive wheels of the car. Called constant velocity (CV) joints, they can, like other U-joints, turn and move in any direction—up, down, and from side to side. They need periodic lubrication, which should be done professionally.

9 The **differential** is another box of gears which takes the movement of the spinning driveshaft through a 90° angle to the **axle** that turns the drive wheels. It also allows each side of the axle to rotate at a different speed, because when you go around a sharp curve, the outside wheel travels farther than the inside wheel and is going to have to move more quickly than the inside wheel, just like the ice skater at the end of a snap-the-whip line.

10 The differential also provides the drive wheels with extra power by using its gears to convert every three revolutions of the driveshaft into one revolution of the drive wheels. This is called a "3 to 1 **gear ratio**."

Now, let's go back and look at each one of these components again, in greater detail:

**The Gearshift**  Gearshifts can be located on the steering column or on the floor in front of, or between, the front seats.

Generally speaking, floor shifts are more desirable because they connect more directly with the transmission (which is under the front seat of most cars). Older cars designed for the general market used to have shifts with three forward speeds located on the steering column (very old cars had a 2-foot gearshift located in front of the driver). Then the sportier models emerged, with four forward speeds. The gearshift in these cars was located on the floor, and this gave rise to the term "four on the floor." Today most cars with manual transmission have floor shifts.

There isn't much you have to know about gearshifts except that they may occasionally become hard to move. This can happen if the *gearshift linkage,* which connects the shift lever to the rods that go to the transmission, needs adjustment, lubrication, or minor repair. This is not expensive and should certainly be investigated before you let anyone talk you into major transmission work.

**The Clutch**

You use the clutch when you start, stop, and shift gears. In each of these cases, you step on the clutch pedal to disengage the clutch disc from the flywheel, so that the engine and the crankshaft can turn independently of the transmission. Otherwise, if you attempted to shift gears without using the clutch, the gears in the transmission would be rotating at different speeds and would clash and break their teeth.

The major parts of the clutch are:

1 The **clutch pedal**, which is located on the floor of the car to the left of the brake pedal.
2 The **clutch disc**, which moves back and forth on the *input shaft* to engage and disengage the **engine flywheel**, and to connect and disconnect the engine from the transmission.
3 The **pressure plate**, which moves back and forth on that same shaft to force the disc to engage and disengage the flywheel.
4 The **throw-out bearing**, which is linked to the clutch pedal. It activates the release levers that move the pressure plate back and forth.

Once you've got the engine going at its new speed (or going at all, for that matter), you release the clutch pedal to bring the clutch disc into contact with the flywheel again. The **friction** caused by the asbestos covering (it's the same stuff that brake linings are made of) causes them to grab each other lovingly and turn at the same rate once more. If your car responds erratically when you shift, it might be that the coverings on those plates are worn and that the clutch is "slipping." The engine will rev up loudly, but the car won't respond well—it won't change speed properly.

By keeping your clutch pedal properly adjusted, you can cut down on the wear on your clutch disc. Your clutch pedal should move down from ¾ to 1 inch without effort and then require a good deal more effort to travel the rest of the way down to the floor. This **free pedal play** insures that when you release the pedal, the disc will be fully engaged. Too much free pedal play is not good either, as too much pedal travel is used up doing nothing. There is not enough movement left at the bottom of its travel to compress the clutch springs and allow the flywheel and the clutch disc to separate. In this case, the gears would clash whenever you shifted into "First" or "Reverse" from a stopped position.

**How to Tell If Your Bearing's Wearing**

If there is no **free pedal play** on your clutch pedal, another problem can occur, even if there is enough play to allow the clutch disc to engage. In this case, the **throw-out bearing**, which responds to pressure on the clutch pedal by causing the disc to disengage, may go on spinning. If the throw-out bearing is allowed to revolve constantly in this way, it will wear out. If that happens, getting the car into or out of gear will become difficult.

Don't "ride the clutch." Riding it can cause the throw-out bearing to wear out too. You'll know that something is wrong because it will make whirring, whining sounds. If the sounds disappear when you release the clutch pedal, and resume when you step on it, you have a bad throw-out bearing. If you think you have one, or your clutch has been misbehaving in other ways, you might as well go to a reliable mechanic and have the clutch checked out.

Your clutch can be good for from 5,000 to 50,000 miles.

This varies widely, depending on the type of car, the way you drive, and how much maintenance the car receives. It could go as far as 100,000 miles, or it could break down after 10,000. If you are having a clutch disc replaced, be sure to have the pressure plate and the flywheel checked at that time to be sure they aren't badly worn. Here are some tips about what to expect:

1 If the flywheel is worn, have a garage mechanic re-surface it. This means that it is ground down to a new flat surface and then polished to a mirrorlike finish. If you fail to do this, the worn flywheel can wear out the facing of the new clutch disc very quickly. And if you've had to have the disc replaced, the chances are that it managed to score the flywheel by the time you recognized the trouble signs and had the disc attended to.

2 If the **pressure plate** is excessively worn, scored, or glazed, it should be replaced. If you replace it with a **rebuilt** unit, you can turn your old one in and receive credit for a **core charge**.

3 If the springs on the pressure plate become loose, replace them.

Since, as I've mentioned before, excessive wear on any part of your clutch will result in wear on the other parts, it is generally a good idea to have the clutch assembly, levers, clutch disc, and throw-out bearings checked and, if necessary, replaced at the same time. You can also have the *pilot bearing,* which is located where the shaft meets the flywheel, checked then too. In this way you can save money on labor charges by eliminating the necessity of getting into your clutch and putting it back together a second time. This is a good practice to keep in mind when dealing with other parts of your car as well. If your mechanics have to open your transmission, be sure they check the whole thing and replace gaskets, etc., that look as though they are about to go. If they have to open your cylinder head or get into the engine, be sure they look for potential trouble from the rest of the stuff in there. Of course you will want them to show you the parts that are wearing before they proceed with any unauthorized work—you are not giving them *carte blanche* to replace anything they please—but keep in mind that a good part of the labor costs are associated with just getting the thing apart and back together, so if they have to do it only once, you save money.

Easy so far, right? Now to the toughies. I'm sure you are dying to know what goes on in that mysterious transmission gear box. Well, here goes!

**How a Manual Transmission Works**

A Gear with 10 Teeth Will Rotate Completely When a 30-Tooth Gear Has Only Traveled a Third of the Way Around.
Jack Herlihy

Generally speaking, the faster your engine runs, the more power it puts out. If you need extra power to get your car up a hill, or to overcome inertia and just get that heavy monster moving in the first place, your engine must run faster than it would run simply to maintain speed once your car is on the road. Low gears supply that power, by making your wheels turn at a slower rate than your engine does.

Imagine, if you will, a large gear placed next to a small gear so that their teeth mesh. If the large gear has 30 teeth, and the small gear has 10, the large gear will turn once to every three turns of the small gear. Another way of saying this is that it would turn only a third of the way around for every complete revolution of the small gear. The gears in your transmission work on this principle. If you imagine the turning crankshaft ending in a gear that will be brought into contact with other gears of different sizes, you can see that the transmission sets up a situation where the crankshaft that runs between your engine and the transmission is turning at the same rate of speed as the engine, but the driveshaft that leaves the transmission and carries the power to the rear wheels will turn at a different rate of speed, depending on which gears in the transmission are engaged.

In low gear, the gears in the transmission make the driveshaft (and therefore the wheels) turn *more slowly* than the engine. In fact, it may turn only once for every four revolutions of the engine. All the power of the swiftly running engine is channeled into those few turns. The wheels turn more slowly, but they have more power to put into each turn, so your car can start, climb a hill, or pull a trailer. Not only does the engine run faster, but you have the mechanical advantage of having the big gear provide more leverage by turning slowly but with more force.

In second gear, the engine turns more slowly than it did in low, putting out less power but more speed, because the wheels can turn more quickly. In this gear the driveshaft may turn once for every two revolutions of the engine, or twice as fast as in low gear.

In high gear, the ratio can drop to around 1 to 1. This means that the engine and the driveshaft are turning at relatively the same rate of speed. The wheels can go very fast now; yet the engine is not putting out additional power to produce that speed. Since you have overcome inertia by the time you shift into high gear, and generally have nothing more to contend with than the wind resistance and the surface of the highway, it does not take a lot of power to keep moving at a good clip once you've gotten there. As Newton said, once something gets moving, it tends to keep moving unless it encounters something that stops it. So you don't need much power to ride the freeway. What you need is power to stop, and that is the job of your brakes.

As far as the way things look inside the transmission is concerned, I've included a simplified cutaway of a manual transmission for those of you who are curious.

Basically, all that a manual transmission consists of is a group of gears of varying sizes which are moved into and out of mesh with each other by the gearshift lever. The number of gear wheels depends on the number of forward speeds the car has. Then, there is one more gear that reverses the direction of power, so your car can move in reverse. This reverse gear works in conjunction with your lowest gear, and your car moves backward fairly slowly but with a good deal of power. Since we bring the car to a stop before we back up, and since we rarely want to hit high speeds in reverse, this low gear provides the power to get the car moving efficiently in the "wrong" direction.

**Low Gear**

**Second Gear**

**High Gear**

Cutaway of 3-Speed Manual Transmission Gears
Automotive Information Council (AIC)

## Automatic Transmissions

There are mechanical computers and electronic computers, but did you know that an automatic transmission has a very efficient **hydraulic** computer built into it? It is a unique piece of equipment that allows the car to shift gears because little valves sense the changes in hydraulic pressure caused by changes in the speed of a pump that reacts to changes in the speed of the engine. When the engine goes faster, the pump pumps harder, and this causes the hydraulic pressure to rise. As a result of these changes in pressure, the computer helps your car to shift gears automatically.

The automatic transmission works on the same basis as a manual transmission does, with a **gear selector** on the steering column or floor to allow you to tell the car manually to park, idle, go into reverse, or into lower gears for special occasions. But instead of a manual clutch, the automatic transmission uses hydraulic pressure to change gears automatically.

This hydraulic pressure is caused by oil (**transmission fluid**), which fills the transmission system. As the speed of the engine changes, a pump, which pumps the transmission fluid to develop hydraulic pressure, also changes speed. The transmission fluid responds to the changes in pressure by flowing through the transmission at different rates. When the car is moving slowly, the pressure is low, and only the low gears respond. As the speed of the car increases, so does the pressure, and higher gears are brought into play.

There are several different types of automatic transmission systems. They are all based on principles of hydraulic pressure, which drives the transmission gears by means of friction **bands** and plates. These bands and plates do the same thing that the clutch on a manual transmission does—they pull various gears into and out of action. When mechanics tell you that your bands need adjusting, these are the bands they are talking about. This can usually be done by external adjustment, but certain jobs involve opening the transmission, draining out the oil, taking the whole thing apart, and replacing defective parts. This kind of job is expensive and must be done properly by people who really understand automatic transmission systems in general, and the kind your car has in particular. Well then, if you can't do the job yourself, how do you keep from being ripped off?

First, have your automatic transmission serviced periodically, according to the manufacturer's recommendations (usually around every 24,000 miles). Then you should know what the basic kinds of transmission work involve:

**If your transmission needs "servicing" they will:**

1 Change the transmission fluid, if necessary.
2 Adjust the bands if this can be done externally.
3 Replace the transmission filter.
4 Replace the gasket around the pan and change the oil it holds.

**If your transmission is leaking:**

1 If the *front seal* is bad the mechanic must remove your transmission to replace it, but he doesn't have to take the transmission apart. Front seals usually have the biggest leaks.
2 If it's the *rear seal* the mechanic must remove your driveshaft, but your transmission can stay in place.

**If your transmission must be "overhauled" they will:**

1 Remove and disassemble the transmission.
2 Replace the seals, clutches, bands, and bushings that are worn or defective.

So you can see that the ability to tell the kind of transmission work that is necessary can save you from paying for more work than you need. There are also a number of other things that can go wrong and seem to indicate that you need major transmission work to correct them; yet they really can be fixed for very little money. An unscrupulous mechanic can diagnose one of the problems as a major transmission breakdown and charge you hundreds of dollars when the real solution could be achieved for much less. Here are two of these:

**How to Keep from Being Ripped Off on Transmission Work**

**The Malfunctioning Vacuum Modulator Caper**

Many vehicles with automatic transmissions have a device called a **vacuum modulator**. When it goes wrong, the car tends to stay in low gear all the time or shift with a bang—especially into lower gears. These little devils can suck up transmission fluid and burn it, causing white or gray smoke to emerge from the car's tail pipe as you shift gears. If your car has a vacuum modulator, and it's easy to reach, it's worth the gamble to replace it before considering more costly remedies. Vacuum modulators are inexpensive, and you usually only have to unscrew the old one to replace it.

**Those Low Transmission Fluid Blues**

1 *If your automatic transmission seems to be acting up*—by hesitating when you change gears, or by shifting with a "clunk"—first check your transmission **dipstick**. Your transmission fluid may be low, or dirty, or it may have dried. Chapter 5 tells you how to find and check your transmission dipstick, and how to buy the proper kind of transmission fluid for your car. It's a good idea to do this fairly often anyway as part of your regular under-the-hood check. A good many "band jobs" have been bought and paid for when a quart of transmission fluid would have solved the problem for pennies.

2 *If your fluid level is low,* use a funnel to add a teeny bit at a time down the dipstick hole until the level just reaches the "Fill" mark on the stick. *Do not fill beyond the line;* driving with too much transmission fluid can damage your car. If the level is low again in a couple of days, look under the car for a leak around the transmission; you may need a seal replaced.

3 *If your fluid level is fine but your transmission isn't working well*—or if your fluid keeps disappearing and no leaks are evident—you probably need some transmission work. We'll get to that in a moment.

4 *If your transmission fluid looks or smells burned or dirty,* you might want to consider having the fluid, filter, and pan gasket changed. Transmissions should be serviced every 20,000 to 25,000 miles, but if your car has over 100,000 miles on it and the fluid has never been changed, don't change it unless there are really serious reasons for doing so. The old transmission fluid has formed a deposit around the front transmission seal. If it's totally replaced with fresh fluid, the new stuff can dissolve the deposit and the old seal may start to leak. In this case I'd just add enough new fluid to bring the level up to the "Fill" mark on the dipstick or as close to it as possible. Then, when the poor neglected beast dies,

have it rebuilt (unless the rest of the car is dying, too). This does *not* mean you shouldn't have the transmission serviced. Since you'll probably lose only 3 quarts in the process of servicing, replacing the lost fluid should not disturb the seals.

**How to Keep Your Drive Train Running Smoothly**

Your manual or automatic transmission system will work better and live longer if you have the **U-joints** in your drive train checked and replaced with new ones if they are loose, and have your **differential** lubricated at regular intervals. Even if you are now lubricating your steering linkage and suspension system yourself, you should still take the car to a service station to have *everything* lubricated at least once a year. Be sure to check to see if your rear end (sorry, that's the way they refer to the differential) needs lubrication. Here's how to do it:

Find the inspection plug in the differential (that's the gear box between the two rear wheels of the car). You can usually remove this plug by putting the square end of a ½-inch drive **ratchet** into the square hole in the plug. If, when the plug is removed, fluid drips out, you're O.K. If nothing comes out, add differential/manual transmission grease until it is full. If your car has a "limited slip" or "positraction" rear end (very few cars do), it will require a special fluid. Check the specifications in your owner's manual, or call your dealer, to find out for sure.

Checking the grease level on a manual transmission is the same as checking the differential on cars with either a manual or an automatic transmission. You just locate the inspection plug, remove it, and see what comes out. If nothing does, you use the same differential/manual transmission grease to fill it up again. (On cars with an automatic transmission, the transmission dipstick does this job for you, as we've already mentioned, and automatic transmission fluid instead of gear grease is used.)

**How to Undertake Transmission Repairs Wisely**

For transmission repairs, take your car to reputable transmission specialists and ask them to diagnose the trouble and give you an *estimate* of the costs. *Do not let them take the thing apart.* Once your transmission is in pieces, you are a sitting duck. Have them drive the car, listen to it, ask you questions about its history and its symptoms, and give you their ideas. They may say, "You may just need your bands tightened, or you may need a new transmission; we can't tell until we open it up." Fine. Ask them for estimates for both jobs and move on to the next place.

Get three estimates, or more if the first three vary widely. Discard the high estimates. Discard a *very* low one, too, if it seems way out of line with the others. It may be a hustle. Then return to the place with the lowest price and/or the best vibes. Of course if someone you know who is fairly knowledgeable about cars recommends a place enthusiastically, this is usually worth extra points when you are deciding. But I'd get estimates anyway.

Once the work is underway, ask to be notified about what they find when they open it up. Will it be a simple adjustment? Or a major rebuild? Get the estimated costs on the receipt, signed by you, *before* the actual work begins, and ask to be called if that estimate changes because they uncover other problems. Ask them to save you the parts they replace so that you can see what you paid for. There are consumer laws in many states which hold the mechanic responsible for failing to give the customer a written estimate, for failing to notify the customer if the estimate becomes way out of line because more serious problems have been uncovered in the course of the work, and for failing to turn over parts that have been replaced when the customer asks that they be saved.

Now go home, cross your fingers, and wait for the operation to be over. Of course you may still be ripped off, but you'll know that you've done everything possible to prevent it. And since you've been so canny about estimates, open about shopping around, familiar with the transmission itself (drop words like "hydraulic pressure," "modulators," and "bands," etc.) and insistent about written estimates and such, you just might scare someone who would like to cheat you into doing a good job and charging you properly for it.

If this whole thing sounds paranoid, that's just because there are bad apples that give the good, honest, hard-working, car-loving, competent transmission specialists a lot of competition. Most specialists are all of the above positive things. But the baddies are the ones you tell your friends about, and so we have all become a bit paranoid when dealing with an unkno___ shop for delicate and expensive work. Go ahead a___ be paranoid. It can't hurt. You haven't done anything to insult the shop. You've just been careful. The owner's probably the same way about dealing with other people when faced with an expensive job that must be done by strangers. And if the shop does the job well, for a reasonable price, you can always sing their praises to your friends and refer them to them when they have problems. Chapter 20 has lots of advice on how to find a good mechanic, how to keep one happy, and what to do if you get ripped off anyway.

There is one thing more that you can do to keep from ripping *yourself* off, and that is to learn some driving habits that will extend the life of your transmission.

## How to Keep From Driving Your Transmission Crazy

Driving your car with expertise can prevent many of the most common causes of transmission failure. This means getting into the proper gear to reduce the strain on the engine and on the transmission, and not riding your clutch. Remember, an automatic transmission works with gear, too. If you are in low gear, you are transmitting more power to your rear wheels, and your transmission will be feeling the strain. If you attempt to speed in a low gear, you will be straining the transmission even more. On the other hand, if you attempt to climb hills in high gear, you will be forcing the car to make the effort in a gear that lacks the power for the job. Result, more strain. People with a manual transmission learn to watch the **tachometer**, or just "feel" the car's need for more power or more speed, and shift into the proper gear for each occasion. But people with an automatic transmission tend to shift into drive and GO—up hills, with heavy loads, and into jackrabbit starts—happily oblivious to the fact that even automatic transmissions have gear selectors that provide one or two lower gears for these occasions.

Using a lower gear can save wear and tear on your brakes too, especially if your car has a manual transmission. If you are driving along in high gear and you see that a traffic light is changing to red or that traffic is slowing ahead, instead of using your brake to take on the full job of slowing the car down, try **downshifting** (shifting into the next lower gear) after the car has slowed down a bit. The lower gear will help your car to slow down still further, and this will save your brakes. Also, if you are going down a steep hill, use a lower gear to help your car move at a slower pace without the need to ride your brakes all the way down.

On cars with an automatic transmission, **passing gear** provides the same kind of help as downshifting does. In this case, you use passing gear when you are already in high gear and need an extra burst of power to pass a car or enter a freeway. If you have been traveling at less than 50 mph, the sudden flooring of the gas pedal will make your car downshift automatically from high to second, which provides more power by speeding up the engine. When you release the pedal, the car goes back to high.

If you have a car with **overdrive**, you have an extra, higher, gear that allows your rear wheels to turn even faster while maintaining the same engine speed. Once you are really traveling along, shifting into overdrive means that your car can move at the same speed but the engine can turn more slowly and consume less fuel as you cruise along.

Once you have the car moving along swiftly, it is always a good idea to shift into the higher gears as soon as possible. There is no need to speed the engine to supply extra power when it is not needed. But if you come to a steep hill—or if you are carrying four kids, everything you'll need for a month in the country, and those two dogs—go for the lower gears instead of trying to haul the whole mess as fast as you can. This way, you avoid engine strain (this is called "lugging") and the power goes toward carrying the load rather than into maintaining speed. When the engine is lugging, always shift into a lower gear so that it can turn faster and carry you along with less strain. Once you get everything moving freely, you can return to a higher gear—until you reach the next steep hill. Then back to low again for the power to carry the load up the hill against gravity, with less strain on the car. In this way, even drivers of cars with automatic transmissions can extend the lives of their engine and their transmission.

Although this has been a "clean-hands" chapter, rather than a work chapter, it is probably the most difficult one in the book. If you understood the whole thing, fine—you probably would have made a terrific engineer or mechanic. If the principles of transmission design have failed to penetrate, don't worry— that's what we pay transmission specialists for. Just go over the parts of the chapter that deal with driving properly until it gets to be a habit, and you may never have to worry about your transmission at all. If your luck turns bad and your transmission acts up, reread the parts about diagnosing and getting help wisely. If you "fake it" you can probably get everything taken care of with a minimum of pain.

Having survived the intricacies of the internal combustion engine and the automatic transmission, you are now ready to confront **diesel engines**, which differ considerably in design and in maintenance from all that has gone before. The next chapter will also unravel the mysteries of **turbocharging** and **supercharging** both conventional and diesel engines. After you read it you should be able to swagger down to the corner garage and join the "guys" standing around with their heads under the hood of a local dragster. If you're convincing enough they might even let you drive it around the block...

# Diesels for Dummies

Traditionally, **diesel engines** were used mainly on large trucks, buses, and London taxicabs. Diesel-powered passenger cars existed, but they had a reputation for being noisy, underpowered, smokey, and cantankerous. However, with the onset of the fuel crisis, the spectacular mileage achieved by diesel engines—over 25 percent greater than that of gasoline engines—caused many car manufacturers to take another look at diesel design and, for a while, there were many diesel models available. Then, gasoline prices fell while taxes drove the price of diesel oil up until it cost as much as—or more—than gasoline. Gasoline engines were perfected which competed with diesels in mileage. As a result, many of the hastily designed diesel engines dropped out of the market. But Mercedes-Benz, who pioneered the diesel car as a luxury vehicle decades ago, still makes diesel-powered cars and station wagons that many consider unsurpassed for beauty, performance, high resale value, and high price tags. Volkswagen, whose VW Rabbit was the first peppy, moderately priced diesel car, still offers diesel-powered vehicles, and other manufacturers also offer diesel cars and trucks. So a choice still exists. But before you commit yourself to one type of car or another, there are a number of pros and cons to consider:

PRO: Diesel cars get great mileage.

CON: So do the newest gas-saver compact cars. And these generally cost a couple of thousand dollars less to buy. You can buy a lot of gas for a couple of thousand dollars!

PRO: Diesel cars run on diesel oil, which contains more usable energy than gasoline.

CON: But diesel fuel is still not available at many gas stations, and although it used to be cheaper than gasoline, in these inflated times it has risen in price to where it can often cost as much as gasoline. Since it is quite similar to home heating oil, kerosene, and jet fuel, in the future it may become even more expensive, depending on availability and demand. Although diesel fuel is considered more efficient because it converts heat into energy rather than sending it out the tailpipe as gas-powered cars do, it doesn't result in flashy "high performance." A gasoline-powered car is like a race horse—high-strung, fiery, and fast out of the gate—whereas a diesel car is more like a work-horse—slow, strong, and enduring.

PRO: Diesel cars have no carburetors, spark plugs, or distributors. Therefore they never need a tune-up.

CON: But they must have regular maintenance to keep them running. You will have to change the oil; change the air, oil, and fuel filters; and probably have to bleed the excess water out of the system every now and then. True, you can do these things yourself, but if you neglect the maintenance and the fuel-injection system gets clogged or breaks down, you will have to pay a mechanic to get things unsnaggled and it will probably be expensive.

PRO: Diesels are built more ruggedly, to withstand the rigors of higher compression. Consequently, they usually go much longer before they require major repairs than conventional cars do.
Mercedes-Benz holds the longevity record with several vehicles clocking more than 900,000 miles on their original engines!

CON: True, but do you really want to hang on to the same car for 900,000 miles? And will the newer low-cost diesels hold up as well as the old ones?

PRO: The new **turbocharged** diesels are a new breed indeed. They have even better fuel efficiency, and are much more powerful and responsive than those dowdy old models were.

CON: This is so. But turbocharging is still being developed, and it will probably get cheaper and even more efficient in the near future. The early bird may get the worm, but the later bird might get the butterfly...

PRO: Diesel cars put out much less carbon monoxide than ordinary cars do. That means less air pollution.

CON: But they also put out 30 to 90 percent more nitrogen oxides and carbon particles (soot). Since cutting down on one of these emissions seems to increase the other, diesel manufacturers currently are having a hard time meeting the increasingly stringent EPA standards.

PRO: New innovations have made diesels easier to start in cold weather.

CON: Although they are better than they used to be, diesel engines are still more difficult to start on cold days than gasoline engines are.

Before I try to sum up all of the above, please remember that this is just my opinion as of this writing. By the time you read this book, diesel pros and cons may have changed into a whole new ball game. So you are going to have to go out, check on what's available, and make up your own mind in the long run. However, based on the current situation, here are my conclusions: If you need a big car with a large carrying capacity, and if you plan to drive it a great deal and keep it a long time, you may want to consider buying a diesel car now. If, on the other hand, you like fast, peppy, small cars, you don't plan to drive many thousands of miles each year, and you don't have a lot of money to spend, then I would lay back for a while and closely watch developments in the diesel field. By the time they are really perfected, super-efficient, and priced to compete effectively with conventional cars, you may have enough money saved to buy one.

If you do decide to buy a diesel car, be sure to choose one that will allow you to do most of the maintenance yourself, without a lot of time, money, or skill required. Check the owner's manual and talk to the dealer or to the mechanics to be sure that the oil can be changed easily (because it's going to have to be changed quite often), that the oil, air, and fuel filters are easy to reach and change, and that the fuel system can be bled and primed easily. Before you buy the car, make them show you where things are under the hood and what you must do to maintain them.

**What Makes It Go?** Since diesels differ from conventional cars in several ways, this chapter will be a mini-version of the entire book. We'll explore in general terms the way diesel cars work, what needs to be done to maintain them, and how to buy fuel and oil for them. If you then want to get down to the details, there are a few books available that deal specifically with diesels and are written for amateurs rather than mechanics.

The basic difference between a diesel engine and a gasoline engine is that the fuel is not ignited by an outside power source like a spark plug, nor is it mixed with air in a carburetor. Instead, it is sprayed into the **combustion chamber** through a **fuel injector nozzle**, just when the air in the chamber has been placed under such great pressure that it is hot enough to ignite the fuel spontaneously. Most conventional engines have **compression ratios** of around 8:1. Diesel engines may employ ratios of above 20:1. Because of this, and the fact that the compressed air can reach very high temperatures, diesel engines must be built for great strength and endurance.

Because diesel fuel is less volatile than gasoline and is easier to start if the combustion chamber is preheated, manufacturers have installed little **glow plugs**, which work off the battery, to prewarm the air in the cylinders when you first start the car. They have also designed a variety of heaters to help get things going in extremely cold weather. I'll discuss these right after the section on regular maintenance.

First, let's go step-by-step through the things that happen when you start up a diesel-powered vehicle. (The details may vary from one car to another, but the action remains pretty much the same.)

1 When you first turn the key you will be asked to wait until the car has built up enough heat in the **cylinders** for satisfactory starting. (Most cars have a little light that says "WAIT," but I'm sure there will be a sultry computer voice doing the job in the near future.) Usually you don't have to wait very long— probably no more than half a minute in moderate weather, and new developments in glow plugs have reduced starting time even more dramatically.

2 When everything is warm enough, a "START" light will go on. This tells you to step on the **accelerator pedal** and turn the key to "Start."

3 Fuel pumps deliver the fuel from the tank to the engine. On its way, the fuel passes through a couple of **fuel filters** which help to clean it before it can get to, and clog up, the injector nozzles. Proper mainte-

Precombustion Chamber

1 Piston
2 Intake valve
3 Fuel injector nozzle
4 Glow plug

Diesel Fuel Filters
Robert Bosch Sales Corporation

Anatomy of a fuel injector nozzle
Robert Bosch Sales Corporation

**KEY**

1. **High Pressure Inlet**
2. **Leak-off**
3. **Shim**
4. **Pressure Spring**
5. **Pressure Spindle**
6. **Intermediate Plate**
7. **Pintle Nozzle**
8. **Nozzle Nut**

nance of these filters is especially important in diesels, because fuel contamination can clog up the tiny holes in injector nozzles more easily than it can interfere with carburetors, which are better equipped to handle dirty fuel.

4 The injection pump is truly the "heart" of the diesel car. Located inside it are a series of mini-pumps, each of which is responsible for delivering fuel at a pressure of over 1000 psi to one of the **fuel injector nozzles**.

Cutaway View of a Diesel Engine
Robert Bosch Sales Corporation

The injection pump's "brain" is a **governor**, which controls the exact amount of fuel that is sent from each mini-pump. The governor has a very important job. It makes sure that the engine doesn't go so fast that it damages itself with excessive heat and pressure. Some governors are built right into the injection pump; others work off the **crankshaft** or the pump's timing gear; still others measure the speed of the air coming into the engine. All of them are affected by the pressure of your foot on the accelerator pedal, by the temperature in the cylinders, by altitude, by the speed of the car, and by the load the car is carrying.

Now the action moves to the cylinders. What has been taking place there to prepare the scene for the final fiery "power play"?

5  On conventional diesel cars, the air comes in through an **air cleaner** that is quite similar to those in ordinary cars. However, in recent years **turbochargers** have been developed which ram greater volumes of air into the cylinders and may provide greater power and fuel economy under optimum conditions. We'll talk more about these fascinating devices a bit farther on.

6  As you recall, turning the key started the glow plugs warming up the air in the cylinders. On many engines the glow plugs are located right in the combustion chambers of the cylinders. On others, they have been placed in a little **pre-combustion chamber**, which the glow plug can heat more quickly and easily. From here, combustion spreads from the smaller amount of fuel that is placed under pressure in the pre-combustion chamber to the fuel and air in the combustion chamber itself, in much the same way as it does on cars with **stratified charge engines**.

Fuel Transfer Pump
Robert Bosch Sales Corporation

Fuel Injection Pump with (1) Governor, (2) Fuel Supply Pump, (3) Timing Device Built Into It.

Although some diesel engines operate with two-stroke power cycles, the chances are that the cars you may encounter use a four-stroke power cycle, which is comparable to the power cycle of a gasoline engine, shown on pages 130–131. Here's how the diesel's four-stroke power cycle works:

**The Diesel Four-Stroke Power Cycle**

**Intake Stroke**  The **piston** descends, the **intake valve** opens, and air is drawn into the **cylinder**.

**Compression Stroke**  The intake and exhaust valves are closed as the piston moves upwards and places the air under extreme pressure. As the pressure increases, the air heats up to the flash point—the point at which it will cause the fuel to undergo spontaneous combustion. Just before that point is reached, **fuel injectors** spray fuel into the combustion chambers at the precise instant when ignition is to take place—much in the same way that a distributor is timed to send electricity to the spark plugs of a gasoline engine.

**Power Stroke**  With intake and exhaust valves closed, the fuel ignites, and combustion forces the piston down. This driving power is transmitted through the **transmission** and the rest of the **drive train** to the wheels, which causes the car to move.

The **exhaust valve** opens, as the piston rises and pushes the burnt gases out of the cylinder.

**Exhaust Stroke**

That's how it works for conventional four-stroke diesel engines. Now let's see how turbocharging the engine changes things in a very exciting way!

**Turbocharging** means to use a blower or a turbine to force greater amounts of air into the cylinders of an

**Turbocharging**

Five-Cylinder Turbocharged Diesel Engine
(cutaway view)
Mercedes-Benz of North America

AIR OUTLET

COMPRESSOR

TURBINE

AIR INLET

EXHAUST OUTLET

TO TURBINE

TO WASTEGATE

EXHAUST INL

WASTEGATE BOOST CONTROL

Turbodiesel Engine
Mercedes-Benz of North America

engine. This produces more power in both diesel and conventional cars because, as I've said before, cars run on air more than they run on fuel. So, the more air the engine can take in, the bigger the "bang" is during the power stroke. At first, cars were turbocharged to perform better on racetracks, but when car manufacturers began to use smaller engines on larger cars, to lighten their weight and conserve fuel, turbocharging provided a way to increase the power of the engine so the big cars wouldn't be sluggish on the road.

When it came to designing diesel cars, the problem was even more pressing: how to change a car with a reputation of being noisy, underpowered, and smokey into a faster, quieter, more efficient vehicle which would meet the EPA requirements. The results have been heartening indeed. *A turbocharger can increase the power on a diesel car by 50 percent while lowering its fuel consumption by 20 to 25 percent!* And, what is more, since the turbine itself is powered by the hot gases which would normally go out of the exhaust pipe, you need provide nothing extra to drive it. What a wonderful example of recycling! It seems that every time we set out to create something new from something we used to throw away, the grateful environment showers bonuses on us...

If you're sufficiently impressed, let's get a bit more specific about how turbocharging works:

1 The hot exhaust gases leave the **exhaust manifold** in much the same manner as they usually do, but instead of going directly through the exhaust system and out of the car via the tail pipe, they first pass through a **turbine**, which is nothing but a fan that is set in motion by the velocity of the passing gases.

2 A shaft connects the fan to a **compressor**, which blows fresh, filtered air into the cylinders. (On a gasoline-powered car, it would take the fuel/air mixture supplied by the carburetor and blow it into the cylinders.)

3 The excess and used exhaust fumes pass from the **turbine** to the **exhaust system** and continue on their way to the **tail pipe** and out into the air in their usual manner.

4 The more load on the engine, the hotter and faster are the exhaust fumes which turn the turbine. The faster they turn it, the more air the compressor will send to the engine and the faster the engine can go. This unique way of converting exhaust gas energy into mechanical power has a nice merry-go-round effect.

Sounds simple, doesn't it? Well, usually the first thing an engineer learns is "the simpler, the better," or, as the Zen monks put it, "less is more." Wow! Ecology, engineering, and philosophy all in a couple of paragraphs! Maybe I ought to change the name of this book to "Zen and the Art of Auto Maintenance." Sounds familiar somehow...

**Turbocharging Kits**

There are turbocharging kits available which can be installed on conventional cars to increase their power and performance. However, since turbocharging places considerable stress on engines which were not designed with that in mind, you run the risk of dam-

000-301

aging your engine and voiding all existing warranties if you decide to boost Old Faithful with a turbo kit. Therefore, investigate the situation carefully before you go this route. Some owners have had marvelous success, and their engines have lived to tell the tale; others weren't as lucky. Generally speaking, I would never attempt to turbocharge the original engine of an older car, nor would I tinker with anything but a ruggedly built engine in top condition. If Old Faithful is beginning to show the strain of passing years, it would be wiser to recycle the old workhorse and buy yourself a turbo-powered filly!

**Supercharging**

Do not confuse turbocharging with **supercharging**. A supercharger is a pump which compresses the fuel/air mixture and forces it into the cylinders of a gasoline-powered car. Since superchargers are usually belt-driven by the engine instead of by exhaust gases, they use engine power to increase engine power. Because they are not fuel efficient, they are generally used only to increase the speed of "high-performance," low-efficiency vehicles.

**The Electrical System**

Diesel cars require more stored energy for starting than conventional cars do, especially on cold days. Instead of just using the **battery** to enable the starter to crank the engine, a diesel car must have sufficient power to enable the glow plugs to warm the combustion chambers and then must build up enough heat and compression in the cylinders to ignite the fuel. For this reason, diesels must possess considerably more battery capacity than do conventional cars. Some come equipped with two batteries, while others feature a single oversized battery, which may be more than 50 percent bigger than one found on a conventional car. It would be useless to try to jump-start a diesel from a conventional gasoline-powered car with a battery of lower capacity. Aside from this, electrical systems on diesels are pretty much the same as those on conventional cars, with **alternators, regulators, solenoids**, and **starters** performing their usual functions.

As we've seen, there will be no need to change plugs or **points**, or adjust a **carburetor** on a diesel car. However, there are occasions when the **timing** or the **idle speed** will need to be adjusted. Because these jobs require expensive special equipment, it is probably better for you to have them done professionally. If you aren't sure whether or not the car is idling properly, check the dashboard **tachometer** against the recommended idle speeds in the owner's manual, and head for help if you don't like what you see.

**Diesel Fuel**

Diesels run on **diesel oil**, which is an all-around better type of fuel than gasoline. For one thing, it contains 10 percent more energy per gallon than gasoline does. It is also safer than gasoline because it doesn't give off vapors that are as noxious or as explosive, and it doesn't ignite as easily, unless it is in a diesel engine.

Diesel fuel is sold in two grades: Diesel #1 and Diesel #2 (also called 1-D and 2-D). Just as gasoline is rated by its octane, diesel oil is rated by **cetane**. To arrive at a cetane rating, they measure the time lapse between the injection of the fuel and its ignition to determine how easy it is to ignite and how fast it will burn. (The higher the cetane number the more volatile the fuel.) Most diesel cars use fuel with a rating of 40 to 55. Diesel #2 is less volatile than #1 and provides greater fuel economy. That's why truckers tend to use it to carry heavy loads for long distances at sustained speeds.

Most diesel car makers specify Diesel #2 for normal driving conditions, but there can be other factors to consider. Diesel fuel is also measured by its **viscosity**, which, as you may remember from the section on motor oils, has to do with its thickness or "flowability." As is the case for any oil, at low temperatures diesel oil tends to thicken and cloud up. Under extreme conditions, it can even turn into a gel and refuse to flow at all. Diesel #2 has a higher cloud point than #1, usually about 20°F. So some companies offer "winterized" Diesel #2, which is usable down to 0°F. Diesel #1 flows more easily, and therefore it has a temperature range which is lower still. The two fuels can be mixed safely, but it is always wise to consult your owner's manual for the proper fuel for your car. If you aren't sure and you're going to be driving in cold weather, be sure to choose fuel rated at least 10 degrees lower than the coldest temperatures you expect to encounter. Luckily, most service stations sell diesel fuel that is blended and rated for local weather conditions and appropriate for passenger-car use.

**A Word About Emergency Substitutes**

Although diesel engines theoretically should be able to run on kerosene, certain airplane fuels, and home heating oil, *do not* try to use these in your car under any circumstances, unless your name is Clint Eastwood! Standards of refining, filtering, and blending these oils differ widely and they can ruin your engine, void your warranties, and create a whole lot of trouble for you.

If you find yourself getting low on fuel in a remote area, look for diesel fuel at trucking companies, food processing plants, electric plants, hospitals, and farms. These are all places that usually have diesel engines on the premises and some Good Samaritan may take pity on you and let you have some.

If you absolutely cannot find a source of diesel fuel, it might be better to try to borrow some home heating oil or buy some Jet-A fuel at a local airport, rather than resorting to other substitutes. Diesel mechanics consider this stuff to be like "rot-gut" whiskey—it will get you there, but it's not the best stuff for your system! So run on these fuels only long enough to get to the nearest source of proper fuel, and remember that you do run the risk of voiding your warranty, and damaging your engine, unless your owner's manual specifically says you can use these substances.

**Where to Buy Diesel Fuel**

These days, as diesel engines are becoming increasingly popular, more and more service stations are carrying diesel fuel. If it is still relatively scarce in your area, the following hints may apply:

Under normal conditions, try to buy diesel oil at popular truck stops. It may be cheaper there than at local filling stations, and the fuel will be fresher (which is important, as you will see shortly). If possible, plan to tank up on a Saturday morning, when the commercial trucking action is virtually nonexistent. Weekday evenings are the worst times to buy. It isn't easy to muscle your way into a crowd of "big rigs" in a compact diesel car!

It is best to buy diesel fuel at a truck stop or a busy station because many small local stations with few diesel customers carry it only as a "convenience" and don't sell enough of it to ensure a fresh supply. This can create problems, because diesel fuel tends to easily become contaminated by the water that condenses in fuel tanks and by fungus and other microbes that can clog filters and fuel injectors. All diesel cars should have a **water separator** to remove excess water from the fuel before it goes to the engine. If you should buy a car without one, you can have one installed without too much trouble. I'll discuss them shortly under "Regular Maintenance." If you find yourself at a station which arouses your suspicions, you can check it out by looking for slimy stuff on the nozzle of the pump. An even better idea is to carry a small jar with you and pump a small quantity of fuel into it before you fill your tank. Take a couple of minutes to let the liquid settle, and then check to see if there are unidentifiable objects at the bottom of the jar, or if the diesel oil is floating on a layer of water. But squeeze the pump handle gently to avoid splashing the fuel out of the jar and onto yourself.

**How to Cure a Sick Diesel**

If you suspect that your car has caught a dose of fungus, check its filler pipe and cap for yucky-looking matter, or dip a clean stick into the tank and inspect that. An advanced case of fungus smells like rotten eggs. To cure it, use a **biocide** designed to kill fuel fungus. Your dealer can probably suggest the proper product and the right amount to use. Or you can ask someone at an auto parts store, or a home heating or chemical company, for advice.

Only add biocide when you are filling the tank with fuel, never to an empty or almost empty tank. If your tank's really been fouled up, it is probably best to drain it and have it steam-cleaned or clean it yourself with a commercial cleaner designed for fuel tanks. Then refill the tank and add the biocide.

If you are planning to store your car for a while, fill the fuel tank completely, so that there is no space left for water vapor to condense out of the air. Then dose it with biocide to prevent fungus from forming.

**Diesel Fuel Permits**    Until recently, several states required fuel permits to buy diesel fuel (usually because there was no tax collected at the pump as it generally is for gasoline). Today this is a rarity, and in most cases permits are waived for tourists who are just passing through the state. If you want to check out the situation in a particular state, ask the AAA or the state's Department of Motor Vehicles.

**Regular Maintenance**    Although the engines on diesel cars tend to last longer without major repairs and require no ignition tune-ups or carburetor adjustments and rebuilds, they do require regular low-cost maintenance, mostly in the form of frequent oil and filter changes. If you own a conventional car and you get sloppy about maintenance and don't change the oil often enough, you will probably end up with an engine that's aged prematurely. If you own a diesel car and do the same thing, you may end up with an engine that's prematurely dead. The same goes for changing filters: a dirty fuel filter can impair the performance of a conventional car, but dirty fuel will clog a diesel's fuel-injection system, and it may take some expensive professional help to get the car on the road again. As a rule, you won't be able to clean or adjust the fuel injectors yourself, but they can last 100,000 miles or more if you take care of the car properly. If you maintain your vehicle according to the instructions in the owner's manual, you should have few problems. After all, truckers have always preferred diesels because they have found them to be cheap to run and maintain, tough and reliable.

Most diesel cars are designed so that the owner can

perform the regular maintenance chores without an undue investment in time and money. I'll cover them in general terms and your owner's manual should contain the rest of the information you'll need. If it doesn't, amble on over to the dealership's parts department and ask to see the **service manual**. A quick look at the proper sections in the manual should tell you whether or not you can do it yourself. If you're not sure, ask someone in the service area where the filters are located and what's involved in changing or servicing them. Most mechanics are pretty nice about that kind of thing. If the job really is easy, they won't make enough on it to make it worthwhile to lie to you; if it isn't, you'll be happy to have them do it for you.

**Finding a Reliable Diesel Mechanic**

If you need professional help, either with maintenance or for repairs, and the car is out of **warranty**, you might want to check around for a good independent diesel mechanic, if only to compare prices or get a second opinion on major surgery. One way to find a good independent diesel mechanic is to look in your local Yellow Pages under "Automobiles, Repair" for a shop whose ad carries the logo of the Association of Diesel Specialists. The ADS authorization goes to repair facilities that send their mechanics to factory schools for instruction, maintain standards of cleanliness, and meet requirements for stocking the tools and parts to deal properly with a variety of diesel systems. The last chapter of this book is devoted to finding and maintaining a good relationship with a mechanic, and discusses how to get satisfaction in a dispute over labor or services.

**Changing the Lubricating Oil**

Since diesel fuel is sometimes called diesel oil, be aware of the fact that the oil you are going to have to change is not the fuel oil, but the oil that is used to lubricate the engine. To do this you will need lubricating oil that is specially designed for diesel engines, rather than the lubricating oil designed for conventional cars. O.K.? Once you've got that distinction, the actual work involved is the same as it is for conventional cars—except that you have to do it more often. Be sure to check your oil **dipstick** at least once a week, when the car is on level ground, and change the oil filter when you change the oil. Don't be surprised if you change the lubricating oil in your diesel car, run the engine for two minutes, and check the dipstick only to find that the new oil is pitch black already. This is normal. Your owner's manual will tell you what kind of oil to use and the maximum intervals you can wait between changes, but I believe that the more often you change the oil on any car, the longer the car will live and the healthier it will be, and that goes double for diesels because the extreme heat and pressure help to contaminate the lubricating oil more quickly.

You can find instructions for changing oil and oil **filters** in Chapter 12. Since the procedure is the same, that entire chapter is relevant with the following exception:

**Classification Codes for Diesel Lubricating Oil**

There are classification codes for automotive oils which tell us which oil to use under a specific set of conditions. These are the codes for diesel lubrication oils:

> CA—For use with low-sulphur, high-quality fuels only.
>
> CB—For use with high-sulphur, low-quality fuels on cars subjected to low to medium stress.
>
> CC—Protects against rust, corrosion, and high temperatures under medium to severe conditions.
>
> CD—For use under severe conditions.

CC is the lubricating oil designated for most popular diesel cars, but check your owner's manual to be sure. It will also specify a viscosity grade in the form of a number preceded by the initials SAE. This refers to the "weight" of the oil and the temperature conditions under which it will flow. Diesel lubricating oil comes in the same range of weights as oil for conventional cars, and you can find all the necessary information beginning on page 245 under "How to Tell Which Kind of Oil to Buy."

**Tips on Changing Oil and Oil Filters**

1 Be sure to check your dipstick with your car on level ground when you are adding oil. If you overfill a engine with oil, it can be damaged.

2 Change the oil and the filter when the engine is warm. Warm oil drains faster and more completely than the oil in a cold engine.

3 Keep the proper **oil drain-plug gasket** on hand and check to see if the old one needs replacing. It's a nuisance to have to drain all the oil out of the engine if the old one starts leaking between changes.

4 Be sure to moisten the seal of the new oil filter with oil before installing it. It makes it seal better.

The **air filter** set-up on most diesel cars is the same as it is for conventional vehicles, with the filter located inside the air cleaner under the hood of the car. You'll find directions on how to reach it on page 140. There is one big difference, however:

**Changing the Air Filter**

You must always shut off the engine of a diesel car before you try to change the air filter. Diesel engines produce exceedingly powerful suction and the air intake goes directly to the engine. Since almost anything can fly or drop into it, from nuts and bolts to your favorite hairpiece, you risk serious damage to the engine if you open the **air cleaner** with the engine running.

Most diesel cars have two **fuel filters**—a "primary" filter located between the **fuel tank** and the engine, which cleans the fuel before it gets to the fuel transfer pump; and a "secondary" filter up near the engine, which gives the fuel a final cleaning before it gets to the injectors. Both are usually easy to change, and your owner's manual should show you how to do it. On some cars the job is much like changing the oil filter on a conventional car: you unscrew the old one, moisten the gasket of the new one with fuel, and screw it into place. Other cars have filters with replaceable cartridges; you just remove the old one and pop in the new one.

**Changing the Fuel Filters**

There is one catch, however. Whenever you change the fuel filter or run out of fuel in a diesel car, you must **bleed** the air bubbles out of the system and then prime it to get a new supply of fuel circulating. Be-

**Bleeding and Priming the Fuel System**

cause cranking the engine will do the job but will also wear down the battery, most cars include a manual primer pump and an air-bleed screw for this purpose. On many cars you simply pump the handle of the primer to get the fuel moving, then turn the air-bleed screw until a hissing noise tells you that the air is escaping. Just keep pumping until all the air leaves and the noise ceases, then tighten the air-bleed screw and replace the pump handle. Since bleeding and priming the fuel system is something that may occur fairly often, I would suggest that you check the equipment and procedure for any model you are interested in purchasing, to be sure that this can be handled quickly and easily.

**Water Separators**

Because diesel fuel can easily become contaminated by water, many diesel cars feature a gadget called a **water separator**, which is usually located on or near the primary fuel filter. If your car doesn't have one, I'd strongly suggest you get one. You can have a water separator installed for under $100. Both "integral" and "optional" water separators are usually drained by just turning a little petcock and emptying the water from the collection chamber of the separator. It is a good idea to check it weekly at first, to see how fast it fills up under normal conditions when you are driving on fuel from your usual source of supply.

**Getting Started on a Frosty Morning**

Because the metal cylinder walls become very cold whenever the temperature drops, most cars are harder to start in cold weather. On conventional cars, as we've already seen, this problem is handled by the **choke** and the **thermostat**. Because diesel engines require much higher temperatures to fire the fuel, they have always been harder to start in cold weather than conventional cars are. It is a matter of warming things up before the engine can run, and so a variety of heaters have been developed that keep various parts of the car warm and snuggly even when it is not being driven. Some of these gadgets may be on the car when you buy it; others can be bought and installed later on, if the need for them arises. If you are planning to buy a diesel car, be sure to ask which heating devices are included in the purchase price. If you live in a cold climate or do a lot of traveling, it might be a good idea to have several devices available for extreme weather conditions.

Many diesel cars come equipped with electrically powered **block heaters** that are built right into them to keep the **engine block** warm overnight. You simply park the car and plug the heater cord into a heavy-duty three-pronged extension cord. Then plug the extension cord into any 110-volt electrical socket. Don't skimp on the length of the extension cord—it can be 50 feet to a socket from a motel parking lot! I've been told that in Alaska, where a heater is a vital necessity, electrical outlets have been built right into some of the parking meters. I doubt that anyone tries to beat those meters, especially at −40°.

**Block Heaters**

If your car doesn't have a block heater, you can buy one and have it installed. There are various types available, but immersion-type heaters are the most popular. When buying a heater, consult the charts at the dealer's to match the wattage of the heater to the size of your engine and the range of weather you expect to encounter. A high-wattage heater will run up your electric bills unnecessarily if you have a small engine or don't expect the temperature to go below zero very often.

If your car won't start in cold weather and you've remembered to plug the block heater in, your **battery** may be the culprit. Batteries can lose 35 percent of their power at 32°F, and as much as 60 percent at 0°. Since the battery has to supply the glow plugs with sufficient "juice" to get things warmed up, a frostbitten battery isn't going to be of much use on an icy morning. There are two remedies to the problem: you can buy a battery with greater capacity (providing there is room for one under the hood), or you can buy a battery warmer. The two most popular models are the "hot plate" warmer, which simply slides under the battery like a cookie sheet and warms its little toesies, and the "electric blanket," which wraps around

**Battery Warmers**

000-311

the battery and uses more current to deal with really frigid situations. Both just plug in to a nearby 110-volt socket.

**Oil Warmers and Other Gadgets**

You can buy a heated **dipstick** to heat the oil in the engine **crankcase** (just trade it for your normal dipstick and plug it in) and a host of other gadgets to warm the coolant in the engine and the fuel in the fuel lines. Most of us don't need all this stuff, but they tell me that this book sells in Alaska, so I thought I'd cover the subject thoroughly...

I recently came across a handy hint which might work in a pinch. On a day when your block heater isn't able to combat the cold effectively, try turning on your electric hair dryer and putting the nozzle into the car's air intake. The warm air should help your engine warm up faster.

**What Not to Do on a Frosty Morning**

Never use engine starting fluids to start your engine—no matter how anxious you are to get under way. The ether in these fluids can ignite at such low temperatures that you risk a fire or an explosion—either of which can mean severe damage to both yourself and your precious car. Although there are instructions on the containers, it's just too hard to measure the "safe" proportions required. If you feel that you must use this stuff, there are starting-fluid injection kits that are safe and effective and you might want to have one of these installed. Just stay away from those "convenient" spray cans!

Well, dear friends, we've covered all the basic systems found on cars with both conventional and diesel engines. You now know more about cars than most people do and are equipped to do the basic maintenance on all but the most exotic vehicles. So let's shift our focus from the garage to the roadways and talk about driving, traveling, and coping with the unexpected. In short, let's get the show on the road!

# 15

# On the Road:
# How to Drive Economically,
# Travel Safely, and What
# to Do If Your Car
# Drops Dead on the Freeway

This chapter can really expand your life, if you let it. After all, you are no longer a dummy about cars, and you are as well-equipped as most other people to head for the high adventure of the open road. It's time to get out of the neighborhood/office/shopping rut and onto the busiest freeways and the most remote byways. There may be bumps and surprises ahead, but the joy of exploring the unknown will be well worth it. Here's how to save fuel, pack and travel by car and trailer, cope with accidents, and diagnose and deal with breakdowns. In short, everything you need to know in order to get out there and really let your car take you places!

**How to Drive "Eco-logically"**

In previous chapters, I have touched on the relationship between good maintenance and fuel economy. If your car is well tuned and lubricated, it will burn less fuel and contribute less pollution to the ecology. This is no longer news to anybody, and if you have become involved to the point where you are regularly changing your oil, tuning your carburetor, replacing your points and plugs, and generally keeping your car at the peak of efficiency, you are probably already happily aware that you are now getting better mileage than you ever did in the past. But there are several other ways to save fuel. Fuel crises may come and go, and we may all be rolling in money someday, but unless every driver learns to drive efficiently, we are going to go on wasting fuel and dumping the unburned residue into the ecology. So here are some ways to do your bit for the ecology when you and your car are on the road. I call it "eco-logic" because it makes sense to view your car and your driving techniques from an environmental perspective as well as from an automotive point of view. The two are intimately related, as you will see.

**Starting Up Without Warming Up**

When you start your car in the morning, do you warm it up before you drive off? No good! Most manuals will caution you not to indulge in lengthy warm-ups. They waste fuel, pollute the air, and increase wear on your car.

What exactly happens when you start your car? When you kick the gas pedal once or twice, the **choke** on your **carburetor** automatically closes (unless you have a manual choke). It does this to cut down on the amount of air that is going into the carburetor. This increases the vacuum in the **venturi** and draws more fuel than usual into the engine. This enriched **fuel/air** mixture helps the car to heat up more quickly. It is also necessary because part of the fuel will condense on the cold metal walls of the **intake manifold** and not get to the engine at all. The whole thing takes only a minute or two, and once the car is warm, the choke opens and things go back to normal. At this point you simply waste fuel by sitting there with the engine **idling** at zero miles to the gallon. And if you happen to be sitting in a closed garage, you can waste *yourself* with carbon monoxide fumes.

If your car keeps stalling unless you warm it up and your car has a carburetor, check the choke:

**How to Check Your Choke**

Before you start the car in the morning, remove the **air cleaner** and look into the **carburetor barrel**. The choke is probably open. Have someone kick the gas pedal once or twice, and the choke should close. (If you can get someone to help, you'll save yourself a lot of running around. If that doesn't work, try jiggling the **throttle** linkage; it may just be stuck.) Have your helper start the car and let it idle. After a minute or two the choke should open again. If it doesn't, or if it never closed, it could be stuck. A little carburetor cleaner can be squirted in to free it, or a teeny drop of oil might help. If it still won't work properly, check the choke adjustment according to the instructions in Chapter 7.

If your choke appears to be working properly but the car continues to stall if you don't warm it up, then check the **carburetor settings** with a tach/dwell meter after the car has heated up. You may find that the idle speed is too low, which can cause the car to stall when it should be idling; on the other hand, a too-rich fuel mixture or a too-fast idle speed will waste fuel. Chapter 7 can help you here, too.

If your carburetor is properly adjusted and the car still doesn't seem to warm up properly until you've driven it for several miles, it might be the **thermostat** that's at fault. As you probably remember, the thermostat simply keeps the water from circulating out of the engine until the engine warms up. This helps the engine to warm up more quickly. If your thermostat is on the blink, the whole process will take longer. Consult Chapter 8 for instructions on locating, testing, and replacing your thermostat.

**Checking Your Car Out Eco-logically**

While you're at it, take another look at your air cleaner. If the **air filter** is dirty, you can lose a mile per gallon at 50 mph. Remember, if you can improve your mileage by only 10 percent, you can save an average of 77 gallons a year! And according to the Automotive Parts and Accessories Association (APAA), if every car owner saved just one gallon a week, the nation could save more than 300,000 barrels of fuel per year!

Other things to check while you are under the hood:

**The PCV Valve**

If your **PCV valve** is not functioning properly, you are going to be running your engine less efficiently, and you might be burning and polluting your oil, too. Check it according to the instructions in Chapter 7.

**The Points and Plugs**

Misfiring **spark plugs** can cost you up to 25 percent in mileage! If your **ignition system** is overdue for a tune-up, do it—or have it done—now! A simple **tune-up** can reduce carbon monoxide and hydrocarbon exhaust emissions (that's air pollution, folks) by 30 to 50 percent! It is also a good idea to check your **dwell** and examine at least one spark plug every 5,000 miles, to be sure your car is running efficiently. If the dwell is off, the **rubbing block** could wear away and your **points** would stop opening and closing. If you check at least one of your plugs against the chart in Chapter 5, it will tell you if you are running too hot, burning oil, or losing power in some other manner.

**The Fan Belt and Other Drive Belts**

Since these belts connect your **fan, water pump, alternator**, and a variety of other devices, a belt that's too loose or too tight can result in a serious loss of efficiency. It should have about half an inch of "give" and should not be frayed or badly worn. A properly adjusted **fan belt** will keep your **battery** charged and help you to start faster, with less fuel consumption.

O.K. Now you are ready to get in and drive away.

**Eco-logical Driving Techniques**

First, you must view your driving techniques in terms of *fuel consumption*. In other words, if you are driving at 55 mph and you accelerate to 65 mph and have to

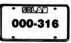

step on the brake after a block or two, you have wasted the gasoline it took to accelerate the car, because you've had to return to the original speed so soon. So check before putting on extra speed to be sure you won't have to waste that effort by slowing for a blinker, crossroad, or curve ahead. This kind of thinking is the key to driving efficiently. Every time you step on the gas pedal you are using gas. Every time you step on the brake pedal you are losing the speed that you used the gas to achieve.

It takes power to move a car from a stationary position. Either you can apply that power efficiently, by starting and accelerating slowly, or you can blow the whole thing by slamming on the accelerator for a quick getaway. A fast start may cost you 8 miles per gallon for the first 4 miles. A slow start can carry you 50 percent further on the same amount of gas! Try to go slowly, at least for the first mile. Once you are underway, keep an eye on the speed limits and pace yourself accordingly, especially in city traffic. Unless you are racing the stork to the hospital, you will probably want to keep within the speed limits anyway. So if the limit on a city street is 35 mph, don't jump off at each light, speed down the street, and have to stop for the light at the end of each block. Those traffic lights are set for the speed limit. If you maintain a nice, steady 35, you will find that the lights will magically turn green as you approach them and you will not have to stop—or start—so often. Results: less work for you and 15 percent less fuel consumed. The AAA reports that your gasoline efficiency could be increased by as much as 44 percent if all your stop-and-go driving techniques were improved!

What about changing lanes and passing other cars on the freeway? Each time you do this you accelerate to pass or change lanes and then usually have to step on the brake to fit back into the traffic pattern. The result is up to 30 percent more fuel wasted. Try to stay in lane if you can. And when you get stuck behind a slowpoke, wait for the opportunity to pass without any automotive histrionics.

My mother used to tell me that the mark of a fine chauffeur was that the passengers were never aware that the car was moving. She never had a chauffeur, to my knowledge, but she was—and is—a good driver. She taught me never to stop short if I could help it, but to anticipate the stop and to slow down gradually. Sometimes you can slow down by just taking your foot off the accelerator. Great! You can't use extra gasoline when your foot is off the gas pedal. The same goes for dramatic changes in speed. Try to set a steady pace on the road and around the curves. If you are not speeding, you may be able to account for a lot of the slowdowns by decelerating, rather than by braking. You won't wear out your brakes as quickly, and you will save fuel. If you have a **manual transmission**, you can **downshift** to slow down, as well.

Try to accelerate slowly and smoothly. It may fool your **accelerator pump** into not supplying an unneeded extra squirt of fuel to your carburetor. And, if your carburetor has secondary barrels that cut in at higher speeds (some two-barrel and all **four-barrel carburetors** have this feature) try to stay below the cut-in level, especially if you are going to have to slow down soon, anyway.

Arrange your car seat so that you are as comfortable as possible. Research has shown that a comfortable driving position will help you to tread lightly on the gas pedal. A light foot on the gas pedal saves gas. By traveling at 50 mph, a "featherfoot" can get 20 percent better gas mileage than someone can who is tromping on the pedal and doing 70. This is because wind resistance increases at higher speeds, and every mile per hour over 50 costs you more than 1 percent in mileage. An extra 5 mph will cost you 7 percent, and so on. Besides, your car's **chassis** will age twice as fast at 70 mph! It may get you there sooner, but will it be waiting for you when you're ready to go home?

When you approach a hill, try to build up speed slowly before you get there. The extra momentum will carry you at least part of the way up the hill. Don't accelerate to maintain your speed while you are climbing unless you are holding up traffic. Try to keep the gas pedal steady, and never, never crest the top of a hill at high speeds; you'll only have to brake on the way down, wasting the gas that got you up there so quickly in the first place. Try coasting down the other side, using the weight of the car and its momentum to carry you down with your foot off the accelerator.

You can use your **transmission** to save fuel, too. If you have an automatic transmission, ease up on the gas pedal at around 18 to 22 miles an hour. This will allow the transmission to shift into high gear more easily. As you may remember, the higher the gear, the less strain on the engine—and the less fuel consumed. Does the car have **overdrive**? It can save another 10 percent! Owners of cars with manual transmissions can do the same thing by shifting into higher gears as soon as possible. The APAA suggests that you shift into second gear at about 5 to 8 miles per hour and into higher gears at the lowest speed that the engine will take without laboring or lugging. If you haven't already practiced this, start now.

Here's a really way-out way to save gas. Did you know that a *left turn* uses more gas than a right turn? That's because you generally have to wait, with the car idling at 0 mph, until the road is clear for the turn. Then you have to overcome inertia and get into low gear to get moving again. If you really want to be a gas saver, try to structure your trips around the city to include as few left turns as possible. By the same thinking, it is more eco-logical to go around the block than to make a U-turn if the turn involves a lot of stopping and starting as you shift from forward to reverse, and to forward again. A nice slow cruise around the block uses less gasoline and probably won't take much more of your time.

While you are tinkering around with structuring trips to save gas, try the following:

1 Don't make a lot of little trips; keep a list and combine them into one longer one. A one-mile trip on a cold engine can cut fuel economy by as much as 70 percent.

2 Eliminate unnecessary trips by letting your fingers do the driving through the phone book, or by writing letters.

3 Arrange a car pool to work or to school if you can. These are not only eco-logical; they often result in new friendships as well.

4 Have you ridden a bike lately? How about the bus?

5 A local store may have slightly higher prices than the one at the edge of town, but in terms of time, gasoline, and wear and tear on your car, the neigh-

borhood store may be cheaper. If you are committed to the distant markets, experiment with shopping only once a week, or every ten days, instead of hopping over there whenever you run out of something. You can car-pool to those distant shopping centers too.

6 If you can, choose your routes carefully. A "short-cut" over a poorly paved road can cost 15 percent in fuel penalties—and a gravel road ups that figure to 35 percent!

**Streamlining Your Car Eco-logically**

We've already mentioned *wind resistance* and its relation to mileage. Take a tip from racing drivers and from the designers of fast cars and planes. Look at your car to see what you can do to cut down on wind resistance and otherwise improve its fuel consumption:

Did you know that a highly *waxed* car cuts wind resistance dramatically? And it looks good too.

Those light-looking *roof racks* are deceptive. They create quite a bit of drag, especially when fully loaded, and the ensuing wind resistance substantially interferes with the air flow around the car. As a matter of fact, a small trailer loaded with the same gear is probably not as big a liability. Trailers travel in the "wake" of the car and meet with less air resistance. Of course they weigh more too, but once underway, they follow along easily if you don't try to speed. Besides, you always disconnect the trailer when you don't need it, but you tend to carry the empty roof rack around even when you have no load to put on it.

*Open side windows* also increase wind resistance. Try to use the interior vents and the vent windows whenever you can. An air conditioner may seem to be a good answer in terms of wind resistance, but you will still lose mileage if you have one. First, the car has to carry around the weight of the air conditioner and its coolant. Second, it has to put out extra power to make the air conditioner work. You pay your money and you take your choice—air conditioners consume an extra 2½ miles per gallon!

Did you know that **radial tires** can save you up to 10 percent in fuel consumption? They roll more freely than conventional tires do. If your car cannot use—or does not need—radial tires, you can compromise with bias-belted tires the next time you need tires. Underinflated tires consume about 1 mile per gallon of extra gasoline. And they wear out faster too. Air costs nothing, so be sure your tires are getting all they need. On long trips, add about 4 pounds more than is recommended to your tires, but don't go above 32 psi. To get an accurate reading, always put air into your tires in the morning before you drive the car (except to get to the air pump, of course). After a car has been driven for a while, the tires heat up and the air in them expands. Get the snow tires off the car as soon as possible—they consume a lot more fuel, too.

Check your *brakes* if you haven't already done so. Sometimes a poorly adjusted brake will "drag" while the car is in motion. It takes more power to move the wheel against the dragging brake, and the result is that your brake linings—and the gas in your tank— won't last as long. To check for dragging brakes, jack up each wheel and spin it. If a brake shoe is dragging, you will feel it as you try to turn the wheel on the hub.

*Worn wheel bearings* will cut fuel mileage in the same way. Check them at the same time by listening for a rumbling sound as you spin each wheel. If your bearings or your brake shoes seem to be preventing your wheels from moving freely, have the situation remedied quickly or you will soon be paying for new brake linings, a new brake drum, or a worn axle.

The overall *weight* of your car is significant, too. Every 500 pounds of chrome, steel, and power accessories which you haul around will cost you from 2 to 5 miles per gallon! A car that weighs only 2,500 pounds can get you twice the mileage of a car that weighs 5,000 pounds. And it will get you there just as fast....

While you are at it, clean the junk out of the *trunk compartment*. You use extra fuel to haul that weight around, too.

Possibly the most dramatic way to save fuel is to trade that faithful old gas-eater in for a good used *compact car*. Most small cars don't need power accessories either, so you win twice. And while you are considering it, did you know that a car with a big, wide front-end creates enough wind resistance to substantially increase its fuel consumption over that of a car with a smaller, narrower front-end?

How about this one for eco-logical sophistication: A car with a 10-percent-higher **rear axle ratio** can save you from 2 to 5 percent in mileage. It really doesn't matter if you don't know what rear axle ratio is; just look at the specs the next time you are trying to choose another car and pick the one with the higher ratio if everything else is equal. The higher the rear axle ratio, the slower the engine has to turn at any given speed. That's why it saves you fuel.

**Filling 'er Up Eco-logically**

Did you know that, like everything else, gasoline expands with heat? Ten gallons of gas will expand by 8/10 of a quart (that's the same as 4/5—as in a bottle of whiskey) with a temperature increase of 30 degrees? So if the day is going to be a scorcher, try to fill up in the early morning or in the evening, when the air is cooler. This way, your gas tank will hold more gasoline at no extra cost, and you won't have to make as many trips to the filling station.

If you really want to fill the tank efficiently, shake the car a bit while it is filling, to get rid of trapped air in the tank. If you think this is compulsive, consider that gas expands 1/10 of 1 percent for every 10 degrees of heat. If you are judging your fuel consumption by dividing the number of gallons in your tank into the number of miles you drove before it needed refilling, you will get more impressive results if the tank is *really* full to begin with—and not partially full of heat-expanded gasoline and partially full of air.

This does *not* mean that you should jam those extra ounces of gasoline into the tank after the filler hose has automatically shut itself off. Many station attendants like to do this because it means extra money for that extra gas, but it also increases the danger that the overfilled tank will simply run over and spill that gasoline on the ground if you should travel up a hill soon afterward or park in the heat of the sun. The lost gasoline is not only a waste of fuel, but the fumes from it contribute substantially to air pollution. So fill your tank efficiently, but don't overfill it. And check your fuel tank cap to be sure its gasket is in good shape.

As the enlightened gurus of the East say, "On any path the Way is of more importance than the Goal." This is especially true of car trips. If getting there and back again is dismal, the short time you spend enjoying the object of your journey often is simply not worth the effort. The key to happy tripping by car or camper lies less in *how much* you take than in *what* you take and *how* you pack it. It is important to travel light for fuel economy, since it takes gasoline to lug every pound around. How then do you evaluate what you need and what you can leave behind? Here are a couple of tips that work for me:

Your car may be the most important member of your entourage. See that it is roadworthy and be sure to pack its necessities as well as those of the others making the trip. Check the car out thoroughly to be sure it's ready for the road. Do this a couple of days beforehand to provide time to handle any problems you discover. Use the following as a checklist:

**There and Back Again: How to Prepare Your Car for a Long Trip**

**Tires**

1 Check the treads for signs of misalignment, following the instructions on pages 237 and 238. A couple of hundred miles at highway speeds can finish off a pair of new radials if they are out of alignment.

2 Check also to be sure that the tires have enough tread left to make the trip. It's better to buy a new set a few miles early when you can shop for the best prices than to risk the dangers of a blowout in some out-of-the-way place where tires (and medical help) may not be readily available!

3 Be sure to reread Chapter 9 so that, if you get a flat tire on the road, you will be prepared to jack up your car and change the tire. Before the trip, you may want to follow the instructions on using a hollow pipe to remove and replace power-tightened lug nuts so they'll be easier to handle in an emergency.

4 Check the pressure in each tire according to the instructions beginning on page 239. Consult your **owner's manual** or your dealer to find the correct pressure for your tires, and to see if it would be O.K. for you to add a couple of extra pounds of

pressure to help you carry an extra-heavy load. Don't exceed the maximum embossed on the tire. If you are going to be driving where it is very hot, remember that hot air expands and the pressure inside the tires will rise along with the thermometer. The same goes for high-speed driving—freeway speeds dramatically increase the heat and pressure in your tires. Check them in the morning when they're cold to be sure that they are not too far over or under the limits. This will extend the life of the tires and give you the best ride and maximum fuel efficiency. Generally speaking, nothing horrible will happen if your tire pressure goes a bit over the maximum when it gets hot, as long as both tires on an **axle** remain equal in pressure. If you find excessively unequal pressure developing in a tire, have it checked for a slow leak or for damage to the inside of the tire. DON'T FORGET TO CHECK YOUR SPARE TIRE!

**Cooling System**

If you haven't changed the **coolant** and flushed the **cooling system** in a year, do it now, especially if you are going to be traveling to an area with extremely high or low temperatures. Easy instructions start on page 175.

**Under-the-Hood Check**

Go through the complete under-the-hood check on pages 99–110. It will prevent about 70 percent of the problems that cause highway breakdowns. This may be the most important thing you do to prepare for any trip!

**Give the Car a Tune-up**

This is no time to get lazy. Take the time to tune the car before you leave. Proper **carburetor** adjustments, clean **spark plugs**, and accurate **timing** will really pay off in fuel economy and performance, and that couple of extra miles to the gallon really adds up to big savings on long trips!

**Pack a Bag for Your Car**

It is bad enough to have something go wrong with your car while you are on the road, but if you have to wait hours for a tow truck, just to replace a **fan belt**—

or if you have to unpack the entire trunk compartment to have access to the remedy for the situation—you are really going to be miserable. To avoid this, be sure to take the following items along, packed in a box or a bag, and placed where you can get at them easily:

**Jumper cables** to start your car if your battery goes dead

A **jack** and a **lug wrench** for changing tires

Clean lint-free rags

The wrenches and screwdrivers you use most frequently

A couple of old **spark plugs** that have been gapped properly

An old or new set of **points, rotor**, and **condenser**

A spare **fan belt**

A tire gauge

Extra fuses

A can of inflator/sealant to be used only for flats that occur when you can't change the tire on the spot

Spare radiator hoses

A can of engine **oil**

A can of **brake fluid**

Flares, lights or reflectors

A gallon of water

Some tinfoil to prevent **vapor lock** in your **fuel line** if you are going to be driving under conditions that may overheat the car

Tire chains, a small bag of sand, and an extra blanket if you are headed for snowy areas

Your copy of *Auto Repair for Dummies* with the **Specifications Record** on page 436 filled in

A **service manual** for your car, if you have one

**If You Drive a Diesel**

If you drive a **diesel** car and are going off the beaten path, be sure to bring along a couple of cans of **diesel oil**, a few cans of the proper lubricating oil, and any special tools your car may require. On winter trips, also remember to bring an extension cord at least 50 feet long for your **block heater** and any other heaters your car may need.

Check the diesel chapter for tips and information on how to find diesel fuel or acceptable substitutes in emergency situations, or remote areas, and how to get your car started in unexpectedly cold weather.

**Wash and Wax Your Car** This is not to impress the public! A highly waxed surface improves the air flow and will decrease your fuel consumption. It will also make it easier to remove dead bugs and dirt after the trip. For instructions, see Chapter 16.

**Travel Light** When packing your gear for a trip, view the entire car as a backpack. This is not a joke. It takes a great deal of energy to tote a heavy pack around, and carrying extra weight in the car will consume energy, too—the kind you pay for at a gas station. So, weigh each decision carefully when packing for the trip. Follow the old camping adage: *When in doubt, leave it out!* Remember, the less you tote along, the less you will have to pack and unpack, as well.

**Roof Racks and Bumper Racks** Make sure that the bindings which hold the racks in place are secure, and be sure that everything is tied down and covered so that it can't shift or be blown away.

Inspect all the straps, rubber parts, and other gadgets involved with the racks periodically to be sure they aren't deteriorating from age, wind, sun, etc.

Be sure that front- or rear-bumper bike or ski racks don't obstruct visibility. They should not interfere with access to the trunk or the hood, but if this is unavoidable, be sure you know how to remove them easily in case of emergency.

**Renting or Buying Trailers** If you must take along an enormous amount of gear, consider renting a small trailer. It will cost you less in fuel consumption than a roof rack, because the trailer will follow along in the wake of the car, while the roof rack will interfere seriously with the air flow. Although the trailer weighs more, it should roll along easily, and the only time the car will have to exert much energy to move it is when it starts up from a dead stop or has to climb a steep hill. This is what makes freight trains so fuel efficient, too. However, if your car has a diesel engine, it may not be suitable for towing heavy loads. Most diesels should not pull more than 2,000 pounds—they lack the power, and the undue stress will shorten their lives (as it shortens ours). Be sure to check with your dealer to find out what your diesel car can handle. If you are thinking about buying a new car and fully intend to travel with a trailer often, it would be wise to buy the car with a **trailer-towing package** installed. See page 409 for more about this useful **optional equipment**.

Here are some tips about towing trailers:

**Tips on Towing Trailers**

1 Be sure that the trailer sales or rental agency provides you with an adequate tow bar or trailer hitch. There are several different types with varying rates of efficiency. If you are only renting a small unit for one job or trip, any of the standard varieties designed to adapt to ordinary bumpers will probably be sufficient. Remember that trailers must not swerve from side to side, and must be secured by a strong safety chain as well as a rear trailer hitch.

2 If you are buying a trailer, or are going on a long trip with a large live-in unit, consider the alternative towing devices carefully. The proper towing equipment affects the way the trailer follows your vehicle around curves, and governs its movement when you stop abruptly, back up, and park. Your dealer will be glad to demonstrate the latest equipment, and friends with trailers can provide insights as to what you need and what frills to avoid. Remember, good towing equipment is an investment in safety as well as in traveling easy.

3 When packing a trailer, distribute the weight evenly and don't overload. Tie down the contents securely, to avoid weight shifts and the loss of items that could blow away at highway speeds. Use strong materials for covering—I've had paper bags remove themselves completely from things in the back of my convertible, leaving everything that was in the bag exposed. The heavier objects remained, but the light stuff vanished in the breeze. And lightweight plastic drop cloths will do the same disappearing act!

4 When the trailer is loaded, check the headlights on the car to be sure that they are not tilted upward because of the weight on the rear **suspension**. By law, headlights must be properly aimed at all times.

5 Check the rear of the car to be sure that the weight isn't pulling it down too far. If the car is riding very low, you may need to modify the suspension or install heavy-duty **shock absorbers** to carry the load.

6 Law requires that vehicles towing trailers must have a rear-view mirror mounted on each side of the car so that the driver can see at least 200 feet behind the vehicle.

7 Have the company where you get the trailer connect the trailer's brake lights and directional signals to those on your car so they operate together.

**Driving Rules for Trailers and Other Recreational Vehicles**

Many of the rules below have been taken from the *California Driver's Handbook.* Since California has excellent traffic laws, I felt that this was a good source. However, since my intention was not to write the definitive *Handbook for Driving RVs and Trailers* (although writing one may not be a bad idea!), I want to caution you to check the laws that apply in the state you live in and in any areas you may be driving through. Contact the AAA, or if you don't have access to their services, contact the state Motor Vehicles Bureau in each area. Some companies which sell or rent RVs provide such data as a public service. However, most of the rules below are good common sense for safe driving anywhere and should be followed whether a particular state requires them or not.

1 Stopping a trailer or a heavily loaded RV or camper places a heavy load on your brakes. Remember that the load you are hauling tends to want to keep going after you've come to a stop. Your car may be able to pull a heavy trailer, but are your *brakes* in shape to stop both vehicles in an emergency? Check to be sure your brakes are adequate and are in good condition, and keep plenty of distance between you and the car in front of you to allow plenty of time and space for stopping. Drive with your eyes a mile ahead to anticipate any circumstances which may cause you to have to stop quickly.

This includes cars waiting to turn onto the highway from side roads, cars that are signaling to change lanes up ahead, cars that appear to be driven by drunken or erratic drivers, road work, and so on. Defensive driving techniques are twice as necessary when you are controlling twice as many vehicles or twice the normal load!

2 Vehicles towing trailers must keep to the right lane of the road, except to pass slower cars or to use left-lane exits. Remember that most freeway accidents are the result of a lane change.

3 If there are five or more vehicles following you at reduced speeds because you are negotiating a winding road or a hill, you must pull into any available turnout and let them pass.

4 In some states, it is illegal to tow a trailer coach or camp trailer with a passenger in it. Certain "fifth-wheel" trailers are sometimes exempt from this. Even if you are driving a truck with a camper, it must have an unobstructed exit door that can be opened from outside and inside if you want to drive with passengers in it.

5 Recreational vehicles with stoves or heaters must carry fire extinguishers. Check yours now and then. Even if you have a properly rated fire extinguisher on the vehicle, if it doesn't work in an emergency, you may find your insurance company most unco-operative.

6 Know the net weight (what it weighs unloaded) of your vehicle as well as its gross weight (the maximum it can weigh loaded). If its net weight is less than 4,000 pounds it should not tow more than one other vehicle with a gross weight of under 6,000 pounds. You should check the Highway Patrol or DMV in the states you visit for other weight regulations.

## What to Do in Case of an Accident

Now that you're all charged up to travel, let's get to the down side of the deal. Things can go wrong with your car on the freeway and on remote roads as well. Up to now, you may have shied away from touring by car because you felt you would be helpless in an emergency. At this point, you know as much as or more than most drivers do about how your car works and what it requires. So, if you learn how to troubleshoot and deal with breakdowns and accidents, you will be pretty well equipped to cope with the unexpected. That is just what the rest of this chapter provides. Read it thoroughly, and be sure to take the book and basic tools with you when you travel. Remember, the most exciting roads are often the least traveled. They may be relatively bumpy and filled with unexpected potholes and pitfalls, but the joy of exploration and the lure of the unknown more than make up for the inconveniences and occasional unpleasant surprises. One of the best reasons for getting involved with your car is that you will feel more secure in your ability to cope with the unexpected. If you keep it feeling fit and powerful, it will be willing to take you where you have never ventured before. And how many of our friends are willing to do that for us?

Nobody likes to think about the possibility of being involved in a car accident, but the fact is that they do happen occasionally, despite our best efforts to prevent them. Working on the "fire-drill principle," it's better to know what actions to take before such an emergency occurs than to be caught short in a crisis. Accordingly, let's talk about what you should do if you find yourself in such unhappy circumstances. The following guidelines should be followed, whether you are the one who caused the accident or the unfortunate victim of one:

**Aiding the Injured**    Obviously, anyone who is injured should command your first attention. Don't attempt to move an injured person, unless there is a danger of the car catching fire or of their getting hit by traffic. People with neck and back injuries can be more seriously injured if you move them. Although the Good Samaritan Act says you are not liable if your act is reasonable and in good conscience, you may still be sued if something you did to aid or comfort an injured person had negative effects. So unless you are qualified to administer first aid, be sure to summon help. In many communities, simply dialing 911 or the local emergency number will bring whatever aid is necessary. Coinless emergency telephones are also available along most major highways and freeways. And the highway patrol or other law-enforcement agency may monitor certain CB channels for emergency help calls.

Of course, if someone is bleeding profusely, it is of paramount importance to try to control the flow of blood rather than worrying about the legal implications. My copy of the *California Driver's Handbook* says "Bleeding: Apply direct pressure. Even severe bleeding can almost always be stopped by putting continuous pressure on the bleeding site."

If the injured person is suffering from shock, place a blanket or a coat over him to keep him warm. Aside from this, just providing love and support is probably the most effective way you can help anyone who has been hurt, unless you are trained in first aid (which isn't a bad idea, is it?).

If you injure or kill an animal, stop and try to find the owner. If you can't, call the local Humane Society and the police and stay with the animal until help arrives. If there are witnesses who can testify that you could not avoid hitting the animal, it would be wise to get their names and addresses.

**Turn Off the Ignition**

If any of the cars which were wrecked in the accident are still running, turn off the ignition, to avoid fires from spilled gas. No matter how shaky you are, don't smoke around the vehicles involved!

**Protect Oncoming Traffic**

If you can, move the vehicles out of the flow of traffic. If not, or if there is glass or oil or gasoline all over the roadway, get someone to wave approaching vehicles away from the scene, to avoid pile-ups. If you wish to use flares, be very careful not to set them anywhere near spilled gasoline! They should be placed far enough away from the accident to give oncoming traffic a chance to slow down and change lanes.

**Search the Area for Victims**

In a severe accident, people are sometimes thrown some distance from their vehicles. You may want to take a look around to make sure that no one is lying nearby, unobserved.

**Notify the Police**

In any traffic accident, you must notify the authorities. If you don't, you may have trouble recovering expenses from your insurance company and can be open to prosecution as a hit-and-run driver. Send someone to summon them, or use a roadside emergency phone, if one is available. In many states, you must fill out a written police report about even minor accidents and send a report to the state Department of Motor Vehicles as well. If you don't, you run the risk of losing your driver's license.

If you can, make a quick sketch of the accident, noting any nearby cross streets or other topography and the direction and speed of every vehicle involved and where it ended up. If there are skid marks, put them in your sketch. Don't forget the proper time and date and any unusual weather conditions that may have had a bearing on the accident.

**Exchange Information**

No matter how small the accident appears to be, it is important that you get the following information from the driver of each car involved and from anyone else who may have been injured:

Name

Address

Phone number

License number

Insurance company

You will need this information in order to report the accident in the event the police don't arrive at the scene, and also for your insurance company. If you leave the scene of an accident without exchanging this information, you may be liable for legal prosecution.

**Get Witnesses**

All too often drivers who have talked over a minor fender-bender at the scene and agreed that there was little or no damage suddenly find themselves sued for "whiplash" injuries or damages to the other car—or cited for negligence, unsafe driving, or traffic violations. Therefore it is best to take whatever steps are necessary to get the details of the event down and recorded with the proper authorities right away. If there are witnesses to the accident, make every effort to get their names, addresses, and phone numbers, too. If they are uncooperative, write down the license plate numbers of their cars.

If you hit a parked car or accidentally damage someone's property, and you can't locate the owner when the accident occurs, leave your name, address, and phone number on the car you've hit, or attached to the site of the damage. If you are driving someone else's car, leave their name and address, too. To avoid "hit-and-run" prosecution, be sure to notify the local authorities.

**If You Are the Only Person Involved**

## What to Do if You Lock Yourself out of Your Car

Here's an "emergency" that may not be dangerous, but certainly can be exasperating! If you tend to be featherheaded and leave the keys in your car fairly often, you may be tempted to hide an extra key somewhere on your car. However, I must warn you that unless you are very clever about where you hide it, you may be inviting someone to steal your car or its contents. Those little magnetic boxes that stick to the metal surface of the body or frame are the best bets here, but be sure to place it in an obscure and hard-to-reach area where it will not jiggle loose and fall out. I leave the choice of area up to you—if I publish a list of suggestions, then the Car Thieves of America will have me up for their annual "Helpful Dummy Award"! Be imaginative. It is better to have to struggle a little to reach that extra key than to give the car away easily. And don't hide your house key with it. You don't want to give *everything* away, do you?

Assuming that you have decided not to risk hiding that extra set, here's how to get into your car without a key:

If you have conventional door locks on the car, obtain a wire coat hanger, straighten it out, bend the end of it into a little hook, and insert it between the rubber molding and the window or vent window. Then, carefully, with the dexterity of a jewel thief, hook it around the door button and pull it up.

If you or your auto manufacturer has had the foresight to replace these buttons with the new, smooth, cylindrical ones, your car has less of a chance of being stolen, and you have a harder job getting into it without a key. You might be able to hook the door handle, but most of them will straighten out your hanger before they condescend to budge.

If you call a locksmith, you will have to prove that you own the car before any work will be done and you will probably also have to pay immediately. So let's hope that you didn't lock your wallet in there, along with your keys. If your key has been lost outside your car and your steering wheel locks, they may have to dismount the steering wheel and remove the lock—and this can run to $70 or more, plus time and aggravation, before you can drive off again. However, there is good news! Each car key is coded by the manufacturer and, if you have the key code number, a locksmith can make you a new key as long as you have identification and can describe the car in terms of its vital statistics. GM car keys have little coded tags you knock out of the key and keep; other U.S. cars come with little metal tags with the number on them, and most foreign car makers engrave the number right on the keys. As a valuable favor to yourself, write down the code number where someone at home can read it to you in an emergency, and also record it, without identifying what it is, in your pocket address book or in your wallet *before you lose your keys.* If you don't know the code number for your keys, and you bought the car, new or used, from a dealer, they may still have the number on file. Failing that, a good locksmith may be able to analyze a key in fairly new condition and come up with the proper code for it. This kind of preventive work is worth doing right away, before you get into trouble!

If you should happen to lock yourself out of the car while you have the trunk open, it is sometimes possible to move the rear seat out of the way and gain access to the rear of the car or you can hide an extra ignition key in the trunk.

If you get totally freaked out and decide to break a window, break the little vent window, if you have one. It's cheaper to replace, and sometimes the latch will break before the glass does. If you have to break the glass, wrap something around your hand and use a stone or a heavy object. Keep your head away from flying glass, although most auto glass should be shatterproof. Don't break a window that will interfere with visibility when you are driving home to face the jeers of your family and friends.

If you'd like to keep your car locks in good working order, or unstick them when they get too gummed-up to work properly, a squirt of spray lubricant such as LPS1 or WD-40 works wonders. Some people use graphite, but too much of this stuff can cause the lock to malfunction.

**What to Do If Your Car Drops Dead on the Freeway**

This is really a trouble-shooting section. Whether the car has died on the freeway or in front of the house, it is always a time of unrivaled panic and stress. But an informed, well-organized approach to diagnosing your sick monster's ills will pay off by getting you moving again with a minimum loss of time, money, and composure. The problems involved are seldom serious, and you can usually solve them by keeping a cool head and following these instructions.

First, if you are on a freeway, try to get to the righthand shoulder of the road. Very often, if a car is going to do its swan song while in motion, it will give you a couple of hints first. Be alert to any sudden loss of power. Do you suddenly have to floor the accelerator to maintain speed or to keep moving at all? Have any of your warning lights gone on? It is worthwhile to stop immediately and check the cause. Is the car suddenly running roughly? Is the engine misfiring? Are there any new noises? Is the car pulling to one side? All of these are good reasons to head for the side of the road.

**Safety Precautions**

While the car is still going, try to coast down the shoulder until you are well away from any curves behind you. This will pay off when you are ready to get back onto the freeway, because you will be able to spot oncoming traffic before it's on your tail.

If the car has died right on the freeway and you can't get off the road, *don't do anything!* I know that it is unnerving to sit in a dead car, with traffic piling up behind you. But it is literally suicide to attempt to cross a high-speed freeway on foot. Most freeways that are heavily traveled are also heavily patrolled, and some nice highway patrol officer will be along before you know it. Once the officer is on the scene, it will be a simple matter to stop traffic long enough to push your car to the right shoulder.

Once you have reached the side of the road, take these additional safety precautions:

1 Don't work on your car from the left side, unless you will be standing well away from the right-hand lane. If you can't move the car farther off the road, climb into the area from the front or the right, if necessary, but keep away from traffic. That goes for changing left-hand tires, too.

2 If it is daylight, put on your emergency blinkers or your left-turn signal to alert oncoming traffic to the fact that your car is not moving.

3 If it is nighttime and you carry flares, place them about six feet behind the car to alert traffic. If you don't have any flares, you may carry a lantern, a large battery-operated light, or a couple of milk cartons filled with wax and a wick. If you have nothing, leave the right-hand car door open so the interior lights will go on and alert traffic.

Once you are safely off the road and ready to deal with the problem, try to view what happened in dietary terms. Your car lives on a mixture of air, fuel, and fire—as you probably remember. If it won't go, it is not getting one of these ingredients.

**Air** This is simple and probably not the problem. The car gets its air through the air cleaner. Unless the **air filter** is totally clogged, it should get enough air to keep it going. Of course your **choke** or **throttle** may be stuck in a closed position, and this could keep your car from breathing properly. Remove your air cleaner and look into the carburetor barrel. Is the choke open? Move the throttle linkage with your finger (that's the arm that makes the car rev when you push it). Does it seem to be moving freely? Then that's not your problem. Check your **PCV valve** to be sure it's clear and functioning. Look at those hoses—have any of them become disconnected or broken? Do you hear air whistling while the car idles—if it can? One strategic hose lost can slow or stop your car. Reclamp the wanderer or tape the hole, and you'll soon be on your way. Of course if you've made a habit of checking and replacing worn hoses before disaster strikes, you have avoided this trouble completely.

**Fuel**

If the car will **turn over** but won't start running, it may not be getting any fuel. Are you out of gas? Even if your **gas gauge** says you still have some, the gauge may be on the blink. When did you fill the car last?

Did you lose power before the car died? Look down the carburetor again and push the **accelerator pump** arm. Is fuel squirting into the **venturi**? Then the **float bowl** is full. Still, it may not be getting a fresh supply when it needs it. Disconnect the hose that leads from the carburetor to the **fuel pump**. Somewhere along that line is the **fuel filter**. This could have jammed—especially if it hasn't been changed in ages. Place the end of the hose in a jar or plastic bag. If you don't have anything to put it in, let it hang down so the gas can run onto the ground. Don't let gasoline run out of the hose onto your clothes or all over the engine. If it's very hot, fan the area to disburse the fumes. Bump the starter and see if gasoline squirts out of the hose. If it does, then your fuel filter and fuel pump are probably all right. If nothing comes out of the hose, you probably either have a plugged fuel filter, a defective fuel pump, a broken fuel line, or you are out of gas.

If you can, try to eliminate the fuel filter as the villain by taking it out to see if gas comes out of the hose. If you have changed the filter recently, ignore this step and look under the rear end of the car to see if fuel is leaking from a broken fuel line. If you find nothing and you fail to find any other cause of trouble, tie a white rag to your door handle or antenna and wait for help, or try to get to a phone and contact a rescue unit or the AAA. With luck, help should arrive within half an hour.

Sometimes the problem is *too much* fuel. If you open your hood and find that everything is covered with gasoline, *don't try to start the car!* Gasoline is too inflammable to monkey around with. Just hoist that white flag and get some help.

If it's a very hot day and you've been on the road in stop-and-go traffic, you may have **vapor lock**. Chapter 8 tells you everything you need to know about it, and about all the other causes of overheating. For the time being, simply wrap a wet rag (assuming you are near a source of water) around the fuel line between the fuel pump and the carburetor and wait for things to cool down. If you haven't got a wet rag, try some tinfoil, and leave it in place after you get started. No tinfoil? Then just sit there and wait for the darn thing to cool down, and the vapor lock will go away.

Testing for Spark
Richard Freshman

**Fire** If the fuel is entering your carburetor as it is supposed to, then you are probably having ignition trouble. As you know, the "fire" is really electric current that is stored in the **battery**, replaced by the **alternator**, amplified by the **coil**, and directed by the **distributor** to each **spark plug**. If something along the way goes wrong, all the air and fuel in the world will not produce **combustion** in the car's **cylinders**, and it won't go. Since the car was running before it died, it's probably not the fault of the battery, **solenoid**, or starter, which brings you to the distributor cap. *With the engine off,* check to see if the cables that run from the distributor cap to the spark plugs are pushed down securely at each end. Check the cable that runs from the center of the cap to the coil to be sure it, too, is secure. How about the smaller wires that come out of the coil? *Please note that because many cars now have high-energy ignition systems that operate at 47,000 volts or higher, it is unsafe to pull a distributor or spark plug cable to test for a spark.* In fact, if you have an **electronic ignition system**, skip the rest of the checks under this heading. If your car has a nonelectronic ignition system, you can remove the distributor cap and look at the **points**. Do they open and close when you bump the starter? If not, adjust them so they do and check again for spark. If there is still no spark, your points could be oxidized, or fouled by a bit of grease or oil. Bump the engine so the points are closed, and insert the tip of a screwdriver, fingernail file, matchbook cover, or feeler gauge to rub the point surfaces to eliminate the oxidation or dirt. If you *still* don't get a spark, there's still another thing to try.

It is a good idea to keep your old **rotor**, points, and **condenser** in the trunk of your car after you replace them during a tune-up. First, try replacing the rotor with the old one. If that doesn't work, replace the condenser. If that doesn't work, replace the points. Don't worry about gapping them; as long as they open and close, the car will run. I have been told that the most frequent cause of car failure is improper lubrication of the **cam** when the points were changed. Because of this, the little **rubbing block** gets worn down, and then, even when the block rests on the **cam lobe**, there is not enough surface to force the points apart. That's why it's important to check your **dwell** every 5,000 miles and replace points at every tune-up.

If you've checked everything out and the car still won't go, then you are probably going to have to wait for help. Sometimes it's your coil or part of your engine that has given out. Sometimes it's the **transmission**. If that's the case, you may be saying good-bye to Old Faithful. All the comfort I can offer is that Chapter 18 will tell you how to buy a good used car. Most of the time, however, you will find the cause of the trouble by checking as I've outlined above. Or you will have plenty of warning before the car gives up the ghost. If you have not checked and maintained your car properly, if you have ignored the warnings, the **knockings**, the smoke from the **tail pipe**, the hesitations and the stalls, well—you asked for it.

As you work on your car, you will get to know it better. Before long you will find that you are becoming more sensitive to its signals. If something "sounds funny" or "smells funny" or just doesn't feel "right," you will soon sense it. This will help you forestall those sudden-death routines, because you will be preventing trouble or catching it before it reaches the terminal stage. Here's some "funny" things to be alert to:

## Symptoms of Trouble Ahead

1 *If a fan belt (or any other belt) is singing,* readjust or replace it. It should have at least half an inch of play in it and shouldn't be frayed, cracked, or glazed on the underside. Some belts tend to sing more than others. Rubbing a bit of petroleum jelly on the V-shaped undersides of these usually quiets them down. Don't drive with a broken **fan belt**. If you carry a spare or an old belt in the car, you may be able to save yourself towing charges.

**Sounds**

2 *If your radiator is singing,* check the cap. The rubber gasket may be worn and steam from the hot engine may be escaping past it.

3 *If your tires are squealing on curves,* and you aren't speeding, check treads and **alignment.**

4 *If your tires are "tramping,"* check inflation, tire wear, and wheel balance.

5 *If something is ticking rhythmically while your engine is idling,* shut off the engine, wait ten minutes and then check the oil level. The hydraulic lifters that operate your valves can make these noises if you are down as little as a quart of oil. If the level is low, add oil up to the "Full" line on the dipstick and check again in a couple of days. If you have enough oil, have a mechanic check the valve adjustment if your car has adjustable valves—some do not. Faulty valves can seriously affect your car's performance and fuel consumption.

6 *If there's a knocking sound in your engine,* stop the car and call for road service. It may just be a loose **rocker arm,** but if it's a loose bearing or a faulty **piston,** it can destroy the whole engine if you let it go unheeded.

7 *If there's a whistling noise* coming from under the hood, check the hoses for vacuum leaks. If it's inside the car, patch the weatherstripping according to the directions in Chapter 17.

8 *If there's an unlocatable sound,* get an old stethoscope from a medical supply house or ask the family doctor. Take off the rubber disc and insert a piece of tubing in its place (about 1½ inches will do). Then put the plugs in your ears, run the engine, and move the tube end of the stethoscope around the hood area. It will amplify the sound as you near the part that's causing it. A metal wrench will work this way too. Place one end of the wrench on the bone behind your ear, and, leaning over, place the other end of the wrench on the parts that seem to be the source of the noise. Be careful not to get a shock or get your hair tangled in the fan.

9 *If your brakes are squealing,* the brake linings may be greasy, glazed, or worn. Some disc brake pads have built-in wear sensors that squeal when it's time to replace them. Even though some disc brakes tend to squeal under normal circumstances, it's safer to have the brakes checked, or follow the instructions in Chapter 10 and check them yourself.

Small tube

A Piece of Tubing and an Old Stethoscope Make an Efficient Trouble-Shooting Device
Alexandra Soto

SGLAD
000-340

10 *If the car sounds like an old taxi,* especially when it is driven on a bumpy road, it probably just needs **lubrication**. You may get used to the squeaks and groans, but they also indicate wear, because they are caused by parts rubbing together or moving without the proper lubrication.

11 *If the car is idling with an offbeat rhythm,* it is not becoming creative, it is probably **misfiring**; one of the **spark plugs** or one of the cables that connect them to the **distributor cap** may be at fault.

   a *With the engine off,* check the spark plug cables for breaks or shorts in the wiring.

   b *With the engine off,* remove the spark plugs one at a time and check to see if they're clean and properly gapped. Replace any that are fouled or burned.

   c If that doesn't help, have a mechanic check the ignition system with an engine analyzer. People used to check spark plugs by holding them close to a metal surface to see whether a spark jumped across when the engine was cranked, but the high voltage in most ignition systems now makes that procedure extremely dangerous.

12 *If the idling is rough but even,* the **carburetor** may need to be adjusted. Chapter 7 shows how to do this yourself. If that doesn't work, you may need a new carburetor. Fuel-injected cars don't have carburetors, and a mechanic must check and adjust these complex electronic systems. Check the **compression** in each cylinder, following the instructions on the next two pages. If the engine needs rebuilding, you may prefer to get another engine—or another car.

13 *If you hear something squeaking, rattling, or vibrating,* Chapter 17 tells you how to locate the sound and remedy the situation.

An easy way to see whether or not your car is **idling** evenly is to place your hand, or a stiff piece of paper, against the end of the **tail pipe** while the car is idling (with the **emergency brake** on, please). Either will amplify the sound and enable you to hear the rhythm. A misfiring **cylinder** will come through as a pumping or puffing sound. An even but rough idle is a clue that it's time to retune your **carburetor**—especially the **idle mixture** and **idle speed screws**. Go back to Chapter 7 for instructions on how to do this easy job.

If Your Horn Gets Stuck, Pull the Wire to Silence It.
Richard Freshman

14 *If your car sounds like a jet plane* or makes some other kind of really loud abnormal sound, a hole in the **muffler** is probably the cause. Replace it immediately: traffic cops hate noisy mufflers, and carbon monoxide hates people!

15 *If the horn is stuck,* your car is producing probably the worst noise it can make. Before this happens, have someone honk your horn until you can locate it under your hood. There are usually two horns. Each has a wire leading to it. If your horn gets stuck, pull these wires and it will stop. (Sometimes you have to pull only one.) When you have the horn fixed, tell the mechanic that you pulled the wires, and find out why the horn got stuck. (If you can't get at the horn wires, disconnect one battery terminal or pull the fuse that goes to the horn to stop the noise.)

### How to Check the Compression in Your Cylinders

A Compression Gauge
Karcheck Products, Otsego, Michigan

For this job you need a **compression gauge**. This is a device that tests the amount of pressure that the **piston** exerts on the **fuel/air mixture** before the **spark plug** fires it. If there isn't enough pressure, the mixture won't explode. If there is less pressure than there should be, the mixture won't explode as efficiently. If one or more **cylinders** have a good deal less pressure than the others, the car will not run evenly, and this is what you are checking to see. Now, why shouldn't there be enough pressure? Because something is letting the pressure escape from the cylinder. Where can it go? Basically, two places. Either out through one of the **valve** openings, because the valve is improperly adjusted or so worn that it doesn't close properly, or down past the **rings** on the piston. These rings are supposed to keep the pressure at the top of the cylinder in, and the oil that lubricates the engine from entering the cylinder. When the rings get worn, oil gets in and pressure gets out. Your compression gauge can tell you whether or not your cylinder is firing efficiently and whether your rings or valves are worn or out of adjustment. And it doesn't cost much to buy one of these gauges or take much time and effort to use it.

a Unless you want to buy or borrow a remote starter switch, have someone sit in the driver's seat with the engine off, the car in "Park" or "Neutral" (if it's a manual transmission), and the emergency brake on.

On non-GM cars, pull the big wire that leads to the **coil** from the center of the **distributor cap** and lean the metal connector against a metal surface as far away from the plugs as possible. Note that on GM cars the coil is built right into the distributor cap. On the side of the cap there are two plugs. One has three wires leading to it, the other has one wire. Pull this second plug and get it out of the way.

b Remove all the spark plugs. Lay them down in a clean place. Keep them in order, or label them.

c Have your friend turn the ignition key until the engine cranks over about half a dozen times. (The car won't run because the ignition has been disabled.)

d If your car has a manual choke, open it. If it has an automatic choke, prop it open with a screwdriver. (If you're not sure, read about chokes, pp. 120–122.)

e Insert the compression gauge into the hole where the first spark plug screwed into the cylinder.

f Ask your friend to crank the engine about five times. Be sure to keep the gauge plug firmly inserted while the car is cranking.

g Look at the gauge and write down the reading. Then go on to the next cylinder. Don't forget to reset the gauge and crank the car each time.

h When you've done this to each cylinder, look at the readings. The highest and lowest should not vary by more than 15 percent. If one or more of the cylinders read way below the rest, use a trigger-type oil can to send a good squirt of motor oil down the spark plug opening and retest with the gauge. If the reading stays the same, the valves either are worn (and letting pressure escape) or are out of adjustment. If the reading rises dramatically after you insert the oil, you probably need new rings on the piston in that cylinder. If the pressure is less than 100 psi, the cylinder definitely isn't mechanically sound. Once you know what's wrong, you'll have to decide whether or not it's worth correcting. If the car is on its way out anyway, get rid of it. If it is otherwise in good shape, you may want to have the engine rebuilt or replaced with a new or remanufactured one.

i Replace each spark plug in the cylinder it came from. *Be sure the ignition is off before you reconnect the wires.*

Checking Compression
Actron Manufacturing Company

Some Gauges Have Long Hoses That Screw into the Spark Plug Opening, So You Can Do the Check Unaided
Actron Manufacturing Company

**Smells**

1 *Do you smell rubber burning under the hood?* One of your hoses might have come loose and landed on a hot part of the engine. Rescue it before it melts through.

2 *Do you smell burned rubber with the hood closed?* Feel your wheels. If one is hot, a **brake shoe** may be dragging or you may have left the **parking brake** on.

3 *Do you smell oil burning?* First check the **dipstick**; your **oil gauge** may be lying and you may be out of oil. Or your engine may be overheating and your temperature gauge may be broken. If neither is the case, look around the engine for an oil leak that may be frying in the heat of the running engine. If the oil situation seems to be O.K., check the **transmission fluid dipstick**. Sometimes a faulty **vacuum modulator** can siphon the fluid out of the transmission and feed it to the engine, where it is burned. Also, if the transmission fluid is very low, it can be burned in the transmission because the gears are not lubricated enough and are getting very hot.

4 *Do you smell oil or exhaust fumes in the passenger compartment?* The cause could simply be burned oil from the engine area—but it could also be a faulty **exhaust pipe** under the car which is letting **exhaust gases** get into the car through the floorboards. Exhaust fumes are full of carbon monoxide, so if you smell oil or exhaust in the car, be sure to keep your windows open at all times and have the problem checked out as quickly as you can. We've all heard stories about people who have died on the highway from carbon monoxide or from passing out at the wheel because of it. Such stories are true.

5 *Do you smell gasoline?* Check your **carburetor** to be sure it isn't leaking fuel. If it seems all right, check down the **fuel line** all the way to the **fuel tank** for leaks. A look under the car, after it has been parked overnight, may help, but remember that fuel evaporates quickly, so the clues may be stains rather than wet spots. Check your **fuel pump** for fuel leaks. The gasoline will wash a clean streak across it, which can be seen with the naked eye.

**Smoke and Leaks**

You'll find a full range of "smoke signals" on page 395 and how to check for leaks on pages 165 through 167.

**Strange Sensations**

This is a catchall category for those things that just "feel funny." Use the process of elimination to check anything that may cause your car to run roughly: **hoses, tires, brakes, oil** levels, and **spark plug** connections; the **carburetor, cooling system, clutch, gearshift**, and **steering linkage.** If steering is difficult and you have **power steering**, page 108 shows how to check the dipstick in the reservoir attached to the power-steering unit to see if there's enough power-steering fluid in it. If it's low again soon after you've filled it, check for leaks in the hoses leading from the unit to the front wheels.

**If Your Car Won't Start**

Before we end this section, let's consider those wonderful days when your car simply refuses to start. We've covered most of this before, but there are a few more things that you should know.

If you have left your lights, heater, radio, or some other electrical gizmo on after you parked the car, then you know what the trouble is. Your **battery** is dead. You can use jumper cables to get going again if you know how to jump a start from some Good Samaritan's car, with an important exception: If either car has electronic systems, the use of jumper cables *may* damage it. If your car is one that may be damaged in this way, there may be a warning to that effect in the owner's manual or on a decal under the hood. To be sure, ask your dealer. Here's the safest way to jump-start your car:

**How to Jump a Start**

1 If you have found a Good Samaritan, be sure his or her battery has at least as much voltage as your own. It doesn't matter if your car has negative **ground** and the GS's car has positive ground, or if your car has an **alternator** and the GS's car has a **generator**, as long as you hook up the cables properly (and the proper way is the same in every case).

2 Take out those nice **jumper cables** you bought as soon as you read about them in Chapter 2. If you didn't, you'll have to find a Good Samaritan who has cables too.

3 Place both cars in "Park"—or "Neutral" for cars with manual transmissions—with ignitions shut off and emergency brakes on. Remove the caps from

Connect the Positive Cable to Each Battery and Then the Negative Cable
Delco-Remy Division, General Motors Corp.

both batteries (unless they're sealed) because batteries produce explosive hydrogen gas and a spark could set it off. If the caps are open, you can avoid such an explosion.

4 The positive cable has red clips at either end, and the negative cable has black clips. First, attach one of the red clips to the **positive terminal** of your battery (it will have "pos" or " + " on it, or it will be bigger than the negative terminal). Then attach a red clip to the positive terminal of the GS's car.

5 Now attach one of the black clips to the **negative terminal** on the GS's battery and the last black clip to an unpainted metal surface on your car that isn't near the carburetor or battery and isn't aluminum.

6 Get into your car and try to start it. If it won't, check to be sure the cables are properly connected. If they are, your battery may be beyond help, but have the GS run his or her car for 5 minutes with the jumper cables connected, and try to start your car again.

7 Disconnect the cables, thank the Good Samaritan, and resume your life.

If your alternator light stays on, or your gauge continues to point to "Discharge" after your car's been running, check your fan belt to see that it is tight enough to run your alternator properly. If your battery keeps going dead, have it and your alternator checked professionally. In any case, do not drive around with a light or gauge that reads "Trouble"; have it checked out immediately—that's why they put those gauges in there.

Now let's run through the rest of those Won't Start symptoms for one last time:

*Car is silent when key is turned in ignition.* Check **battery** terminal cable connections. If they look very corroded, force the point of a screwdriver (with an insulated or wooden handle) between the connector and the post and twist it to lodge it firmly. Then have someone try to start the car. If it starts, you need to clean or replace your cables.

*Car makes a clicking noise but won't start.* Usually a dead **battery**. If not, check the **starter** wiring for a loose connection.

*Car cranks over but won't start.* Check the fuel supply to your **carburetor**. If that's O.K., check your **distributor cap** to see if the spark is getting through.

*Car starts but dies.* Check your **carburetor** adjustment and your **choke** to see if the choke is first closing, then opening.

*Car won't start on rainy days.* Check inside the **distributor cap** for dampness. If you find moisture, carry some mechanic's solvent in the car (get some from your friendly service station—they use it to clean car parts—and it's also sold in aerosol cans). When you find dampness inside the distributor cap, turn the cap upside down and pour some solvent into it. Swish it around and pour it out. Then dry the cap as best you can and replace it. The solvent will evaporate the water; just be sure to only use *clean* solvent. Gasoline won't do; the spark can ignite the fumes.

*Car won't start on cold mornings.* Check the **choke**. Is it closed? Does it open?

Here are some more trouble symptoms:

*Engine misses while idling.* Check the **points** and the **idle speed screws** on the **carburetor**, and look for leaky vacuum hoses.

*Engine misses at high speeds.* Check the **points, spark plugs, fuel pump, fuel filter**, and **carburetor**.

*Engine misses or hesitates during acceleration.* Check the **accelerator pump** in the **carburetor**, the **spark plugs**, the **distributor**, and the **timing**.

*Engine knocks or pings.* Check your **timing**; check the octane of the fuel you are using. The owner's manual will tell you the proper octane and whether the fuel should be leaded, low-lead, or unleaded. Check the **cooling system**. Do a **compression check** on the engine cylinders.

Two things should have emerged as a result of all the above. The first is that most of the things that go wrong with your car can be avoided by simply maintaining it properly—lubricating it frequently and replacing fan belts, wiring, hoses, points, plugs, brake

**Preventive Medicine**

linings, and other parts *before they fail.* It is much simpler to diagnose car failure if you know that you've checked certain parts and systems recently and that they are in good shape. This is preventive medicine, and it is well worth the effort!

The second is that by understanding the way your car works, by exploring a failure logically in terms of what is happening (or not happening) and which part or parts are involved in that function, and by checking them to see if they are working properly, you will be able to quickly diagnose—and sometimes remedy—the situation. You won't feel helpless or bewildered, perhaps just frustrated by the time it sometimes takes to fix the trouble. And once you become familiar with the way things *should be,* and know why, you will be much more alert to the signs of disaster *before* disaster strikes.

If your car exhibits many of the symptoms in this chapter and seems to need major surgery such as an engine rebuild, a complete valve job, or major transmission work, I suggest you go right on to Chapter 18, "Auto Recycling Without Tears," so you can decide whether Old Faithful is worth the extra investment or not. The idea is to evaluate it as though it were a used car you were considering buying, and estimate the amount of money it will cost to fix it up. If you decide it's time to retire the old workhorse, there are chapters in this book that can help you to decide whether you want to fix up another used car with good potential, or buy a new one before your present car bites the dust.

Whether you decide that Old Faithful is well worth preserving or you intend to trade it in for a peppy young colt, it will be important for it to look its best. You may laugh, but I have found that a clean, sparkly car runs better than one that is dusty and shabby. And you look better driving it, too. So let's talk about what you can do to keep your car bright and shiny inside and out.

# Good Housekeeping: How to Keep Your Car Looking Young and Beautiful

Up until now, this book has focused on explaining and maintaining the basic systems that make cars go. But cars are more than a collection of parts and systems. When you drive your car, or try to trade it in or sell it, it will be judged on its appearance as well as performance, the same way a house is. Contrary to popular belief, the main reason for washing your car often and keeping a good coat of wax on it is not to keep it looking good, but to wash away the salt, mud, and chemical-laden dust and dirt that provide breeding grounds for rust and accelerate the deterioration of the paint. If you live in an area that is near the seashore, or where a lot of salt is used on the roads in the winter, or where there is industrial air pollution, it is especially imperative that you wash your car as often as once a week. If you have no access to a hose or a place to wash your car, or if the weather in your area gets so cold that the water freezes on the windshield, take the car to one of those coin-operated do-it-yourself car washes and use their facilities. The steamy hoses will keep both you and your car warm enough to wash away the mud and salt in the winter and will do an even better job than you could do at home, if your water pressure is low. It's not a matter of being a fanatic who spends every second of free time washing and waxing and dusting; just spending an hour or two each week will keep your new car young or brighten up Old Faithful.

Those of you who don't care how your car looks, and who intend to drive the same machine until it spontaneously destructs like the Miraculous One-Horse Shay, should consider this: After years of driving and restoring cars, I have found that clean cars run better! You may think this is silly, but after all, humans, plants, and animals respond to being kept clean, cared-for, and happy, so why shouldn't your car? And if you think that your car is an insensitive, inanimate object, you haven't been reading this book very carefully! At any rate, why not try it and see—all it will cost you is little more than elbow grease and a couple of soap bubbles!

**The Lazy Person's Guide to Good Housekeeping**

If you have no time or inclination for cleaning your car, my advice to you is simple: Hire someone else to do it for you. The expense will more than pay off in the increased life of your car. At the very least, take the car to a car wash every week or two and be sure they clean and vacuum the interior as part of the deal. Car washes vary considerably in efficiency and reliability. Be aware that your car will probably respond to the rather rough and impersonal scrubbing it will receive from the machines by acquiring scratches and losing a bit of paint around the edges. Still, it's better than nothing.

Forget about the optional hot-wax sprays offered by car washes. They are simply not strong enough to offer sufficient protection. Every car needs a good coat of wax or one of the new polymer products to protect it from rust and fading. This should be done at least twice a year, in the spring and the fall, to protect the car from hot sun, rain, salt, and snow. If you don't want to wax the car yourself, then hire someone to do it by hand.

If you drive a convertible or a luxury or classic car, and you can't keep it clean yourself, please hire someone to wash it by hand, at least every couple of weeks. Running such a special car through commercial car washes is tantamount to murder. You would be better off selling the car to someone who will give it the treatment it deserves and buying yourself a durable old clunker or a cheap, flashy "disposable" model every couple of years.

Most people think there is nothing special to know about washing a car, but this is not the case. If you do it properly, the job will be easier in the long run, and the car will come out looking great. If you do it in a haphazard way it will take much longer, and you run the risk of scratching the finish, streaking the surface, and leaving it vulnerable to rust. Here's a set of easy steps that can make washing a car as casual a chore as shaving or washing the dishes:

**How to Wash a Car**

1 Never wipe or "dust" a car with a dry cloth. The tiny particles of dust and grit on the surface will scratch the paint, leaving it looking "cobwebby" wherever the sun hits it.
2 Never wash a car in the hot sun; you can ruin the finish. Park it in the shade or wait until morning or evening. That way, you can water the garden, too!
3 Use cold or lukewarm water and use a hose rather than a bucket. Hoses with spray nozzles can project a stream of water forceful enough to loosen the mud, bug bodies, bird waste, and other baddies that stick to the surface. Buckets hold a finite amount of water. As you rinse out your rag or sponge, the dirt is transferred to the water and back to the rag, where it can scratch or streak the car. If you've never washed the car with a hose before, spray lightly around the edges of the windows and the rear deck lid for a short time and then check to see if the weatherstripping leaks. If it does, consult the instructions in Chapter 17 on how to patch or replace weatherstripping, and try to avoid spraying these areas until you remedy the problem.

4 Use a soft rag (old terry towels are wonderful), a sponge, or a chamois to wash the car. Follow the contours of the car, rather than going in circles, to avoid cobwebby scratches. Rinse the rag often to get rid of the grease and dust particles.

5 Your car's sensitive skin requires gentle cleansers just as your own body does. You can use a mild soap, mild liquid dish detergent, or a commercial car washing product. Just remember that soap and detergent will remove the wax from the car and that this is only an asset if you are in the process of cleaning and rewaxing the car. Between waxings, I like to use a liquid car-washing solution that comes with a little wax blended right into it.

6 Always wash a car body from the top down, and remember to get to all the corners where dirt can collect and rust can form: behind the wheels, inside the fenders, behind the bumpers. Don't forget the underbody—this is usually the muddiest and greasiest place of all and the most prone to rust. Don't use the hose under the hood, however. This has to be done differently, as you will see.

7 Wash one section of the car at a time: hose it down, soap it up, rinse it off. When you have finished the entire car, hose it all down again to get every last bit of soap off. Then towel the car dry with terry towels or a chamois to get rid of water spotting that can mar the car's surface. Chamois are especially good for this and can be washed and rinsed and used for years. But they are expensive, and I find that old dry terry towels work pretty well, too. Besides, what else can you do with towels that have not only become too faded for the bathroom but are too torn even for the beach? Be sure that no water is allowed to collect unseen in the tiny rust-prone spaces around the trim and behind the bumpers.

8 Don't scratch at hard-to-remove dirt. Soak it loose by placing a wet rag on it. If your car is befouled with tar or dead bugs, there are commercial products that will remove them safely. Be sure to remove these intense cleansers thoroughly, and wash the surface with soap and water immediately afterward.

9 Speaking of commercial products, here are a few safety tips:

a Always read and follow the directions on the package. Some products can damage your skin or your car's surface if left on too long or applied and removed improperly.

b Never use a spray in an unventilated area. Never get your face close enough to inhale it or risk getting it in your eyes.

c Don't smoke when using chemicals or petroleum products. As a matter of fact—don't smoke!

10 Before you wash the car body, hose it down to get rid of the surface dust, and then clean and polish such exterior surfaces as vinyl hardtops, convertible tops, glass, chrome bumpers and trim, side mirrors,

wheel covers, whitewalls and tires. Then, when you wash and rinse the car itself, you will be sure to get off the last residue of all of the substances you've used for those jobs. Here's how to clean and restore some of those special surfaces:

**Windows**

Clean the glass windows and mirrors with the same products you use in your home. There are products that simply spray on and wipe off without rinsing. If you are really a hardy soul, you can use ammonia with very good results. Be sure to use a lint-free soft rag, or sturdy paper towels, to avoid scratching the glass. Use vertical strokes on the outside and horizontal strokes on the inside of each window, so you can see at a glance which side the streaks are on when you are wiping off the cleaner. I always carry a little spray bottle of glass cleaner and a clean soft rag in my car to spruce up the windshield when visibility gets cloudy. Your windshield wipers will lift away from the glass to allow you to clean under them, and don't forget to wipe the wipers, too. A dirty blade can streak or scratch the glass.

**Plastic Rear Windows**

If your convertible has a plastic rear window, it may become cloudy from oxidation, especially if the hot sun shines on it constantly. There are excellent conditioners especially designed to keep plastic windows clear and supple without scratching them. If your car's rear window is already clouded beyond visibility, Meguiar's Plastic Cleaner is a unique heavy-duty product that will polish the cloudy stuff right off the window, leaving it relatively clear again. If you must park your car where the sun can shine directly on its plastic window for long periods of time, cover the outside of the window with an old towel to protect it from the sun.

**Chrome and Metal Trim**

There are excellent polishes designed specifically to clean chrome without scratching the delicate layer of plating. These preparations will not only clean the metal without scratching it, but will retard rust and leave the surface bright and shining. You can use chrome polish on other metal surfaces, too. Try not to get the polish on the surrounding paint, however; it can discolor it. Be sure to do the inside surfaces of the bumpers if you can reach them, and don't forget the metal hubcaps and wheel covers, and the metal frames around the lights and side mirrors. If you find rust on any metal area, rush directly to the section on rust removal (page 367) and get rid of the stuff immediately! After cleaning, metal surfaces should be waxed to prevent rust from forming. Use a special wax designed for chrome bumpers and metal surfaces, because they require more protection than painted surfaces do.

**Tires** Be sure to clean the tires when you wash the car. You wouldn't take a bath without washing your feet, would you? Use mild soap or dish detergent to remove dirt and grease. A brush or kitchen scouring pad will remove the stubborn stuff, but be sure to wet the tires first. Never use gasoline or kerosene to clean tires. If your car has whitewalls that are extremely dirty or greasy, you may have to resort to a special whitewall cleaner to restore them to their original pristine good looks. If you want your tires to look extremely shiny and spiffy, here's an inside tip: Car dealers and people with show cars have been known to wax their tires with Lemon Pledge furniture polish! Extremely scuffed tires can be painted with "tire black," a preparation for that purpose sold at auto supply stores. Whether you are going for appearances or not, I'd suggest you spray your tires with a silicone lubricant every once in a while to preserve the rubber.

**Convertible Tops** If your top has a plastic rear window, follow the instructions on page 353 to clean it without scratching it.

Go over the metal mechanism that raises and lowers the top and polish it occasionally to keep it shiny and beautiful. Put a coat of wax on it to retard rusting, and oil the hinges now and then to keep things working smoothly. Use the oil sparingly to avoid staining the top, however.

Remember to dust or vacuum the well into which the top folds and to keep it free of objects that can puncture or mar the top. I remember a friend who had a convertible with a glass rear window. The top was up for most of the winter, and that well seemed like an ideal place to stash her umbrella and other paraphernalia. Then one day the sun shone, and she happily put her top down. Crunch! End of story...

**"Ragtops"** If you have a convertible with a cloth top, keep it clean by vacuuming it often, or use a whisk broom, to get the dust out of the areas around the trim. This is not just a matter of cleanliness; the dirt can cause the fabric to rot away if it is allowed to remain there. Check the top occasionally to be sure that it is not getting caught in the mechanism which raises and lowers it, since this can leave greasy streaks on the fabric, weaken it, and cause it to tear. Check to be sure that there are no weak spots or tears, and check the seams for threads that are beginning to break. Seams that are loosening up can be restitched by hand before they become major problems. Try to use the same holes as the original stitches, stitching right on top of them, and use strong thread in the same color as the original. Convertible tops are under considerable tension, and a tiny rip can swiftly tear right across the top. If you see a weak place or a small hole, reinforce it by placing a patch on the inside of the top, and glue it into place with a good adhesive or stitch it down securely.

**Vinyl Tops**

Vinyl hardtops and convertible tops usually clean up easily with mild soap or dish detergent and water. If the top is very dirty, you may want to try a commercial product made especially for vinyl tops. Use a fairly soft brush to get the dirt out of the tiny crevices in the finish (a recycled tooth brush or nail brush will get into the areas around the trim easily). Brush in circles, since the crevices run in every direction, and rinse often to wash the dirt away. Vinyl hardtops respond nicely to a light coat of wax, or the proper silicone preservative, too.

If you find that your vinyl hardtop has bubbles in it, prick the areas with a pin and try to press the air out. If any adhesive comes out of the holes, wipe it off the vinyl immediately. When the air is out, press the vinyl against the roof to reseal it. If the adhesive has dried out, you can use a glue injector to insert a tiny amount of vinyl adhesive under the surface. It is important to deal with air bubbles, because they can create holes in the vinyl if something catches them. If you find holes or rips in the vinyl, use a vinyl repair kit to correct them. There is a wide variety of these on the market: tiny bottles of liquid vinyl that will fill in scratches, major repair kits that include vinyl liquid that can be mixed to match the color of the surrounding area, patches, and sophisticated adhesives. Be sure to select the simplest kit that will suit your purposes by reading the instructions right there in the store.

If your vinyl top has become faded and discolored, there are excellent sprays on the market that will renew the color for you. Be sure to mask the surrounding areas of the car. Always choose the same color or a slightly darker shade to cover up spots.

**Cleaning and Polishing the Car**

Let's get clear on the distinction between *washing* and *cleaning and polishing* the exterior of a car. Washing gets rid of the dirt on the surface. Cleaning and polishing goes a little deeper. As a car gets older, especially if it is exposed to the sun and other elements, the top layers of paint begin to fade and oxidize, giving the car a hazy or smokey surface. Regular washing and waxing will usually retard this process, but an occasional good cleaning and polishing will remove tiny scratches and dead paint to leave even a well-kept car shining with unusual brilliance. There are a variety of products you can use, including some which combine wax with the cleaner to reduce the number of steps you have to go through. These combined products are easy to use and work well if the car is not too filthy, but they will not substitute for a thorough waxing when it comes to long-term protection. Most commercial products contain fine particles of abrasive which effectively remove an infinitely small top layer of paint and grime. For this reason, do not use these cleaners more often than once a month. If your car is a dark color, or has a delicate lacquer finish, look for a cleaner or wax/cleaner which contains chemicals rather than abrasives, since scratches really show up on these finishes. Do not use abrasive cleaners on chrome or plastic unless the label specifically says you can. If you do, you run the risk of scratching the surfaces and removing the chrome plating.

**Rubbing Compounds**

Whereas most polishes have a mild abrasive action, the abrasives in rubbing compounds are designed to dig a bit deeper into the surface, discard the top layers of paint, and get down to the fresh stuff underneath (assuming there is any). As a rule of thumb, it is generally wise to avoid any polishing preparation that contains such strong abrasives because it can go right through your car's painted finish. However, if your car is in really sad shape, with paint that has faded and dulled to where there is little reflection or shine, and you are considering painting the car anyway, you might want to try using rubbing compound to restore the finish before you spring for a paint job. Most newer cars are painted with an acrylic lacquer or enamel that has a hardener in it which helps to protect the finish and keep the color from fading for a long time. These cars should not require rubbing compound to keep their colors bright. Rubbing compounds come in fine, medium, and coarse grades. I would always try the fine grade first, since the others may be too harsh. The coarse grade removes so much paint that it is usually used for prefinishing jobs, where the surface is going to be taken down, restored, and repainted. Use rubbing compound sparingly. Follow the directions on the package and don't bear down too hard. Go easy at first, to avoid removing patches of paint that have loosened from the surface, bubbled, or chipped around the edges. You can always apply a bit more elbow grease if your initial efforts prove to be too gentle. Always wax the car after using a rubbing compound unless, of course, you are going on to paint it.

You may have seen professionals using electric buffers to apply cleaners and wax and to shine the car up to a high gloss. Although there are lamb's-wool pads available that can be attached to the shaft of an electric drill, do not use these, or any other high-speed gadgets, to buff or polish your car. Professional buffing equipment works gently at slow speeds to avoid scratching or grinding the paint right off the car. Most of this power equipment requires the light, experienced touch of a professional. **Electric Buffers**

If washing the car removes the surface dirt, and cleaning and polishing it removes the dead layers of paint, waxing the car preserves that clean and shiny finish and seals its "pores" against dirt, water vapor, and rust. If water does not bead on the surface of the car when it rains or when you hose it down, it needs waxing badly. Don't neglect this. Even if you use a car-washing product that has wax in it, you must still plan to give the car a thorough waxing at least twice a year, in the spring and fall, to protect it from heavy weather. There is literally nothing more vital if you want to keep your car rust-free and young-looking for years to come. **Waxing the Car**

Always be sure to wash the car before you wax it, no matter how clean it looks, to avoid scratching the surface and trapping minute particles of dust. There are a variety of waxes to choose from, ranging from the previously mentioned combination products to liquid, soft, and hard waxes. Again, if you drive a dark-colored car, or one with a sensitive lacquer finish, make sure that the cleaners and waxes you use have no abrasives in them.

Generally speaking, the liquid waxes are very easy to use but will not last as long as the soft or hard waxes, although some of the abrasive-free liquid wax/cleaners specially formulated for cars with delicate finishes are quite effective. Liquid waxes are excellent as a touch-up between major waxings or for general use to replace the wax you lose if you wash your car with a wax-free detergent or soap.

Soft waxes are my favorites. They are light and fluffy and very easy to apply and remove. My favorite is mixed with a light cleaner and leaves the car shining beautifully. (I don't let this keep me from washing it thoroughly first, however.) These products are applied with the applicator pads provided, or with a soft terry rag. You simply wipe it on, following the contours of the car, allow it to dry to a haze, and wipe the haze away. The soft waxes that contain no cleaner are excellent for sealing the surface if you've used an abrasive cleaner or a fine-grade rubbing compound. Because the waxes that contain cleaners usually contain abrasives, do not use them for every car wash or more often than once a month. In between, use the liquid car washes that come with a little wax already in them.

Hard or paste waxes provide the most protection and should be used for your semi-annual major wax job. They last longer than anything except the new polymer products mentioned below. These waxes are harder to apply and require rubbing and buffing to bring up a high-gloss shine. Always do a small area at a time to avoid letting the wax harden to a point where it's hard to remove. Apply according to the directions on the can with an applicator or soft rag, use another clean soft rag to remove it, and use still another clean soft rag to rub the car all over until it shines.

**Polymer Preservatives**

Recently, a new group of products has appeared on the market. These contain polymer substances that are reputed to protect the surface of the car more effectively than wax, and for longer periods of time. These products literally bond with the surface of the paint and prevent it from fading and oxidizing. You can buy poly-sealants at the auto supply store which are easy to apply and are supposed to protect your car for from six months to a year. Professionals and auto manufacturers offer polyglycotes that are supposed to last for from two to three years. If you would like to use one of these products, be sure to wash the car thoroughly and give it a good cleaning and polishing first. Some of these products say that they can be applied over wax, but I prefer to get all of the wax off the car before applying them. When the car is really clean, shiny, and dry, apply the protective coating, following the directions on the label. Make sure it gets into all the little crevices around the trim, and on the painted metal inner surfaces of the doors and deck lid. Since I am a fairly cautious person, I still inspect my car regularly for rust, and to make sure that this new miracle stuff is really doing its job.

**How to Clean Your Engine**

Many car owners never bother to deal with the dirt under the hood on the assumption that "what you can't see can't hurt you." Although it is true that only people who exhibit show cars or are compulsively fastidious would set much store by having the engine area constantly at its pristine best, there are practical reasons for having a gross accumulation of grease, oil, gasoline, and dirt removed from under the hood and for making an effort to keep things under control from then on. Engines are made of metal and are dependent on rubber hoses and gaskets and wiring if they are to work properly. Since all of the aforementioned baddies can cause rust to form or can seriously deteriorate nonmetal parts and wiring, it is a good idea to keep the under-the-hood area as clean as possible. If the area under the hood of your car is beginning to look grubby, get a rag and wipe off as much of the dirt and grease as you can. If the situation has reached the "unspeakable" stage, then I would strongly urge you to have the area steam-cleaned by a professional. Although there are engine degreasers available at the auto supply store, and coin-operated steam-cleaning facilities at do-it-yourself car wash centers, I would not recommend that you try either of these alternatives for the following reason: Most engine cleaners and degreasers must be washed off thoroughly—usually with a hose—and there is a risk that moisture will penetrate the distributor cap and prevent the car from starting. The steam produced by the steam cleaners is even more insidious. There have been cases where the car started and went home, only to fail to start the following morning after the moisture from the steam had condensed. That's why I urge you to have your engine cleaned professionally if it is too dirty to wipe clean yourself. When the job is done you should be able to keep it in good condition by wiping off the area every now and then.

If, in spite of my warnings, you are determined to do the job yourself, here are some tips to remember:

1 Be sure to remove the **air cleaner** and cover the **distributor** and the **carburetor** throat with plastic bags to prevent water from getting into them. Try not to spray the hose directly at these areas.

2 Follow the directions on the can of engine cleaner carefully.

3 Avoid getting chemical cleaners on the body of the car. They can remove the wax and stain the surface.

4 Hose off the cleaner thoroughly after it has had time to act.

5 Unless directed to do otherwise, start the engine after cleaning it, and let it idle long enough to dry out the under-the-hood area.

6 If your engine fails to start, you can try to remove the moisture from inside the distributor cap by following the instructions for starting the car on a rainy day, on page 347, but I'm not promising anything. Never try to do this with gasoline! A spark from the distributor can cause an explosion.

When you have the engine cleaned, be sure that the **blow-by** on the inner surface of the hood above the engine is cleaned too, and that the mud and dirt that has accumulated on the inner walls of the car body and near the wheel wells is removed.

If you find that oil is accumulating very quickly on your newly cleaned engine, the first thing I'd check is the **PCV valve** to see if it is plugged up. This little gadget is responsible for rerouting the exhaust fumes from the **crankcase** back to the engine, where they are burnt again and then released through the exhaust system. If the valve gets plugged, pressure can build up in the crankcase and create oil leaks around the engine. A PCV valve can be checked and replaced very easily. Read all about it, starting on page 144.

Oil may also seep from under the **valve cover gasket** if the cover needs to be torqued down properly or the gasket needs to be replaced. If this seems to be your problem, check with a mechanic.

If you think cleaning your engine is compulsive, think of my uncle who sprayed the under-the-hood area of his second-hand Cadillac with gold paint so he could impress the service station attendants!

## Cleaning the Interior of Your Car

The interior of your car is like your living room at home: it is "decorated" with carpeting, paint, fabric, plastic, vinyl, and glass. Some cars have leather and wood as well. Although, unlike the interior of your house, your car stands out in public and reflects your personal habits (and you certainly don't want everyone to think you're a slob!), keeping the interior clean is more than a matter of pride. Because dirt contains grit and chemicals that can eat away the surfaces of your "furniture," it is vitally necessary that you practice the same good housekeeping techniques on your car as you would on the place you live in, if you want to keep it in decent condition for a long, long time.

Generally speaking, the same procedures and products you use in the house will work quite well in your car. If you're an "old hand" at housework, read the following information just to make sure you don't forget anything. If good housekeeping has never been your bag, or if you have spent your life in hotels, here's how to clean and care for the interior of your car:

### Keep Things Tidy

The most effective thing you can do is to vacuum the carpets and seats and dust the dashboard, rear window shelf, and other surfaces regularly. There are little hand vacuums that work on batteries, if getting your usual equipment to the car is a hassle. Keep the little vacuum in the trunk so you can use it if a spontaneous fit of cleanliness overtakes you.

Keep the clutter under control and the seats free of everything but you and the seat belts. Objects left lying on seats may rip or stain them as people move about or enter and leave the car. Maps and guidebooks belong in the glove box. Store the flashlight, tools, and a copy of this book in the trunk or under the front seats. Your fire extinguisher takes precedence over any other candidate for front-seat storage, however, since you have to be able to reach it quickly in case of an emergency (and the trunk is right over the gas tank).

Don't keep heavy objects on the rear window ledge or the dashboard. They can obscure visibility, and can fly around and hurt someone if you have to stop suddenly.

If you have children who require a supply of toys, keep them on the floor in an open carton that fits snugly between the rear seat and the back of the front seat, and make putting the toys away a regular part of each driving experience.

## Upholstery and Carpeting

You can use the same products to clean car upholstery and carpeting as you use to clean your chairs and sofas and rugs. Avoid using large quantities of water; you don't want to get the padding under the fabric wet or rust the buttons, if there are any. Avoid sponges; work with damp rags wherever possible. If you think you've gotten things too wet, use a portable hair dryer to dry the padding quickly and evaporate water from around the base of the buttons. The best products for fabrics and rugs are the ones which spray on, turn to powder, and are removed by vacuuming. Stain-repellent sprays are excellent if the fabric is clean and new; otherwise they will simply preserve your stains forever.

## Vinyl and Plastic

Vinyl seats and interiors and plastic surfaces such as dashboards, steering wheels, and interior moldings usually respond well to water and a mild soap or dish detergent, but you may have to resort to special vinyl-cleaning products if things have really been allowed to get out of hand. You can use a soft brush on vinyl, to get at the dirt in the graining, along the welting, and around buttons, if there are any. Water can soak down to the padding between the stitching and around the buttons of vinyl-covered seats too, so use it as sparingly as possible. Preserve all vinyl and plastic surfaces against sunlight and heat with products such as Armor All. While you're at it, use it, or a spray silicone lubricant, on weatherstripping, vinyl or rubber floor mats, and on your tires, too, to prevent them from cracking and drying out and to keep them supple and new.

## Leather

If you are lucky enough to have leather seats in your car, be sure to take care of them properly. Leather looks and feels wonderful, and it smells good, too. Since it "breathes," it doesn't get as wet and sticky as vinyl does on hot days. If properly cared for, leather will last a long time, but like all skin (including ours), if it is not kept clean and moisturized, it will dry out and age prematurely. Use a high-quality product like saddle soap, Hide Food, or Lexol to clean and preserve your leather seats. Neatsfoot oil will waterproof, soften, lubricate, restore, and preserve leather which has been cleaned first. If you must park where the sun can get at your leather seats, lean them forward or drape something over them to protect them. If this is impossible, take comfort from the fact that they don't get as hot as vinyl and you can probably sit down without screaming.

**Stains**  Since stains are caused by a wide variety of substances and can be enlarged or set permanently if you try to remove them improperly, in the interests of brevity, and because I believe in leaving specialized areas to the specialists, I suggest you refer to a stain-removal guide before tackling stains on fabric upholstery or carpeting. Be sure to get them while they're fresh; the older a stain gets, the harder it is to remove. If something spills and you can mop it up swiftly and dab at it with some water to dissolve it, it's probably worth a try. They say that chewing gum can be removed more easily if you freeze it with an ice cube first and then chip it off. That may be, but be sure not to scratch at it or you will risk ruining the nap of the fabric or scratching or tearing vinyl upholstery. I'd tend to consult the experts on things like chewing gum, tar, blood, and other hard-to-remove substances. You may be able to cut the stains off high-napped carpets and then replace it with loops cut from a hidden area and glued in with clear adhesive. I'd try this procedure on an area that doesn't show, first, just to see whether my handiwork looks better than the original stain.

**Repairing Tears and Holes**  Car seats get considerable wear and tear and reupholstery is very expensive these days. If you catch small tears and holes early, you can save yourself a lot of money in the long run. Sew up tears in fabric seats with strong thread, or use patch kits which allow you to put the patch under the fabric and seal the "wound" with a colorless adhesive. Repair small tears and holes in vinyl seats with the special kits that are on the market. If you have to patch an area where the vinyl no longer exists, be sure that the patch is at least half an inch larger than the hole, so that when you slip it under the hole, the adhesive will not contact the padding. Check out the various vinyl repair kits available and choose the simplest one that can do the job. If your seats need major surgery, go to a professional who can do the work properly.

Headliners are cleaned and repaired just like upholstery, but you have to work at it upside down. Rinse both cloth and vinyl headliners with a clean rag and cool water. Dry with a terry towel to avoid drips.

**Headliners**

Floor mats are useful to protect the floorboards of cars without carpeting—and the vinyl floor coverings that substitute for rugs on many new cars don't look very sturdy to me. Mats also help to keep the noise level down, which is one of the main functions of carpeting. You can use mats to protect existing carpets, especially in rainy or muddy areas, and they will also hide carpets that are stained or torn.

**Floor Mats**

Clean vinyl and rubber floor mats with cold water and soap. You can take them right out of the car and hose them down as you wash the car. Be sure to rinse them thoroughly. Use a brush on vinyl mats and a kitchen scouring pad on rubber ones to remove caked-on dirt.

Use old or worn mats on the floor of the trunk or hatchback area to reduce the noise level and protect the interior.

Clean the interiors of all your windows, and the rear view mirror, to remove the film caused by smoke and by the vapors given off by vinyl and plastic. Wash them the same way you wash your windows at home or refer back to the car-washing section of this chapter for instructions.

**Glass**

Clean interior metal and chrome in the same way as you dealt with the exterior surfaces. And don't forget the door handles and window cranks if your car has metal ones.

**Chrome and Metal Trim**

Ah, for the days of wooden steering wheels and dashboards! There are very few left now, and if your car has these elegant appurtenances, be sure to oil and polish the wood often to keep it from cracking and drying out. Use the same stuff you would use on fine furniture—which it is, when you come to think of it!

**Wood**

Just to "touch all the bases," oil the hinges of the doors, hood, and rear deck lid now and then, and spray the door and trunk locks with graph-

**Final Touches**

ite to keep them working smoothly. Be happy that you don't have to put fresh flowers in a little crystal vase in the passenger compartment, as some chauffeurs used to do!

Now that wasn't so bad, was it? When you are ready to go on your cleaning campaign, try to pick a day when you have some time to spend puttering about. Line up all those groovy cans of special cleaners, festoon the area with clean terry-cloth rags or other softees, and tackle the entire interior in one glorious effort. Unless you plan to take the car out into the bush, chauffeur a horde of wild kids armed with ice cream cones and other goodies, or the weather gets really terrible, you probably won't have to go through this more often than once a month—longer if you are very fastidious and don't travel around a lot.

Now that the car is clean inside and out, let's talk about how you can deal with damage to its body from rust, dings, dents, and other uglies.

# Bodywork: Getting Rid of the Dings, Dents, and Other Hard Knocks

These days, when "Forever Young" seems to be more of a national anthem than an old love song, many of us have begun to devote a regular portion of our time to "bodywork." The bicycle lanes are crowded with people who eschew their cars for the pleasures of combining errands with exercise, the streets are thronged with joggers as well as walkers, and aerobic dance, jazzercise, and yoga classes are filled. We've faced the fact that the only way to stay forever young is to be vigilant about keeping our bodies in shape and to repair minor damage before it has a chance to develop into something really difficult to deal with. I guess by now you know what I'm leading up to, but I'll say it anyway for those of you who have spent the last paragraph with your minds on something else: Yes, pals, your car's body is subject to the same ravages of time and hard knocks as your own body is—and is exposed to weather a great deal more. If you want Old Faithful (or the new pony) to stay forever young, then you must be willing to keep a careful eye on it and to forestall major damage by taking care of the minor stuff as soon as possible. We've already talked about proper nutrition and regular maintenance for your car's innards, and how to keep it clean inside and out. Now it's time to deal with the dings and dents that the world has dealt it, and to forestall America's Number One Car Killer: RUST!

## Seeking Professional Help

Before we begin, here's a word of warning that will apply to all of the tasks outlined in this chapter. No matter how optimistic and ambitious you are, do not tackle anything larger than a couple of inches in size. If the car has suffered fairly extensive body damage, such as major rusting or large holes, dents, creases, or tears in its metal skin, forget about trying to fix it yourself and rely on a professional body shop for appropriate surgery. You wouldn't try to set a broken leg yourself, would you? Remember that, even if you remove the dent or the rust successfully, you will still have to mask, sand, apply the filler, shape it to the contours of the car, sand some more, and then prime and paint the surface. Unless you have considerable skill in working with your hands and really enjoy getting into challenging and time-consuming jobs, you will probably find that having a professional tackle the big stuff is well worth the money. That way, you can spend the time it would have taken doing something that will be profitable enough to pay the restorer's charges, and you can both walk away happy. The car will look better, too. Amateur attempts usually give themselves away with uneven surfaces or uneven color, and you run the risk of having the filler or the paint remove itself prematurely from an improperly prepared surface.

If you need to locate a reliable body shop, consult the section in Chapter 20 on finding and evaluating a good mechanic. Be sure to get several estimates, which must include a list of all the parts that will need to be replaced or rechromed (such as trim, lights, bumpers, etc.). Straightening and rechroming has become so expensive these days—and it must be done properly if it is not to flake off quickly—that it is often less expensive to buy a new bumper or piece of trim, or to locate an unflawed one at a wrecker's, than it is to restore the damaged one.

If extensive areas of the car body have to be repaired, damaged body panels should be replaced, rather than simply filled in with plastic body fillers. Unless you are a metalworker and are really familiar with torches, have this done professionally. It's a good idea to ask each body shop you consult whether they are planning to replace large damaged areas with sheet-metal body panels welded in place of the old ones, or if the old ones are going to be straightened and finished with a thin skin of plastic body filler wherever it is necessary.

If it is just a matter of a superficial dent, ding, or rust spot, you can probably fix things up yourself by following the advice and instructions below. The key to all the work described in this chapter is to keep things small. It is relatively easy to repair a small area. If you end up damaging the surrounding surface enough to significantly enlarge the problem until it is more than a couple of inches in size, you will either have to have a professional restore the situation, do a tacky-looking patch job on it yourself, or ignore the mess until the car falls apart.

## Getting Rid of Rust

Since rust is the "heavy" of this chapter, we'd better get to it first. Rust might better be known as "car cancer." It arrives unheralded, eats corrosively into the car's body in unsuspected nooks and crannies, and if you are foolish enough to simply paint over it, goes right on with its deadly work unseen. This imagery may seem unduly grim to you, but I honestly believe that over the years, more fine cars have given way to the ravages of rust than have been demolished in accidents.

## How to Check for Rust

If you live in an area where they put salt on the streets in winter, or where it rains or snows a great deal, or near the seashore—anywhere your car is exposed to moisture and/or salt—you must be especially vigilant about detecting and getting rid of rust quickly. However, even if you live in a dry climate, you must still make it a habit to check carefully every few months and, if you find rust forming, to get rid of it before it can do major damage.

We've already talked about how washing and waxing the car regularly will help to protect your car from rust. The paint on your car is there not only for beauty, but for protection as well. Check for small scratches, nicks, and spots where the paint may have flaked off, and following the instructions later in this chapter, touch up the paint in those areas before rust can form on the bare metal. Look for dark spots in the paint, which may indicate that the metal is rusting out from underneath. Look for pitted places in the paint and on the chrome and metal trim and treat them with a rust remover, following the directions on the package. Most removers are simply applied, left to work for several minutes, and then washed off thoroughly. Look for one which can be used on painted surfaces, and test the stuff on a small hidden area first, to be sure it doesn't affect the color—no matter what the package says.

Each time you wash the car, take a flashlight and check around the fenders and the wheel wells and behind the bumpers, where salt, mud, and dirt accelerate rust's growth. Shine the light into the little crevices between the car body and all the trim and moldings that are affixed to it. Dirt and moisture tend to collect in these areas. Don't forget to look all around the lights, the windows, the side mirrors, and the aerial, too. If you live in a damp area, check the metal stuff on the inside of the car, also, and around the window frames.

Next time you have the car serviced, have them put it up on the hoist and check its underbody thoroughly. If you are afraid they won't be thorough enough, arrive at the end of the day, armed with a flashlight and a paper sack with a six-pack of the mechanic's favorite beer in it, and ask them to put the car up and let you have a look around. While you are at it, get them to show you all the fascinating things under there: the **transmission**, the **oil pan**, the **brake lines**, the **emergency brake**, the **differential**, where the **grease points** are, etc. It's quite an education! Note that, even if you have a car with a fiberglass (and therefore rustproof) body, the underbody is still the most sensitive area where rust is concerned. I have driven in venerable old cars where the floorboards had rusted through so completely that you could see the road flash by underneath. And if the rust attacks the frame, the car can be on its way to "The Great Car Lot in the Sky" before you know it.

**How to Deal with Rust If You Find It**

O.K. The worst has happened. You've checked and found some rust spots on the car. Don't panic, there's still time to save the patient—unless it's pretty far gone. If there are large rust holes in the body of the car, or if the frame has been badly weakened, get a couple of estimates from reliable body shops on what it would cost to repair the damage and check those against what your car is worth by calling your local bank, insurance company, or loan agency and asking them to look up the car's value in the **blue book**, or by looking in the newspaper to see what cars of that year, make, and model are being sold for these days. If the car seems worth the effort and the money, and is mechanically sound, then bite the bullet and get it fixed up. Otherwise, move on to the next two chapters and get yourself another car.

If the rust is underneath the car, on the underside of the body or bumpers where it doesn't show, or is still confined to very small areas that can be touched up easily, you can probably take care of the matter yourself.

Here's what to do:

1 Gently scrape away the rust with a single-edged razor blade. You may want to try fine sandpaper or a brush with stiff (but not metal) bristles for slightly larger painted areas, and coarse sandpaper to grind the rust off large areas that are out of sight and not surrounded by paint. Always work inward from the edges to avoid extending the area by damaging the paint. Don't make a large job out of a small one by carelessly damaging the surrounding area! Rust remover may make this job easier, if you apply it after you get the crusty stuff off the surface.

2 When all the rust is removed, apply some rust arrestor to keep the rust from spreading further. Rust, like fire, is a form of oxidation. There are products like Meta-Prep and Extend that change the chemical nature of the rust and prevent it from further oxidizing the metal. Be sure to follow the directions on the package. Most rust arrestors are just brushed or sprayed on, allowed to turn from white to black, and then washed off thoroughly. As soon as the area is dry, prime and paint it to protect it and restore it to its former beauty.

**Undercoating to Prevent Rust**

There are special **undercoatings** which prevent rust from forming on the undersurface of a car, and these work quite well, if the car is so new that absolutely no rust exists. If there is rust, undercoating will simply lock the rust away, where it will continue its insidious work unseen. Many new cars come with undercoating as part of the package, and this is fine and worth bargaining for. If it is an "optional extra," it might be cheaper to have the work done by a professional independent undercoating shop. Get an estimate of costs before you deal for the car, so you will know where the best deal lies. If your car is fairly new and has not begun to rust, it still might be a good idea to have it undercoated, especially if you live in a snowy area. Be sure that they treat the underside of the car with a rust arrestor first, just to be sure. There are spray undercoats for amateur use which are probably better than nothing, although I would continue to watch closely for rust. If you decide to try one of these, be sure to work in a well-ventilated area, and don't spray the undercoating (or anything else, for that matter) on any cables, pipes, or parts under the car that get hot, or they will smell awful when the heat hits the undercoating.

## Removing Dents and Dings

Before we get to priming and painting the car, let's consider what you can do to remove the small dents and tiny dings that may be marring your car's surface, whether there is rust or not. By taking care of all of these things at once, you can then put the final coats on all of them at the same time and have a car that really looks wonderful.

It takes special tools and equipment to yank, hammer, or otherwise coax large dents back into place. The little dents and dings are another matter. These may respond to simple measures and not require much work at all. It's worth trying to deal with these because, if you fail, you can always take the car to the body shop anyway, right?

If the paint has simply flaked or been scratched off the surface, follow the instructions on touching up paint later in this chapter.

If the metal has been pushed in and has not been badly creased, you can try to pop it back into place with a rubber plunger (the kind they call a "plumber's helper"). Just moisten the edge of the rubber, place the plunger over the dent, establish suction by pressing down on the handle, and then pull it towards you. It may take a couple of tries before things pop back to normal. This works especially well on large expanses of metal like doors and fenders if they have just been bent inward.

You can attempt to hammer out small dents by placing a flat piece of metal, with a rag wrapped around it to protect the paint from scratching, on the outer side of the car and banging the dent on the underside with a flat-ended hammer. Be very careful to bang the underside of the dent only, or you will end up with a couple of bumps to deal with as well! Work from the shallow sides of the dent towards the deeper areas and avoid overworking the metal, which will stretch it.

You can fill very small dings or places where the paint has been chipped with glazing putty, which is very easy to handle. Use a putty knife to apply it, following the directions on the package, and then prime and paint the area. If the damaged area is larger than a very small shallow ding, you will have to resort to a plastic body filler.

## How to Fill a Dent or Hole in Your Car's Body

Dents and holes are usually repaired in one of two ways. As I've already mentioned, large damaged areas should be repaired professionally by replacing the body panels or straightening them. Smaller indentations can be filled with plastic body filler. Many people refer to this process as "bondoing," but, although "bondo" has become a synonym for all car body fillers, it is really the commercial name of a variety of car body-repair products put out by one company. There are many plastic compounds on the market for filling small holes, dents and creases in the surface of your car. Buy a good-quality product (the cheap stuff may break loose or flake away), and follow the directions on the package closely. My body-repair kit came with an instruction folder filled with photographs of each step of the work, and with a floppy vinyl phonograph record which provided advice and encouragement in dulcet masculine tones! Most kits contain at least two substances: the filler itself and a hardener, which must be mixed with the filler before you use it. My all-purpose kit contained filler, hardener, spot-and-glaze putty, screening for filling holes, applicators, and a can of spray primer. Check carefully at the auto supply store to find the kit with the easiest instructions that can do the job for you as simply as possible. The salespeople should be helpful here, if you tell them that this is your first attempt at bodywork.

To give you an idea of how it's done, here are a few general instructions that will suit most situations, but be sure to read and follow the directions on the product you buy:

1 Clean the area thoroughly to remove all traces of dirt, wax, or rust.

2 Because body fillers will not stick to paint, you must sand the area before you apply it, with #180 or #220 aluminum oxide sandpaper (you can find it in the auto supply store). When sanding, be sure to "feather-edge" (blend) the paint edges to prevent the old paint from chipping up through the new paint in the future and to ensure a good bond. Work inward from the edges of the dent to avoid enlarging the area.

3 Because the hardener-filler combination starts to harden immediately, it is important to mix only as much as you are going to use right away. Just mix up a relatively small batch at a time, using the proportions recommended on the can, and then mix up some more when you need it. This allows you to work without rushing and gives you time to allow each layer to dry before you apply the next.

4 If there is a hole in the car's body, fiberglass screening or fine aluminum chicken wire should be placed beneath it, on the underside of the car, to keep the filler from falling out. Be sure to clean the area under the car thoroughly to get rid of any dirt or paint that may be present. Then, mix a very small proportion of filler and hardener and apply it to the edges of the screen and the edges of the area to be patched, to hold the screen in place. If there is no applicator, use a putty knife or a plastic kitchen scraper to apply the filler. Let the screen patch dry for several hours before going on with the work.

5 Apply the plastic filler, working slowly and as carefully as possible, to avoid spreading the filler outside the dent and marring the surrounding area. When you finish, the filled portion should be slightly higher than the surface of the car around it. As soon as the plastic starts to harden (about to the consistency of hard cheese) use a perforated file (some people call these "cheesers") to bring the level down almost to the level of the paint.

6 Wait at least 20 minutes to half an hour until everything is bone dry, and then sand the area with medium sandpaper until it conforms perfectly to its surroundings. If you are working on a curved surface, like a fender, this may take some skill.

7 When everything is smooth and even, it is time to prime the area and touch up the paint. Primer can be used as a last layer of filler to fill tiny holes or irregularities. You can apply several layers, sanding each with a sanding block, until the area appears perfectly smooth (to check, wet it and look at the way light reflects off the surface).

**Priming and Painting**

The techniques used to paint the body of a car will vary, depending on the size of the area you are working on. Larger areas require spray painting, and unless you possess an experienced and steady hand and the car's original paint has not changed color since it was new, it will be almost impossible to conceal the fact that the area was repainted if you attempt to do it yourself. Spray paints must be applied in a well-ventilated area that is free from dust and dirt. A good spray gun can cost a lot, not to mention the air compressor. Besides, using a spray gun can be similar to flying a fighter plane! I would never attempt to repaint a good car until I'd first tried my hand on a couple of old wrecks where even a bad paint job might increase the resale value and I could afford to make mistakes. If you fail to prepare and prime the surface properly, the new paint will peel, blister, or flake away before very long. So, if the area to be painted is large, it would be best to have the job done by a professional car painter who can match the paint and do the job right. If you want a cheap but decent job that will last a year or so, find out where the new-car dealers take the used cars they get as trade-ins to have them spiffed up before resale. Remove rust and spotfill and paint the small areas yourself, and then have the rest of the job done professionally. Of course, if even a cheapo job is beyond your budget, it is certainly better to do your best with a can of spray paint rather than to simply let the car rust away. You can use the instructions below to help you find the color paint you need, and follow the directions on the can carefully. Be sure to mask the surrounding area well and use even, sweeping strokes to apply the paint. Practice on a piece of scrap metal before you tackle the car, and don't expect it to turn out looking terrific.

On the other hand, it is very easy to touch up a small spot with a little bottle of touch-up paint:

1 Look on the **firewall** of your car for a little plate with the body number and the paint code number on it. If you can't find it, consult your **owner's manual** or ask your mechanic or your car dealer to point it out to you. You can buy little bottles of touch-up paint to match the code number at the dealership parts department. If that's not possible, you can try a professional auto-paint supply house. They are often good sources of semiprofessional advice. If neither source is available, your auto supply store should have a chart that indicates the proper paint to match your car's make, model, and year. These little bottles of paint usually come with a brush in them. You will also need a small bottle of primer, unless the paint specifies that it doesn't require one.

2 Make sure there is no rust in the area. If it is only a deep scratch or a tiny spot, you may only need a dab of rust arrestor to stop the rust from continuing to form under the new paint. If the area is any larger than that, you must remove all the rust carefully, following the directions I gave you.

3 Sand the spot carefully with a tiny bit of #220 sandpaper to rough up the surface so the primer will adhere properly. Work in teeny dabs, feathering the edges and working inward from the surrounding area to avoid enlarging the spot.

4 Wash the area thoroughly to remove any rust arrestor, dust, dirt, filler residue, and wax, and let the area dry thoroughly before you begin.

5 Primer is used to seal the surface of the metal against rust from air and moisture and to provide a surface for the paint to adhere to. It also fills in tiny holes and imperfections in the surface. Paint then protects the primer from the sun, dust, and heavy weather. And, as you know, wax protects the paint. If you are dealing only with a surface scratch or chip that has not gone down to the bare metal, you can probably get away with simply applying the paint. Paint should never be applied to bare metal, so if any metal is exposed, or if the spot is larger than a fraction of an inch, be sure to prime the area first.

6 Apply the primer sparingly, using a tiny brush or a matchstick. You shouldn't need more than a drop to cover the area. If the directions call for it to be applied to a sanded surface, use a fine sandpaper and work inward from the edges in little dabs to avoid damaging the surrounding paint. Avoid getting primer on the original paint. If you do, wipe it off immediately. Let the primer dry thoroughly before going on with the job. Then apply the paint immediately. If you use glazing putty, you can paint right on top of it without priming first.

7   Mix the paint in the bottle thoroughly to get the color pigments properly blended. Unless your car is very new, it probably won't match exactly, which is another reason for keeping the area as small as possible. The paint on new cars doesn't fade as quickly or badly as the old paints did.

8   Apply the paint, covering the surface of the spot completely, working inward from the edges. If you are painting a scratch or a very small area, you can cut down the brush or use a matchstick or a toothpick instead. The paint should be no thicker than the surrounding surface or it will show, run, bubble, or peel off.

9   Wait several days for everything to get completely dry and then polish the car to blend the painted area and bring everything up to a high gloss.

10   Be sure to give the car a coat of wax or polymer to protect your hard work.

## How to Get Rid of Rattles, Squeaks, Whistles, and Leaks
### Rattles and Vibrations

If you find that there are suspicious *rattles* and *vibrations* going on when you drive, check and tighten these first before seeking professional help:

Loose screws and bolts (both inside the car and under the hood)

Rear view and side mirrors

Dashboard knobs and trim

Radio speaker grills

Window and door cranks and locks

Ashtray (is it empty? does it fit snugly?)

Glove box (is the door tight? is anything in it rattling around?)

Hub caps (remove and check inside for pebbles)

Outside trim

If none of these checks out, or if the noise persists, have a mechanic find the cause. Often something inside the passenger car will vibrate sympathetically because another part of the car is running roughly.

### Squeaks

Most *squeaks* respond well to a **"lube job."** If you have a persistent squeak under the car, your mechanic may be able to install an additional **grease fitting** in the squeaky area at a low cost. Tweety Bird, and other Mustangs of her vintage I've met, were prone to squeaks in the A-frame under the front bumpers. A grease fitting on each side of the upper **control arms** cured the sound effects quickly and cheaply.

*Whistles* and *leaks* are usually the result of worn, torn, or faulty weatherstripping. If the interior or trunk of the car gets wet when you wash it or when it rains, use the hose to locate the areas on the weatherstripping that have been letting the water in. If the car windows whistle when you drive with them closed, check the weatherstripping for the cause of the sound effects.

If you notice leaks under the car, refer to page 165 for ways to find the source and end the problem.

**Whistles and Leaks**

If the weatherstripping is old, dried, cracked, or worn, you can probably buy a whole new piece, designed just for your car's year, make, and model, at your car dealer's service department. Here's how to install it:

**Installing New Weatherstripping**

1 Be sure to check to see if it is the same as the old piece you are replacing. The pieces should be the same shape and thickness and should have holes, channels, and rubber studs on the inner side which match the ones on the original.

2 Remove any screws and gently peel the old weatherstripping off, prying any rubber studs out of the holes they are inserted in without damaging the paint or scratching the metal window trim. If it is hard to remove, spray weatherstrip remover around the area and wait until the adhesive softens before continuing.

3 Use the same remover to remove any old adhesive that remains on the frame after the seal is gone.

4 Insert the new weatherstripping into the frame to be sure it fits the holes and contours of the frame. Then, gently, remove it.

5 Make sure the new weatherstripping is clean. You can rinse it off and dry it thoroughly or use fine sandpaper to remove any unauthorized bumps and rough spots.

6 Apply weatherstripping adhesive (it comes in a tube) *sparingly* to the strip and to the surface of the frame. You don't want it to squoosh out the sides because if it gets on anything it may become permanently affixed to the surface. Then, before the adhesive can dry, replace the new weatherstripping. Make sure every rubber stud or other fastening device is securely in its hole. Replace any screws that were removed. Make sure the ends of the weatherstripping meet and that they are glued down securely.

If your old weatherstripping is in pretty good shape but is admitting air or water, you can try applying weatherstripping adhesive under the loose portions, or use a clear silicone sealer (it comes in a tube) to seal around the areas that are leaking. A quick and easy way to patch things

**Patching Old Weatherstripping**

up, if you don't care how it looks, is to get a roll of black household weatherstripping around ½ inch wide with an adhesive back and simply stick small pieces of it onto or under the weatherstripping in the trouble areas. This stuff is also useful to keep camper hatches and sun roofs from leaking or banging if they don't fit quite perfectly, and to keep the rain from coming past the rubber sleeve where the camper shell meets the cab of a truck. And, of course, you can always use it around the house, too!

**Car Covers**  Once you have your car looking wonderful, inside and out, it pays to keep it that way. If you have no garage and the car must be parked outdoors, you may want to invest in a car cover to protect it from the sun and keep the dirt and dust off it. The first thing you should realize is that a car cover is not used to protect a car from moisture (except to the extent that it will keep a strong rain from driving the water into the car through the windows). Many people go out and buy vinyl or waterproof car covers to keep their cars dry and innocently cause more trouble than they prevent. The reason for this is that the moisture gets under the car cover anyway, from underneath, and then is trapped under the cover and prevented from evaporating quickly. Thus, a car that is covered with a waterproof cover will remain damp longer than one that has been unprotected and has dried in the air and sunlight following a storm.

O.K., now that you know what *not* to buy, here's what to look for: The best covers on the market are cotton or cotton and polyester, woven so closely that they keep out the sunlight, prevent a good deal of moisture from getting through, dry out quickly and allow the moisture to evaporate easily, and are durable enough to last a couple of years. The fabric is also soft enough to avoid scratching the paint. These covers come in shapes and sizes designed to fit specific cars and you order them by year, make, and model. The best can cost up to a couple of hundred dollars, but they'll save you money in the long run, if you have an expensive car to protect. Some come with cables that slide under the car and lock onto the cover to keep it from being stolen, and you may want this option, especially if your car sits unattended for long periods of time. Other people simply paint their names or license numbers on the cover in supergraphics. If you do this, just be sure the paint is waterproof and will not dry hard enough to scratch the surface of the car. There are cheaper car covers designed for small, medium, and large models that work fairly well, at much lower prices. If you buy one of these be sure it has no metal cleats or grommets that can scratch the car, and that it will stay on the car securely in gusty weather. Look for mail-order ads in car magazines for some of the best buys.

Perhaps, while reading this chapter, it has occurred to you that Old Faithful may not be worth all the work it will take to fix it up. You may be right, but before you make a final decision it would be wise to read the next two chapters. They will tell you how to appraise your own car to decide if it is worth repairing, and how to test and get the best deal on a new or used car.

# 18

# Auto Recycling Without Tears: How to Buy a Good Used Car and Evaluate Your Own

We've come a long way, friends. You are no longer "dummies" when it comes to cars. You know how they work, and by this time you have probably formed a pretty good idea of how well *your* car is working. If you've tuned it and fed it properly, and if you have been driving it efficiently and it still isn't performing well—or if you find that it needs a lot of expensive professional work (and I'll show you how to evaluate that at the end of this chapter)—then you may decide to get rid of it and buy another car. On the other hand, if your car is pretty old but is now in surprisingly good shape, you may want to hang on to it instead of risking the chance of getting involved with a shiny new lemon. New cars have definitely improved, but it's still wise to hang onto an older one in good condition, unless you drive so much that fuel economy will compensate for the high cost of a new car.

Although today's cars have **electronic ignition systems** that don't need tuning, **fuel injection systems** that offer better mileage, and computer brains that hook up to electronic analyzers for instant diagnosis and do everything except order your coffee at the drive-in, they're often not built to last as long as old ones were. New cars are made with much less hand labor; machines are building machines, and robots aren't programmed to care about people. If you think that's unfair, just look at the number of recalls in recent years and the dangerous situations that prompted them. Metal parts have been increasingly replaced with plastic in order to lighten the costs and the weight, and the thinner metal or fiberglass bodies they're using now don't always withstand the effects of accidents as well as the heavier-bodied old cars did. Even though the new electronic systems tend to run better with less maintenance, if anything goes wrong they're too complicated for most laypeople (and some mechanics!) to tackle, and the chances are that the cost of repairs will be quite high. In recent years, manufacturers have spent enormous sums on research and development, and the cost of this is being passed on to the consumer, along with the growing cost of labor, import duties, and interest.

On the brighter side, there are dramatic new developments in the works which will probably revolutionize cars in the near future: ceramic engines that will last longer, weigh less, and be more fuel-efficient; new sources of fuel; even cars with independent rear-wheel drive to make parking and passing easier. So why not hang in there and see what happens before you commit yourself to a new car?

If your old car is not worth keeping, you might want to buy a used car in good condition. Older cars are going up in value, and many of them are considered classics. Although most of us think our cars are played out at half the mileage, a well-built car that has been properly maintained can stay on the road for over 150,000 miles. If you decide to go this route, I suggest that you avoid buying a car that was built in the early seventies. Many of them were less fuel-efficient than their forerunners because they employed emission control devices that wasted fuel, reduced engine performance, and produced other dangerous pollutants in the process of controlling carbon monoxide emissions. Happily, around 1974 car makers finally decided to respond to the oil embargo by developing cars that could achieve better fuel economy with more efficient emission control systems and engines. So used cars from around 1975 on are pretty good buys.

Consider this: If you buy a new car, your payments can run to several hundred dollars a month, and a new car can depreciate to half its value in a few years. If you buy or hang onto a well-made older car, you can keep it running for a lot less than you'd spend on car payments, even if you have to rebuild the engine. I'm not the only one who thinks this way; today people are keeping their cars for an average of 7 to 10 years—twice as long as they used to—and more used cars are on the road than ever before.

Here's another way to go: Many of us cannot help viewing cars as status symbols, and car freaks like me dream about owning a really superb piece of automotive engineering. But if you're on the market for a status symbol, it might be wiser (and perhaps more impressive) to forget the new expensive models and look for an older **classic car** instead. I bought Tweety for a little over $500 in 1973 and spent about $200 to fix her up, including a classy red paint job. Today, she's worth over $5,000. Consequently, when the macho-mobile died, we went looking for another Tweety and found Sylvester. Over the years there have been a total of three Mustangs in our family, and now they're all considered **classic cars**! In the late seventies, with the advance from the first edition of this book, I bought and restored Honeybun, a 1959 Mercedes 190SL roadster (talk about a suitable reward!). Not only has she turned out to be a prime investment—she's now worth at least four times her original price and twice what she cost me to buy and rebuild—she's brought me years and miles of sheer delight. Such oldies have increased in value because they're beautifully made of the best materials—by hand, in many cases. And although their previous owners usually loved and pampered them, because of accidents the supply will diminish as years go by—and the demand will increase.

Of course, the classic "oldies" are getting pretty pricey, too, and the cost of having someone rebuild them has gone up (except for the stuff you do yourself!). Rarer models are sometimes difficult to maintain because parts can be hard to find and expensive to buy, but many of them were popular enough to ensure a fairly large selection of parts through classic car clubs and specialized automotive salvage yards. Look in the Yellow Pages under "Automobile Wreckers." As far as I'm concerned, the current appreciation rates on these darlings far outweighs the expense—and besides, you can't put a price on fun!

SCLAR

000-381

Whether you are going to look for a new, used, or classic car, please be professional about it. Ever since I've become automotively involved, I've been horrified at car ads because they almost never deal with the most important thing you're buying. Most ads reflect the ignorant concerns of the majority of potential auto buyers. They talk about externals like racing stripes, sun roofs, whitewalls, and "luxury packages," but there is little or no mention of what has been put under the hood. Be sure to ask what kind of engine the car has. What kind of transmission? How fuel-efficient is it? Can you reach the spark plugs and oil drain plug easily? How about the oil filter? I've been amazed to find small cars that have been optionally equipped with large V-8 engines which burn more fuel to provide speed that is useless at current speed limits. There is so little room under the hoods of these hybrid darlings (which were usually designed for straight 4-cylinder engines) that you have to hoist the engine right out of the car in order to change the spark plugs! Not only is it impossible for the owner to do this at home, but the labor costs for dismounting the engine, hoisting it, and replacing the engine mounts when the tune-up is over are astronomical. What's more, any engine that has to be repeatedly disconnected and hauled out is just not going to be as silent and stable as one that stays put. Any owner of this "super sports model" is going to pay more for the car, more for the fuel it consumes, and much more for maintenance. If, because of the high cost, the owner doesn't spring for the required maintenance as often, the car will run less efficiently, burn even more fuel, and contribute more to air pollution.

This chapter will help you decide if you want to get rid of your old car and will help you choose a good used one. It will show you how to evaluate a used car to determine what it would take to fix it up, where to buy used cars, how to sell your own, and how to strike a good deal with Smiling Sam once you've found the car you want. Oh, and if all of the above has failed to convince you, and you simply won't be happy without a brand-new car, Chapter 19 tells you how to get the best possible deal on one.

**Where to Shop
for a Used Car**
*Auctions*

There are three major sources for used cars—auctions, dealers, and private parties. Rule 1 is: Stay Away from Auctions! Although cars go very cheaply at auction, there is little or no chance for you to inspect the car, determine its past history, or get your money back if you find you've bought a terminal basket case with a lovely paint job. Car dealers go to auctions prepared to take risks. You can't. So forget them.

Sometimes you will hear of an auction or sale of police cars, fleet cars, or taxis, at very good prices. Forget these too. Although such cars have usually been pretty well maintained, they have been driven for long hours over thousands of miles by people who neither owned them nor cared for them. As a result they are often worn out and ready for pasture. The same often goes for used station wagons. These are sometimes owned by traveling salespeople who put 50,000 miles a year on them. So unless you know the former owners, a used station wagon should be checked out very thoroughly before you consider buying it.

It is usually cheaper to buy a car directly from the owner rather than from a used-car lot. But there are drawbacks here too. The owner usually wants to sell the car quickly because the money is needed to buy a new car. Consequently, private owners are not too happy if you want to take the car and check it out thoroughly. Some will let you, but if they have had fifty answers to their ad, they are more inclined to keep the car close to home and wait for another, more impetuous, buyer to come along. Also, if you buy the car and get ripped off, it is harder to get the old owners to give you your money back. They have no reputation to protect as a car dealer, and most private deals carry no warranty, guarantee, or money-back promises. You pay your money and you take your lumps—unless you arrange, *in writing,* that you can return the car for a full refund in a day or two—after you've had it checked. If the car is as good as the owners say it is, they may be willing to do this. There is also the chance of buying a stolen car from a private party. If they take off and you are left holding the car, it is your loss if the police come to repossess it. Of course if you buy a used car from a friend, relative, or business acquaintance, you may have better luck returning a lemon. But the relationship is going to go a little sour, too. I wouldn't recommend it, unless you need the car more than you need the former owner. Remember the federal ruling on cars sold in "as is" condition: If you sign it and you buy it, you own it *without recourse!*

**Private Parties**

Car dealers come in two flavors. There are the new-car dealers who have facilities for selling the used cars they take in as trade-ins, and there are independent used-car dealers who buy cars from the public and from the new-car dealers for resale.

*New-car dealers* are generally the safest sources for used cars. They are not really in business to move the trade-ins, so they generally keep only the nicest trade-ins on the lot and sell the lemons to independent used-car dealers or to wreckers. Also, they have spent years building their reputation in the community, and if trouble develops, they will often go out of their way to see that you are satisfied. Many dealers have service facilities to handle new-car warranty work, and so if you find that your new used car has defects, they may fix the car at less cost to you and to themselves. There are two drawbacks, however. First, if new car sales are

**Car Dealers**

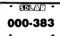

SOLAR
000-383

really down, a new-car dealer may become as hard-nosed as an independent about moving the used merchandise. Second, new-car dealers generally charge top prices for used cars, higher than independents and much higher than private parties. If you can argue them down a bit, it may be worth a slightly higher price up front to have safe recourse if trouble develops.

It is a good idea to go to the classiest neighborhood around when shopping the new-car dealers for a used car. In high-income areas there is usually little demand for used cars and a high turnover in new ones, so the dealers are eager to move the trade-ins off their lots. Also, well-heeled people tend to have maintenance work done regularly, with the best mechanics and the finest parts, because they can afford it. So the used car they trade in is often in pretty fine condition. It may not have as much mileage on it either, because wealthy families often have several cars to choose from, instead of running just one car into the ground. This may be the only time you will find the best bargain in the high-rent part of town!

*Used-car dealers* can be good sources for bargains if they have been around long enough to have established a stake in being a reliable part of the community. An established used-car dealer is probably totally trustworthy, considerate, and worth checking as a source for a used car. But it is wise to avoid the hit-and-run independent who springs up in an unused lot like a weed, unloads a group of lemons on the local public, and vanishes before the cars fall apart. It is these fellows that have made us ask, "Would you buy a used car from this man?"

When we were shopping for Sylvester, I got a good view of the used-car hierarchy in my home town. For some reason, Santa Monica has a very large number of auto dealers. It is probably one of the main sources of cars for the Los Angeles area. The dealers vary from new-car dealers who have been in the same location since the manufacturer invented the car and gave them the franchise, through a good many established used-car dealers, to the weed-grown independents on the edges of town. Oddly enough, we got the most accurate view of the hierarchy when we were trying to unload the macho-mobile. We went first to the new-car dealer who sold m-m's. He looked at our car and said, "I don't handle anything more than a year or two old. If I take a car that's little older in trade, I generally sell it to Dealer X, down the block. You might look there if you want a model from the early seventies. But this car is a '68. We sell those to Dealer Y, who is about a mile away. And if you can't sell it to him, then check out Dealer Z, on the edge of town. He's the one who gets the cheapest and the oldest cars." Dealer Y bought our car. I hope it didn't end up with Dealer Z.

Of course, when you are looking for a used car, check the newspaper ads to see what they are going for. Also check to see what cars like the one you currently own are selling for, so you will know how much money you can expect to get from selling yours. You will see that cars that are sold by private parties are generally lower in price than those from dealers. That's because the private party will still do better selling at the lower price to another private party than he or she would have done if the car were sold to a dealer. A car that is sold by a dealer for $2,000 was generally bought or taken in trade for $1,500 or less. The owner could probably have sold that car easily for $1,800 through a newspaper ad to a private party. Remember that newspaper ads are usually a bit inflated because the owner wants a chance to deal for the best offer.

**How to Determine the Price of a Car**

Other good places to check prices are the *NADA* (National Automobile Dealers Association) *Used Car Guide,* the *Kelly Blue Book,* and the *Red Book* published by National Market Reports, Inc., which provide the current wholesale and retail prices for every car—sometimes referred to informally as "**blue book** prices." These books tell you how much you can expect to get for your car and how much you can expect to pay for the car you want. They generally break down the price in terms of accessories, power extras, body condition, engine size, transmission, etc., so you can pretty well zero in on the price range for a car of the same age, quality, and general condition as your own. You can find blue books at banks, at insurance or loan companies, and at some public libraries. Be sure you are reading the most recent copy. Car values change drastically according to competition, economic conditions, and current fads. The best time to buy a used car is in the fall, when there are lots of trade-ins because people are buying the new models that have just come out.

You can get more for your car if you sell it yourself, especially if it is in good condition. If it is terminally ill, be reasonable and don't try to unload it on an unsuspecting stranger. I'm firmly convinced that deeds like that eventually come home to roost. If, however, it is not terminally ill but does need some fairly major work, you might be better off trading it to a car dealer for a newer used car. The dealer will not give you much, but it may be worth his while to make the sale. And *he* can worry about unloading your monster, or fixing it up in his own shop for less money than a private buyer would have to pay. Still, in general, selling the car privately is more lucrative—if you have the time and patience to sit through dozens of phone calls, answer silly questions, and wait while several prospective buyers kick your tires.

**How to Sell Your Old Car**

Incidentally, if you want to sell a sports car or a convertible, try to wait until spring. Convertibles are notoriously hard to sell during the winter or the rainy season.

**Free Advertising** The first thing to do is advertise. How can you sell something if nobody knows it's for sale? The cheapest form of advertising is *free*. Just place a "For Sale" sign in one of the car's rear side windows, with your telephone number on it in large black numbers that can be read from across the street. Then drive the car around town, or leave it parked in a large shopping area where it will get lots of exposure. If you want to avoid a lot of silly inquiries, put a price on the sign. If you'd rather wait for the best deal, just the phone number will do.

There are also a number of consumer-oriented newspapers that accept free ads from people who want to get rid of second-hand stuff. Many of these exist only on the price they get for the paper. Others will take the ad free but expect as much as 5 percent of the selling price in return if you make a sale. Check out the possibilities, and go for the most popular paper, which will reach the largest audience.

A third way to advertise free is to use the bulletin board at your local school, church, shopping center, community center, or at the office where you work. You can get a couple of index cards, write your sales pitch on them, and stick them up all over town. Use colored cards, add a colored border, or use colored lettering to make your card stand out from the crowd.

**Cheap Advertising** Most local newspapers now have a Bargain Box, or a column for the sale of second-hand merchandise by private parties. Most of these cost about $1 per line and most are one-liners. Just the make, year, price (if you like), and phone number will fit. It's worth a dollar.

Newspapers also have classified sections for second-hand car advertising. Rates vary, and you can get a cheaper rate if you agree to run the ad for a week. Get an idea of the circulation of the paper and estimate how many prospective buyers you will hit per dollar of advertising cost. Also, choose a paper that will be read by people who live fairly near you—or by very large numbers of people all over town. Take ads on weekends in the winter and on weekdays in summer (when people tend to get out of town on Friday).

**How to Write Your Ad** What can you say about Faithful Flash? It's been carrying you around for years, and you have a personal love for it, but to the eye of a stranger, old Faithful is just a heap. Well, the best ads convey the fact that the owner cared about the car. So if space permits, try to establish the fact with copy like, "Good home needed for Faithful Mustang. High-spirited, fuel-saving 6-cyl. engine, lovingly maintained, housebroken," etc. Convey whatever enthusiasm you can muster, but don't misrepresent what you are selling. If the car is only in fair shape, don't say that it is in mint condition. That isn't honest and you can be sued. "Needs minor body work," and other bad-news items are better left unsaid. But tell the customer the truth when asked. Sometimes you will find someone who is looking for a bargain and is quite willing to undertake some work themselves, if they know that the car will be worth the effort when they are through. In fact, if you get proficient enough at car repair, you might want to go looking for a classic oldie, such as we've discussed before, that is for sale cheaply because it needs some work that is within your range of expertise.

Be sure your ad contains the following information: year, model, condition (if good), mileage (if low), major equipment (air conditioning, automatic transmission, tape deck, radio, power stuff, etc.), price (if low), your phone number, and when you can be reached. If you have the time to wheel and deal, you can include the words "best offer," or "highest bid" and then sit around and wait for the best deal. You will have to put up with an awful lot of silly phone calls and tire kickers, however, because a lot of people are going to try for a bargain at a price that is much lower than the one you have in mind. Still, a golden goose may fly in and make it all worth while.

**How to Get the Best Price for Your Car**

When the prospective buyers come around, you will want to show your car to its best advantage. Also, by knowing what to do to make your old car look its best, you will also be wise to similar tactics on the part of those who want to sell you their cars. Here's what should be done to bring out the best in your car:

1 Clean your car inside and out. Wash the car, the upholstery, and vacuum the rug. Empty the ash trays. Make it look loved!

2 This is important. Wash the car's windows inside and out. This may sound silly, but most people drive around with a layer of dirt on their car windows. The only ones that get washed are the windshield and rear window—if they have a conscientious gas station. When a prospective buyer gets into a car with clean windows, the effect is scintillating. The car seems spacious and roomy, the world looks brighter as they drive around. No kidding, this really works!

3 Have the car waxed. A nice shiny finish can add $50 to the price.

4 *Don't* have the car painted. Most prospective buyers will assume that the new paint job is there to cover up recent body work after a smashup.

5 Repair torn upholstery, worn pedal covers, and floor mats. But don't wait till the last minute to make the replacements. If you replace a brake pedal or an accelerator pedal, do it a couple of weeks in

advance so the new pedal will be a bit scuffed. This is because a badly worn pedal cover or floor mat is a sure sign of high mileage, and a sparkling new pedal or mat will convince the alert buyer that the old one must have been worn through.

6 If your engine looks really cruddy, you can clean it with an aerosol can of engine degreaser. Be sure to cover the distributor before you wash the stuff off, however. But before you turn the under-the-hood area into a Mr. Clean fantasy, you should be aware that many buyers consider a totally clean engine to be a cover-up for the fact that some mechanic opened the engine and found a terminal illness inside, then closed it up and eliminated the signs of his exploratory surgery by cleaning everything. But do clean the worst parts up, because a well-kept engine is generally a good selling aid.

7 To give your car a well-maintained look, clean off battery deposits with 1 tablespoon of baking soda in a cup of water. Then take a look at the underside of the hood. A sure giveaway of a poorly functioning PCV valve, or bad rings, is a huge greasy spot on the undersurface of the hood, right over the air cleaner. This is called **blow-by.** It is usually worse-looking than the condition that causes it. Wipe this off before you show the car.

8 If you can, have the receipts from past maintenance handy to prove mileage and show the car's history of maintenance and repair. Also try to have an up-to-date service sticker on the door. It is a good idea to tune your car and get it into good working order so that the test drive will be a positive experience for the prospective buyer. Avoid major repairs, however; they very rarely raise the price enough to compensate for what they cost. The same goes for new tires.

**How to Shop for a Used Car**

You should have a good idea of what you want, and how much you are prepared to pay, before you go shopping. Read the ads, look at the **blue books**, car-watch a bit on the street, and talk to people who own the cars you like for a firsthand view of the pleasures and problems associated with that particular model.

Be wary of the following kinds of cars:

1 Car models that have gone completely out of production unless the one you want was so widely sold that there are still lots of parts available. Of course you may want to buy an Edsel as a collector's item....

2 Cars with engines that have been modified. If a major change has been made by the owner, find out what went wrong with the original equipment and ask a professional what damage the defective part might have done to other parts of the car.

3 Sports cars with racing modifications. Most of these souped-up darlings are miserable in stop-and-go traffic and at lower speeds. Many have been worn out by leading fast lives and aren't good for anyone anymore.

4 Very new cars that are up for sale. These may be lemons or might have been wrecked.

5 Any car that has been in a wreck. Although the car may have been completely restored, it's possible that the frame is bent and less stable, that the spot welds may not hold, or that the steering may be damaged. And remember, even though you may be convinced that the car has been restored and is as good as new, when the time comes for *you* to sell it, you may have trouble finding a buyer who feels the same way.

6 Station wagons owned by traveling salespeople, fleet cars, police cars, ex-taxis, etc. As I've mentioned before, these are usually driven hard and may be worn out.

Now that you know what you *don't* want, figure out a general range of makes and models that appeal to you. Don't limit your choice to just one car. But if you have a favorite brand, go to a dealer who sells new cars of that make, because they will tend to have more used cars of the same kind that they have taken as trade-ins.

Follow these guidelines:

1 Do your shopping during daylight hours. Floodlights tend to make cars look more exotic, and they can hide a lot of damage, especially to the underbody of the car.

2 If you are looking for a trade-in on your old car, park it about half a block away and *walk* to the dealer's lot. This is a good procedure to follow even if you are shopping for a new car. Most dealers will appraise your old car to decide how much they are going to have to give you in trade for it (whether you say you want to trade it in or not). They'll tack that onto the price they'd like to get for the car you are looking at. It is better to get a nice low price on the car you want and *then* talk trade-ins, so keep your car an unknown quantity until you are ready to deal.

3 Shop several places. Buying a car is like hiring a mechanic for an expensive repair job. Establish that you are shopping around. They will be more eager to offer you a good deal to keep you out of the hands of the competition.

4 Make it clear that you are looking for a car in *fine condition* and that you value condition over price. This will prevent the dealer from trying out the lemons on you. They will know that you are going to be very upset if they sell you a car that is not in good shape.

5 Check each car that you really like, and road-test it according to the instructions in the next part of this chapter. It will help you to identify the cars that you want to consider and will impress the dealer a lot, especially if you are female. If you can, bring a friend to help you test the car.

6 Visit several dealers this way. Then go back to the car you liked best and tell the dealer that you are there to buy if the deal is good. (In all of this, it is wise to remember that you want to *buy,* not *be sold,* a car.) Now is the time to trot out your trade-in and deal for the best price. It is your turn to be the car dealer here, so talk up your old car. Say that you've had better offers (even if you haven't) if you feel your car is being undervalued. And it will be undervalued at first. That's car trading. Tell the dealer that you know that the "blue book" value is above what was offered and that you know what other dealers are selling your model for. Eventually you will reach a price that is less than you'd like to get but more than the original offer. If the new price seems in line, take it.

7 Before you drive the deal home, tell the dealer that you want to take his car to a mechanic to have it checked. Dealers will usually let you do this, although some may have reservations about letting the car off the lot overnight.

8 Do have the car checked by a mechanic. It shouldn't cost more than $25 to $50, and a mechanic has the ability to *hear* things you'd miss, a sixth sense to diagnose them, and the hoists and equipment to check the car fully. Unless the mechanic is a personal buddy, don't tell where you got the car.

**Financing Your New Used Car**

When you are satisfied that the car is the one you want, go back and buy the car. If you have to finance the cost, be sure you can pay down at least 30 percent of the total price of the car, including sales tax, license, and registration fees. Check the various finance deals offered by the dealer, your bank, and local finance companies. Car financing is very complex, with a great deal of opportunity for you to lose your shirt, so check carefully. There have been books written on the subject, and I'd rather you got professional advice than the superficial coverage I could offer you here.

**Getting a Guarantee or Warranty**

Most dealers have some sort of **guarantee** arrangement, although almost no used cars carry warranties. If the car is a very late model, its original **warranty** may still be in effect, but I'd question why such a new car has been traded in so soon.

The basic guarantee is a 50–50 split between you and the dealer to cover any repairs that have to be made within the first 30 days. I don't care for it, because if the car turns out to need major work, you are going to get hung for half the retail cost of the parts and labor involved in the job, while a dealer with service facilities or good friends is only going to pay cost for parts and about half the retail cost of the labor. So it isn't really a 50–50 split. However, if that's the best you can do, and if a good mechanic has checked the car and it seems to be in good shape, then take the deal and cross your fingers. But try for a full money-back guarantee over the first few weeks to cover surprises. One major used-car dealer offers "a full refund toward the purchase of any of our other cars if you are not satisfied with the one you've bought." Of course a dealer may not have another car you want, so this is not the best deal.

If a dealer refuses to let you take the car to a mechanic for a checkup or refuses to consider any kind of a guarantee, RUN! If he has no faith in your chances of happiness with that car, he probably knows what he is *not* talking about.

**How to Check Out a Used Car Yourself**

This is not meant to replace having a professional mechanic check a car you are ready to buy. But it is the best way to determine whether the car is worth considering, and it may be your only chance if you are buying from a private party who has a lot of other interested people waiting to view the car. Besides, as I've already pointed out, it will impress the dealers no end, and possibly prevent them from trying to sell you a car that is not in good shape.

When Herb and I went looking for Sylvester, I had the most marvelous time checking out the prospects. Most used-car dealers we encountered tended to be "old-boy" types, who were convinced that the only thing the "little lady" would be interested in was the color of the car. When I asked one of them to open the hood, he said, "Will you know what you're looking at if I do?" That fellow's eyes popped as I wrenched open the master cylinder and poked around. "What is she doing?" he asked my husband in astonishment. "Oh, she's a mechanic," Herb replied. "I'm just along for the ride." The salesman wiped his brow. "Now I've seen everything," he murmured. After I got through telling him what was wrong with the car and what it would probably cost to fix it we left.

**Checking the Outside of the Car**

1 First, walk around the car and just form a general opinion of it. Does it have "good vibes," or do you get a general impression of seedi-ness? If that's how it looks to you, that's how it will look to others when you drive it.

2 If the car has severe dents or very chipped paint, then prepare to add the cost of body work and maybe a paint job to the price of the car.

3 Sight along the sides of the car to catch ripples in the light reflections from the surface of the body. If the reflection is distorted, it can reveal body work, spot welds, and paint cover-up after an accident.

4 Look at the chrome trim. You can have a bumper rechromed for about half the cost of a new one, or you can find a good bumper at a wrecker's if the car is a popular model. Trim is usually cheap to replace, ditto hub caps; but a grill is hard to find and expensive, even at a wrecker's.

5 Check for rust around the headlights and trim and on the underside of the car. This will need immediate removal and a paint touch-up because rust is a "disease" and tends to spread if not checked immediately. If the car is old and has recently had an undercoating, this may have been done to hide the fact that the bottom has rusted out. If you live in an area that gets snow in the winter, check the underside for corrosion due to the salt put on the streets. You may have trouble finding a car in such an area that has not rusted through because of these conditions.

6 Look at the windshield and at the rear window. The glass is expensive to replace, and cracks tend to enlarge with time. If the glass is cracked or severely scratched by the wiper blades, you will have to replace it. Side windows and side vents are generally much cheaper to replace.

7 Look for sagging doors, loose door handles, and trunk and hood lids that don't fit properly. These could mean that the car has been thrown out of line in an accident. If it's been driven a lot since then, parts of that car are now dangerously worn.

8 Check under the hood, in the trunk, and around the door jambs for signs of repainting. If the car is new and has recently been repainted, it has probably been wrecked and restored. If it is quite old and is otherwise in good condition, consider the new paint a plus.

9 Look under the car for signs of a bent **frame**, spot welding, etc. These are clues to accidents. If you see them, don't buy.

10 Check the **tires**; they will tell you how the car was driven.

   a If the outside treads of the tires are worn, the car has probably been driven hard and is worn out. (See the tire chapter for pictures of tire wear.) If only the front tires show this kind of wear, the car probably just needs wheel realignment.

   b If the tires are unevenly worn, either the car is out of **alignment** or, simply, the wheels are poorly **balanced**. Having the wheels realigned or balanced is not expensive, but you may have to get new tires if the present ones are in bad shape.

c If the tires simply show signs of overinflation or underinflation, correction is no problem.

d If the tires are worn *very* unevenly, or cupped, steering, suspension, shock absorbers, or brakes may be defective. Draw this to the attention of your mechanic if the car is otherwise O.K. and you are having it checked.

e If the tires are worn evenly but are very worn, the car has at least 20,000 miles on it no matter what they tell you.

f Is there a spare tire? Is it in good shape? If not, you will have to pay for a new one. Does a **jack** go with the car? Do you need one?

g Grab the top edge of each of the front tires and try to pull it toward you and push it away from you. If you hear a clunking sound or if there is a lot of movement, the **wheel bearings** may be worn or out of adjustment.

h If you can, get a rear wheel off the ground, jiggle it up and down. If there is any up-and-down movement of the wheel while the axle housing remains stationary, the rear axle bearing may be worn. The **axle** and the wheel should move as a unit.

11 To check for sagging **springs**, look at the profile of the car as it sits in the lot. The front and rear ends should be on the same level—also the left and right sides of the car. Lean on the front and rear fenders on each side and let go. Do you hear squeaks? Sometimes these mean that lubrication is needed; sometimes they mean that the suspension has had it.

12 Check the **shock absorbers** by stepping on the front and rear bumpers and placing your weight on them. Then take your weight off the car abruptly. If the car continues to bounce up and down for a while, the shocks are worn. The car should return to its former level and stay there when you take your weight off it. Look for special sales when buying new shocks. If you want to save the cost of installation, do it yourself at an auto class.

13 Back the car up a car length and take a look at the surface of the lot where it was parked. Are there fresh spots or puddles on the paving? Dip your finger into each one:

a If it's water, check the **radiator** and hoses for leaks.

b If it's black oil, figure out which part of the car was over the puddle and check for leaks around the **oil drain plug,** the **crankcase,** the engine, etc.

c If it looks like a light fluid, check around the **master cylinder, brake lines,** and in back of the wheels for **brake fluid** leaks (depending on which part of the car had been parked over the puddle or spot).

d If the leak seems to be pink oil and is coming from under the center part of the car, check the **transmission** for leaks. In all cases, just run your hands around the area, if you can reach it, and *feel* for wetness.

e If it smells like gasoline, check around the **fuel pump** and the **carburetor** if the leak is near the hood area. If it came from the center of the car, check the **fuel lines**. Check the **fuel tank** if it came from the rear.

14 Ask how long the car has been standing in that spot; it's possible that the leaks have come from another car. Later, if you take the car off the lot for a test drive or to have a mechanic check it, park it and let it stand for about 15 minutes; then back up and again check the pavement for leaks.

**Checking the Inside of the Car**

Now open the door and get in. Look around you.

1 Is the rug in good shape? Is the upholstery torn? It will cost money to buy a new rug or to repair or recover the seats.

2 Is the lining of the roof torn? More expensive.

3 Are the springs in the seats sagging? Forget the car—new seats are expensive.

4 Worn floor mats and pedal covers are cheap to replace, but they may mean that the car has been driven many miles.

5 Try to move the steering wheel without starting the car. If there is more than 2 inches of play in the steering wheel before the wheels begin to move, the steering is unsafe.

6 Put the **emergency brake** on, and turn the key in the ignition. With the car in "Park," look at the gauges. A broken gauge can be replaced cheaply, but if the gauges are operating and indicate low oil pressure, a discharging **alternator**, brake trouble, etc., then be wary of buying the car.

a While you have the motor running, try out the windshield wipers and washers, the clock, and the radio. Are they working properly? How about the heater, the defroster, and the air conditioner (if there is one)?

b Turn on the headlights. Check to see if the directional signal flashers on the dashboard are working. If they aren't, check the directional lights in the front and rear. Have a friend look to see if the headlights are on and if they go to high beam when you press the button. Have your friend look at the brake lights to see if they go on when you step on the brake, and at the back-up lights to see if they are functioning.

Now race the engine, still in "Park" or "Neutral," with the emergency brake on. Have someone look to see if there is smoke coming out of the **tail pipe**.

1 If it is a cold morning, you may see some white water vapor. Disregard it if it stops when the car warms up.

2 If white vapor continues to come out of the tail pipe after the car is warm, a cracked **engine block** or **cylinder head** may be letting water leak into the engine.

3 If black smoke comes out of the tail pipe, you may need only to adjust the carburetor because the **fuel/air mixture** is too rich. You can check this by running your finger around the inside edge of the tail pipe (make sure first that it is not hot). If carbon comes off on your finger, the mixture is probably too rich. Ask your mechanic to adjust it if you take it in for a checkup.

4 If there is light or dark-blue smoke coming out of the tail pipe, the car is burning oil. This can indicate that the car needs its **piston rings** replaced because oil is leaking into the **combustion chambers**. Forget the car. Rebuilding or replacing the engine can cost $1,500 or more, which is probably why the previous owner got rid of it. Even if the smoke means only that the oil was not changed and has been allowed to get so low and cruddy that it is smoking, this would indicate that the moving parts of the engine are worn owing to improper **lubrication**.

5 If the smoke is light gray, the car may be burning **transmission fluid**. Check the transmission **dipstick**. Is the fluid dark and burned-looking, or does it smell? Have the transmission checked carefully by your mechanic if you are still interested in the car. If there are signs of transmission trouble, forget the car completely. Sometimes a faulty **vacuum modulator** can suck transmission fluid into the engine, where it is burned in the **cylinders**, causing the same type of smoke to come out of the tail pipe. If this is the case, you can usually replace the vacuum modulator yourself quite easily. All you usually have to do is unscrew the old one and screw in the new one. A mechanic will be able to tell you if this is true of the car in question.

Shut off the engine and step on the brake (leave the engine running if it is a **power brake**). Check for sinkage of the brake pedal. It should stay put after you have depressed it. If it continues to sink slowly toward the floor, the master cylinder is probably defective. Get out and check the brake lines around the master cylinder, and behind each wheel for leaks.

Run the **gearshift** through each gear if the car has a **manual transmission**. Does it move smoothly, or does it stick?

Now lift the hood and peek in. How do things look in there? Most used-car dealers have the engine area cleaned so that it will look as though it is in mint condition. But remember that this can hide signs of repair work, or that the dealer may have opened the engine, taken a look at a worn **crankshaft**, and closed it up again. Be wary and look for signs of leaks (these don't have to be wet; sometimes stains can clue you in).

1 Look at the **radiator** and the principal hoses. Run your hands around them. Are there signs of wetness, or are there stains that show that coolant leaked the last time the car was driven (because of the pressure) and then dried up? Make a note to have the cooling system checked with the pressure tester we talked about in Chapter 8. Leaky radiator hoses can be replaced for a couple of dollars; leaky radiators can cost a lot of money to fix or replace.

   a Open the radiator cap and look in. Is there much rust floating around inside? The radiator may need flushing (which is easy to do), or it may need replacing, if it is rusted through. Ask if they've replaced the **coolant** recently.

   b Look carefully around the **water pump** to see if there are rusty areas that can indicate leaks. (In case you've forgotten, the fan is usually mounted on the water pump.)

2 Look at the **battery**. If it is very corroded (they'll have cleaned up the acid deposits, but the cables will tell the story), you will need a new one. Maybe the dealer would like to throw one in as part of the deal. Look inside the battery. Is it filled with water?

3 Look at the engine.

   a Run your finger around the edge of the **cylinder head** where it meets the **rocker arm cover**. Is oil leaking out? You may need a new **gasket**. That's not too expensive if you replace it yourself. You'll have to unscrew the bolts, pull off the valve cover, remove the old gasket, put in the new one, and screw everything back. Just make sure to tighten all the bolts a little at first, then go back and tighten them all down, skipping from front to back and from side to side to get the pressure even. Don't tighten them so hard that you crush the gasket, however, or it will leak again.

   b Look at the **core plugs** in the sides of the engine. Are there signs that these have been leaking? If only one plug looks rusty, the others probably have as much rust and will soon begin to leak, too. Replacing them all can add up to a lot of money.

   c Check the engine block, cylinder heads, and **manifolds** for cracks or rust (which can indicate leaks). If you find cracks, RUN!

   d Check around the **crankcase** and the **oil pan**. Are there leaks there?

e Check the oil dipstick. Is the oil clean? Does it have particles in it? Is the level low? This can indicate a leak or just poor maintenance. Does the dipstick have drops of water on it? They could be there because the car has been driven too long without an oil change, or they could be clues to a blown head gasket or a cracked block that has allowed water to leak into the oil. Ask when the **oil, oil filter, air filter**, and **fuel filter** were last replaced. Most dealers will replace these as a matter of routine when getting a car ready for resale. If they haven't, they should do it as part of the deal. If you're buying from a private party, you'll have to do it yourself.

f Feel the hoses that run into and out of the engine. Are they cracked or leaky? Sticky? Soft and mushy? Stiff or brittle? If they have any of these symptoms they will have to be replaced or they could blow at any time. Again, not a big expense if you do it yourself. Actually, the dealer should do it for you.

4 Now ask the dealer to take off the air cleaner (or do it yourself). Notice if the filter has been changed recently. If it is really filthy, the car may not have been properly maintained.

5 Look at the carburetor. Are there signs of leaking fuel from the bottom or from the gasket area where the top of the carburetor meets the **float bowl**? If you haven't run the engine yet, is the choke closed? It should be.

a Look at the inside of the hood itself, above the carburetor. Can you see a **blow-by** stain? Have the **PCV valve** and the compression checked.

b Start the car again, with the **air cleaner** off. Did the choke open after a while? Remember to be careful about looking down a strange **carburetor barrel** while the engine is running; it could possibly backfire in your face.

c Move the **throttle** linkage with your finger. Does it move easily? Does the car rev up promptly? Shut off the engine and move the throttle linkage again while you peer carefully into the carburetor barrel. Does fuel squirt into the **venturi** when you move the throttle? It should. A carburetor may simply need adjusting to make it run well—or it may need to be taken apart and cleaned (that's called "rebuilding"). If you think the carburetor needs to be rebuilt or replaced, think twice about the car. At any rate, checking the carburetor is a good way to shake a dealer into a better deal. Replace the air cleaner.

6 Take off the **oil filler cap** and listen to the engine. How do the **valves** sound? Are there ticking, rattling, or clunking noises coming from inside the engine? Valve jobs are expensive, and even worse things could be happening in there.

7 Is the engine shaking around a lot while the car is running? One or more cylinders could be **misfiring** because of a loose connection, bad wiring, or a carburetor that needs adjusting. If the shaking occurs only when you are stepping on the gas and accelerating, the cause could be the engine mounts. These can be replaced—for more money.

8 With the emergency brake on, the transmission warm and the engine running, put the car in "Park" or "Neutral" and check the **transmission dipstick** if you haven't already done so.

9 Take a screwdriver and open the top of the **master cylinder**. If you've forgotten how, see Chapter 10. Look inside. Is the **brake fluid** clean? Is it up to the fill line of both compartments? If it is low, there may be a leak in the lines or in a wheel cylinder. Does the rubber diaphragm on the lid look to be in good shape? Replace the cover and run your hands around the sides and base of the master cylinder. Are there any signs of leaks? Look at the **firewall** behind and next to the cylinder. Are there any signs of wet or dried leaks?

10 Wiggle the **distributor** to see if it is loose. If there is a lot of play, the timing will be off. Check the **distributor cap** for frayed wires and cracks.

11 Remove the wire from the center of the distributor cap and lay it on a metal part of the car to ground it. Have someone crank the engine. Listen for uneven cranking. This can clue you in to uncovering a poor **starter**, or broken teeth on the flywheel.

**How to Road-Test the Car**

Now you are ready to take the car on the road.

1 Find a quiet nearby street where you can check the **brakes**. With your seat belt on, check to be sure that there is no one behind you and then hit the brakes. Does the car pull to one side? This can indicate a leak or worn linings. Do the brakes squeal? They may need to be replaced. How long does it take to stop the car comfortably at the end of the block?

2 Drive slowly down the block with your hands off the wheel. Does the car pull to one side? The **steering linkage** may be damaged, or the front end may need **alignment**. The first is a no-no. The second is not costly.

3 Vary your speed; shift from forward to reverse. The engine should not race, and there should be no slams, jerks, or howls from the **transmission** during these shifts.

4 If the car has a **manual transmission**, check the **clutch** for slippage Run through the gears. Does the **gearshift** work smoothly? Does the car hesitate or make grinding noises when you shift? What about the **clutch free pedal play**? Is there ½ to 1 inch of movement before it starts to disengage? Does the clutch chatter?

5 Drive a car with a manual transmission at a low speed and shift it into high gear. Then accelerate. The engine should stall and die if the clutch is in good shape. If the clutch is slipping, the engine will speed up but not the car. This is a bad sign. It is one of those few circumstances when stalling out is good news.

6 Have a friend watch while you drive the car slowly. Do the wheels wobble? The cause may be a bent wheel. If you really want the car, try the spare.

7 Are you comfortable in the car? Adjust the seats. Can you see well? How about the rear and side mirrors? Do you feel at home?

8 Head for the freeway if there is one nearby. Does the car handle well? If the front wheels shimmy, you may need an **alignment**, or the front end may be badly worn.

9 What is the car's pickup like when you accelerate, pass, or start? Is there enough power? If it has an **automatic transmission**, does it move smoothly from low to higher gears? Is there **overdrive**?

10 Drive up a hill if you can. How does the low gear feel? Does the car "just make it" up the hill? Or does it sail up smoothly, with power to spare?

11 Drive down an alley or driveway. Open the car windows and shut off the radio if it's been on. Can you hear clanking or grinding noises coming from the rear wheels? This can indicate worn rear-**axle bearings**. Check them when you get back according to the instructions in the early part of this chapter, or have a mechanic take a look.

12 When you get back home, look at the engine again for signs of leaks that may have opened up under the pressure of driving. If the car seemed to lack power, or felt "funny," you might want to run a **compression check** on the engine. This will tell you how well the **cylinders, pistons, rings**, and **valves** have worn. Look for instructions on page 342, or have a mechanic do it.

## How to Evaluate What You've Found

Before you get back to the dealer, stop and evaluate what you've discovered about the car (of course, you've been taking notes, right?). On the next page is a chart that will give you a general idea of what your findings mean in terms of expense and the future performance of the car. Actually, all these items should be taken care of by the dealer as part of the deal. A used car, bought from a dealer, is supposed to be in good condition unless it is advertised as needing work. Some states require a recent state inspection sticker before a car can be sold or reregistered. If your dealer is *required* to furnish this, then he will have to fix anything found below standard if you have the car reinspected after you buy it. If you are buying from a private party or must undertake the work your-

## Repair Evaluation Chart

| Major Problems | Think Twice About These | Relatively Cheap |
|---|---|---|
| **I. Wreck Indicators** | Needs new shock absorbers | Minor dents |
| Extensive dents, rust, and chips | Needs new springs | Needs front-end alignment |
| Misalignment of hood, trunk lid, or doors | Needs new carburetor | Needs new throttle linkage |
| Welded or bent frame under car | Needs new master cylinder | Needs carburetor adjustment |
| New paint job on a new car | Needs complete brake job | Needs new gauges, knobs, switches, wiper blades, lighter, etc. |
| **II. High Expense Items** | Self-adjusting brakes out of adjustment (possibly expensive) | |
| Transmission leaks or poor performance | | Radio needs to be repaired |
| Blue smoke coming from tail pipe (unless due to faulty vacuum modulator) | Needs new alternator, radiator, starter, muffler, flywheel, or distributor | Clock doesn't work |
| Cracked block, head, or manifold | Needs seats recovered | Needs horn, lights, or signals repaired |
| Valves need to be reground or replaced | Needs new side windows or vents | Needs hoses replaced |
| Grille missing or damaged | Needs a new rug | Needs a tune-up |
| Needs four new tires | Needs new chrome, or new bumper | Needs manual brakes adjusted |
| Needs new windshield or rear window | Needs pollution device required by law | |
| Clutch worn or defective | | Needs a spare tire, or just two tires |
| Rear axle worn or damaged | | Needs new fan belts |
| Steering linkage and front-end suspension worn or damaged | | (The dealer should definitely supply all of the above. In some states the law requires that the brake system, muffler, pollution devices, steering, suspension, horn, and lights be in safe condition before the car is sold.) |
| Needs extensive body work or complete paint job | | |
| Needs new seats because seat springs are shot | | |
| Needs new convertible top, or interior | | |
| Needs new crankshaft, driveshaft, etc. | | |

self for some reason, a good rule of thumb is, if any of the conditions listed as a major problem exists, forget the car. These problems are either unsolvable, and will lead to the quick demise of the vehicle, or they are much too costly to handle. The only time you might want to fool with any of these problems is if you are dealing with a truly classic car that will go up in value by *thousands* of dollars once it is restored. Add up the probable cost of the work required plus the cost of the car, and see if it compares favorably with the going price for that car in recent newspaper ads.

Repairs in the middle column can cost $100 and much more. It may be worthwhile to invest if only one of these repairs is needed; but more than one of these repairs will mean a considerably larger outlay of money, even if you do the work yourself. Unless the car is really outstanding, you should probably find another one that does not require such expensive work.

The last column lists repairs and replacements that many used cars require. You can do most of these yourself with little or no expertise, but if much work is required, the car is probably more trouble than it's worth, unless you have a lot of time on your hands or it is a classic car worth restoring completely. Be sure to use the information in the Bodywork and Good Housekeeping chapters to restore, preserve, and clean any car you buy.

One final thing: Even if you are not in the market for a used car and have just read this chapter on your first sweep through the book, it might be useful to go out to your own car and run it through these checks. This will give you a good idea of the car's general condition and tell you whether or not it is worth investing your time and effort. These checks will also pinpoint the areas to concentrate on when you are ready to put down the book and go to work.

**Evaluating Your Own Car**

If you should decide that Old Faithful simply isn't worth the time and effort, then you should think seriously about buying a good used car and fixing it up or buying a new car. Before you make your decision, read the next chapter for hints on getting the best deal on a new car, and reread Chapter 14, "Diesels for Dummies," to have a complete picture of all the fascinating ways you can spend your money.

# How to Get the Best Deal on a New Car

If, after reading all the wonderful advice I gave you about auto recycling, you still feel that nothing can make you happy except a brand-new car, well, I can understand how you feel and I'm prepared to help. A couple of things have tempered my previous conviction that buying and refurbishing used cars was the only way to go. For one thing, the supply of good used cars dating back to those halcyon days of the sixties is diminishing rapidly as the years move inexorably onward. And the really good fifties and early sixties models that have survived are now considered to be classic cars and are priced accordingly. I'm still in love with them but it takes a lot of time, effort, and money, and since some of those huge finny fifties darlings were prodigious gas hogs, my dream car may not be the answer to your daily needs. Today, many new cars are equipped with engines and systems that really do operate more efficiently, and there are cars on the market at competitive prices that can get 40 to 50 miles per gallon. If you drive a lot, that's a great reason for buying a new car.

However, to be totally honest, the thing that really changed my mind was the fact that after spending eight years restoring and driving two wonderful old cars I finally woke up one morning yearning for a new vehicle that would not require any kind of coddling to make it perform. Something that I could just jump into and take off in, in any kind of weather, with any kind of load, to any place I cared to visit. A vehicle that would get at least 25 to 30 miles to the gallon, with enough room in it to haul my surfer son and a couple of his friends—with wet suits, surfboards and the usual sandy and soggy stuff—home from the beach. Something with the strength to haul home a load of firewood. A recreation vehicle that could hold a good supply of camping gear and get it over fairly rough roads for a little wilderness camping. A haven on wheels where I could cuddle down and sleep if I found myself away from home late at night and not particularly inclined (or in shape) to get there. Something which would wear the dents and dings of constant use with pride and, yes, a bit of macho. In other words, a brand-new, long-bed, five-speed, shiny blue truck complete with sunroof and camper shell!

Now, your reasons for wanting a new vehicle and the type of vehicle you want may be very different from mine, but in the process of choosing and buying Baby Blue, I learned a great deal that I am quite willing to pass along to you. Basically, the way the process breaks down is: Be very clear about exactly what you want, investigate thoroughly to see what your options and alternatives are and which cars offer them, then deal wisely and from a position of enlightened power to get the best possible vehicle at the lowest possible cost.

First, let's take a look at some questions you should ask yourself in order to decide what kind of new car you want and what sort of options and features it should possess. (I realize that you may be in the market for a truck, or a motor home, or even a motorcycle with a sidecar, but I'm going to refer to the vehicle as a car from here on because the word has fewer letters to type.)

What are you going to use it for and who else is going to use it? Is the car going to be used as a commuting vehicle? On the highway or through city stop-and-go traffic? Do you plan to travel a lot by car? Or is your route mainly the home-school-stores routine? How many people do you expect to carry on most trips? Just you? Do you have kids who need infant seats or carriers? Do you chauffeur amateur athletes and their gear? Old people? A large dog?

Compact cars cost less, but it's difficult to load your kids into the tiny rear seat of a two-door compact. And if you travel a lot, you may find that you lack luggage space or are forced to leave your possessions exposed to public view at the rear of a hatchback compact car.

What is your main reason for wanting a new car? Fuel economy? Status? (Be honest, this is just between you and me!) Business depreciation? Or have you been struck by the beauty and power of a newcomer to the automotive field?

What are your priorities? Make a list and weight each from one to ten to see what's really important to you: low cost, high power, fuel economy, versatility, space to carry large loads, beauty, etc.

How much power do you really need? Do you carry heavy loads? Do you have to climb steep hills regularly? Is there any place where you can hit high speeds or are you going to be tied down to 55 mph anyway no matter what you drive? Big engines not only burn more fuel, they weigh a lot too! And, as I've said before, many of them fit so closely under the hood that you cannot reach the spark plugs, when tune-up time comes, without hoisting the engine right out of the car! However, if you do a lot of freeway driving in areas where it is important to accelerate swiftly in order to merge into traffic, you would probably be better off with a bit more power. There is nothing more frightening than trying to move a sluggish, underpowered car into high-speed traffic.

Can you put off buying until the most favorable time of the year in order to save money? It is always good to wait for sales, for the end of the month when the salespeople are trying to fill their quotas, or until the end of the summer when the new models are coming in and this year's models are a lot cheaper than they were in January. True, they will be considered a year older in terms of depreciation, but if you intend to keep the car for quite a while this difference may be insignificant compared to what you'll save when you buy the car.

**Getting Clear on What You Want**

**Evaluating the Options**

What **optional equipment** is important to you? (You might want to weight these, too.) Here are some pros and cons about several popular options:

**Air Conditioning**

If you live in a very hot climate, then air conditioning is a feature that you would not care to live without. For those of us who live in areas where the heat is rarely unendurable, it may not be that great an idea. Here's why: An air conditioning unit weighs enough to cost you a couple of miles per gallon in gasoline. If fuel economy means a lot to you, then you may want to forget the air conditioning and simply open the side windows. I opted for a sunroof, which provides great air flow even when I choose to keep the windows shut. It's almost as good as having a convertible, and it cost a fraction of the price of air conditioning. Another air conditioning drawback is the fact that the unit and its hoses tend to crowd the space under the hood and interfere with do-it-yourself maintenance at tune-up time. However, if you do decide to include an air conditioner, have it installed while the car is still at the factory. "Factory air" takes up less room and is tailor-made to cool your car more efficiently than units installed by independents after the car is finished.

**Power Options**

Today's cars often feature a variety of power options. Some, such as **power brakes** and **power steering** on large vehicles, are not only useful, they are indispensable. Others, like power seats, are of relatively little use. They add significantly to the up-front cost of the car, weigh enough to lower the car's fuel economy, and are very seldom used. Unless you share your car constantly with someone who is very different in size, or are too old or weak to slide your seat forward and back yourself, I would advise you to pass on the power seats. Power windows have never taken my fancy either. I guess my main complaint is that I always forget to put the windows up when I park the car. By the time I remember, I have to fish the key back out of the depths of my handbag (which can be a major project), turn the car's ignition back on, and slide up the windows. Also, I don't feel secure that I'd be able to get the windows down if I had to escape through them in a car wreck. The last thing I'd want to do would be to turn the engine on and risk igniting any spilled gasoline. Call it claustrophobia, but I have always needed to be in charge of my ability to get into or out of anything. And so, I guess that might go for power door locks, too. If it turns out that my fears are unfounded (and I'm sure the car manufacturers will be swift to call that to my attention, if they are), then I still object on the grounds that the switches that operate power windows tend to start going bad when the car gets older and that kids can literally drive you crazy by playing with them. You can add power-operated side mirrors and all those other classy but unnecessary gizmos to my list, too.

On the other hand, I'm totally in favor of rear-window defoggers and even windshield wipers for those big windows at the back of hatchback cars. Anything that increases visibility appeals to me.

**Cruise Control**

Optional **cruise control** is useless in stop-and-go rush-hour traffic and on city streets. Its extra cost can be justified only if you drive a big gas-burner for many miles per week, on the highways at sustained speeds. And if that is the case, you might give some thought to whether having to watch your speed is helping to keep you awake. Just cruising along, mile after mile, without having to do much, might trip you out completely! I would consider this option only if you tend to be terribly lead-footed on the accelerator pedal, and spend most of your time on the freeways.

**Sound Equipment**

Many of us consider a radio to be an indispensable friend in a car. I love to drive along to music; it's rather like dancing. But when I bought my truck I took one look at the quality and price of the AM/FM/cassette offered by the manufacturer and decided to have one installed privately after the truck was delivered, because there is a wide range of sound systems available at extremely competitive prices and tailored to each individual's tastes and needs. Do you want a powerful FM receiver that can bring your favorite station in from far away? Or would you rather spend your money on a fully automated tape deck with maybe a less powerful radio to keep the cost down? How many speakers do you need to satisfy your ears? My only suggestion is that you choose an integrated system, rather than one that's hung under the dashboard. Those are too visible and can therefore be targets for theft. They can also be hazards in an accident. I'd avoid those spectacular many-buttoned LED readout gizmos because thieves just adore them, and even if you get to keep yours, you'll find that the simpler the equipment you buy (and this goes for everything), the less the chances of something going wrong and needing repair. Check the Sunday papers for sales on sound equipment and wait for the best prices.

**Radial Tires**

These are definitely an advantage. Radials ride smoother and actually save gasoline. If the car you choose comes without radials, ask to have them included in the price. You'll probably have to pay a bit more, but it will be worth it. However, be sure to specify that you want 40,000-mile steel-belted radials, since you will certainly put at least that much mileage on your new car and it would be silly to accept anything but the most durable equipment. Reread the tire chapter to be sure you know what you are getting.

**Dashboard Gadgets**    We are just getting into the wonderful world of the dashboard, as far as cars are concerned. LED displays in a variety of gorgeous colors can be fun, or just plain distracting. There is at least one car out that features a lush feminine voice telling you "Your oil is getting low," etc. (I hope they put one out soon with a sexy male counterpart for lonely ladies.) Some of these are standard equipment, and others will cost you money. It's up to you. Briefly, I would favor real oil, water, and temperature gauges over **idiot lights** or voices that simply inform you when it's already too late to avoid damaging your car. I also like a tachometer on a car with a manual transmission. Most of the other stuff I can do without.

**Automatic vs. Manual Transmissions**    And speaking of transmissions, here is a question to be considered carefully. **Automatic transmissions** are much easier to drive—you just step on the gas to go, on the brake to stop, and steer the car in the direction that appeals to you. But they also cost more, can get fewer miles to the gallon, and are less powerful than **manual transmissions** applied to the same-size engine. In some cases, automatic transmissions can be cheaper to repair than manual transmissions; in others it's the other way around. Generally speaking, manual transmissions with **stick shifts** are great for small cars, especially those that are relatively low-powered. If large, heavy cars with big engines appeal to you, you'd probably be better off with an automatic transmission. Which of these features matters the most to you?

For my money, manual transmissions are much more fun to drive, although they require more driving skill. I really feel a rapport with my car as we glide through the gears together, and I've had a lot of fun developing fuel-saving routines by considering what gear I'm in on hills, around curves, and the like. The five-speed transmission on my truck is especially wonderful. In fifth gear, the wheels are turning faster than the engine and the mileage is improved geometrically. But if you are driving mostly from one city stoplight to another, these options aren't going to do much for you and you may really get tired of shifting from gear to gear at every light. Some cars with automatic transmissions are equipped with overdrive to accomplish much the same thing, and you may want to consider that instead. There is an add-on torque converter available that can provide this option if the car you buy doesn't have it, and there are also cars available that have an automatic transmission with a torque-converter clutch to provide additional fuel economy.

Seat Options

Many car makers offer a variety of seating options and coverings. If this is the case, ask yourself how many people you have to be able to carry in the front seat of your car. Bench seats will accommodate three people, or two people and a baby in a safety car seat. Bucket seats accommodate only two people safely, but can be individually adjusted for comfort and leg room. There is also a "split bench" seat available on some models which combines the best features of the two—room for three plus individual adjustment of each half.

Rear seating also varies widely, from the roomy couchlike seats found in large sedans to the tiny vestigial shelves that offer little more than package room in the back of some subcompact cars. Some hatchbacks provide rear seats that can be folded down to create room to carry larger loads, and there are a variety of station wagons and vans that can carry from eight to fifteen people in comfort. As far as seat coverings are concerned, whether you opt for washable vinyl, gorgeous leather, or cut velvet will depend on your individual taste and on the dependability of the people and animals who are regular passengers.

**Rustproofing and Undercoating**

Many cars come already undercoated and rustproofed these days. This can be a blessing indeed, especially if you live in an area with salty ocean breezes or salted snowy roads, both of which can literally eat away the metal surfaces on your car. If the car you choose doesn't feature this treatment as part of the basic package, you may find it cheaper to have it undercoated at a shop which specializes in it, rather than paying the car dealer to have it done before the car is delivered. You can also buy and apply **undercoating** yourself. This is cheaper than having it applied professionally, but generally doesn't last as long.

As far as rustproofing is concerned, many new cars come with **polymer coatings** that are said to protect your car's paint and body for a couple of years. You can also have these products applied professionally, if it is only an optional extra and not part of the original package. There are also new polymer coatings that you can apply as easily as car wax. These generally last about half as long as the substances used by professionals, but cost a good deal less. Check Chapter 16 for more about these alternatives.

**Trailer-Towing Packages**

If you plan to tow a trailer, it is important to pick a vehicle with a large transmission and to have it delivered with a **trailer-towing package** installed. This option usually includes a heavy-duty **suspension system** with **springs** and **shock absorbers** that can cope with the extra weight and shifting loads, a cooler to prevent the transmission from overheating, and a rear bumper that can be hitched to a trailer. If you have no immediate plans but would like to tow a trailer in the future, you might want to buy this package anyway, since they are usually priced very reasonably by the car manufacturers. Your car will be tougher and easier to handle and it is infinitely less expensive to buy a car equipped this way than to scrap your existing equipment and buy all this stuff in the future. At the very least, find out if the car you are considering can handle a trailer, should you decide to invest in one at some future date. And by the way, there's a whole section on trailers in Chapter 15, "On the Road."

**Fuel Economy**    As I've mentioned before, many of the new smaller cars are now extremely fuel-efficient and if you plan to do a great deal of driving, you may want to place a high priority on one of these. If you want a long-lasting, larger car with good fuel economy, you may want to consider a diesel-powered car, with or without a **turbocharged** engine. Read the **diesel** chapter for information that will help you to come to a decision. Compare the **EPA estimates** for each car that interests you. You can find them on the window tickets of each car, or ask for a free copy of the EPA Gas Mileage Guide at a car dealership. Don't expect the car you buy to achieve the EPA estimates, however. They are really averages, for comparison purposes only. The mileage for each vehicle varies with the driver, the load, and the road conditions.

**Evaluating**    To keep abreast of all the new cars and new features you have to choose
**What's Available**    from, make it a habit to talk to people about the cars they drive, especially if they have just bought a new one, and read the car magazines that carry feature stories on new vehicles. Be sure to check the consumer magazines, especially the annual issues that report on the performance, economy, special features, and repair records of each year's new models. AAA publications in many states also review new cars and compare them for handling, safety, fuel economy, and other features.

To check out the depreciation record of the cars that interest you, consult the consumer magazines, the *Kelly Blue Book,* or the *NADA Used Car Guide* at your local insurance company or lending agency for a good view of how well the cars made by different companies keep their value as they get older. Generally speaking, a line of cars that has depreciated at a slower rate in the past will continue to do so in the future.

While you are checking the **blue books**, be sure to find out what your old car is worth, if you plan to trade it in. The listings are by make, model, and year, plus "extras" such as air conditioning, etc. Look in the automotive sections of the newspapers to see what cars like yours are selling for. Appraise your car objectively, as a prospective used car, using the criteria in Chapter 18. Be honest about its condition. When you have a pretty good idea of what you are looking for, and the value of what you have to trade, it's time to visit the dealerships and interview the pretty new models.

**Find Out What Your Old Car Is Worth as a Trade-in**

It is always a good policy to park down the street and walk into a dealership, whether you want to trade in your old car or not. It is also wise not to wear your most expensive outfit, and to leave the jewelry at home, too. Salespeople are trained to size up a customer, and there's no point in having to start bargaining at a higher price just because you look well-to-do.

**Visiting Car Dealerships: A Study in Creative Paranoia**

Remember that the first visit to any dealership is only a preliminary visit. Never buy a car on a first visit. Wait until you have checked out the competition. It pays to give car salespeople a chance to worry a bit about whether they can sell you a new car at all. They will probably ask you early in the game whether or not you want to trade your old car in, but be evasive at that point. Refuse to talk about it until you are in the final phases of dealing for the car you know you want. As you will see when we get to that situation, it is important that you know what the lowest possible price would be without a trade-in before you bring it up.

There are several things to check out when you are looking over a prospective car at a dealership. Bring along a notebook, or a pad, on which you've provided space to list the base price and the costs of all the optional extras you want, plus any charges for preparation, transportation, fees, and taxes that will be included in the price you pay. Leave room for noting the size of the engine, **warranties**, financing deals, **EPA estimates**, and other things that are important to you. Fill in the information as you talk. This shows you are a serious customer and also that you intend to compare cars at several dealerships. It will help to motivate salespeople to provide the most competitive prices they can quote. Nevertheless, be prepared to bargain for an even better deal later. Be sure you cover each of the following items:

If you plan to do the basic maintenance on the car yourself (and I can't imagine your having read this book and feeling otherwise!), be sure that

**Do-It-Yourself Maintenance**

you will have easy access to the **oil filter** and **oil filler hole**, every **spark plug**, the **distributor** (unless it is the electronic kind that needs no service), and the **carburetor** (unless the car has **fuel injection**). Even if you are not sure you will be taking care of this stuff yourself, ease of access can mean lower costs to have the work done by a mechanic.

**Electronic Gadgets and Systems**

If a car has a lot of electronic features, ask how long these features have been in use. It may take a year or two to work the bugs out of a new gadget and to provide the mechanics in the service department with enough experience and training to deal with it efficiently. I like to wait until a new system establishes a track record before I buy. Ask if the new system breaks down into components that can be repaired, or if large portions of it have to be replaced if something goes wrong.

**Availability of Options**

Compare the standard equipment on various cars. Are some of your options standard on some models? If not, is the dealership willing to supply them, and at what price? Ask to see the list of **optional equipment** that is available for the models you like. You may find some reluctance to special-order a car with unusual optional equipment because the dealers may be afraid of being stuck with the car on their hands if you back out of the deal. If you look at the list, you will know what is available and be able to demand that it be part of any deal you make.

**Check Out the Service Department**

These are the people who will be doing the work on your car for as long as it is under warranty. Read Chapter 20 to be prepared to evaluate how efficient the dealership's service department will be. Have a chat with the **service writer** and ask if the mechanics have been trained to handle the new electronic components. Ask about the availability of parts at the parts department (or ask some of the independent mechanics who may be at the desk buying parts for the cars they are working on at their own shops).

**Test-Drive the Car**

When you've found a car that attracts you, ask to take it for a test drive. If they will let you take it out alone, that's terrific, because you can put the car through any paces you want to. If the salesperson has to come along, insist on driving the car yourself. If there is someone who will be sharing the car frequently as a passenger or driver, be sure to take them along, too. Make sure you test-drive the car under all kinds of conditions. Up steep hills, at high speeds (if that matters to you), on the freeway, in stop-and-go traffic, etc. Find a deserted street or alley, make sure everyone is safety-belted, and put the car through some short stops and hard turns to see how well it responds. Chapter 18 lists a thorough procedure for test-driving cars. Try to duplicate, as closely as possible, the traffic and road conditions that you will encounter most often.

Before I test-drove my truck I told the salesman that since I intended to use it for camping, I had to see how well it could handle hills and rough roads. He agreed, and since he insisted on coming along, he soon found himself out of town and climbing up a pass that leads straight into the wilderness. "Where are we going?" he asked nervously, positive that I was abducting him. "My boss is going to be upset if we're gone too long." "Well, I told you I have to check it out in the country, and this is the nearest country we've got," I said, as I gained the top of the mountain and headed down a winding dirt road that led back toward town. Half an hour later, when we returned to the dealership, I was convinced that this was the truck for me. The salesman was not only relieved to be back in civilization but was mighty glad that I had decided to buy the truck, since it was now too dusty to show again without a bath!

**Check for Hidden Costs in the First Price They Quote You**

Does the price include tax, transportation, the optional extras you want, license plates, registration, and other hidden items? If "dealer preparation" is added to the price, question them closely concerning what this item involves. In some cases the cars arrive at the dealership in fine condition and this is merely a gimmick for building in additional profits. Be sure the price you are quoted is the full price you will have to pay. Say, "If I wrote you a check for this amount, would I have to pay anything else in connection with buying and owning this car?" Of course you will not, under any circumstances, end up paying the first price they quote you. Just make a note of the first prices quoted at each dealership so you can compare them when you decide which car you are actually going to deal for. Remember to carry a little notebook and jot down the pertinent details of each car offered. It will drive them crazy to see that you are really going to subject their products and prices to a close comparison with those of the competition.

**Service Contracts**

If you are interested, ask what kinds of service contracts they offer. Some contracts stretch the time period covered by the basic **warranty** for up to five years or 50,000 miles. Unless the dealership is offering a very special deal, you will usually have to pay quite a bit for an extended service contract, so consider this option carefully. As a rule, unless you expect to subject the car to unusual wear and tear during the first few years, you are probably better off with the regular warranty and an occasional helping hand from Lady Luck. Most cars don't begin to need major repairs until after 50,000 miles—which is when most extended contracts run out. Still, check it over. Maybe the dealership is offering an especially good deal...

**Warranties**  If you are seriously interested in a car, ask about warranties on standard and optional equipment. Is the warranty readable? Do you understand it? Which parts and systems are covered by the car manufacturer? Does that include labor? Which parts and systems are covered by separate manufacturer's warranties? (Tires, sunroofs, and other special equipment probably will fall into this category.) Which parts are not covered at all? How long does the warranty run? What do you have to do to obtain parts and services under the warranty? Is there anything you might do that would void it? Be sure to read the small print carefully before you buy!

**Financing**  New cars cost so much these days that many of us have to pay for them in installments. If this is the case for you, it would be wise to check with your bank, local lending agencies, credit unions, and other money sources to locate the lowest interest rates available before visiting the dealerships. Compare these with the terms offered by the dealership and pick the best deal for you. If you are confused, consult your accountant. Beware of vendor-related loans, where the dealer refers you to a specific finance company; and split loans, where the dealer finances a large down payment and then sends you to a particular finance company for the balance. Many dealerships do their own financing; ask to know what their terms are. Ask about any current factory rebates that are in effect or may be coming into effect in the near future.

**Leasing vs. Buying a Car**  There are circumstances in which it is more profitable in the long run to lease a car than to buy one. Depending on your financial picture, type of business, and the uses you envision for the vehicle, leasing can be of considerable value to you, or it can be a waste of money. Generally speaking, the people who benefit most from auto leasing are self-employed people who can deduct all or part of the lease from their income tax as a business expense, and those who simply cannot live without a new car every year. Your accountant can tell you if leasing would be a good idea for you.

There are two basic types of leasing arrangements: *open-end* and *closed-end*. The main difference between the two kinds is that at the end of the closed-end arrangement, you return the car to the company you leased it from. At the end of the open-end arrangement, you ante up additional money and get to keep the car. One of the benefits of leasing is that there is no down payment required, which frees up a lot of cash, although the first month's bill is larger to cover licensing and taxes.

However, you may have to come up with a chunk of money at the end of the lease if you choose an open-end contract. Since the cost of a lease is determined by the car's rate of depreciation during the duration of the contract, it is wise to check the consumer magazines and **blue books** to determine which cars depreciate the least, and to lease your car as soon as the new models come out in the fall in order to get the highest valuation at the end of the lease.

If you do decide to lease, be sure to read the agreement carefully. Check the rules regarding maximum and minimum mileage, payment for licensing and registration, terms of ownership at the end of the lease, who pays for maintenance and repair, whether or not there are restrictions on who does the work, insurance coverage, lease renewals, etc. Service contracts are generally more expensive than having the work done on the car yourself during the terms of the lease, but if the convenience of just dropping the car off at the agency every time it needs work is of value to you, you might want to consider it. Have your lending agency or your accountant check the contract as well.

## How to Bargain with the Best of Them

When you have checked out all the cars that interest you and have carefully compared the deals at each dealership, it will be time to return to the dealership of your choice and bargain for the best deal on the car you have selected. Remember that you are about to make the most expensive purchase of your life (unless you are into large diamonds or small houses). It's an exciting game, played against well-trained and intelligent professionals, and the prize is the best possible car at the lowest possible price. You can walk away a winner if you pay close attention to all of the advice that follows, and remember that "All's fair in love, war, and buying a car!"

Don't deal for a car when you are pressed for time. Return to the agency when you have at least a couple of hours free. Tell the salesperson you dealt with before that you are now ready to buy. Pull out your list of options and the prices they gave you and tell them exactly what you want. Through all of the proceedings take your time. Don't be swayed by super salestalk. Salespeople love to make you feel that there are ten other people just waiting to get their hands on the only model you like. They may tell you that if you don't act *today*, the deal will be off. Don't believe it. To any good salesperson, closing the deal is the most important thing. If they can't do it now, they will be just as eager to sell you the car when you are ready. If the car that you liked is no longer on the lot, they will turn heaven and earth to find a similar one for you, rather than let you buy from someone else. So relax and refuse to be high-pressured into a commitment until you know it is the best deal you can get.

Assume that the first price you heard was simply their first offer. Keep asking "Can't you do better than that?" If you live in a fairly small city, you might want to visit a dealership for the same manufacturer in a larger city first. The big-city prices are usually lower, but of course it is generally more convenient to buy from a local dealer in order to have access to their management and service department if problems arise or when the car needs regular maintenance during the warranty period. However, it is always useful to be able to say "I can buy the same car for $———in the city," because this will often jog the local dealer into meeting the price. Be sharp. This is a game of wits.

A fairly common practice is for the first salesperson to call in someone else—a "closer"—to take over and close a deal that seems close to fruition. If this second person attempts to raise the price or to steer you onto another, higher-priced model, be very firm about sticking to your original choice and refusing to be conned into unnecessary expenditures.

If their "absolutely rock-bottom price" is just too high for you, hang in there if your heart is set on that car. Just sit around, have another cup of coffee, smile, talk about the weather or the local sports scene, and say, "Gee, I sure wanted that car, but it's just more than I can spend." Pretty soon the salesperson will probably go off to "consult the boss" and come back with another figure or a different deal. Occasionally they will be willing to add an option you'd considered and dropped as too costly, in order to justify the price. Salespeople can be amazingly creative in order to close a deal that is threatening to dematerialize at the last moment. They may even offer optional equipment at low cost or an additional discount off the price to save the deal. Be open-minded and willing to consider their alternatives to get the car you want at a price you can afford.

When they've come down as far as you believe they will, then, and only then, is it time to mention the possibility of a trade-in. "I guess I could trade in my old car. I was hoping to keep it to give to my kid [or kid brother] next year." Or whatever. Ask them how much your old car would be worth as a trade-in, and if they are close to the blue book price or within $200 of the going price (they have to make a profit too), have them subtract that figure from the lowest price they've quoted. If you don't feel they've offered you enough for your old car, tell them you will probably sell it yourself and will postpone buying the new car until you've done so. They are not going to want you to walk out of the agency at that point, and their trade-in offer may go up.

**Closing the Deal**  Get everything in writing. Don't accept verbal estimates or agreements. Most dealerships are honest, but there have been cases of "highballing" or "lowballing" where customers are told at point of sale that the figures they have been given are too low, or do not apply to the exact car they've selected. If this sort of thing happens, either with the salesperson or with the sales manager who has to authorize the final deal, just get up and head for the door. Make sure that the final papers list every option you asked for and contain the warranties you've been promised. Run lines through any blank spaces and initial all changes in the contract. In any business deal there is no substitute for caution and for hard, written facts. And the less chance you have for a misunderstanding when you buy the car, the better the chances of a good relationship with the dealership in the future.

Take a final look at your list of options and features to be sure that the deal includes all of them. Check the vehicle you get carefully. I'm ashamed to say that when I bought my truck, I drove it home and then discovered that it lacked an "optional" rear bumper and side mirrors! It never occurred to me that a rear bumper could be considered an optional extra, and I had simply forgotten that I wanted extra-large mirrors on each side for better visibility. When I returned to the dealership the sales manager said soothingly, "Don't worry, I'll give them to you at our cost because I want you to be a happy customer." Luckily, I had taken the precaution of calling their parts department and getting the retail prices for those items before returning to the dealership. "How can this be your cost when your own parts department is selling them for less?" I asked innocently. The manager exhibited great shock and surprise. "The prices must have changed recently," he gasped, and proceeded to call the parts department for "verification." I ended up paying about 50 percent less on those items than I would have if I had blindly accepted his "cost" prices!

Before you drive your new car away, here are some final tips that may pay off in the future:

**Be Prepared to Keep the New Car Running Smoothly**

1 Be very clear about what basic maintenance must be done to keep the warranty intact, and when that maintenance should be undertaken. Find out if they will contact you, or if you must keep track of the time and mileage and bring the car to them at the proper point.

2 Be sure you have an **owners manual**, and if it fails to provide instructions for doing the basic maintenance yourself after the warranty period, buy a **service manual** as well. I always buy the service manual so I can check what's involved in any repairs that come up. If it looks easy, I tackle them myself. If not, at least I know what's involved and can deal with my mechanic from an informed point of view. I also offer to lend the service manual to the mechanic, if the shop is an independent and doesn't have one for my car's year, make, and model.

3 Ask the service manager or the mechanic who does the **lubrication** work where the **grease points** are on the car. If there are very few, find out if there are any trouble areas that could benefit from **grease fittings**. I found out that there were several such spots on my truck and had extra fittings installed before things had a chance to begin to wear away.

4 If you are going to park your new car outside all the time, invest in a car cover to protect it. You'll find some tips on choosing a cover at the end of Chapter 17.

At this point, you know how cars work, how to do the basic maintenance necessary to keep them happy, healthy and new looking, how to drive them efficiently, and how to appraise and buy new and used cars. You not only are no longer a Dummy, you are better informed than an embarrassingly large segment of the American Public. However, sometimes things go wrong that we cannot or do not want to do ourselves. In such cases, even experts rely on professional help. So, the only thing left to include in this book is information on how to find a good mechanic or specialist, how to establish a long and happy relationship with one, and what to do if you get ripped-off anyway. I'll tell you all about it in the next chapter.

# 20

## How to Find and Deal with a Good Mechanic— and What to Do If You Get Ripped Off Anyway

**Where to Find a Good Mechanic**

You've just moved into a new town and your trusted former mechanic is too far away to be of any use to you. Or, you've bought a new car and your old mechanic doesn't work on that particular vehicle. Suddenly you're lost in the unfeeling and unfamiliar marketplace without the faintest idea of where to go for help if an emergency should arise or whom to hire when your car requires even normal servicing that is beyond your abilities. The Yellow Pages are full of ads and the streets are full of service stations, but how can you tell which shop is reliable and which is just waiting to take advantage of you? Relax, dear friend, you have come to the right place for advice...

There are several kinds of shops that repair and service automobiles. Each has its drawbacks and advantages. Look over the following list and try to judge which type seems best for you.

**Dealerships**

When you buy a new car you generally use the dealership's service facilities at least until the **warranty** period is over. This gives you the opportunity to see how well you like dealing with them. If you don't, you are free to seek service elsewhere. In some states you can have warranty work done by a licensed independent mechanic, but check to be sure this is the case if you want to leave your dealership before the warranties expire. Of course, you may want to stay, since dealerships may offer the following advantages:

1 They often provide extra service to insure goodwill so you will come back to them when it is time to buy another new car.

2 They usually have a variety of specialists right on the premises so you can have brake work, transmission work, even bodywork done by the same company.

3 They stock a wide variety of parts and **original equipment** made specifically for your vehicle.

4 If you have a complaint you will be dealing with an established company that is financially able to reimburse you and insured to cover any major lawsuits that may result.

However, there are disadvantages to consider, as well:

1 It generally costs more to have your work done at the dealership than it would at an independent shop which has a lower overhead to support.

2 Since the sales and service departments of a dealership are generally run separately, you may find that the mechanics don't really care all

that much about your goodwill and whether they'll sell you another car or not. Instead, the attitude may be, "We have more work than we can handle so if you're not happy here, you can go somewhere else."

3 Because you generally deal with a **service writer** at the dealership who then assigns your car to whichever mechanic is available when its number comes up, you will not receive the personalized service you might get from an independent. Of course, if you build a good relationship with the service writer he might honor your request for a specific mechanic or at least see that the car doesn't get handed to a new one every time.

**Large Chain Stores**

Large chain stores that have automotive service departments offer another set of pros and cons:

1 They are generally less expensive than dealerships.
2 They usually stock a wide variety of parts, many of which are made specifically to their specifications and carry their brand name. How these parts compare to the original equipment supplied by the car manufacturer to the dealership will vary in price and quality, depending on which chain you are dealing with. The only time you absolutely don't want to use anything but original equipment is when you are restoring a **classic car**.
3 Chain stores usually provide good guarantees on parts and labor. And if there is a complaint, they are generally motivated toward keeping your goodwill.
4 National chain stores maintain branches all over the country which will honor their warranties and guarantees. This can be very beneficial if you travel a lot.
5 Large chains also use service writers and the work may tend to be impersonal, with a new mechanic working on your car each time.

And, speaking of new mechanics, large chains are good training grounds for inexperienced mechanics who are just out of school and working on their first professional jobs. Your car may turn out to be a guinea pig as well as a gas hog if it falls into incompetent hands, or it may be lucky enough to be tended to by bright, enthusiastic young mechanics with all the latest techniques still fresh in their minds.

**Specialists**

If you know that the trouble with your car resides in a specific area, such as a leaking radiator, holes in the muffler, or transmission problems, you may want to look for a well-established specialist who focuses on a single automotive system.

SCLAR
**000-421**

A reliable specialist can provide the experience, specialized tools, and extensive inventory that may be unavailable at a shop that handles everything in general and nothing in particular.

Check out brand-name specialists in consumer publications to be sure that the one near you has a good reputation for durable parts and quality service. Some chains that sell and install cheapo parts seem to me to be more interested in selling new parts than in repairing old ones. I've always felt that they would rather give you a "lifetime guarantee"— which will keep you coming back to pay for the labor to install those "free" replacements—than provide high-quality service and top-quality parts.

**Independents**

An independent mechanic or shop can offer the best—or the worst—of all the alternatives.

Honest, reliable, and experienced independent mechanics can provide personal service based on personal standards of excellence. They can offer you the opportunity to communicate directly with a professional who knows you, knows your car, and cares a great deal about maintaining a good reputation, since most independent business comes from referrals.

Many independent shops offer lower prices than those charged by dealerships. Others, especially those which service only expensive luxury cars or sports cars, may offer the finest workmanship at relatively exorbitant rates. A cherished few provide fine workmanship at low prices— these mechanics are probably saints disguised in greasy coveralls!

Expertise, the availability of specialized tools, and the variety of special parts on hand may vary from one independent to another, so it is especially important to check carefully to be sure you are getting a good one. A good independent will know where to find the proper talent, borrow the tools, and buy the parts at a good price if the shop lacks any of these for a specific job. An unreliable one will patch things together and hope for the best.

**How to Find a Reliable Mechanic**

There are several organizations that test, rate, and certify good mechanics. If you are unsure about a particular shop, you can feel pretty secure if you see a sign or a mechanic's patch which shows that the shop or the individual has achieved recognition from one of the following sources:

The AAA has a rating program for auto-repair shops in several parts of the country. They visit and evaluate them, just as they do hotels and campgrounds. These shops must meet the AAA's high standards for service, attitude, efficiency, and speed. They must provide customers with written estimates of all costs and offer a minimum warranty on parts and labor of 90 days or 4,000 miles. Any history of customer complaints about the shop to the local AAA office is also taken into account in the evaluation. Since this program operates at no cost to the accredited shops, there is no way that a shop can "buy" AAA approval. The AAA does not impose price limitations on approved shops, either. They cover the full spectrum from low-cost to high-priced repair shops.

The AAA is willing to arbitrate disputes between AAA members and approved shops with two exceptions. It will not go to bat for you just because you found that you could have gotten the work done more cheaply somewhere else, and it will not decide whether a specific job is covered by a manufacturer's warranty. However, if you are an AAA member with a complaint about the service you received, you can fill out a form at a local AAA office and get proceedings under way.

You can look for the AAA logo on display at a shop, contact your local or regional AAA office to find out if there is a Garage Approval Program in your area, or write to the National Headquarters of the American Automobile Association at the following address for a list of AAA Approved Repair Facilities:

Automotive Engineering and Road Division
American Automobile Association
8111 Gatehouse Road
Falls Church, VA 22047

The Canadian Automobile Association has a similar program and a reciprocal agreement with AAA-affiliated clubs in the United States.

**AAA-Approved Repair Facilities**

The National Institute for Automotive Service Excellence (ASE) certifies mechanics by giving tests twice a year in a variety of automobile-repair specialties. You can look for the blue and white ASE patch on your mechanic's uniform (ASE certifies the individual mechanic, not the shop) or obtain a list of certified mechanics in your home state by writing to:

ASE
1920 Association Drive
Reston, VA 22091

**ASE-Certified Mechanics**

**ADS-Authorized Diesel Mechanics** Owners of diesel cars that are out of warranty who are looking for a reliable diesel mechanic can look in their local Yellow Pages under "Automobiles, Repair" for a shop which displays the logo of the Association of Diesel Specialists (ADS). The ADS-authorized shops must send their mechanics to factory schools to keep abreast of new parts, techniques, and systems; they must meet high standards for cleanliness and stock sufficient tools and parts to deal efficiently with most diesel repair and maintenance jobs.

**IGO—Independent Garage Owners Association** An IGO shield or sign indicates that the owner of the garage is a member of this association. Although the IGO has nothing to do with the qualifications of the individual mechanics, it does have a code of ethics that members are pledged to live up to if they want to stay in the organization.

**Better Business Bureau** You can also check with your local Better Business Bureau to see if a shop has been the subject of numerous consumer complaints.

**Referrals** I've always felt that the best way to find a good mechanic is the same way you find a doctor, a lawyer, or a plumber—through referrals. Ask people who drive the same make car as you do where they get their car repaired and then check out the shops that are the most conveniently located. As a fringe benefit, you'll also learn which shops to avoid, since most of the people you ask will have horror stories to tell you, too.

**How to Evaluate a Mechanic for Yourself** A quick way to do a preliminary check is to call a shop and ask for their basic prices on easy jobs like tuning the make and model car you drive, flushing the cooling system, changing the oil and the oil filter, and lubricating the car. It is also a good idea to ask what their hourly rate for labor is, and whether they stock parts for your car. A telephone interview can give you a good idea of whether or not the shop's prices are competitive, and will also give you a sample of its "vibes." If they are surly and uncommunicative over the phone, chances are you are going to run into trouble when you have to deal with them in an emergency. I'd follow up a positive phone interview with a drive-in appearance to check on the following things:

1 *Is the place clean and well organized or filthy and cluttered?* This is a good indication of general attitude. Automotive mechanics is a trade which calls for patience and precision. If the shop is sloppy and disorganized, chances are the work may be, too.

2 *Do they have modern electronic diagnostic and testing equipment?* These machines save time by pinpointing trouble areas and checking adjustments and tolerances. And saving time means saving money when it comes to paying those labor charges. Of course, this equipment is only as good as the person using it. You might ask if anyone at the shop attends factory schools and seminars run by manufacturers to learn how to use the more sophisticated analyzers and keep up to date on new systems.

3 *Does the shop have a good up-to-date service manual for your vehicle?* I usually buy one for my car's year, make, and model and offer to lend it to the mechanic. After all, they can't stock one for every car in the world.

4 *Does the shop have the necessary tools to do your job?* Ask if any part of the job will have to be sent out to a specialist.

As I've said before, a big repair job is like major surgery. Not only do you want to have the best possible surgeon, but you also want to be sure the surgery is necessary and that it will be done under the best possible terms. Therefore, whenever you bring your car in for maintenance or repair, it is wise to follow these guidelines:

**Getting the Best Possible Deal**

1 If you are dealing with a new mechanic or are faced with major repairs, it is wise to *get at least a second opinion and an estimate of costs* from another repair shop. If there's a big discrepancy, additional estimates and opinions are in order. If one shop is much lower in price than the others, this is not necessarily the best place to go. Be sure that the work will be of the same quality before you go for the cheapest job.

2 *Ask for a written estimate.* Many states require one anyway and require the shop to call you if they find that it will cost more than originally estimated. Beware of general statements; try to get as detailed an estimate of what is involved as is possible.

3 *Ask that all the parts they replace be returned to you,* whether the laws in your state require that they do so or not. That way you can be sure that you got what you paid for.

4 *Ask for credit for the **core charge*** on any *rebuildable* part that is going to be replaced with a new part. If you are buying a rebuilt part as a replacement, the core charge should be deducted from the price of the part you buy in exchange for trading in your old part, which will then be rebuilt and sold to someone else.

ALL PARTS INSTALLED ARE NEW UNLESS SPECIFIED OTHERWISE

**JENNINGS UNION 76**
5755 Hollister Ave. — Phone (805) 967-5416
Goleta, California 93117

No 827

# REPAIR ORDER ②

LABOR CHARGE

| QTY. | PART NO. OR DESCRIPTION ③ | SALE AMOUNT |
|------|---------------------------|-------------|
| | | |
| | | |
| | | |
| | | |
| | | |
| | | |
| | | |
| | | |
| | | |
| | | |
| | | |
| | | |
| | TOTAL PARTS | |
| | CUSTOMER INITIAL OUTSIDE-SUBLET REPAIRS ④ | |
| | | |
| | | |
| | | |
| | TOTAL SUBLET REPAIRS | |
| | FOLLOWING REPAIRS RECOMMENDED | |

| MAINTENANCE INSPECTION ☐ |
| LUBRICATION ☐ |
| CHANGE OIL GRADE ☐ |
| CHANGE OIL FILTER CART. ☐ |
| TRANS. ☐ |
| DIFF. ☐ |
| ROTATE TIRES ☐ |
| ALIGN FRONT END ☐ |
| ☐ |

NAME _____ DATE _____

ADDRESS _____ CITY _____

PHONE _____ YEAR _____ MAKE _____ TYPE OR MODEL _____ ⑦ YES NO

MILEAGE _____ LICENSE NO _____ SERIAL NO _____ MOTOR NO _____

TIME REC'D A.M. P.M. TIME PROM. A.M. P.M. TERMS ORD WRITTEN BY CUST. ORDER NO

OPER. NO. REPAIR ORDER - DESCRIPTION OF WORK ①

⑤

ORIGINAL ESTIMATE $ ⑥ DATE _____ TIME _____ BY _____
REVISED ESTIMATE $ _____ DATE _____ TIME _____ BY _____

I acknowledge notice and oral approval of an increase in the original estimated price.

**Replaced parts requested by customer** YES ☐ NO ☐

TOTAL LABOR
TOTAL PARTS
GAS. OIL. GREASE
SUBLET REPAIRS
TAX

**PAY THIS AMOUNT**

I hereby authorize the above repair work to be done along with necessary materials. You and your employees may operate above vehicle for purposes of testing, inspection or delivery at my risk. An express mechanic's lien is acknowledged on above vehicle to secure the amount of repairs thereto. You will not be held responsible for loss or damage to vehicle or articles left in vehicle in case of fire, theft, accident or any other cause beyond your control. I have read and understand the above and acknowledge receipt of an estimate.

X ⑧ _____

SCLAR
000-426

Be sure that the invoice for the job includes a written guarantee on parts and labor, and find out if any of the parts they have installed come with their own warranties. This is especially important if it is a big job that involves expensive parts. It always pays to know just where the responsibility lies, in the event of a dispute or a malfunctioning part. There are separate areas on the standard invoice shown on page 426 for:

**Checking the Invoice**

1 *Itemizing the work:* This should list each job that needed to be done. Be sure to check this item-by-item to see that everything was taken care of.

2 *Labor charges:* These are given in terms of fractions of an hour. If a job seems to have taken an excessively long time, ask to check the **flat rate manual**, which is a listing of every job that can be done on a car, with the amount of time it should take to accomplish it. Most shops will charge you for the amount of time listed in the manual, no matter how little time it actually took them to do it, and few shops will keep a mechanic who can't "beat the book" by a substantial amount of time. If the hours seem right, multiply them by the shop's hourly rate to make sure they've done the math right. Then check to be sure the "labor" total is the same as that shown in the "totals" column below.

3 *Parts used:* Each part should be listed, with its price. Make sure they have added correctly and that the "parts" total is the same as that shown in the "totals" column of the invoice.

4 *Subcontracted repairs:* This should show all the work that was sent out of the shop to be done by a specialist. The total costs should be repeated in the "totals" column.

5 *The "totals" column:* All charges are listed here. You pay the final figure.

Every invoice should also have a space for (6) *a written estimate* and for (7) *a number where you can be reached* if necessary. You will be asked to (8) *sign the estimate*. Be sure to read the small print above the signature before you sign. It should only cover your approval of the estimate, and the fact that you are willing to allow them to drive the car in order to diagnose, repair, and test it.

The reverse side of the invoice often contains information on the shop's warranty and on the **mechanic's lien**, which allows mechanics in some states to sell your car if you refuse to pay for services. For this reason, it is important that you pay your bill, and then seek restitution if a dispute occurs. I'll get into complaint procedures later in this chapter.

It is not enough to find a mechanic who is reliable, honest, intelligent, efficient, and relatively inexpensive. If you have been lucky enough to discover such an automotive guru, the ball is now in your court when it comes to establishing a good and lasting relationship. Even though most

**How to Make Your Mechanic Happy to Serve You**

small businesses are struggling to stay alive these days, a good mechanic is an exception. Every outstanding one that I've ever encountered has had more business than time to deal with it. When I moved to a new city and needed someone whom I could trust to do major work or emergency surgery on Honeybun, my precious little classic car, I literally had to beg the man who came most highly recommended to take me on as a customer. He hadn't accepted a new customer in over five years, and it took a referral from an outstanding car restorer, plus my credentials as an automotive writer and car freak, plus the fact that I had restored Honeybun myself, plus all my charm and my assurances that I would never bother him with mickeymouse maintenance, to get him to agree to be there for me if something came up that I could not handle myself. We have since become very good friends, in no small part because I faithfully follow these guidelines:

1 *Call for an appointment.* **Don't just show up and expect them to drop everything and take care of you.**

2 *Get your car into the shop early* (at least by 8:30 or 9:00 a.m.) if you hope to get it out the same day. If you are on your way to work, allow sufficient time to give the mechanic or service writer a full account of what you want done, or what you have found to be wrong with the car. Sometimes a test drive helps to demonstrate the problem, so be sure you have the time to go on one, if they seem favorably inclined to the idea.

3 *Bring along a written list* of the things you want serviced or repaired. *Include a phone number* where you can be reached if questions occur, or if the work is going to cost more than was originally estimated.

4 *Be as specific as possible about the symptoms* you've experienced. For instance, it helps to know:

    a *What is happening* (e.g., the car stalls, it pulls to the right, it runs roughly, it seems to be losing power, it is overheating).

    b *When it happens* (e.g., the car hesitates when I accelerate, it won't start when it rains, it smokes when I change gears, it pulls to the left when I brake).

    c *Where on the car the trouble seems to be located* (e.g., I smell the gas more powerfully when I sit in the rear seat, there's a vibration under the front seat, there's a squeak under the right front fender).

You can find a whole list of symptoms on pages 339–345, just to give you an idea of what kinds of things to look for.

If you can provide information such as this to help them diagnose the trouble more easily, you can avoid paying a mechanic to drive your car around just to find out that it is only a matter of turning a screw on the carburetor! However, note this distinction carefully:

Provide the clearest information you can regarding all of the symptoms, but DO NOT DIAGNOSE THE PROBLEM YOURSELF! If you tell a mechanic that your car needs a specific job done on it, then that is the work that will be done, and you will pay for it, whether you needed it or not. If you want to inquire whether it is possible that the trouble is being caused by a malfunction in a specific part, then do so, but keep it in the form of a question. The final diagnosis must be up to the repair shop, so they can be responsible if the diagnosis turns out to be wrong.

5 *Keep a maintenance record* on your car and bring a photocopy of it for their records, if they haven't done the past maintenance themselves. You will find a blank Maintenance Record and a Specification Record that you can use on pages 436–439.

6 *Don't press to get the job done fast,* unless you're really in a bind. It takes time to make a diagnosis, get the proper parts, do the work, and test the results properly. Nobody likes to work under pressure. A great way to get the pressure off everybody is to see whether the shop has a spare car, or "loaner," that you can borrow while the work is being done on yours.

7 *Call to be sure the car is ready* before you come to pick it up. If it isn't, try to be understanding, unless the shop is chronically slow about getting work done. If it's a matter of parts that must be ordered, there is very little that they can do about it. If it is just that they are overbooked with work, then be polite but firm about your need to get the car back as soon as possible.

8 When the car is ready, be prepared to *spend a little time test-driving* it to be sure the job's been done to your satisfaction. It is better to return immediately with your complaints than to show up several days later, when any number of things might have happened to mess things up.

9 *Show your appreciation* for a job well done. A phone call to the manager, praising a mechanic's work—or a letter they can display—means a lot to a service facility. If you notice that your mechanic likes a particular brand of beer, bring along a six-pack in a paper sack when you come to pick the car up at the end of a busy day. If you're lucky, you might get invited to share it. I've received some of my most valuable tutoring strolling around a garage after working hours, brew in hand, while my mechanic expounded on the secrets of his art.

Even if you've followed all of my advice on how to find good mechanics and stay on the best of terms with them, there is still a chance that you may get into a dispute over the services they've performed. If you've maintained a good relationship with a shop, you will usually find them willing to be cooperative about redoing work that fails to correct a problem, replacing defective parts they've installed, and the like. If you ap-

**Complaint Procedures**
**How to Get Some Satisfaction**

proach them with an attitude that assumes that they are going to treat you fairly and honestly, chances are they will. If you attack immediately on the assumption that they are out to get you, you will put them on the defensive and make things much harder for yourself. I have found that it pays immensely to maintain a friendly attitude in all disputes, while refusing to be swayed from my purpose. I learned the following technique from an excellent human-potential trainer, and I pass it on to you:

1 *Approach the proper person in a friendly way* that assumes they will do everything they can to settle the issue fairly. (We'll get to who that person is in a moment.)

2 *State the problem and what you'd like them to do* about it clearly, and be prepared to back it up with as much documentation as possible, if that should prove necessary. This is why it is so important to keep maintenance records, invoices, guarantees, and warranties.

3 *Listen patiently to the person's responses.* If they give you a hard-luck story to explain their negligence or inability to give you satisfaction, be sympathetic. Show that you care about their problems; it will encourage them to care about yours.

4 In a friendly fashion, *keep reiterating your problem and what you want them to do* to rectify the situation. Say things like, "Yes, I understand the difficulty—and I must have this corrected," or, "Gee, that's really a problem, I know how hard it is to deal with something like that—and what can you do to correct this situation?"

5 If the person says that he or she cannot give you what you want, *ask who has the authority* to do so, and go and repeat the process with them and keep repeating it until you get satisfaction. There is a whole hierarchy of people who can help you if you are willing to make an effort in your own behalf.

This combination of *friendliness, sympathy,* and *inflexibility* really pays off. I have seen people go out of their way to help me once they realized that I expected them to be the kind of loving and creative people who could remedy the situation and that I cared about the difficulties they might have in doing so. I know we've all been programmed to believe that "squeaky axles get the most grease" and that people will take advantage of you unless you take a hard line with them, but to my amazement, this technique has shown me that most people who handle complaints have been trained to deal with hostility, suspicion, and anger, but very few have any defenses against friendliness, trust, and compassion. So try it. What can you lose? You can always bring the big guns out as a last resort!

It is always good policy to take a complaint first to the person you dealt with and then to work your way up to people at higher levels of power. "Going over someone's head" rarely pays off unless that person has proven to be unsympathetic or unable to help you. Once you get out of the structure of the shop itself, however, it pays to get to as high a person as you can, on the theory that even if they send your complaint back down the ladder, it will have come from their office, and their "underlings" must deal with the chance that they will follow up to see how well your complaint has been dealt with. Here's a list of the steps to climb if you are working your way up the complaint ladder:

**Climbing the Complaint Ladder**

1 *The mechanic* you dealt with.

2 *The manager* of the shop, or the service manager if it is a dealership or a large chain.

3 *The owner* of the shop or dealership.

4 If you've had no satisfaction from a dealership, then go to *the factory representative* at the car manufacturer's nearest regional office. Write to them and tell them what happened and what you want in order to resolve the issue. Be sure to include the following information:

   a The name and address of the dealership.

   b Whom you dealt with at the dealership.

   c The make, year, and model of your vehicle and its ID number. You can find it on your registration, or up near the windshield where it can be seen from outside the vehicle.

   d Copies of any documentation you think is required, such as invoices, warranties, previous correspondence, etc.

5 *The president* of the corporation that built the car. Some people suggest going to the corporate public relations department first, but since I've found that both the president and the PR department often send the matter back to the regional office for action, I'd rather have the president's initials on the letter when it shows up at regional headquarters again.

   I've even gone directly to the president and bypassed the regional office in the past, but since the president usually gives the regional office a chance to handle it, you might save time by referring the matter directly to them and then going to the president if they fail to satisfy your complaints.

6 If you still "can't get no satisfaction" or if you have problems with an independent shop that has refused to settle the matter properly, then write to your local *Better Business Bureau* and to your state's *Consumer Protection Agency*. They may suggest taking the matter to a mediation service or they may apply some pressure of their own. Some states have special bureaus dedicated solely to handling auto-repair disputes.

7 If the shop has AAA, ASE, IGO, or ADS accreditation, write to those *organizations* with the full specifics of your complaint.

8 If your problem is with a dealership, write to:

AUTOCAP
National Automobile Dealers Association
8400 West Park Drive
McLean, VA 22101

to see if your state has this service. These people have no clout with independents, however.

9 You can also take either an independent or a dealership to *Small Claims Court.* In many states new laws have raised the maximum of small claims settlements to levels which will cover all but the most expensive auto-repair disputes. The fees involved are generally negligible, and you don't need a lawyer. From my experience, small claims procedures are usually swift and fair and aimed at allowing "the little guy" to bring a case of litigation without the need for legal or technical expertise, or for great amounts of time and money. If all else fails, don't hesitate to avail yourself of this alternative. Many independent mechanics would much prefer to settle a dispute than to lose valuable time in court and have the fact that they have been sued by dissatisfied customers known to the general public and to the Better Business Bureau.

10 If you're really riled, you can complain to:

Federal Trade Commission
Bureau of Consumer Protection
Pennsylvania Ave. at 6th St. N.W.
Washington, DC 20580
(they also have regional offices)

11 To register complaints about defects and obtain data on recalls, fuel, tires, child seats, seat belts, and other safety-related issues, call:

Auto Safety Hotline
1-800-424-9393

12 Another excellent guide to obtaining satisfaction is:

*The Consumer's Resource Handbook*
Dept. 579L
Pueblo, CO 81009

A word of caution: No matter which line of recourse you decide to follow, it is always a good policy to pay the disputed bill first if your state still honors the "mechanic's lien" mentioned earlier in this chapter. Check it out, and if they do, it is better to pay the bill than to have your car towed away and sold to pay a bill for a fraction of its value. So pay up first, and then go get 'em!

Well, folks, that about wraps it up. I've given you everything I think you should know about understanding, buying, maintaining, restoring, driving, and loving a car. If this book has turned you on, then by all means extend your knowledge in the days to come by reading more and more sophisticated literature on your favorite automotive topics. There are excellent books that deal with specific systems, cars, and repairs, written for the amateur mechanic. But there is no substitute for "hands-on experience," so remember, whether you want to keep a good car in good condition without paying dearly to have someone else do the maintenance, or you simply want to keep your old heap running just a little longer without spending a lot of money on it, and whether you want the satisfaction of "doing it yourself," or are convinced that a well-tuned, well-maintained car will consume less fuel and contribute less air pollution, you won't be able to realize any of these goals unless you stop procrastinating and start *working*. Don't finish these pages and say, "Yes, I must try some of these things someday." You'll never find the time or the opportunity that way, and this book will just join all the others on the shelf. So *make a commitment* right now! Whether you run your car through these checks, or go out and buy a set of socket wrenches, or just change your air filter, DO IT NOW. Once you've made any kind of an effort to get intimately involved with your car, you will find you'll want to carry the relationship further.

If your car hasn't had a tune-up lately, pick a day when you know you'll have a couple of free hours, and plan to change your spark plugs and install new points and a condenser in your distributor (assuming, of course, that you don't have an electronic ignition). Before the big day comes, buy the spark plugs and the distributor kit and round up the tools you'll need—even if you have to borrow them. Or, plan to change your oil (anybody can do that!) and buy the oil and oil filter *now*. Once you've spent a couple of dollars, you will make the time to get the job done. Don't put things off by planning to do *everything* in this book when your next vacation rolls around. Most of these things can be done in from fifteen minutes to three hours. Then you can spend your vacation driving your happy, peppy car to all those lovely places you've been meaning to visit.

And the best part of all will be that both you and your car will have the satisfaction of knowing that, when it comes to auto repair, you're not a dummy anymore!

On the following pages you will find a Specifications Record and a Maintenance Record. If you make photocopies of them before you fill them in, you'll have them for several cars and be able to take them to the store with you when you go to buy parts.

# Specifications Record

| Item | Car #1 | Car #2 | Car #3 |
|------|--------|--------|--------|
| Manufacturer | | | |
| Make | | | |
| Model | | | |
| Year | | | |
| Number of Cylinders | | | |
| Auto. or Standard Transmission | | | |
| Type of Transmission Fluid or Grease | | | |
| Type of Power Steering Fluid | | | |
| Engine Displacement | | | |
| Type of Carburetor or Fuel Injection | | | |
| Air Conditioned? | | | |
| Smog Devices? | | | |
| Horsepower | | | |
| Electronic Ignition? | | | |
| Dwell | | | |
| Contact Point Gap | | | |
| Distributor Kit Number | | | |
| Spark Plug Gap | | | |
| Spark Plug Number | | | |
| Cylinder Firing Order | | | |
| Ignition Timing | | | |
| Oil Weight | | | |
| Oil Capacity | | | |
| Oil Filter Number | | | |
| Coolant Capacity (½ total cooling system capacity) | | | |
| Air Filter Number | | | |
| Fuel Filter Number | | | |
| Tire Size | | | |
| Min. & Max. Tire Pressure | | | |
| Disc or Drum Brakes | | | |

# Maintenance Record

**CAR:**_____  **FROM:**_____  **TO:**_____

| | J | F | M | A | M | J | J | A | S | O | N | D |
|---|---|---|---|---|---|---|---|---|---|---|---|---|
| **I. Under-the-Hood Checklist** (once a month or every 1,000 miles) | | | | | | | | | | | | |
| Checked Coolant Level | ☐ | ☐ | ☐ | ☐ | ☐ | ☐ | ☐ | ☐ | ☐ | ☐ | ☐ | ☐ |
| Flushed System and Changed Coolant (once a year) | ☐ | ☐ | ☐ | ☐ | ☐ | ☐ | ☐ | ☐ | ☐ | ☐ | ☐ | ☐ |
| Checked Fan Belt | ☐ | ☐ | ☐ | ☐ | ☐ | ☐ | ☐ | ☐ | ☐ | ☐ | ☐ | ☐ |
| Changed Fan Belt (if frayed) | ☐ | ☐ | ☐ | ☐ | ☐ | ☐ | ☐ | ☐ | ☐ | ☐ | ☐ | ☐ |
| Checked Battery | ☐ | ☐ | ☐ | ☐ | ☐ | ☐ | ☐ | ☐ | ☐ | ☐ | ☐ | ☐ |
| Replaced Battery (as needed) | ☐ | ☐ | ☐ | ☐ | ☐ | ☐ | ☐ | ☐ | ☐ | ☐ | ☐ | ☐ |
| Checked Oil Level | ☐ | ☐ | ☐ | ☐ | ☐ | ☐ | ☐ | ☐ | ☐ | ☐ | ☐ | ☐ |
| Changed Oil (every 3 to 6 months or 3,000 miles) | ☐ | ☐ | ☐ | ☐ | ☐ | ☐ | ☐ | ☐ | ☐ | ☐ | ☐ | ☐ |
| Replaced Oil Filter (every oil change) | ☐ | ☐ | ☐ | ☐ | ☐ | ☐ | ☐ | ☐ | ☐ | ☐ | ☐ | ☐ |
| Checked Automatic Transmission Fluid Level | ☐ | ☐ | ☐ | ☐ | ☐ | ☐ | ☐ | ☐ | ☐ | ☐ | ☐ | ☐ |
| Last Added Automatic Transmission Fluid | ☐ | ☐ | ☐ | ☐ | ☐ | ☐ | ☐ | ☐ | ☐ | ☐ | ☐ | ☐ |
| Checked Brake Fluid Level | ☐ | ☐ | ☐ | ☐ | ☐ | ☐ | ☐ | ☐ | ☐ | ☐ | ☐ | ☐ |
| Last Added Brake Fluid | ☐ | ☐ | ☐ | ☐ | ☐ | ☐ | ☐ | ☐ | ☐ | ☐ | ☐ | ☐ |
| Checked Power Steering Fluid Level | ☐ | ☐ | ☐ | ☐ | ☐ | ☐ | ☐ | ☐ | ☐ | ☐ | ☐ | ☐ |
| Last Added Fluid | ☐ | ☐ | ☐ | ☐ | ☐ | ☐ | ☐ | ☐ | ☐ | ☐ | ☐ | ☐ |
| Checked Windshield Washer Fluid Level | ☐ | ☐ | ☐ | ☐ | ☐ | ☐ | ☐ | ☐ | ☐ | ☐ | ☐ | ☐ |
| Checked Windshield Wiper Blades | ☐ | ☐ | ☐ | ☐ | ☐ | ☐ | ☐ | ☐ | ☐ | ☐ | ☐ | ☐ |
| Replaced Windshield Wiper Blades | ☐ | ☐ | ☐ | ☐ | ☐ | ☐ | ☐ | ☐ | ☐ | ☐ | ☐ | ☐ |
| Checked Tire Pressure (don't forget the spare!) | ☐ | ☐ | ☐ | ☐ | ☐ | ☐ | ☐ | ☐ | ☐ | ☐ | ☐ | ☐ |
| Replaced Tires (record details below) | ☐ | ☐ | ☐ | ☐ | ☐ | ☐ | ☐ | ☐ | ☐ | ☐ | ☐ | ☐ |
| Checked Wiring | ☐ | ☐ | ☐ | ☐ | ☐ | ☐ | ☐ | ☐ | ☐ | ☐ | ☐ | ☐ |
| Replaced Wires (record details below) | ☐ | ☐ | ☐ | ☐ | ☐ | ☐ | ☐ | ☐ | ☐ | ☐ | ☐ | ☐ |
| Checked Hoses | ☐ | ☐ | ☐ | ☐ | ☐ | ☐ | ☐ | ☐ | ☐ | ☐ | ☐ | ☐ |
| Replaced Hoses (record details below) | ☐ | ☐ | ☐ | ☐ | ☐ | ☐ | ☐ | ☐ | ☐ | ☐ | ☐ | ☐ |

(continued)

CAR 000-437

# Maintenance Record

|  | J | F | M | A | M | J | J | A | S | O | N | D |
|---|---|---|---|---|---|---|---|---|---|---|---|---|

## II. Tune-Up Time Checklist
(non-electronic ignitions: every 12,000 miles or 1 year—more
    often if necessary)
(electronic ignitions: every 18,000 miles or 2 years)

| | J | F | M | A | M | J | J | A | S | O | N | D |
|---|---|---|---|---|---|---|---|---|---|---|---|---|
| Checked Air Filter | ☐ | ☐ | ☐ | ☐ | ☐ | ☐ | ☐ | ☐ | ☐ | ☐ | ☐ | ☐ |
| Replaced Air Filter (once a year or every 20,000 miles) | ☐ | ☐ | ☐ | ☐ | ☐ | ☐ | ☐ | ☐ | ☐ | ☐ | ☐ | ☐ |
| Checked Fuel Filter | ☐ | ☐ | ☐ | ☐ | ☐ | ☐ | ☐ | ☐ | ☐ | ☐ | ☐ | ☐ |
| Replaced Fuel Filter (every tune-up or as manufacturer recommends) | ☐ | ☐ | ☐ | ☐ | ☐ | ☐ | ☐ | ☐ | ☐ | ☐ | ☐ | ☐ |
| Checked PCV Valve | ☐ | ☐ | ☐ | ☐ | ☐ | ☐ | ☐ | ☐ | ☐ | ☐ | ☐ | ☐ |
| Cleaned or Replaced PCV Valve (every 12,000 miles) | ☐ | ☐ | ☐ | ☐ | ☐ | ☐ | ☐ | ☐ | ☐ | ☐ | ☐ | ☐ |
| Checked Spark Plugs (cleaned and regapped them) | ☐ | ☐ | ☐ | ☐ | ☐ | ☐ | ☐ | ☐ | ☐ | ☐ | ☐ | ☐ |
| Changed Spark Plugs (every tune-up—more often if burnt or worn) | ☐ | ☐ | ☐ | ☐ | ☐ | ☐ | ☐ | ☐ | ☐ | ☐ | ☐ | ☐ |
| Checked Points, Dwell, & Point Gap | ☐ | ☐ | ☐ | ☐ | ☐ | ☐ | ☐ | ☐ | ☐ | ☐ | ☐ | ☐ |
| Changed Points, Condenser, & Rotor (every tune-up—more often if burnt or worn) | ☐ | ☐ | ☐ | ☐ | ☐ | ☐ | ☐ | ☐ | ☐ | ☐ | ☐ | ☐ |
| Checked Timing | ☐ | ☐ | ☐ | ☐ | ☐ | ☐ | ☐ | ☐ | ☐ | ☐ | ☐ | ☐ |
| Adjusted Carburetor | ☐ | ☐ | ☐ | ☐ | ☐ | ☐ | ☐ | ☐ | ☐ | ☐ | ☐ | ☐ |
| Cleaned or Rebuilt Carburetor (when needed) | ☐ | ☐ | ☐ | ☐ | ☐ | ☐ | ☐ | ☐ | ☐ | ☐ | ☐ | ☐ |

## III. Lubrication & Brake Checklist

| | J | F | M | A | M | J | J | A | S | O | N | D |
|---|---|---|---|---|---|---|---|---|---|---|---|---|
| Checked Grease Fittings (every 3,000 miles) | ☐ | ☐ | ☐ | ☐ | ☐ | ☐ | ☐ | ☐ | ☐ | ☐ | ☐ | ☐ |
| Lubricated Steering & Suspension (every 3,000 miles or as needed) | ☐ | ☐ | ☐ | ☐ | ☐ | ☐ | ☐ | ☐ | ☐ | ☐ | ☐ | ☐ |
| Had Complete Professional Lube Job (once a year or as needed) | ☐ | ☐ | ☐ | ☐ | ☐ | ☐ | ☐ | ☐ | ☐ | ☐ | ☐ | ☐ |
| Checked Brakes (every 10,000 miles) | ☐ | ☐ | ☐ | ☐ | ☐ | ☐ | ☐ | ☐ | ☐ | ☐ | ☐ | ☐ |
| Had Brakes Rebuilt (record details below) | ☐ | ☐ | ☐ | ☐ | ☐ | ☐ | ☐ | ☐ | ☐ | ☐ | ☐ | ☐ |

|  | J | F | M | A | M | J | J | A | S | O | N | D |
|---|---|---|---|---|---|---|---|---|---|---|---|---|
| Checked Wheel Bearings (every 10,000 miles) | ☐ | ☐ | ☐ | ☐ | ☐ | ☐ | ☐ | ☐ | ☐ | ☐ | ☐ | ☐ |
| Repacked Wheel Bearings (every 20,000 miles or as needed) | ☐ | ☐ | ☐ | ☐ | ☐ | ☐ | ☐ | ☐ | ☐ | ☐ | ☐ | ☐ |
| Checked Shock Absorbers | ☐ | ☐ | ☐ | ☐ | ☐ | ☐ | ☐ | ☐ | ☐ | ☐ | ☐ | ☐ |
| Replaced Shock Absorbers (as needed) | ☐ | ☐ | ☐ | ☐ | ☐ | ☐ | ☐ | ☐ | ☐ | ☐ | ☐ | ☐ |
| Had Front-End Alignment (as needed) | ☐ | ☐ | ☐ | ☐ | ☐ | ☐ | ☐ | ☐ | ☐ | ☐ | ☐ | ☐ |
| Had Automatic Transmission Serviced (every 20–25,000 miles) | ☐ | ☐ | ☐ | ☐ | ☐ | ☐ | ☐ | ☐ | ☐ | ☐ | ☐ | ☐ |

## IV. Parts Replacement Record

Part | Date and Details

Wiring
(coil wire, ignition wires, spark plug boots, etc.)

_____

_____

_____

Hoses
(top or bottom radiator hose, vacuum hoses, fuel lines, etc.)

_____

_____

_____

Brakes
(shoes, relined, drums turned, etc.)

_____

_____

_____

Tires
(which one? where did new tire go?) (mileage on odometer at tire change)

_____

_____

_____

Other Parts

_____

_____

_____

SCLAD
000-439

# A Practical Glossary of Automotive Terms

*[Words appearing in italics are defined elsewhere in the Glossary.]*

**accelerator**   the gas pedal.

**accelerator pump**   the part of the *carburetor* which provides an extra squirt of fuel to enrich the *fuel/air mixture* and thus enables the car to respond swiftly to increased acceleration when you depress the gas pedal suddenly.

**additives**   substances that are added to such products as *coolant* and engine *oil* to enable them to perform better, last longer, and provide secondary benefits. Popular additives are rust preventers (in coolant and oil), *viscosity* extenders (in oil), lubricants (in coolant), and preservatives (in foods).

**air cleaner**   a metal can located atop the *carburetor* which contains an *air filter,* which removes dust and dirt from the air before it enters the carburetor. Also acts as a flame arrester in case of backfire.

**air filter**   the element in the *air cleaner* that removes impurities from the air. Some air filters are disposable; others can be cleaned and reused.

**air horn**   the tubular passage through which air travels to the *air cleaner* and the *carburetor.* See *venturi.*

**air-cooled engine**   an engine that uses air instead of water in its *cooling system.* Most Volkswagens have air-cooled engines.

**alignment**   the procedure for adjusting the position of the front wheels to improve handling and performance and to reduce *tire* wear. See *camber, caster, toe-in, toe-out, steering-axis inclination* and *turning radius.*

**allen wrench**   an L-shaped rod designed to remove certain screws and fastenings with hexagonal holes in their heads. These wrenches come in sets of assorted sizes and are sometimes called "hex wrenches."

**alternator**   generates electric current that is stored in the *battery* and is used to start the car and run the electrical equipment. Alternators generate alternating current (AC). Alternators have replaced *generators* that produced direct current (DC) but otherwise performed the same functions on older cars.

**antifreeze**   see *coolant.*

**automatic choke**   a *choke* that automatically adjusts the amount of air entering the *carburetor* by sensing changes in engine temperature. See *thermostatic coil choke, thermostatic spring choke.*

**automatic transmission**   a *transmission* that selects gears automatically by means of a *hydraulically* driven system of *bands* and plates.

**axle**   a solid metal shaft to which the rear wheels of a vehicle are attached. On most cars, the rear *axle* spins at right angles to the *drive train* and transmits the power to the rear wheels. See *spindle.*

**backflushing**   See *flushing the cooling system.*

**ball joint**   a movable joint found on the *steering linkage* and *suspension system* of a car that allows the front wheels to move like a door hinge. See *boot, grease fitting, zerk fitting.*

**bands**   *automatic transmissions* rely on *hydraulic* pressure to change gears by means of a system of friction *bands* and plates. These bands can be adjusted externally without taking the *transmission* apart. Adjusting the bands is part of normal transmission service.

**battery**   a box filled with a solution of water and acid called *electrolyte* which contains metal plates that store current generated by the *alternator* and deliver it to the parts of the car that operate electrically. See *ground, negative terminal, positive terminal,* and *electrical system.*

**bearings**   antifriction devices that are usually found between two moving parts. For instance, in your car the babbit bearings found between the *connecting rod* and the *crankshaft* are lubricated and cushioned with *oil,* and the front wheel *bearings* must be repacked with *grease* at regular intervals. Bearings can be ball- or roller-type.

**biocide**   a product which kills any fungus or microbes that may have contaminated *diesel* fuel.

**bleeding a system**   to remove air bubbles from a *brake system,* a *fuel injection* system, or a *cooling system* so that they won't impede the flow of liquid through that system.

**block heaters**   devices that keep the engine warm when a car is not being used in very cold weather. These are especially important for starting *diesel engines* at extremely low temperatures.

**blow-by**   a *fuel/air mixture* under compression which is lost past the *piston rings* and causes fumes that form acid and *sludge* in the *crankcase* and smoking from the *oil filler hole.*

**blue books**   listings of the current prices for used cars, based on age, condition, and optional equipment, published in the *Kelly Blue Book,* the *NADA Used Car Guide* published by the National Automobile Dealers Association, and the *Red Book,* published by National Market Reports. Available at banks, loan offices, libraries, and insurance companies.

**boots**   the rubber or plastic covers located at either end of the spark-plug cables to insulate the connections between the cable ends and the *spark plug* and *distributor* terminals. Always grasp the cable by the boot when removing it. Also, the protective cover of the *ball joint* that holds the *grease.* See *grease fitting.*

**bore**   the width or diameter of the *cylinder* hole. See *stroke.*

**brake backing plate**   a metal plate, located inside the *brake drum,* on which the *wheel cylinder, brake shoes,* and other brake parts are mounted.

**brake drums**   metal drums mounted on each wheel. The

*brake shoes* press against the inner surfaces of the drums to slow or stop the car. See *brake system.*

**brake fluid**   the liquid used in the *hydraulic brake system* to stop or slow the car.

**brake lines**   a system of hoses and metal tubes through which the *brake fluid* flows from the *master cylinder* to the brakes at each wheel. See *brake system.*

**brake lining**   a heat-resistant asbestos material that is attached to the *brake shoe.* When the shoe is pressed against the *brake drum,* the lining grabs the inside of the drum, which stops the car and also prevents the drum and the shoe from wearing each other away.

**brake shoes**   curved pieces of metal with heat-resistant surfaces that are forced against the *brake drums* to slow or stop the car.

**brake system**   a system that uses *hydraulic* pressure to enable your car to slow and stop safely. Consists of the *master cylinder, brake lines,* and *disc* or *drum brakes* at each wheel. See *brake drums, brake fluid, brake lines, brake lining, brake shoes, parking brake, power brakes, wheel cylinder.*

**breaker plate**   the movable plate inside the *distributor* to which the *points* and the *condenser* are affixed.

**breaker points**   see *points.*

**bushing**   a protective liner that cushions noise, friction, or movement. Rubber bushings on the *suspension system* should be lubricated regularly.

**butterfly valve**   a small metal disc that controls the flow of air into the *carburetor.* See *choke, throttle.*

**calipers**   devices on *disc brakes* which hold the disc pads and press them against the disc to stop or slow the car.

**cam**   a metal disc with irregularly shaped *lobes* used in the *camshaft* to activate the opening and closing of the *valves* and, in the *distributor,* to force the *points* to open.

**cam lobes**   the bumps on a *cam* that contact and activate such devices as the lifters, which operate the *valves,* and the *rubbing block,* which causes the *points* to open and close, as the cam spins with the *distributor shaft.*

**camber**   a wheel *alignment* adjustment of the inward or outward tilt on the top of the wheel when viewed from the front of the car. Improves handling and cuts *tire* wear.

**camshaft**   a shaft with *cam lobes* which causes the *valves* to open and close. See *overhead cam, push rods, rocker arms.*

**carburetor**   a device that *vaporizes* fuel and mixes it with air in proper quantities to suit the varying needs of the engine.

**carburetor barrel**   the tubelike part of the *carburetor* through which air flows and is mixed with *vaporized* fuel. The *choke butterfly valve* is located at the top of the carburetor barrel, and the *throttle* valve is located at the bottom. Midway through, the barrel narrows, and this part is called the *venturi.* Carburetors can have one, two, or four barrels. See *dual carbs, four-barrel carburetor.*

**caster**   a wheel *alignment* adjustment that positions the wheels correctly, like the casters on a chair or shopping cart, so the tires follow naturally in a forward straight line. On a turn, the wheels will tend to straighten out when the steering wheel is released.

**catalytic converter**   a pollution-control device found on many newer cars which acts like an afterburner to reburn unburned gas in the *tail pipe.*

**centrifugal advance**   a device found on GM cars which advances or retards the ignition spark to correspond with changes in engine speed and load. See *spark advance, spark retard.*

**cetane rating**   a method of rating *diesel oil* by measuring the time lapse between *fuel injection* and ignition to determine how easy it is to ignite and how fast it will burn. See *octane rating.*

**charging system**   a system that, using a *fan belt* driven by the engine, enables the *alternator* (or *generator*) to generate electrical current, which is stored in the *battery* and delivered to the electrically operated parts of the car.

**chassis**   the parts of the car which are left when the body and fenders are removed.

**"cherry condition"**   a popular term for a car that has been kept in, or restored to, perfect condition.

**choke**   the device that limits the amount of air allowed to enter the *carburetor,* thus enriching the *fuel/air mixture* and enabling the car to start and run more easily when cold. *Automatic chokes* have a *thermostatic coil* or *thermostatic spring* that activates a *butterfly valve* at the top of the *carburetor barrel.* Older cars have manually operated chokes.

**circuit**   the path of electrical current through an *electrical system.*

**classic car**   a car that is generally considered to be one of the finest models ever built. Unlike antique cars, classic cars do not have to be extremely old. Mustangs and VW Bugs built in the late 1960s are considered to be classics by many people.

**cloud point**   the temperature at which *diesel oil* tends to thicken and cloud up.

**clutch**   a device that disconnects the engine from the *transmission,* to allow the car to change gears, and then allows the engine and transmission to resume contact and turn together at a new speed. See *clutch disc, clutch pedal, engine flywheel, free pedal play, pressure plate, throw-out bearing.*

**clutch disc**   a spinning plate located at the end of the *driveshaft* facing the *engine flywheel* and covered with an asbestos surface. When the *clutch* is engaged, the clutch disc is forced against the flywheel, causing the engine and the *transmission* to turn at the same speed.

**clutch pedal**   a pedal located on the floor of the car to the left of the brake pedal on cars with *manual transmission.* When the clutch pedal is depressed, it disengages the *clutch* so the engine and the *crankshaft* can turn independently of the transmission and the driver can change gears.

**coil**   the part of the *ignition system* which receives a small amount of electrical voltage from the *battery,* amplifies it into a big jolt of voltage, and sends it to the *spark plugs* via the *distributor.*

**coil springs**   large metal coils, like bed *springs,* that cushion and absorb the shocks and bumps as the car is driven. They are usually found near the front wheels, but many cars have them in the rear as well. Often the *shock absorbers* run up the center of the coil springs. See *suspension system.*

**combustion**   the intense burning of the *fuel/air mixture* in the *combustion chamber.*

**combustion chamber**   the part of the *cylinder* where the *fuel/air mixture* is compressed by the *piston* and ignited by a spark from the *spark plug.*

**compression gauge**   a device used to check the amount of pressure created in a *cylinder* when the *piston* is at its highest point (*TDC*) and is squeezing the *fuel/air mixture* into the smallest possible space. A poor compression-gauge reading can indicate the need for a *valve* grind, new *piston rings,* etc.

**compression ratio**   the amount of pressure applied to the *fuel/air mixture* in the *combustion chamber.* It is determined by comparing the size of the combustion chamber, with the *piston* at its highest point (*TDC*), to the size of the *cylinder* when the piston is at its lowest point.

**condenser**   a small metal cylinder, usually located inside the *distributor,* that prevents electricity from arcing across the *gap* when the *points* are open by acting as a "sponge" for the excess current.

**connecting rod**   the metal rod that connects the *piston* to the *crankshaft* and converts the up-and-down motion of the piston into the circular motion of the spinning crankshaft. The term *throwing a rod* refers to a broken connecting rod.

**constant velocity joints (CV)**   see *universal joints*

**contact gap**   see *point gap.*

**contact points**   see *points.*

**control arms**   metal struts located at the top and bottom of the wheel *spindle.* The upper and lower control arms allow the front wheels to change direction. See *suspension system.*

**coolant**   an ethylene glycol solution that raises the boiling point and lowers the freezing point of the water in the *cooling system,* prevents rust and corrosion, and lubricates the *water pump.* Also called "antifreeze."

**coolant recovery system**   a small bottle that acts as a reservoir for liquid expelled from the *cooling system* through the *overflow pipe* and returns the liquid to the system when it cools down. A special radiator *pressure cap* is also part of the kit. Also called a "closed cooling system" when it is part of the original equipment.

**cooling system**   a system that stores, circulates, and cools a mixture of water and *coolant,* which flows through *water jackets* in the *engine block* and keeps the engine from overheating as you drive. See *fan, pressure cap, radiator, thermostat, water pump.*

**core charge**   "core" is an acronym for "cash on return." A sum of money is refunded for a rebuildable part that is being exchanged for a *rebuilt* part of the same type. A common core charge is for *brake shoes* that need relining.

**core plugs**   metal plugs in the sides of the *engine block* which can pop out because of excessive pressure and prevent the engine block from cracking. These plugs sometimes develop leaks and should then be replaced. Also called "freeze plugs."

**cotter pin**   a fastener shaped like a pin but split up the center. After it is inserted, the legs are bent up or around to keep it in place.

**crankcase**   the lower portion of the engine where the *crankshaft* is located. At the bottom of the crankcase is the *oil pan.*

**cranking**   the act of engaging the *starter* by turning the key in the *ignition switch* which makes the engine *turn over.* In the old days, a hand crank was used to do this, hence the term "cranking."

**cranking circuit**   see *starting system.*

**crankshaft**   the main rotating shaft in the engine. The *connecting rods* transmit power from the *pistons* to the *crankshaft,* which, in turn, transmits power to the *driveshaft* and, eventually, to the rear wheels.

**crankshaft pulley**   a wheel attached to the front end of the *crankshaft* which is connected by *fan belts* to the *fan,* the *alternator,* and other devices so that the rotating crankshaft can drive these other parts as well. The crankshaft pulley usually has *timing marks* located on it, and these are necessary for checking and adjusting *timing* with a *timing light.* Also called a "harmonic balance wheel."

**creeper**   a platform on wheels that allows you to move around easily while lying on your back when you work under your car.

**cross-shaft lug wrench**   see *lug wrench.*

**cruise control**   an optional feature that keeps your car cruising at a pre-set speed unless overriden by the brake pedal.

**cylinder**   a hollow tube-shaped pipe in the *engine block.* The *piston* rides up and down in the cylinder to compress the *fuel/air mixture* that drives the engine.

**cylinder block**   see *engine block.*

**cylinder head**   the part of the engine above the *engine block* which contains the *combustion chambers* and, usually, the *valves.* The *spark plugs* screw into the side of the cylinder head. On most cars a *valve cover* or a *rocker-arm cover* is located on top of the cylinder head.

**cylinder sequence**   the order in which the *cylinders* are located on a particular car. It is necessary to locate the #1 cylinder to check and adjust *timing* with a *timing light,* and the #1 cylinder may be at the front of the engine on a U.S.-made straight 4- or 6-cylinder engine and at the rear of the engine on a foreign-made car. See *firing order.*

**diesel engine**   a *fuel system* without a *carburetor* which burns *diesel oil* instead of gasoline. The diesel oil is injected directly into the *combustion chamber,* where it is ignited by the heat caused by intense compression, rather than by a spark from a *spark plug.*

**diesel oil**   fuel for cars with *diesel engines.* (Not to be confused with lubricating oil) See *cetane.*

**differential**   a box of gear wheels, situated between the rear wheels, that turns the power of the rotating *driveshaft* at right angles to drive the rear *axle* and rear wheels. The differential also allows each of the rear wheels to turn at a different speed, when cornering.

**dipstick**   a metal stick that is inserted into a reservoir to check the level of the fluid in the reservoir by means of markings on the stick. The most common dipsticks check the levels of *oil, transmission fluid,* and *power-steering fluid.*

**disc brakes**   brakes that have *calipers* with heat-resistant pads, which grab a disc attached to the wheel and force it to stop turning, thus stopping the car. Many cars have disc brakes on the front wheels and *drum brakes* on the rear wheels. Most disc brakes have a *power booster*.

**displacement**   the volume of the inside of the *cylinders*—that is, the amount of fuel and air they can hold before compression takes place.

**distributor**   the part of the *ignition system* that distributes the proper amount of electrical voltage to each *spark plug*, in the correct sequence, at the precise moment for efficient *combustion*. See *condenser, points, rotor, spark advance, spark retard*.

**distributor cap**   a cap that covers the *distributor*. It has a tower for each *spark plug* cable, plus a center tower where the wire from the *coil* enters the cap to conduct electrical current to the *rotor*. The cap keeps dirt and moisture from getting into the *distributor*.

**distributor hold-down clamp**   a metal bracket at the base of the *distributor* that has a nut or bolt which can be loosened to allow the distributor to be moved on its shaft to readjust ignition *timing* or to open the *points* for gapping.

**distributor shaft**   the metal shaft inside the *distributor* that has a *cam* wheel which revolves with the shaft and forces the *points* to open. (A spring causes the points to close.)

**double clutching**   depressing the *clutch* for a second time, when the *gearshift* is in "neutral," while shifting from one gear to another. This allows the clutch to bring the *engine flywheel* and the *clutch disc* together more smoothly and reduces wear on these parts. Especially useful for cars with *manual transmission* without *syncromesh*.

**downshifting**   shifting the car manually to a lower gear in order to use the engine to aid the brakes in reducing speed. Also called "downgearing."

**drive train**   the path of power from the engine to the rear wheels. Consists of the *clutch, transmission, driveshaft, differential,* and rear *axle*.

**driveshaft**   the spinning metal shaft that transmits power from the *transmission* to the *differential,* the rear *axle* and the wheels.

**drum brakes**   brakes that use *hydraulic* pressure to force curved *brake shoes* against the inner walls of a hollow metal drum attached to each wheel. See *brake system*.

**dual carbs**   two *carburetors* on the same engine.

**dwell**   the distance the *distributor shaft* rotates while the *points* are closed. Also called *cam* angle. The dwell is given in degrees.

**dwell meter**   a device for determining whether your *points* are correctly gapped to allow the *distributor* to deliver a spark of proper intensity and duration to the *spark plugs*. See *tachometer*.

**electrical system**   a system that generates, stores, and distributes the electrical current required to start and run your car and such electrically operated equipment as the radio and headlights. See *charging system, ignition system, starting system*.

**electrodes**   metal rods attached to the center and side of the *spark plug* to conduct current and create a *gap* across which the spark must jump.

**electrolyte**   the mixture of sulphuric acid and water that is found in the *battery*.

**electronic ignition system**   an *ignition system* with a *distributor* that transmits electrical current to the *spark plugs* by electronic means, eliminating the need for replacing *points* or *condensers,* and for checking *dwell*.

**electronic sensing device**   an electronic device found on cars with *fuel injection* which senses changes in engine speed and driving conditions and determines the amount of fuel to be injected into the *combustion chambers,* thus eliminating the need for *carburetors* on these cars.

**emergency brake**   see *parking brake*.

**engine block**   the metal block in which the *cylinders* are bored which runs from below the *cylinder head* to the top of the *crankcase*. Also called the "cylinder block."

**engine flywheel**   a spinning plate located at the end of the *crankshaft,* on cars with *manual transmissions,* which engages the *clutch disc,* causing the engine and the transmission to turn at the same rate of speed. Also helps to dampen engine vibration. See *clutch.*

**EPA estimates**   estimates of the average amount of fuel consumed in city and highway driving by a particular vehicle, based on tests administered by the Environmental Protection Agency. These estimates should be used for comparison only since they vary with the driver, the load, and road conditions.

**exhaust gases**   the burned residue of the *fuel/air mixture* that must be refined and expelled from the car via the *exhaust system*.

**exhaust manifold**   a set of pipes, one for each *cylinder,* through which burned *exhaust gases* can flow from the cylinders through the *exhaust system* and out of the car through the *tail pipe*.

**exhaust system**   a system that conducts the *exhaust gases* from the *exhaust manifold* to the rear of the car and into the air. On the way, pollution-control devices are sometimes used to burn off harmful substances, and a *muffler* (and *resonators* in some cases) controls the noise of the escaping gases. See *catalytic converter*.

**exhaust valve**   the *valve* that opens to allow the *exhaust gases* to pass from the *combustion chamber* to the *exhaust manifold*.

**fan**   situated between the *radiator* and the engine, the fan draws air through the radiator to cool the liquid in the *cooling system* when the car is standing still or operating at low speeds.

**fan belt**   a flexible rubber belt that connects the *fan* and the *alternator*. The operation of the engine turns the fan, and this turns the belt, which drives the alternator, enabling it to generate electric current. Other fan belts can drive air conditioners, *power steering* pumps, etc. Fan belts should be checked and replaced if they seem frayed, glazed, oily, etc.

**feeler gauge**   a device for measuring the distance, or *gap,* between two surfaces. Use a wire feeler gauge to gap *spark plugs* and a flat feeler gauge to gap *points* and adjust *valves*.

**firewall**   the insulated partition that runs from the windshield down between the interior of the car and the engine area. Protects the driver and passengers from engine fires, noise, fumes, and during accidents.

**firing order**   the sequence in which the *cylinders* fire on a particular car to distribute the shock of *combustion* evenly and reduce engine vibrations. This should not be confused with *cylinder sequence*, which refers to the location of the #1 cylinder on a specific car, and where the other cylinders are located with relation to #1.

**five-speed transmission**   a *manual transmission* with a fifth gear that functions as an *overdrive* to allow the wheels to turn faster than the engine. On freeways, where cars can achieve a higher speed and then coast without needing much power, this is a real gas saver.

**flash point**   the temperature at which *diesel oil* ignites.

**flat rate manual**   a listing of almost every job that can be done on a car with the average time required for a mechanic to complete it; it is used by service facilities to estimate labor charges. Many shops require their mechanics to "beat the book" yet charge their customers for the full time suggested by the flat rate manual.

**float bowl**   a small chamber in the *carburetor* that holds a small ready supply of fuel to be *vaporized* and mixed with air by the carburetor. The level of the fuel in the float bowl is controlled by a small float and fuel valve in the chamber.

**flushing the cooling system**   circulating water through the *cooling system* to remove old liquid and clean the system of rust and dirt. "Backflushing" means circulating the water from the engine to the *radiator* (reversing the normal direction of flow) in order to clean the system more efficiently.

**four-barrel carburetor**   a *carburetor* with four barrels that works like *dual carburetors*, with the second carburetor (third and fourth barrels) cutting in only at high speeds. Usually found on large *V-8 engines*.

**four-stroke power cycle**   refers to the four movements of the *piston*—down, up, down, and up—that draw the *fuel/air mixture* into the *combustion chamber* (intake stroke), compress the mixture (compression stroke), transmit the power created by the *combustion* to the *crankshaft* (power stroke), and expel the *exhaust gases* from the *cylinder* (exhaust stroke).

**free pedal play**   the distance the clutch pedal can be depressed before it begins to disengage the *clutch*. About ¾ to 1 inch of free pedal play is normally required to assure that the clutch will be fully disengaged when not in use. Without free pedal play, the *throw-out bearing*, and/or the clutch, would wear out.

**freeze plugs**   see *core plugs*.

**friction**   the rubbing of two moving parts against each other. Friction creates heat and wears down moving parts. The *lubrication system* uses *oil* and *grease* to reduce friction and to increase the life of your car.

**front-end alignment**   see *alignment*.

**front-wheel drive**   a car that is "pulled" by its front wheels, rather than being "pushed" by its rear wheels, has front-wheel drive. This eliminates the long *driveshaft* and the center floor hump found on cars with rear-wheel drive. See *transverse engine, transaxle*.

**fuel/air mixture**   a mistlike combination of *vaporized* fuel and air which is compressed in the *cylinders* and ignited to produce the power that drives the engine and the car.

**fuel filter**   a small device that removes impurities from the fuel before it gets to the *carburetor*. Usually found near the carburetor in the *fuel line* that leads from the *fuel pump* (in-line fuel filter), or inside the carburetor or the fuel pump (integral fuel filter). Must be cleaned or replaced once a year, or every 20,000 miles, or if it becomes clogged and interferes with the carburetor's fuel supply.

**fuel injection**   a fuel system without a *carburetor* that employs an *electronic sensing device* to deliver a specific amount of fuel to each *combustion chamber* in response to changes in engine speed and driving conditions. See *fuel injector nozzles*.

**fuel injector nozzles**   devices that work like hypodermic needles to inject the proper amount of fuel into the *combustion chambers* in response to signals from an electronic sensing device on cars with *fuel injection* systems. Also called *fuel injector valves*.

**fuel lines**   the hoses or pipes through which the fuel passes from the *fuel tank* to the *carburetor*.

**fuel pump**   a pump that draws the fuel from the *fuel tank* and sends it through the *fuel lines* to the *carburetor* or the *fuel* injector nozzles.

**fuel system**   a system that stores, cleans, and delivers the fuel to the engine in proper quantities to meet the varying needs that arise as you drive. Consists of the *fuel tank, fuel lines, fuel pump, fuel filter*, and *carburetor* or the *fuel injection* system.

**fuel tank**   the storage compartment, under the trunk in most cars, that holds the fuel for the car. Also called the "gas tank."

**gap**   the space between the spark plug *electrodes*, or between the *points* when they are as far apart as they can get. Adjusting this space is called "gapping." See *point gap, spark plug gap*.

**gapper**   see *feeler gauge*.

**gas gauge**   a dashboard device that indicates the amount of fuel in the *fuel tank*.

**gasket**   a rubber, cork, paper, or metal plate that is inserted between two parts to cushion against wear and prevent leakage.

**gear grease**   a heavy liquid grease that fills the *differential* and *manual transmission* to lubricate the gears. Also called "differential grease."

**gear ratio**   the speed of the engine compared with the output speed of the *transmission*, and/or the *differential*, in a given gear.

**gear selector**   a *gearshift* located on the side of the steering column on cars with *automatic transmissions*.

**gearshift** the stick attached to the *transmission* which selects new gears in response to the driver's commands. See *gear selector, stick shift.*

**generator** see *alternator.*

**glow plug** an electrical element located in the *combustion chamber* of a *diesel engine* which helps to heat up the air in the chamber so the diesel fuel will be ignited more quickly.

**grease** see *gear grease, lube grease.*

**grease fitting** a device that seals in and allows the addition of more *grease,* or some other type of lubricant, to cushion two moving parts, allow them to move freely, and prevent them from wearing each other away. See *ball joint, steering knuckles, tie-rod ends, zerk fitting.*

**grease gun** a device that can be loaded with *grease* and used for lubricating your car. Grease guns come with extenders for hard-to-reach places and with adapters for lubricating various types of *ball joints* and *zerk fittings.*

**grease seal** a circular, metal-backed, rubber device, that keeps *grease* from leaking out and protects wheel *bearings* and similar parts from dust and water.

**ground** one terminal of the *battery* is wired to the metal frame of the car to utilize the frame as a path for returning electric current to the battery and thus completing the electrical *circuit.* Most U.S. cars are negative ground—the *negative terminal* is wired to the frame of the car. In some other countries, this is called "negative earth."

**guarantee** a promise by the manufacturer to fix or replace a specific part if it does not last for a specific time period or distance.

**head gasket** the seal between the *cylinder head* and the *engine block.* This *gasket* keeps the *coolant* out of the *cylinders* and free from contamination by *exhaust gases.* A "blown" head gasket will cause a serious loss of compression.

**headliners** fabric or vinyl upholstery on the interior of the roof of a car.

**horsepower** the energy required to lift 550 pounds one foot in one second—or, 33,000 foot-pounds per minute.

**hose clamps** adjustable metal rings placed around a hose, where it connects to another part, to prevent leaks and to keep the hose in place.

**hub cap** the cap that fits over the end of the wheel *spindle* to keep dust and water away from the wheel *bearings* and brakes. Considered a decorative accessory on many cars, it is also a safety device that causes quite a racket if a *lug nut* falls off and tumbles around inside it.

**hydraulic** operated by the resistance offered, or pressure transmitted, when a quantity of water, *oil,* or other liquid is forced through a comparatively small opening or tube. Hydraulic devices on a car may include *automatic transmission, power steering,* and most *brake systems.*

**hydrometer** a device to determine the weight of a liquid. They are used to test *battery electrolyte* and the percentage of coolant in the *cooling system.*

**"idiot lights"** popular term for the dashboard indicators which light up only when your car is already in trouble from lack of oil, overheating, etc. (as opposed to gauges which indicate *levels* of *oil* and engine temperatures, thus enabling the driver to prevent breakdowns and damage).

**idle** the engine speed when the car is not moving.

**idle air bleed screw** a screw found instead of the *idle speed screw* on some *carburetors.* It allows air to enter the carburetor when the *throttle* is closed, so that the car can *idle.* It also prevents the formation of deposits in the throttle area. The adjustment of this screw is part of a basic *tune-up.*

**idle mixture screw** a screw located on the outside of the *carburetor* which controls the proportion of the *fuel/air mixture.* It is now illegal to adjust these if limiter caps are present.

**idle speed screw** a screw located at the bottom of the *carburetor* on the outside which keeps the *throttle* from closing completely when the car is idling and thus controls the *idle* speed. This is adjusted as part of a basic *tune-up.* See *idle air bleed screw.*

**idle stop solenoid** a small cylinder located on the outside of the *carburetor* on some cars. It prevents the car from continuing to *idle* after the *ignition switch* has been shut off (this is called *dieseling*). This can be adjusted as part of a *tune-up.*

**ignition switch** the slot in which you turn the car key to close the electrical *circuit* that starts the car. When the key is removed, the switch is shut off.

**ignition system** a system that provides the electric current used to ignite the *fuel/air mixture* in the *combustion chambers* of the *cylinders.* Its parts include the *coil,* which amplifies the current it gets from the *battery* and sends it to the *distributor,* which directs the current to each *spark plug* at the proper time.

**ignition timing** see *timing.*

**in-line engine** an engine in which the *cylinders* occur in a single row with the *crankshaft* running along the bottom. Also called a "straight engine." See *V-type engine.*

**intake manifold** a set of iron pipes, one for each *cylinder,* that conduct the *fuel/air mixture* from the *carburetor* to the cylinders. See *exhaust manifold.*

**intake valve** a *valve* that opens to allow the *fuel/air mixture* to enter the *combustion chamber.* Also called the "inlet valve."

**integral equipment** any device or system that is designed for and installed in a car by the manufacturer, rather than being added on to a finished vehicle at a later date.

**internal combustion engine** an engine that works on power released by *vaporized* fuel and air burning swiftly and violently inside the engine itself, rather than on an outside source of *combustion* as, for example, a steam engine does.

**jack** a device for lifting the car, or part of the car, off the ground to facilitate repairs. The most popular jacks are the tripod, scissors, and *hydraulic* jacks. Some cars come with bumper jacks for *tire* changing.

**jack stand** a safety device that keeps the car from falling to the ground if the *jack* is removed or faulty. Most jobs require two jack stands for safety.

**journal** the area on the *crankshaft* that fits into the lower portion of the *connecting rod*. A layer of *oil* and metal *bearings* cushions the impact during the power *stroke* to prevent the crankshaft from being crushed by the swiftly descending *piston* and connecting rod.

**jumper cables** cables used to "jump a start" by conducting current from one car *battery* to another. This allows a car whose battery has run down to start and begin to generate its own power. See *positive terminal*.

**knocking** a sound that occurs in the *cylinders* when the *fuel/air mixture* is being ignited too soon and the subsequent explosion is hitting the *piston* as it travels up the cylinder on the compression *stroke*. Usually it is due to faulty *timing*, low-octane gas, or fragments of burning carbon in the cylinders. Also called "pinging" or "preignition." It sounds like marbles rattling in a can and can best be heard when accelerating up hills. See *four-stroke power cycle*.

**leaf springs** a series of steel plates, placed one atop the other, which bend flexibly to absorb the bumps and shocks of driving. Most often found near the rear wheels. See *suspension system*.

**leasing** payment of a sum each month in return for the use of a car instead of buying it outright. The two basic types of leases are: *open-end* leases under which you pay an additional amount at the end of the term and acquire ownership of the vehicle, and *closed-end* leases under which ownership reverts to the leasing agency at the end of the term.

**lube grease** super-thick lubricating oil that has a paste-like consistency. Used to lubricate the *steering linkage*, the *suspension system*, and other moving parts outside the engine. See *gear grease*.

**lube job** the greasing and lubrication of the *suspension system*, the *drive train*, and other parts of the car which need it. Should be done professionally once or twice a year.

**lubrication system** a system that stores, cleans, cools, and recirculates *oil* through the engine to lubricate its moving parts and cool them. Includes the *oil pan*, *oil pump*, *oil filter*, and a dashboard *oil gauge*. You can check the level of oil in the system with the oil *dipstick*.

**lug nuts** the nuts that hold the wheel onto the car. You remove them with a *lug wrench* in order to change your *tires*.

**lug wrench** a wrench used during *tire* changes to remove the *lug nuts* that hold the wheel onto the car. The cross-shaft type provides the best leverage. Carry one in your trunk compartment.

**manifold** see *exhaust manifold, intake manifold*.

**manual transmission** a *transmission* system in which gears are selected by the driver by means of a hand-operated *gearshift* and a foot-operated *clutch*. Also called a "standard transmission."

**master brake cylinder** a device that stores *brake fluid* and *hydraulically* forces it through the *brake lines* to the brakes when you step on the brake pedal.

**mechanics lien** recourse available to mechanics in some states by which they can confiscate and sell your vehicle to compensate themselves if you do not pay your bill.

**misfiring** the failure of the *fuel/air mixture* in one or more *cylinders* to undergo *combustion* while the car is running. Misfiring can be due to poor compression caused by worn or improperly adjusted *valves*, worn *piston rings*, or a faulty *head gasket*. Or it can be caused by poor ignition due to worn or dirty spark plug *electrodes*, worn or improperly gapped *points* or *spark plugs*, poor fuel delivery, faulty ignition wiring, or faulty *distributor* components. It can be detected by placing a stiff piece of paper at the end of the *tail pipe* and listening for an irregular puffing sound.

**motor mounts** the rubber-covered brackets that hold the engine and *transmission* to the frame of the car and cushion vibrations.

**mph** an abbreviation for "miles per hour."

**muffler** a device for controlling the noise of the *exhaust gases* before they are released into the air through the *tail pipe*.

**negative ground** see *ground*.

**negative terminal** the *battery* terminal that conducts electric current back to the battery on cars with negative *ground*. The negative terminal is usually smaller than the *positive terminal* and has either "neg" or "-" on it.

**NOS (new old stock)** duplicates of parts for out-of-production cars that are issued by the original manufacturer for the restoration of older vehicles.

**octane rating** a method of rating gasoline by measuring its ability to resist *knocking*, or "pinging," in *internal combustion engines*.

**odometer** a dashboard device for measuring and indicating the number of miles a car has traveled. A trip odometer that can be set to zero in order to register the mileage on a particular trip can be found on some cars, as well.

**OE (original equipment)** parts made by the original manufacturer of a particular vehicle.

**oil** a substance that lubricates and cools the moving parts of the engine and reduces the formation of rust and corrosion. Oil comes in varying weights suitable for efficient operation in cold and hot weather and for engines in varying states of wear. See *viscosity*.

**oil drain plug** the plug that secures the drain hole in the *oil pan*. An oil plug *gasket* lies between the plug and the hole and this gasket should be replaced if leakage occurs.

**oil filler hole** a hole at the top of the engine through which new oil can be added after the filler hole cover is removed.

**oil filter** a canlike device that screws onto the outside of the *crankcase* and cleans the *oil* as it circulates through the *lubrication system*. Oil filters should be replaced at least every other oil change.

**oil gauge** a dashboard device that indicates the oil pressure as the *oil* is pumped through the engine. If this gauge shows a sharp drop, reads "Low," or lights up, stop the car immediately and find the cause before driving any further. Without oil you can burn out your engine in less than a mile.

**oil pan** the chamber at the bottom of the *crankcase* which stores *oil*. The *oil drain plug* at the bottom of the oil pan can be removed to allow old oil to flow out of the car during an oil change.

**oil pump** a small pump located in the *crankcase* which circulates the *oil* from the *oil pan* to the moving parts of the engine.

**optional equipment** any equipment or feature of a new car which is not included in the basic price and is provided only if the purchaser requests it. Beware of new-car deals where you are forced to buy a car equipped with "options" you don't need.

**original condition** an older car that has all of its original paint and equipment and has not been restored or modified.

**oscilloscope** an ignition-system and engine tester that displays variations in electrical current as a visible wave on the fluorescent screen of a cathode-ray tube.

**overdrive** an optional special gear that allows the rear wheels to turn faster than the engine. This lowers fuel consumption during sustained high-speed driving on freeways.

**overflow pipe** a tube located in the *radiator fill hole* that allows excess liquid to escape from the *cooling system* under conditions of extreme heat, pressure, or overfilling. See *coolant recovery kit*.

**overhaul** see *rebuild*.

**overhead cam (OHC)** a *camshaft* located above the *cylinder head* rather than below the *cylinders* in the *engine block*. Overhead camshafts eliminate the need for *push rods* to activate the *valves*. DOHC engines have double (two) overhead camshafts.

**owner's manual** a handbook provided by the car manufacturer to give the owner basic instructions for operating the various devices on the car. Many owner's manuals contain *specifications* for items associated with maintenance, but very few offer instructions for doing-it-yourself. See *service manual*.

**ozone checking** cracks or hard spots usually found on the sidewalls of *tires*. Caused by the action of the ozone in the air on the rubber, this condition is normal but could be dangerous on tires that either are more than 40,000 miles old or have been exposed to the ozone created by electrical machinery.

**parking brake** an auxiliary brake attached to a rear wheel or to the *transmission* which keeps the car from moving accidentally. Also called an "emergency brake."

**passing gear** an *automatic transmission* gear that shifts a car into a lower gear for a short burst of extra power to pass other cars on the highway. This gear is engaged by sharply depressing the gas pedal. When the pedal is released, the car returns to normal driving gear.

**PCV valve** part of the positive crankcase ventilation system, which reroutes *crankcase blow-by* to the *intake manifold* and back to the engine, where it is reburned in the *cylinders* as part of the *fuel/air mixture*. This cuts emission pollution and increases fuel economy because unburned fuel in the blow-by is consumed the second time around. It also keeps the blow-by and water vapor from fouling the *oil* in the crankcase, thus reducing the formation of engine *sludge*.

**Phillips screwdriver** a screwdriver with a pointed tip that is shaped to fit the crossed slots in the heads of Phillips screws.

**pinging** see *knocking*.

**piston** a cylindrical part, closed at the top, that moves up and down inside the *cylinder* to compress the *fuel/air mixture* and drive the engine by means of a *connecting rod*, which is attached to the piston at one end and to the *crankshaft* at the other. See *journal, piston rings*.

**piston rings** metal rings located in grooves on the outside of the *piston* which keep the *fuel/air mixture* from leaking past the piston into the *crankcase* during compression and that keep *oil* from going up into the *combustion chamber*. Faulty rings can cause poor compression, severe *blow-by* and excessive smoking from the *tail pipe*.

**point gap** the space between the *points* when they are fully open. Adjusting this *gap* is a primary part of the basic *tune-up* because the spark that jumps this gap is affected, both in intensity and in duration, by the width of the gap. See *feeler gauge*.

**points** two or more metal terminals, located inside the *distributor*, which are brought into contact and then separated by the movement of the *cam* wheel on the rotating *distributor shaft*. The points regulate the intensity and duration of the current that is conducted to each *spark plug* by interrupting the flow of current from the coil as they open and close. Also called "contact points," "breaker points," or "ignition points." See *gap*.

**polymer coating** a coating that prevents paint from oxidizing and so protects a car from premature fading and rusting. Do-it-yourself poly-sealants last for from 6 months to a year; professionally applied poly-glycotes can last from 2 to 3 years.

**positive terminal** the *battery* terminal that leads to the *electrical system* on cars with negative *ground*. The positive terminal is usually larger and has "pos" or " + " on it. *Jumper cables* and other devices that connect to the battery usually have red clips for the positive terminal and black clips for the *negative terminal*.

**power booster** a device that uses engine vacuum to assist you in braking the car. Helps the brake pedal to activate the *hydraulic* pistons in the *master cylinder*.

**power brakes** a *brake system* that uses a *power booster* to make braking easier.

**power steering** a device that uses *hydraulic* power to help the driver to steer the car more easily. Cars with power steering usually have a reservoir in the power steering pump, which requires the occasional addition of power-steering fluid (usually automatic *transmission fluid*).

**pre-combustion chamber** a small chamber located outside the *combustion chamber* of some cars in which a small amount of rich *fuel/air mixture* can be ignited to increase fuel efficiency and cut emissions. Found principally on *diesel* engines and *stratified charge engines*. Also called pre-chambers.

**pre-ignition** see *knocking*.

**pressure cap** a *radiator* cap that allows the *cooling system* to operate under pressure at higher temperatures for greater efficiency. Safety pressure caps can be used to help to release the pressure before the cap is removed to prevent injuries due to escaping steam or hot water.

**pressure plate** a disc that is forced by springs against the *clutch disc*, which forces the disc and the *engine flywheel* against each other, causing the engine and the *transmission* to turn at the same rate of speed. See *clutch*.

**primary terminal** the clip found inside the *distributor* which allows electric current to pass from the *points* to the *condenser* and provides the insulation to keep the current from contacting other metal parts. See *ignition system*.

**psi** an abbreviation for "pounds per square inch." The term is used to measure the amount of air pressure in *tires* and the amount of compression of the *fuel/air mixture* in the *combustion chamber*.

**push rods** the rods that run between the *camshaft* lifters and the *rocker arms*. The lifters and the push rods are pushed up by the *cam lobes*, causing the rocker arms to make the *valves* open and close. Engines with *overhead cams* do not need push rods, because the camshaft contacts the valves directly.

**radial tires** see *tires*.

**radiator** a device that cools the liquid in the *cooling system* by allowing it to circulate through a series of water channels, which are exposed to air ducts.

**radiator cap** see *pressure cap*.

**radiator fill hole** an opening at the top of the *radiator* through which new water and *coolant* can be added. The *pressure cap* seals the fill hole.

**radiator pressure cap** see *pressure cap*.

**ratchet** a device that allows you to turn a screw or bolt in one direction, then move the handle of the wrench or screwdriver back in the opposite direction to prepare for the next stroke, without removing the tool from the screw or bolt. See *socket wrench*.

**rear axle ratio** the number of times the rear wheels turn compared to a particular *transmission* speed. The higher the rear *axle* ratio, the slower the engine can run and still allow the car to achieve a given speed.

**rebuild** to disassemble a particular device, clean it thoroughly, replace worn parts, and reassemble it. *Clutches*, *carburetors*, and *brakes* are sometimes rebuilt as part of the

maintenance or restoration of older vehicles. You can rebuild a part yourself with a kit containing instructions and part replacements, or you can buy a rebuilt part and turn in your old part for a *core charge*. Rebuilding is sometimes called "overhauling."

**reproductions** cars or car parts that have been duplicated by other manufacturers because the originals are no longer widely available.

**resonator** a small auxiliary *muffler* found on some cars which further reduces the noise of the escaping *exhaust gases*.

**restoration** restoring a car to its original condition (including original parts, paint, chroming processes, etc.) rather than merely rebuilding or repairing one. See *OE*, *NOS*, *reproductions*, "*cherry condition*."

**rings** see *piston rings*.

**rocker arm cover** a metal lid located on top of the *cylinder head* on cars that have *valves* that are activated by an *overhead cam* or by *rocker arms*. See *valve cover*.

**rocker arms** curved levers each of which has one end attached to a *push rod* and the other end attached to a valve stem in order to make the *valves* open and close in response to the pressure of the *cam lobes* on the spinning *camshaft*. Cars with *overhead cams* do not always require rocker arms, because the valve stems may contact the cam lobes directly.

**rotor** a device that sits atop the *distributor shaft* and conducts the electric current to each *spark plug* terminal in turn. See *ignition system*.

**rpm** an abbreviation for "revolutions per minute." A *tachometer* measures engine revolutions in terms of rpm.

**rubber** all the rubber seals, mats, and pads that cushion and protect car windows, trim, handles, bumper sections, carpets, etc. A *restoration* should be a replacement of all damaged or missing rubber with *OE* rubber or exact *reproductions* of it.

**rubbing block** a little block located on the movable point that contacts the *distributor cam* wheel and causes the *points* to open. (A spring causes the points to close.)

**rubbing compound** a polish that contains abrasives harsh enough to remove layers of "dead" paint. Useful in radical restoration procedures, rubbing compounds should not be used on new cars or those with delicate finishes.

**safety pressure cap** see *pressure cap*.

**sealed beam unit** a headlight that usually contains both high and low bulbs, reflectors, and lenses and is sealed to keep out dirt and moisture. When the headlight fails, you replace the entire unit.

**sealer** a substance you can add to the liquid in the *cooling system* to seal leaks. Also called "stop-leak." Other kinds of sealing compounds are used to coat surfaces before installing hoses or *gaskets*. These are effective in preventing leakage but usually make the hose or gasket hard to remove.

**service manual** a handbook published by a car manufacturer or a specialized publishing company that contains instructions and *specifications* for the maintenance and repair of specific cars. Most service manuals deal with only one make, model, or year, and nearly all are intended for professionals or the very experienced amateur. They are useful for locating various parts on your car and for parts specifications. See *owner's manual.*

**service writer** at many dealerships, the person responsible for receiving cars brought in to the service department, in order to estimate the nature and cost of repairs and when the work will be completed.

**shock absorbers** devices located near each wheel to cut down the vertical bouncing of the passenger compartment on the *springs* after the wheels go over a bump or the car stops short. Shock absorbers also improve handling on rough road surfaces. See *suspension system.*

**sludge** a combination of oxidized *oil,* gasoline, water, and *blow-by* that can foul an engine. Some engine oils have detergents to break down sludge.

**socket wrench** a wrench that completely covers the head of a bolt rather than fitting around its circumference. A socket set usually consists of a variety of sockets plus at least one handle (usually a *ratchet* handle), a couple of extenders, and sometimes a *spark plug socket* as well.

**solenoid** a device connected to electrical current which induces mechanical movement in another device. See *idle stop solenoid, starter solenoid.*

**spark advance** to adjust the *ignition timing* so that the *spark plugs* will fire sooner than they have been firing. See *spark retard.*

**spark plug** a device that delivers the electrical spark to the *combustion chamber.* This ignites the *fuel/air mixture* and produces the power that drives the engine. See *ignition system, spark plug gap.*

**spark plug gap** the space between the center and side spark plug *electrodes* across which the spark must jump to ignite the *fuel/air* mixture in the *combustion chamber.* Adjusting this *gap* is a major part of the basic *tune-up,* since the width of the gap affects the intensity of the spark. See *feeler gauge.*

**spark plug socket** a metal cylinder with a rubber lining that fits over the exposed end of the *spark plug* to make it easy to remove the plug without damaging its porcelain surface. Can be purchased as part of a *socket wrench* set, or separately.

**spark retard** to adjust *ignition timing* so that the *spark plugs* will fire later than they have been firing. See *knocking, spark advance.*

**specifications** the size, description, or parts numbers for various items needed to maintain or repair a car. See *owner's manual, service manual.*

**speedometer** a dashboard device that measures and indicates how fast the car is going. The speedometer cable should be lubricated when the needle starts to move erratically, or if the cable begins to make noise.

**spindle** the small shaft located at each front wheel on which the front wheels revolve.

**splash shield** a removable device found on *disc brakes* that helps to keep water and dirt from fouling the brakes.

**springs** devices to cushion and absorb shocks and bumps and to keep the car level on turns. A car can have *leaf springs, coil springs, torsion bars,* or a combination of these. See *suspension system.*

**stabilizers** a variety of devices used to keep the passenger compartment of a car from swaying and lurching on sharp curves and turns. See *suspension system.*

**standard transmission** see *manual transmission.*

**starter** a small motor that causes the engine *crankshaft* to begin to turn, which starts the engine running and so starts the car. Also called the *cranking* motor. See *starting system.*

**starter solenoid** a device that uses electrical current to start and engage the *starter.* See *solenoid.*

**starting system** the portion of the *electrical system* that starts the car. Consists of (1) the *ignition switch,* which closes the circuit and allows current to flow from (2) the *battery* to (3) the *starter,* via (4) the *starter solenoid.* Also called the "cranking circuit."

**static shield** a device found on some *distributors* that reduces radio interference caused by the working of the car's *ignition system.*

**steering-axis inclination** an *alignment* adjustment that allows the steering wheel to return to the straight-ahead position when the car comes out of a turn.

**steering knuckles** a type of *ball joint* located at the ends of the tie rods on the *steering linkage.* See *grease fittings.*

**steering linkage** the system that connects the steering wheel to the front wheels and allows the wheels to change direction in response to commands from the driver. Contains *grease fittings* to cushion against wear and friction. See *alignment.*

**stick shift** a *gearshift* located on the floor between, or slightly in front of, the front seats. A car with a four-speed *manual transmission* and a stick shift is said to have "four on the floor."

**stop-leak** see *sealer.*

**stratified charge engine** an *internal combustion engine* in which a small portion of extremely rich fuel and air is ignited and in turn ignites a much leaner *fuel/air mixture,* resulting in greater fuel economy and a decrease in pollutant emissions.

**stroke** the vertical distance that the *piston* moves as it travels from the top to the bottom or from the bottom to the top of the *cylinder.* See *bore, four-stroke power cycle.*

**supercharging** a method of increasing engine power by forcing larger amounts of air into the *cylinders.* Unlike *turbocharging* this decreases fuel economy.

**suspension system** a system that cushions the passenger compartment of the car from the bumps and shocks caused by the wheels moving over irregular road surfaces. Includes *springs, shock absorbers, steering linkage,* upper and lower *control arms, torsion bars, stabilizers,* etc. The *grease fittings* and rubber *bushings* along this system should be lubricated at regular intervals. See *zerk fitting.*

**syncromesh** a *manual transmission* device that allows two gears to mesh more smoothly by causing them to spin at the same rate of speed before coming together.

**tachometer** a device for measuring engine *rpm*. Many cars with *manual transmissions* have a dashboard tachometer to aid in changing gears. A portable tachometer is used to adjust *idle* speed as part of a basic *tune-up*. Often a tachometer is combined with a *dwell meter* in a single unit. Try to find one with both "Hi" and "Lo" rpm range.

**tail pipe** the last link in the *exhaust system*. Conducts *exhaust gases* from the *muffler* to the rear of the car and into the atmosphere.

**TDC** an abbreviation for "top dead center." This is the point at which the *piston* has reached the top of its *stroke* and has compressed the *fuel/air mixture* to the greatest extent. BTDC and ATCD mean "before" and "after" top dead center. These terms are used to refer to *timing marks*. See *combustion chamber*.

**thermostat** a device that keeps the hot *coolant* and water in the engine to help the engine to warm up more quickly. Then, the thermostat allows the liquid to flow to the *radiator*, where it is cooled and recirculated through the engine to prevent overheating. See *cooling system*.

**thermostatic coil choke** a sensing device mounted on the *carburetor* that automatically controls the choke *butterfly valve* by sensing the heat of the *exhaust manifold*. See *choke*.

**thermostatic spring choke** a sensing device that automatically controls the choke *butterfly valve* by sensing the heat of the *intake manifold*. See *choke*.

**throttle** a device that controls the vacuum created in the *venturi*. The greater the vacuum, the richer the *fuel/air mixture*. The throttle enables the engine to run on a richer mixture and produce more power for high-speed driving. It consists of a throttle arm, located on the outside of the *carburetor* and connected to the gas pedal, which activates a throttle *butterfly valve* at the base of the *carburetor barrel*, where it joins the *intake manifold*.

**throw-out bearing** a part of the *clutch*, activated by the clutch pedal, that allows the clutch to disengage. If you allow the car to *idle* in gear with the clutch pedal depressed, instead of shifting to neutral gear, you can wear out the throw-out bearing. Also called the "clutch release bearing." See *free pedal play*.

**tie rod ends** *grease fittings* or *ball joints* located on the ends of the *steering linkage*.

**timing** the ability of the *valves, ignition system,* and other engine-driven parts of the car to work together for maximum efficiency. Timing is checked as part of the basic *tune-up* because, if the timing is off, the car cannot perform well, just as all the pieces in an orchestra must not only be in tune but must play together to achieve a good performance. Timing is regulated by checking with a *timing light* and then adjusting the *distributor* or the *timing chain*. See *distributor hold-down clamp, spark advance, spark-retard, timing marks*.

**timing chain** a chain that drives the *camshaft* by linking it to the *crankshaft* and assures that the *valves* will open and close at the proper moments for efficient ignition. See *timing*.

**timing light** a device used to check ignition *timing*. The light is hooked to the first *cylinder spark plug* and blinks on and off as the plug fires. When aimed at the *timing marks,* this stroboscopic effect causes the marks to appear to stand still opposite a pointer. Xenon timing lights are usually more useful than the cheaper neon ones because they are more visible in daylight.

**timing marks** a series of marks or notches usually located on the *crankshaft pulley* (also called the "harmonic balance wheel"). When a *timing light* is aimed at these marks, they appear to stand still, enabling you to see if the proper mark is lined up with a stationary pointer located nearby. The proper timing marks are part of the car's *specifications*.

**tire valve** a small valve, mounted on the wheel rim of a tubeless *tire*, that allows air to be added to the tire with an air hose and allows air to be withdrawn from an overinflated tire by pressing on the little stem at the end of the valve. Some tire valves have little caps to protect against leaks and keep dirt from fouling the valve. On tires with inner tubes, the tire valve is mounted on the inner tube. (Today, most tires are tubeless.)

**tires** can be bias-ply, bias-belted, or radial, depending on their construction. The most popular materials used are rayon, nylon, and polyester plies. Belting can be fiberglass, or steel for extra strength. The rest of the tire (treads and sidewalls) is hard rubber. See *alignment, ozone checking, tire valve*.

**toe-in** an adjustment of front-wheel *alignment* so that the *tires* are slightly pigeon-toed when the car is standing still. This improves handling at high speeds.

**toe-out** a wheel *alignment* adjustment to control the way the car tracks on turns. Tires should never toe out.

**torque** turning or twisting power. See *torque wrench*.

**torque wrench** a special wrench that can measure the exact amount of *torque* being applied to tighten a bolt.

**torsion bars** on Chrysler products, these are often connected to the *control arms* to compensate for uneven loads and to allow the front wheels to move up and down freely on uneven road surfaces. See *suspension system*.

**trailer-towing packages** optional equipment which usually includes a heavy-duty *suspension*, a larger *radiator*, a *transmission* cooler, and a rear bumper with a trailer hitch. This improves handling and allows a vehicle to haul a heavy trailer.

**transaxle** a single unit combining the *transmission, differential,* and *clutch,* which connects directly to the drive axle on *front-wheel drive* or rear-engine cars, thus eliminating the need for a *driveshaft*.

**transmission** a box of gear wheels that allow your car to move forward and backward with varying amounts of power to meet a variety of driving situations. *Manual transmissions* are operated by means of a *clutch* and *gearshift*. Automatic transmissions are driven by *hydraulic* pressure.

**transmission fluid** a superthin *oil* that fills the *automatic transmission* system so that it can run on *hydraulic* pressure. Also found in many *power-steering* pumps.

**transverse engine** an engine that is mounted between the drive wheels, often found on *front-wheel drive* cars. See *transaxle*.

**tread-wear indicators**   bars of hard rubber that appear across the treads of *tires* that have been worn below ¹⁄₁₆ inch of surface.

**trim**   nonfunctional metal or plastic moldings, frames, and other decorative additions to car bodies and interiors.

**tune-up**   the process of adjusting and/or replacing the various parts of the *ignition system* to ensure that it delivers a spark of the proper intensity and duration to the *combustion chamber* at the precise moment when the *fuel/air mixture* is compressed to burn at peak efficiency. Adjusting the carburetor *idle speed* and *fuel/air mixture* is a key part of the tune-up, as well. A basic tune-up includes replacing and gapping *spark plugs* and *points;* replacing the *rotor* and *condenser,* checking and adjusting *timing* and *dwell;* and adjusting the *idle mixture screw, idle speed screw,* and sometimes other controlling devices, such as the *idle air bleed screw* and the *idle stop solenoid* on the *carburetor.* Your car should be tuned every 10,000 miles or every six months, whichever comes first.

**tune-up kit**   a kit containing a new set of *points,* a *rotor,* a *condenser,* a little vial of *cam* lube, and a *feeler gauge* of the proper thickness for a specific car make, model, and year. A necessary part of a basic *tune-up* is replacing these parts and lubricating the *distributor.*

**turbocharging**   a method of increasing power and decreasing emissions by rerouting hot *exhaust gases* through a turbine which drives a pump that forces more air into the engine *cylinders.*

**turn over**   an engine is said to "turn over" when the *starter* has caused the *crankshaft* to begin to turn, which starts the *pistons* moving so that *combustion* can begin to take place in the *cylinders,* providing power to move the car.

**turning radius**   the relation of one front wheel to the other on turns. If your tires are "squealing" on turns, have your front-end *alignment* checked to be sure that bent steering arms have not affected the turning radius of the car.

**two-plus-two**   a two-door car with relatively limited seating in the rear for two people. More seating than in a two-seater but less than in a car with a full rear seat.

**U-joints**   an abbreviation for "*universal joints.*"

**undercoating**   a protective material applied to the undersides of new cars to prevent the formation of rust.

**universal joints**   couplings located at either end of the *driveshaft* which allow the shaft to move freely, without affecting the more rigid transmission shaft, and to absorb the movement of the axle and wheels. Also called *U-joints* and, on cars with transverse engines, *constant velocity joints.*

**vacuum advance**   a device located to the side of the *distributor* which advances the ignition spark in response to the vacuum produced by the operation of the engine. You disconnect the vacuum advance before you check the *point gap* with a *dwell meter.*

**vacuum modulator**   a small, easily replaceable, and inexpensive part that can give the impression of *transmission* failure if it malfunctions. If the car tends to stay in low gear, shifts with difficulty or produces whitish smoke, has an *automatic transmission,* and is constantly low in *transmission fluid,* try replacing the vacuum modulator before undertaking major repairs. Most vacuum modulators simply screw into place.

**valve cover**   a metal lid located on top of the *cylinder head* on cars with *overhead cams.* The valve cover is removed when the *valves* need adjusting.

**valves**   metal devices that open and close to allow fuel and air to enter the *combustion chamber* and *exhaust gases* to leave it. Operated from the *camshaft,* by means of valve lifters, *push rods,* and *rocker arms* (except for cars with *overhead cams,* which don't require them), the valves can be adjusted with *feeler gauges* so that they open and close at the proper times. See *exhaust valve, intake valve, timing chain.*

**vapor lock**   bubbles formed in the *fuel line* when the fuel boils because of extreme heat. These bubbles prevent the fuel from reaching the *carburetor* and cause the car to stop running. A wet rag will cool the line and get rid of the problem, and a piece of tinfoil wrapped around the line will prevent its recurrence in extremely hot weather.

**vaporize**   to convert a liquid into a mist by breaking it into small particles and mixing it with air. The *carburetor* vaporizes gasoline to produce a combustible *fuel/air mixture.* If it is not vaporized, liquid gasoline will burn poorly.

**venturi**   the part of the *carburetor barrel* which is narrowed to increase the ability of the air to mix with *vaporized* fuel by creating a vacuum that draws more fuel out of the *float bowl.*

**viscosity**   the thickness or pourability of a liquid. *Oil* comes in a variety of thicknesses, or weights. It also comes in single viscosity (single-weight oil) and in a blend of viscosities (multi-weight oil), which enable it to flow easily in cold weather and prevent it from thinning out in hot weather. The higher the weight, the greater the viscosity of the oil. You can find the weight of the oil embossed on the top lid of the oil can.

**voltage regulator**   an electrical device that controls or regulates the amount of electricity generated by the *alternator.*

**V-type engine**   an engine in which the *cylinders* occur in two rows set at an angle to each other, with the *crankshaft* running through the point of the V. The most popular engine of this type is the 8-cylinder V-8 engine. V-6 and V-4 engines are also available, and Jaguar makes a V-12! See *in-line engine.*

**warranty**   a promise by a car manufacturer and a car dealer to fix or replace parts on a new car if they malfunction before a specific time or distance has elapsed.

**water jackets**   channels in the engine through which water and *coolant* circulate to cool the engine. See *cooling system.*

**water pump**   a device that circulates the liquid through the *cooling system* by pumping it from the engine *water jackets* to the *radiator*.

**water separator**   a device found on *diesel* cars which removes any water that may have contaminated the diesel fuel.

**wheel alignment**   see *alignment*.

**wheel balancing**   a procedure that ensures that the weight of the wheel is distributed evenly to improve performance and cut *tire* wear. Static balancing distributes the weight of the wheel evenly around the *axle* or *spindle* and is done with the wheels off the car. Dynamic balancing distributes the weight evenly as the wheel and tire hang vertically down, also balances the *brake drum,* and can be done with the wheels on the car.

**wheel bearings**   see *bearings*.

**wheel cylinder**   a small cylinder located at each wheel brake that uses *brake fluid* to exert *hydraulic* pressure, which forces the *brake shoes* against the *brake drums* and stops the car.


**zerk fitting**   a small valve that allows *grease* to be added to a *ball joint* with a *grease gun* and prevents the grease from leaking out when pressure is placed on the area. See *grease fitting*.

# Index